Priest & Parish
in
Eighteenth-Century France

Gap in the early nineteenth century. (*Collection Georges Dusserre*)

PRIEST & PARISH
in Eighteenth-Century France

*A Social and Political Study
of the Curés in a Diocese of Dauphiné*

1750-1791

BY TIMOTHY TACKETT

Princeton University Press
Princeton, New Jersey

Copyright © 1977 by Princeton University Press

Published by Princeton University Press, Princeton, New Jersey
In the United Kingdom: Princeton University Press,
Guildford, Surrey

ALL RIGHTS RESERVED

Library of Congress Cataloging in Publication Data will
be found on the last printed page of this book

Publication of this book has been aided by the Andrew
W. Mellon Publication Fund of Princeton University Press

This book has been composed in Linotype Baskerville

Printed in the United States of America
by Princeton University Press, Princeton, New Jersey

For Catherine

Table of Contents

Contents

List of Tables

List of Illustrations

Illustrations

xi

Abbreviations

B.N.	*Bibliothèque nationale*
A.N.	*Archives nationales*
A.D.H.A.	*Archives départementales des Hautes-Alpes*
A.D.B.A.	*Archives départementales des Alpes de Haute-Provence*—formerly called *Basses-Alpes*
A.D.D.	*Archives départementales de la Drôme*
A.D.I.	*Archives départementales de l'Isère*
A.C.	*Archives communales de . . .*
A.E.	*Archives de l'évêché de . . .*
B.M.G.	*Bibliothèque municipale de Grenoble, fonds dauphinois*
Collect. Roman	*Collection Roman*: bound documents held in the A.D.H.A.
BHA	*Bulletin de la société d'études du département des Hautes-Alpes*
AA	*Annales des Alpes*
BD	*Bulletin de la société départementale d'archéologie et de statistique de la Drôme*
RGA	*Revue de géographie alpine*
CH	*Cahiers d'histoire*
RH	*Revue historique*
RHMC	*Revue d'histoire moderne et contemporaine*
RHEF	*Revue d'histoire de l'Eglise de France*
Recueil Giroud	*Recueil des édits et déclarations du roi, lettres patentes et ordonnances de sa majesté, arrêts et règlements de ses conseils et du Parlement du Dauphiné* (Grenoble, Giroud, 1690–1790)
Ord. syn.	*Ordonnances synodales du diocèse de Gap publiées en l'année 1712 par Mgr. de Malissoles* (Grenoble, 1712)

xiii

Priest & Parish
in
Eighteenth-Century France

Introduction

From its inception, the present research into the parish clergy of eighteenth-century France has had two principal objectives. The first has been to learn more about the position and status of the parish priests in society and their relations with their lay parishioners. The important role played by the curés in the local community was widely recognized by the writers and political leaders of the Old Regime itself. A better understanding of this professional group could hopefully give insight into the little-known areas of rural culture and village society at the end of the eighteenth century.

But the parish clergy is also known to have engaged in significant political activities prior to and during the early stages of the French Revolution. Within the Estates General, the decision by the majority of curé deputies to begin sitting with the Third Estate in June 1789 was of considerable importance in the formation of the National Assembly. As one contemporary observer put it, "It is those goddamned curés who made the Revolution."[1] With the enactment in 1790 of the state-imposed reform of the Church, the Civil Constitution of the Clergy, the Revolution would lose the allegiance of many of the parish priests in France. And yet a large segment, probably about half of the entire corps, would continue to embrace and support Revolutionary policy up to and even after the Terror. Thus, a second goal of research has been to broaden our understanding of the process of politicization of the parish clergy at the end of the Old Regime.

Despite their importance, the parish priests have until recently received relatively little attention from historians. Through the middle of the twentieth century, scholars in-

[1] André Latreille, *L'Eglise catholique et la Révolution française*, 2 vols. (Paris, 1970), I, 84.

3

terested in the clergy of the Old Regime focused primarily on intellectual and institutional developments, and on the biographies and political activities of the leaders of the Gallican Church.[2] Only one important book, *Curés de campagne de l'ancienne France*, by Pierre de Vaissière,[3] attempted to examine the parish clergy in its social context. This work is still a valuable introduction to the subject. But de Vaissière based his conclusions almost entirely on the correspondence received by the Agency-General of the Clergy of France in Paris—a valuable though often one-sided source of information—and he never attempted a careful verification in local archives of the observations and complaints expressed by the curés.

As for the parish clergy's experience during the early stages of the Revolution, many of the historiographical observations made by Albert Mathiez some seventy years ago are still applicable. Most works on the subject, Mathiez noted, were written by Catholics who invariably divided the clergy into two groups: the martyrs and defenders of the faith (the refractory clergy), and the group of apostates (the pro-Revolutionary and constitutional priests). Historians on the left, for their part, had shown relatively little interest in the careful analysis of the problems of the Church; and ironically, they had frequently accepted without question the Catholics' evaluation of the constitutional clergy.[4] As recently as 1969 Bernard Plongeron could continue to lament the partisan character of the great majority

[2] Outstanding examples of works written during this period are Augustin Sicard, *L'ancien clergé de France*, 3 vols. (Paris, 1893–1903); Henri Brémond, *Histoire littéraire du sentiment religieux en France depuis la fin des guerres de religion jusqu'à nos jours*, 11 vols. (Paris, 1924–1933); and Edmond Préclin, *Les Jansénistes du XVIIIe siècle et la Constitution civile du clergé* (Paris, 1929).

[3] (Paris, 1933); also de Vaissière's article, "L'état social des curés de campagne au XVIIIe siècle," *RHEF*, XIX (1933), pp. 23–53.

[4] "Coup d'oeil critique sur l'histoire religieuse de la Révolution," in *Contributions à l'histoire religieuse de la Révolution française* (Paris, 1907), pp. 1–41.

of studies concerning the French priest and the Civil Constitution of the Clergy.[5]

In the last twenty years, there has been a broad surge of interest and research in the social history of the Church and the clergy during the final two centuries of the Old Regime. Historians, under the initial leadership of Gabriel Le Bras, have taken advantage of recent developments in socio-economic history in an attempt to place religious practice and its ministers in their temporal setting.[6] The present study is a further contribution to the research being pursued in these areas. Although a number of books, by students of Le Bras and others, have touched on the parish clergy in the context of broader inquiries into ecclesiastical society or pastoral history,[7] this is the first to attempt a systematic social biography of the corps of curés in one diocese at the end of the Old Regime: their careers, their position in lay society, their political aspirations on the eve of the Revolution. In so doing, it seeks also to respond

[5] *Conscience religieuse en Révolution: regards sur l'historiographie religieuse de la Révolution française* (Paris, 1969), pp. 10–11.

[6] Le Bras' articles—primarily methodological in nature—have been collected in *Introduction à l'histoire de la pratique religieuse en France*, 2 vols. (Paris, 1942–1945), and *Etudes de sociologie religieuse*, 2 vols. (Paris, 1955–1956). Among the outstanding works in this school of "religious sociology" are M. L. Fracard, *La fin de l'Ancien régime à Niort, essai de sociologie religieuse* (Paris, 1956); Jeanne Ferté, *La vie religieuse dans les campagnes parisiennes (1622–1695)* (Paris, 1962); and Louis Pérouas, *Le diocèse de La Rochelle de 1648 à 1724: sociologie et pastorale* (Paris, 1964). Le Bras and many of his followers are themselves practicing members of the Catholic Church.

[7] The works by Pérouas, Ferté, and Fracard, cited above. Also André Schaer, *Le clergé paroissial catholique en Haute-Alsace sous l'Ancien régime, 1648–1789* (Paris, 1966); and, above all, John McManners, *French Ecclesiastical Society under the Ancien Régime. A Study of Angers in the Eighteenth Century* (Manchester, 1960). To these should be added a number of important articles by Dominique Julia, listed in the bibliography. For a summary of recent scholarship concerning the parish clergy, see William H. Williams, "Perspectives on the Parish Clergy on the Eve of the French Revolution," in *Proceedings of the Fourth Annual Colloquium on Revolutionary Europe, 1750–1850* (Gainesville, Florida, 1976).

to Plongeron's appeal for a more objective evaluation of
the clergy's reactions to the oath of 1791, particularly in
regard to those clergymen who accepted the Civil Constitution.

The diocese of Gap was chosen as the regional focus for
this study only after a careful examination of several
other possible dioceses. A number of considerations
governed this choice. First, the archival material available
for the diocese of Gap was exceptionally rich and well-
preserved. The series of episcopal registers, existing for
virtually the entire eighteenth century, could serve as the
basis of a study of recruitment and career patterns. Second, the diocese was situated within the province of Dauphiné, a region known to have been the center of a "revolt
of the curés" in the 1770's and 1780's and of a massive
adhesion of the parish clergy to the Civil Constitution
of the Clergy. Third, the diocese was small enough to make
a quantitative approach humanly feasible, and yet it contained unusually diverse geographic and socio-economic
milieux, thus facilitating the study of possible relations
between religious culture and social structures.

As the reader will discover, the chapters of the book
are grouped into five sections. An initial chapter serves to
give a general description of the diocese and the clergy
of Gap in the eighteenth century, with particular emphasis
on the socio-economic and cultural dichotomy between the
north and the south. A second section, Chapters II to V,
deals with the career in the parish clergy, from the initial
entry and intellectual preparation through the problems of
old age and retirement. The third group of chapters, VI
through VIII, seeks to identify the parish priest's status
in society and the patterns of relations in Dauphiné between him and his parishioners. Chapters IX to XI
describe the politicization and revolt of the parish clergy
at the end of the eighteenth century. Chapter XII, which
briefly sketches the movement of de-Christianization and

the careers of the curés during the later stages of the Revolution, may be seen as both conclusion and epilogue. Quantitative techniques have been applied wherever permitted by the documents preserved. A statistical approach is necessary in any collective biography of this kind. But in the interpretation of the data, considerable use has been made of documents less easily quantifiable, such as sermons, court suits, pastoral visits, subdelegate reports, and, especially, the personal correspondence of several individual parish priests. Every effort has been made to observe the curés from as many different perspectives as possible, and to treat the collective of the parish clergy without losing sight of the individuals who composed that collective.

Whenever feasible, attempts have been made to compare conditions in the diocese of Gap with those in other regions of France, to identify the ecclesiastical structures typical of Dauphiné, and those which were typical of the kingdom as a whole. But all attempted comparisons are severely restricted by the limited research previously carried out in this area. Perhaps a future study undertaken in a diocese of western France, an area of very different ecclesiastical structures, in which the parish clergy largely rejected the Civil Constitution, will serve as the pendant to the present work.

I especially wish to express my appreciation to Philip Dawson and Dominique Julia, whose advice and friendship were of immeasurable value in the conception, research, and composition of this study. The initial period of investigation in France was financed by a grant from the Foreign Area Fellowship Program. In the course of research, Michel Vovelle frequently offered his kind assistance and hospitality. I was also greatly assisted by Pierre-Yves and Arlette Playoust, Vital Chomel, Pierre Bolle, Danielle Robert-Lebis, and abbés Jean Godel, Adrien Loche, Lucien

Van Damme, Louis Jacques, and Roger de Labriolle. Abbé Bernard Plongeron graciously read the entire manuscript and offered suggestions for its improvement. Various versions were also read and criticized by Margot Drekmeier, Lewis Spitz, Lynn Hunt, Jean-Guy Daigle, Peter McCormick, and J. Michael Phayer.

CHAPTER I

The Diocese of Gap in the Eighteenth Century

THE MILIEU

In June of 1785, François-Henri de la Broüe de Vareilles, newly appointed bishop of Gap, returned from his first pastoral visit and immediately recorded his impressions of the diocese: ". . . the most fertile imagination could never depict, nor the most energetic style express . . . the horror of the trails over which we have traveled, the narrow paths skirting the base of extremely jagged mountains, surrounded by terrifying gorges."[1] This description, coming, to be sure, from an urbane aristocrat who had spent most of his life in Paris and Poitou, was not untypical of the first impressions of other visitors to the region.[2] Situated near the center of the Alpine massifs of southeastern France, astride the frontier between Upper Dauphiné and Upper Provence, the eighteenth-century diocese of Gap contained within its boundaries some of the loftiest mountains in the kingdom. Yet not all of the diocese was dominated by Alpine peaks. If the bishop's stay had not been curtailed by the Revolution, he might have come to appreciate the extraordinary geographic, economic, and social diversity enclosed within the territory of his diocese, a territory in which the rapid changes in landscape and altitude effected fundamental differences in the activities pursued by the populations of adjoining regions. A brief

---

[1] Register of pastoral visits, entry of June 23, 1785: A.D.H.A., G 791.

[2] Barras and Fréron, representatives on mission in the Hautes-Alpes, made similar comments in letters to the Committee of Public Safety. See, for example, the letter of May 10, 1793: *Recueil des actes du Comité de salut public*, F.-A. Aulard, ed., 28 vols. (Paris, 1889–1933), IV, 92–95.

description of this physical and social milieu is essential for our understanding of the religious and ecclesiastical history of the diocese.

In general, the various natural regions of the diocese might be grouped into three principal zones: the north, the southeast, and the southwest (see Figure A).[3] In the north, a zone of high mountains drained by the river Drac and its tributaries, the greatest natural resource was the pasturage. Vast expanses of Alpine grasslands supported herds of livestock that were often the most important source of local income and a fundamental measure of wealth.[4] In the higher valleys of the Valgaudemar and the Upper Champsaur, the pastoral activities set the rhythms of the peasant's life, with entire families following their flocks—primarily sheep, but also cattle—in a seasonal trek up and down the mountains.[5] The large local herds were

[3] In defining these zones, I have greatly relied on the monumental study of Raoul Blanchard, *Les Alpes occidentales*, 7 vols. (Paris, 1938–1956) and on the numerous monographs appearing in the *RGA* dealing with different regions of the Alps. Blanchard's school of geography generally attempts to put human geography in a historical perspective. I have also made use of the replies of the communities of Dauphiné to a questionnaire circulated by the Interim Commission of the provincial estates in 1789: A.D.D., C 3–5, for the Drôme; and, for the Hautes-Alpes, Paul Guillaume, *Recueil des réponses faites par les communautés de l'élection de Gap au questionnaire envoyé par la Commission intermédiaire des Etats du Dauphiné* (Paris, 1908), supplemented for the Champsaur and Valgaudemar by *BHA*, XXXI (1912), pp. 1–46, 103–150, 294–335 and for Le Poët by *AA*, XIV (1910), pp. 1–11; these will be cited hereafter as *Réponses 1789*. Also, Pierre-Joseph-Marie Delafont, "Mémoire sur l'état de la subdélégation de Gap en 1784," ed. Joseph Roman, *BHA*, XVIII (1899), pp. 73–93, 167–186, 247–264 and XIX (1900), pp. 19–53, hereafter cited as Subdel. Gap-1784; and "Situation économique des Hautes-Alpes en 1801," *BHA*, XXII (1913), pp. 166–197, 226–252, and XXXIII (1914), pp. 23–48. At the end of the Old Regime there were 160 parishes (75 percent) in Dauphiné, 51 (24 percent) in Provence, and 2 in the papal territory of the Comtat-Venaissin.

[4] Philippe Arbos, *La vie pastorale dans les Alpes françaises. Etude de géographie humaine* (Paris, 1922), p. 176. Also Thérèse Sclafert, *Le Haut-Dauphiné au Moyen Age* (Paris, 1926), pp. 472–477, 484, 578–583.

[5] This was the "genre de vie savoyard," practiced, according to Arbos in the Valgaudemar, the Upper Champsaur, and part of the Lower Champsaur: see pp. 383–384 and attached map.

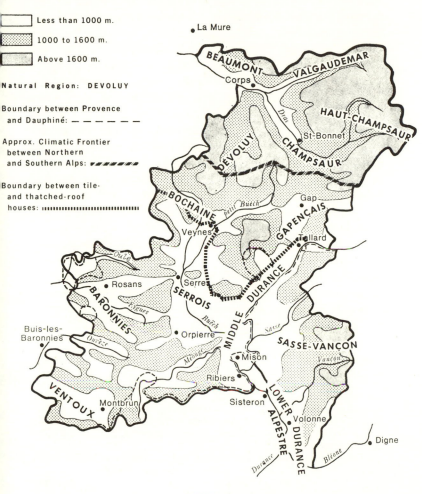

Less than 1000 m.

1000 to 1600 m.

Above 1600 m.

Natural Region: DEVOLUY

Boundary between Provence
and Dauphiné: — — — — —

Approx. Climatic Frontier
between Northern
and Southern Alps: ▰▰▰▰▰▰

Boundary between tile-
and thatched-roof
houses: ııııııııııııııııııııııı

La Mure

BEAUMONT

Corps

VALGAUDEMAR

HAUT-CHAMPSAUR

Drac

St-Bonnet

DÉVOLUY

CHAMPSAUR

BOCHAINE

Petit Buëch

Gap

Veynes

GAPENÇAIS

Tallard

Oule

MIDDLE DURANCE

Rosans

SERROIS

Serres

BARONNIES

Eygues

Buëch

Sasse

Buis-les-
Baronnies

Ouvèze

Orpierre

Méouge

SASSE-VANÇON

Vançon

Mison

Ribiers

VENTOUX

Montbrun

Sisteron

LOWER DURANCE

ALPESTRE

Volonne

Digne

Durance

Bléone

Figure A.

The diocese of Gap: natural regions

11

further augmented by flocks of transhumance sheep driven up each summer from Lower Provence.[6] During the winter months, peasants and animals hibernated together and helped keep each other warm within the large mountain houses. Inevitably, communal lands for grazing pastures were of the greatest importance; several villages in the regions of the Champsaur and the Beaumont were even bound together in joint possession of a "mountain."[7] By comparison, cultivation was less important in many communities. The tiny vineyards and plots of rye and barley provided meager returns during the short growing season. A major exception, however, was the Champsaur. In this broad, gently sloping basin, a plentiful supply of animal fertilizers and a complex system of irrigation canals[8] made it possible to grow substantial crops of the coarser grains (the climate was too cold for wheat). In 1789 the intendant of Dauphiné described this region as "one of the major granaries of the province."[9] With its fields bordered by hedgerows and poplar trees, the Champsaur appeared curiously similar to the *bocage* regions of western France.[10] The southeastern zone of the diocese,[11] drained by the

6 See Arbos, pp. 564–577 and J. Blache, C. Carcel, and M. Rey, "Le troupeau bovin dans les Alpes du Dauphiné et de la Savoie au milieu du XVIIIe siècle," *RGA*, XXI (1933), p. 423.

7 Saint-Bonnet, Bénévent, Charbillac, Les Infournas, La Motte, Saint-Eusèbe, Les Costes, and Aubessagne were in joint possession of one "mountain": A.D.H.A., L 1232, deliberations of Saint-Bonnet on division of communal property, Year II. Chaillol, Saint-Julien and Buissard held another: *Réponses 1789*, replies of Buissard and Saint-Julien-en-Champsaur.

8 The irrigation canals had existed at least since the Middle Ages: Sclafert, *Le Haut-Dauphiné au Moyen Age*, pp. 465–486.

9 In a letter to the subdelegate of Gap, dated Oct. 13, 1789, concerning the foundation of a public granary in Gap: A.D.H.A., Collection Roman, t. LI; see also the "Mémoire général sur la province de Dauphiné," ca. 1730: B.N., Fonds français 8359, f. 17–18.

10 M. R. Livet, "Le bocage du Champsaur," *Bulletin du comité de travaux historiques et scientifiques, section de géographie*, LXXI (1958), pp. 169–182.

11 The Bochaine and Gapençais can be considered as transitional zones between the north and the southeast.

river Durance and its tributaries, contrasted sharply with the north. The mountains were less imperious, the valleys wider and lower, the uncultivated areas were covered only by small pines, brush, or scrub grass; it was a landscape typical of the southern pre-Alps. While the Drac valley partook primarily of weather arriving from the Atlantic, the Durance valley was in the sphere of the Mediterranean, where the winter was milder and the real enemy of crops and animals was the long dry summer. Throughout this zone, the peasants pursued a generalized polyculture characteristic of much of the Mediterranean area.[12] The principal crop, wheat, was supplemented by vineyards, fruit trees, and hemp fields. In the region of the Lower Durance, beyond the narrows at Sisteron, olive orchards were also important. Because the climate was dry, fertility was limited in many places by the possibilities of irrigation, but the irregular terrain prevented the construction of an extensive canal system such as existed in the Champsaur. Livestock was also important, but in many communities insufficient summer grazing lands restricted the size of the flocks or herds that could be kept. The number of animals per inhabitant tended generally to decrease from the north to the south of the diocese, and the percentage of cows declined in favor of sheep and goats.[13] The pastoral activities in the southeast were much more sedentary and nowhere did they dominate the peasant's life as they did in the north. Throughout the year, the animals were left to graze near the village in nearby fallow lands or in plots that had already been harvested; and they were

[12] For the southeast of the diocese, the basic study of economic history and human geography is Paul Veyret, *Les pays de la moyenne Durance alpestre* (Grenoble, 1945).

[13] J. Blache *et al.*, "Le troupeau bovin dans les Alpes . . . ," *loc. cit.*, pp. 419–426 and map. Blache studies mainly the herds of cattle, but concludes, p. 422, that the numbers of sheep also decreased broadly from north to south. One arrives at the same general conclusion via the censuses of livestock made in the Year II: A.D.H.A., L 378, L 380, L 1203.

driven to and from pasture each day.[14] Consequently, communal pasturage was much less important in the southeast than in the north.[15]

Geographically and economically very different, the zone drained by the Durance on the one hand, and that drained by the Drac on the other, were closely linked commercially. An important trade route within the Alps followed the "sub-Alpine depression" through the Drac and Durance valleys from Grenoble to Marseilles. But the third major zone, the southwest, was less closely united with either the north or the southeast of the diocese. Known to contemporaries as the "Baronnies," it was characterized by a series of oval-shaped valleys, isolated from one another and from the outside by mountain ridges and narrow river gorges.[16] Several of the rivers flowed west rather than east toward the Durance, so that the Baronnies tended to fall into the economic sphere of the Rhône valley. It was an especially poor and disinherited zone. The economic activities were largely similar to those of the Durance valley—wheat, grapes, sheep, and goats—but here, in the perpetual fear of a lack of bread, rye and barley and oats might be sown to the highest altitudes. Some peasants even resorted to *essarts* or swidden cultivation, a kind of nomad agriculture in which sections of woods or brush were set afire and crops were planted on the ashes for two or three years until the soil became sterile again.[17] Such practices further reduced the already limited pasturelands and gave the Baronnies the smallest ratio of livestock to human popula-

[14] This is the "genre de vie des pré-Alpes méridionales" as described by Arbos, *La vie pastorale*, pp. 540–541.

[15] The deliberations on the division of communal property, District of Serres, 1793–1794, show that most villages south of the Bochaine and Gapençais were ready to convert their communal lands into private property: A.D.H.A., L 1380. Some had already done so before the Revolution: *e.g.*, Ventavon: Subdel.Gap-1784, p. 78.

[16] See, in particular, Philippe Arbos, "L'évolution économique des Baronnies," *La géographie*, XXXI (1916–1917), pp. 89–112. Also, Blanchard, *Les Alpes occidentales*, IV, 387–397.

[17] J. Blache, "L'essartage, ancienne pratique culturelle dans les Alpes dauphinoises," *RGA*, XI (1923), pp. 553–575. Also, Subdel.Gap-1784, pp. 36–37.

tion in the diocese.[18] Only in the extreme southwest, in the shadow of Mont Ventoux, did a somewhat more prosperous economy exist. With easy communications to the Rhône valley, this area was more market-oriented and produced olives, fruit, and silk cocoons for sale in Provence and the Comtat-Venaissin.[19]

Compared to agricultural and pastoral activities, manufacture played only a minor role in the economy of the diocese. The paucity of wood and of mineral ores, the erratic sources of water power—most streams in the southern Alps were reduced to a trickle in summer—and poor communications, all worked to discourage the growth of industry.[20] To be sure, several of the larger towns had their little teams of cloth and leather workers. In 1788 one man in Gap was said to employ 100 women and a few professional artisans in the production of woolen clothes and blankets.[21] The town of Serres could list 76 heads of household—over one-fourth of the total—engaged in cloth, leather, and hat manufacturing.[22] But these were the exceptions. In general, the two or three spinners or weavers on the tax rolls of many of the villages and towns worked only part-time and for local consumption.[23] The sub-delegate, Delafont, deplored the lack of initiative on the part of the local citizens who sold their raw materials, wool, hemp, and leather, to external markets rather than establishing their own manufactures.[24]

Nevertheless, an important trade in comestibles and livestock brought a lively commercial activity to the little

[18] Blache, "Le troupeau bovin dans les Alpes," *loc. cit.*; see above, note 13.

[19] Blanchard, *Les Alpes occidentales*, IV, 366–379.

[20] Pierre Léon, *La naissance de la grande industrie en Dauphiné*, 2 vols. (Paris, 1953), I, chap. 1.

[21] Camille Queyrel, Un modèle de l'administration éclairée, Pierre Delafont et Pierre-Joseph-Marie Delafont, derniers subdélégués de Gap (D.E.S., Université de Grenoble, 1933), pp. 109–110.

[22] Census of the Year IV: A.D.H.A., L 357.

[23] Subdel.Gap-1784, pp. 51–53. Also, *Réponses 1789*, replies of Barret-le-Bas, Saint-Michel-de-Chaillol, Manteyer, Pelleautier, Eygaliers, Montbrun, Plaisians.

[24] Subdel.Gap-1784, p. 47.

cities and towns of the diocese. In part, this was merely a local commerce reflecting the interdependence of town and country, of mountain regions and lower valleys. Gap itself was the center of a particularly active trade of this sort, which brought wine and fruit from the Middle Durance and grain, livestock, and dairy products from the Champsaur.[25] Some of the smaller towns—especially Serres, Veynes, and Saint-Bonnet—also had important local fairs and markets.[26] In the long-distance trade, almonds, wine, and grain were exported in varying quantities southward toward Provence.[27] But the most important item of trade was undoubtedly livestock. This, in fact, was the real specialty of the mountain peoples of the north of the diocese. Some went as far as Auvergne and Poitou to buy young horses and mules to be raised and resold; and large numbers of sheep and calves, both those born on the farms and those bought elsewhere, were fattened for market.[28] In the interprovincial and in the local trade, the town of Gap was the principal center of activity. Located at the crossroads of the routes from Grenoble to Marseilles and from the Rhône Valley to Italy—via the Montgenèvre pass —Gap was the largest and most animated town in Upper Dauphiné.[29]

THE LAY POPULATION

Attempts to estimate the population of the diocese of Gap in the eighteenth century are seriously hindered by

[25] Paul Veyret, "Le commerce des produits agricoles dans les pays de la moyenne Durance vers la fin du XVIIIe siècle," *RGA*, XXIX (1941), pp. 296–298.
[26] A.D.H.A., C 23, report by the sub-delegate of Gap on the fairs in his subdelegation, 1787. Veynes, with an important wool trade, had the second largest fair after Gap.
[27] Subdel.Gap-1784, pp. 28, 48. On the grain trade to Provence, see the report by the sub-delegate dated Feb. 28, 1787: Collect. Roman, LII.
[28] Subdel.Gap-1784, pp. 46–47. Also "Situation économique des Hautes-Alpes en 1801," *loc. cit.*, replies by the notables of the cantons of Ancelle, Saint-Firmin, Saint-Etienne-en-Dévoluy, and Saint-Bonnet.
[29] E. Sauvan, "Gap et ses foires," *RGA*, XX (1932), pp. 1–57.

the scarcity of demographic research undertaken to date in the Hautes-Alpes. The first somewhat reliable censuses, taken at the turn of the nineteenth century, indicate a total of approximately 92,000 people.[30] This relatively sparse population—about 20 persons per square kilometer, less than half the average density for the kingdom as a whole[31]—was very unevenly distributed (see Figure B). There was a concentration in the regions of the sub-Alpine depression, particularly in the Champsaur, the Beaumont, and the Lower Durance. The mountainous regions on the eastern and western peripheries supported a far less numerous population, with as few as ten persons per square kilometer in the Dévoluy, the Valgaudemar, and the Upper Champsaur.

Demographic trends in the course of the eighteenth century are even more difficult to determine. The minutes of the bishops' pastoral visits sometimes include the number of families or communicants, but not in a consistent form.[32] Unfortunately, there are no complete intendancy censuses in Dauphiné after 1748. In order to evaluate the broad patterns of demographic change in the diocese, we have compared the figures given by the intendant for the number of households per community in 1748[33] with a

---

[30] I have used the census of 1796 for the Hautes-Alpes: Paul Guillaume, "Le mouvement de la population du département des Hautes-Alpes au XIXe siècle," *BHA*, xxvii (1908), pp. 203–217; a census of 1794 for the Drôme; and the census of 1801 for the Isère, the Basses-Alpes, and the Vaucluse. For the latter four departments, figures were kindly furnished by the respective *directeurs de services d'archives*.

[31] If we accept the figure of 26 million for the population of France in 1789, the nation as a whole would have had approximately 48 persons per square kilometer.

[32] It has not been possible to use the population figures calculated from pastoral visits by Raoul Blanchard: "Note sur la population du diocèse de Gap du XVIIe siècle à nos jours," *BHA*, xxxvi (1918), pp. 43–60. Not only are the statistics incomplete, but the method used to convert figures for families into figures for individuals seems imperfect.

[33] B.M.G., U 5210 and R. Vallentin du Cheylard, *Essai sur la population des taillabilités du Dauphiné* (Valence, 1912), pp. 165–202. For the dating of this document, see Jacques de Font-Réaulx, "Note sur certains statistiques et dénombrements . . . ," *RGA*, x (1922), pp. 439–441.

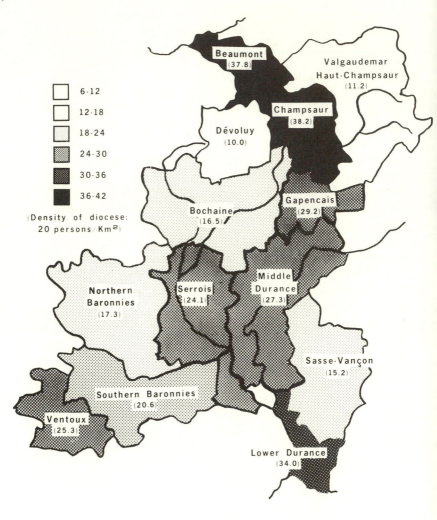

FIGURE B.
Population density at the end of the eighteenth century
(Persons per square kilometer)

partial series of figures available from two sources on the
eve of the French Revolution.[34] While a certain margin of
error must be allowed as to the absolute value of these
figures, they can nevertheless give us an indication of the
relative population change in the various zones of the
diocese during the second half of the eighteenth century
(see Table 1). We thus find an increase of about 10 percent

TABLE 1

Evolution of the Population in the Eighteenth-Century Diocese of Gap[1]
(in Dauphiné only)

Region	Communities in Region for which Data Available (Dauphiné only)	Number of Households 1748	Number of Households 1786–1789	Percentage Increase
ᴇaumont	5 of 13	199	228	15
ᴴampsaur	17 of 22	1214	1402	15
ᴀlgaudemar- Upper-Champsaur	3 of 10	200	221	11
ᴇvoluy	1 of 4	70	80	14
ᴀpençais (excluding Gap)	6 of 7	412	496	20
ᴼchaine	9 of 22	448	498	11
ʀrois	14 of 20	627	698	11
ᴹiddle Durance	13 of 19	1232	1317	7
ᴼorthern Baronnies	16 of 25	867	910	5
ᴼuthern Baronnies	10 of 19	684	694	1
ᴇntoux	4 of 6	332	369	11
ᴅiocese, Total	98 of 167	6285	6913	10

[1] For the limitations of these figures, see the text.

[34] Reports sent by the curés to the bishop of Gap in 1786: A.N., G⁸
68 (Dossier Gap); and those replies of the communities of Dauphiné
to the Interim Commission in 1789 in which the number of households
seems to have been established with care (*e.g.*, some communities gave
careful population breakdowns by age category or by hamlet; others
gave only approximate figures, ending in o): *Réponses 1789*. We have
considered only villages in which parish and community boundaries
coincided.

in the number of households in the diocese within Dauphiné. But the increase was substantially less in the Durance Valley and the Baronnies (1 to 7 percent) and substantially greater in the regions of the Drac Valley (11 to 15 percent).[35] The most rapidly expanding population was in the countryside adjoining the town of Gap. Gap itself may have grown by as much as 50 percent in the second half of the eighteenth century.[36]

Perhaps the salient characteristic of this population was its seasonal mobility. Many of the Alpine peoples temporarily left their homes in winter, or even in summer, impelled by the double necessity of rationing the family's winter stores (it was usually only the men and boys who left) and of finding work to supplement the annual income. The "Gavot"—the inhabitant of the Gapençais—was the generic name for the colorful peddlers and migrant dayworkers who descended from the Alps into Provence and Languedoc each year.[37] Invariably, this seasonal migration also paved the way for the permanent migration of families toward the Mediterranean. The Alps had always been a major reservoir of men for the low countries.[38]

[35] These broad trends seem to be confirmed for the portion of the diocese in Provence by the research of Edouard Baratier. Baratier found that in the zones of the Durance valley there was a slight but continual growth in the number of households between 1702–1703 and 1765; on the plateau of Forcalquier, just south of the Baronnies, there was a population equilibrium or even a decline; while in the mountain valley of Barcelonnette—similar in geography and economy to the Drac valley—there was a very substantial population increase: *La démographie provençale* (Paris, 1961), pp. 103–104.

[36] In 1748, the curés and community officers set the population at 4,747: *AA*, VII (1903), pp. 45–46. In 1796, the census listed 7,197 persons: Guillaume, "Le mouvement de la population dans le département des Hautes-Alpes," *loc. cit.*, pp. 203–217.

[37] Arnold Van Gennep, *Le folklore des Hautes-Alpes*, 2 vols. (Paris, 1946–1948), I, 31; and Veyret, *Les pays de la moyenne Durance*, pp. 354–356. The phenomenon of seasonal migration is difficult to study, but the epicenter would seem to have been in the regions of the Drac, the Bochaine, and the Northern Baronnies: see *Réponses 1789*, in which mention is often made of seasonal migration.

[38] Blanchard, *Les Alpes occidentales*, IV, 471–472; also Pierre Estienne, "Démographie ancienne d'une paroisse haut-alpine (1629–1822)," *CH*,

The Diocese of Gap

One fraction of the lay population, however, must be carefully distinguished from the rest. Since the era of the Reformation, a small but determined Calvinist minority had left its mark on the history of the French Alps.[39] No reliable statistics are available for the Protestant population at the height of its strength in the early seventeenth century. At the beginning of the eighteenth century, after the Revocation of the Edict of Nantes, about 5,100 "newly converted Catholics" remained in the diocese, approximately 6 percent of the total population.[40] They were most concentrated in the Baronnies and in the valleys of the Drac and the Buëch—representing as high as 22 percent of the Serrois and well over 50 percent in certain villages; they were almost absent from the Durance Valley and the Provençal portion of the diocese (see Figure C). In the course of the century, their numbers would decline somewhat further, to about three and one-half percent of the population of 1800.[41] Yet this small, tenacious group of nonconformists would remain a factor to be reckoned with by the representatives of the Catholic Church.

Considering the sharp geographic, economic, and demographic contrasts within the diocese, it is not surprising that community structures also differed considerably from

xv (1970), pp. 215–222. Estienne concludes, p. 222, that the parish in question, Ceillac, ". . . a été incontestablement pourvoyeuse d'hommes pour les bas pays sous l'ancien régime."

39 William Farel, the Protestant pastor of Neuchâtel, was born in Gap and participated in the conversion of his native region near the end of his life. The Duke de Lesdiguières, who conquered the Gapençais and most of Dauphiné for the Protestant armies, was born in Saint-Bonnet in the Champsaur: *Histoire de la ville de Gap* (Gap, 1966), pp. 125–173.

40 Statistics derived primarily from an "état des paroisses" of 1707: A.D.H.A., G 1098–1104; and the pastoral visit of 1740–1741: A.D.H.A., G 788; detailed tables will be published in a subsequent article. See also Paul-F. Geisendorf, "Recherches sur les conséquences démographiques de la révocation de l'Edit de Nantes en Dauphiné," *CH*, vi (1961), pp. 245–264.

41 Statistics taken from a census of the Napoleonic period: A.D.H.A., V 21; A.D.I., IX V¹ 1; and A.D.D., 53 V 1.

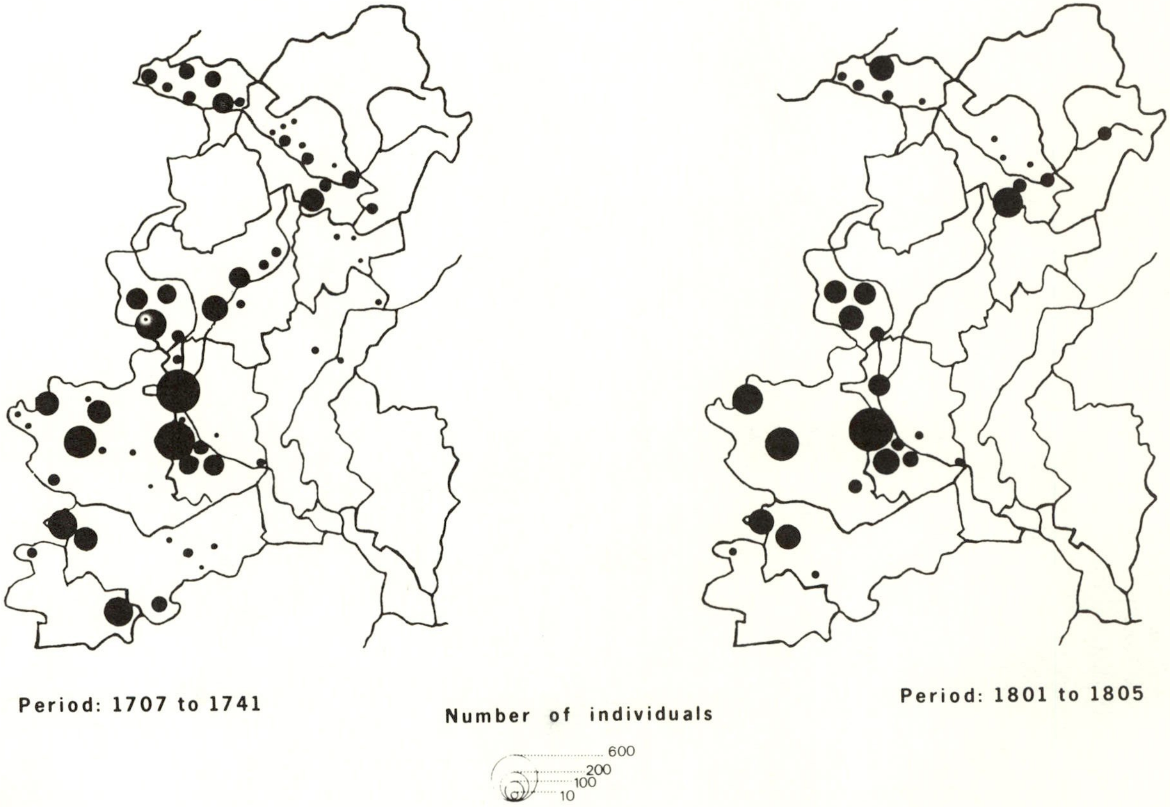

Period: 1707 to 1741

Period: 1801 to 1805

Number of individuals

600
200
100
10

FIGURE C.

region to region. In the valley of the Drac and the adjoining mountains, the large, thatched-roof houses were commonly dispersed through the countryside in numerous hamlets and isolated farms.[42] It was perhaps the hamlet rather than the village that formed the natural unit of local society after the family. Nevertheless, inter-community cooperation was strong. It was necessary because groups of communities jointly possessed tracts of mountain pastures and, in the Champsaur, because the network of irrigation canals that contoured the valley crossed the territory of several villages in succession.[43] The loose associations of communities in the Drac Valley and the Valgaudemar were the distant relatives of the "valley republics" of the Briançonnais. The impression gained from research in the *capitation* rolls of the Old Regime and the censuses of the Revolutionary period is that this hamlet society of the northern portion of the diocese was overwhelmingly rural.[44] The occupational structure, as described in these documents, was simple in the extreme. There were the *laboureurs* and the *journaliers* and a few *rentiers*; but, except in the largest towns, such as Saint-Bonnet, the non-agricultural occupations were rare.[45]

South of the Gapençais and the Bochaine, dispersion of dwellings existed, particularly in the Baronnies, but the central, clustered, hill-top village of tile-roof houses was much more typical. The east-west line marking the frontier between the thatched-roof villages and the tile-roof villages

[42] Blanchard, *Les Alpes occidentales*, II, pt. 2, 598–599, estimates an average of nine hamlets per community in the Champsaur and Beaumont. There were 55 hamlets in four communities of the Upper Champsaur: *Réponses 1789*, replies of Ancelle, Champoléon, Orcières, Saint-Jean, Saint-Nicolas.

[43] The close inter-community cooperation in the Upper Champsaur during the Middle Ages has been noted by Sclafert, pp. 486–489.

[44] A.D.H.A., L 499, L 1234 and L 356–357.

[45] In Saint-Julien-en-Champsaur (population 592) for example, the census of the Year IV gives the following professions for heads of household: 78 *cultivateurs*, 23 *journaliers*, 4 *fermiers*, 1 *tisserand*, 2 *voituriers*, 1 *maréchal*, 2 *notaires*, 1 *mendiant*: A.D.H.A., L 356.

separated the typical mountain communities from the typical meridional communities.[46] Within the southern regions a much more complex division of labor was to be found. Although the agricultural occupations continued to be dominant, there was also a whole array of professional shopkeepers, artisans, and merchants living in the villages along with the masses of peasants.[47] Compared to the villages of the north, those of the Durance Valley seemed already much more akin to that type of "urbanized village"—the village that was almost a town in miniature—so characteristic of Lower Provence.[48]

The geography, the economic activities, the community structures, and the demographic trends of the various regions of the eighteenth-century diocese of Gap all point to the existence of a major dichotomy between north and south. Even in such cultural realms as the patterns of popular folklore and the rates of masculine literacy, the same frontier between a sphere of Dauphiné and a sphere of Provence seemed to exist.[49] The extent to which this

---

[46] *Réponses 1789*, replies to questions concerning the number of hamlets in the community and the type of roof on the houses.

[47] In Aspres-sur-Buëch (population 583), for example, the census of the Year IV gives the following professions for heads of household: 62 *cultivateurs*, 28 *manoeuvriers*, 1 *juge*, 1 *négociant*, 1 *teinturier*, 3 *tisserands*, 1 *tanneur*, 1 *blancheur*, 3 *meuniers*, 7 *cordonniers*, 1 *maçon*, 1 *mineur*, 2 *tailleurs*, 3 *maréchaux*, 1 *menuisier*, 1 *batier*, 1 *muletier*, 1 *peseur d'eau*, 2 *salpêtriers*, 3 *aubergistes*, 1 *berger*, 1 *garde-terre*, 4 non-specified: A.D.H.A., L 357.

[48] Maurice Agulhon, *Société et vie sociale en Provence intérieure au lendemain de la Révolution française* (Paris, 1970), pp. 59–62. The average village in the south of the diocese was smaller than the typical village in Lower Provence.

[49] Van Gennep, p. 29. Careful studies of the percentages of brides and grooms signing their marriage acts—a rough measure of minimal literacy—are presently underway in France. A preliminary examination of two sample parish registers in the Champsaur would suggest that the 60 to 80 percent of bridegrooms signing in the period 1736 to 1741 had risen to over 90 percent by 1786–1790. In two sample parishes in the Middle Durance, the corresponding percentages remained stationary at about 50 percent throughout the century: parish registers of Le Noyer, Saint-Julien-en-Champsaur, Lazer, and Ribiers, preserved in A.D.H.A. It is likely that the 70 to 80 percent masculine signatures indicated for the Hautes-Alpes in 1786–1790 by Louis Maggiolo is

dichotomy was accompanied by differences in the religious culture of the diocese is a subject which we will examine further in the following chapter.

The Clergy

Within the heterogeneous physical and social reality of the diocese of Gap, the local ecclesiastical army, the diocesan clergy, went about its tasks. It was a modest contingent; including the regular clergy, there was a total of about 350 priests present in the diocese in 1790.[50] It would thus have represented something less than half of one percent of the total population, or about 39 clergymen per 10,000 individuals.[51] Not to be included in this group are

the average between a very high rate in the north of the department and a much lower rate in the south: see Michel Fleury and Pierre Valmary, "Les progrès de l'instruction élémentaire de Louis XIV à Napoléon III d'après l'enquête de Louis Maggiolo," *Population*, xii (1957), 71–92. A cultural frontier has also been suggested recently by Michel Vovelle, "Y a-t-il eu une révolution culturelle au XVIIIe siècle? A propos de l'éducation populaire en Provence," *RHMC*, xxii (1975), esp. pp. 94–95.

[50] An estimated 23 canons and *bénéficiers*; 38 regular clergymen; 6 professors in the seminary; 287 curés, vicaires, and chaplains; and 1 bishop, for a grand total of 355 priests. Principal sources for secular clergy: roll of the *décime*, 1789: A.D.H.A., G 2492; Paul Guillaume, *Clergé ancien et moderne du diocèse actuel de Gap* published in the *Inventaire sommaire des archives départementales antérieures à 1790, Hautes-Alpes, Série G,* 7 vols. (Gap, 1891–1913), vi, ix–ccxxvi; plus Guillaume's supplements for the Drôme, the Isère, and the Basses-Alpes (see Bibliography); and the declarations of revenue of 1790: A.D.H.A., L 1024, I Q I 108–09, and I Q I 137. Source for regular clergy: notes by Paul Guillaume taken from series Q in A.D.H.A., ms. 385.

[51] Compare to the 49–51 clergymen per 10,000 individuals in the neighboring diocese of Embrun in 1790: Timothy Tackett, "Le clergé de l'archidiocèse d'Embrun à la fin de l'Ancien régime," *Annales du Midi*, lxxxviii (1976), pp. 182, 186; or the 44 clergymen per 10,000 individuals in the department of the Isère (the Old-Regime dioceses of Grenoble and Vienne) in 1790: Jean Godel, *La reconstruction concordataire dans le diocèse de Grenoble après la Révolution (1802–1809)* (Grenoble, 1968), pp. 58, 244. See also the important article by Michel Vovelle, "Analyse spectrale d'un diocèse méridional au XVIIIe siècle: Aix-en-Provence," *Provence historique*, xxii (1972), pp. 352–451.

the numerous clergymen who possessed benefices in the diocese but who never, in fact, resided there. Among the non-residents was the majority of the sixty-three "priors," secular priests or clerics for the most part, who held their lucrative benefices as simple sinecures.[52] The priests present in the diocese in the eighteenth century fall into four principal categories: the bishop, the canons, the regular clergy, and the parish clergy.

The first member of the diocesan clergy was the bishop. Canon law and royal edict combined to give him near sovereign powers in a vast range of ecclesiastical matters within the diocese. In the sacramental, administrative, and disciplinary questions of the Church and the clergy, his authority was paramount.[53] He also possessed regulatory powers over primary schools, hospitals, poor relief, and mid-wives. Like most prelates of eighteenth-century France, the bishop of Gap was also a seigneurial lord and landholder within his diocese. Prior to the sixteenth century, his holdings had been extensive; but the Wars of Religion, especially violent and disruptive in Upper Dauphiné, had resulted in the loss or alienation of a great many of these possessions.[54] In the eighteenth century, the bishop still held the important title of count of Gap—with an elegant chateau on a hillside overlooking the city—and seigneurial and tithing rights in a number of villages,[55]

---

[52] In the eighteenth century, most of the priories had been secularized or were held *in commendam*. See the *pouillé* of 1755: A.D.H.A., G 1108, and Paul Guillaume's "Introduction" to vol. II of *Inventaire sommaire, série G*, ix–x.

[53] The basic "constitution" delineating the powers of the bishop in his diocese was the royal edict of 1695. See Edmond Préclin, *Les Jansénistes du XVIIIe siècle et la Constitution civile du clergé* (Paris, 1929), p. 28.

[54] Théodore Gautier, *Histoire de la ville de Gap et du Gapençais*, 2 vols. (Gap, 1909–1910), II, 260.

[55] In addition to seigneurial and judicial powers in Gap, the bishop, as count of Gap, also had complete control of the "police" in the city: Gautier, II, 292. The episcopal chateau of Charence was said to have been one of the most beautiful in the Alps: *ibid.*, II, 361–362.

but his total income was only about 18,000 *livres* per year.[56] Most episcopal benefices in France probably yielded between 25,000 and 75,000 *livres* per year.[57]

For the first third of the eighteenth century (1706–1738) the bishopric of Gap was held by a single individual, François Berger de Malissoles. One of the last Catholic Reformation bishops in Dauphiné, Berger de Malissoles made yearly pastoral visits in his diocese and carried to their fullest fruits the efforts of his predecessors toward the renewal and correction of the clergy. He also wrote and published the diocesan statutes that would be in effect until the Revolution.[58] Long after his death, Malissoles continued to be spoken of with reverence and cited as a model bishop by laymen and clergy alike.[59] But after 1738, no one man held the seat of Gap for more than twelve years.[60] Claude de Cabanes (1739–1741) died shortly after arriving in his episcopal city. He was followed by Jacques-Marie de Caritat de Condorcet (1741–1754)—uncle of the philosophe —who was best known as an inflexible opponent of the Jansenists and the Protestants. Then came Pierre-Annet de Pérouse (1754–1763), the most learned of the eighteenth-century bishops, whose personal library held nearly four thousand books, including the most radical of the philosophes and numerous works by Jansenist authors.[61] François

56 In 1763, Vallon-Corse, *receveur des économats* for the diocese of Gap, set the bishop's net revenue at 17,213 *livres* per year: A.D.H.A., G 1497. In 1790, the bishop declared a net revenue of 18,758 *livres*: A.D.H.A., I Q I 108 (1).

57 Norman Ravitch, *Sword and Mitre* (La Haye, 1966), appendix II.

58 *Ordonnances synodales du diocèse de Gap*, 2 vols. (Grenoble, 1712), hereafter cited as *Ord. syn.* These statutes were specifically reconfirmed by bishop Pérouse in 1759: A.D.H.A., G 814, pp. 429–433. For a general biography of Berger de Malissoles, see Gautier, II, 259–328.

59 He was called by his contemporaries the "saint pasteur des Alpes": Gautier, II, 321. Bishop Pérouse gave him the greatest praise and honor in his pastoral letter of Nov. 12, 1756: A.D.H.A., G 814.

60 Paul Guillaume gives brief biographies of all of the bishops of Gap: *Inventaire sommaire, série G*, III, vii–xxx.

61 Catalogue dated 1764: A.D.H.A., G 1178.

de Narbonne-Lara (1763–1774) held the bishopric for the next eleven years; but as personal chaplain to the king's daughters in Versailles, he did not often reside in the diocese.[62] His successor was the pious and scholarly François-Gaspar de Jouffroy-Gonssans (1774–1778).[63] He was in turn replaced by Jean-Baptise-Marie de Maillé de la Tour-Landry (1778–1784). The latter, only thirty-five years old at the moment of his appointment, soon won a reputation of joviality and facile morality that was to inspire a bawdy mock epic, the *Landriade*, probably written by curé Jean-Michel Rolland.[64] The last of the bishops of the Old Regime, La Broüe de Vareilles (1784–1791) arrived in Gap after serving several years as vicar-general of the diocese of Metz.[65] Of irreproachable conduct, he was a dedicated administrator who skillfully handled the financial and organizational affairs of his diocese. But, as we shall see, his authoritarian manners as prelate and seigneurial lord would do little to endear him to a generation of lay notables and parish priests who were particularly jealous of their independence and privileges.[66]

---

[62] Characteristically, he asked the king's permission in order to leave Versailles and visit his diocese: A.D.H.A., G 790, preamble to minutes of pastoral visit of 1772.

[63] The usually caustic *Landriade* poet described Jouffroy-Gonssans as:

> . . . un prélat difficile
> Qui des anciens pasteurs, imitateur servile,
> Connaissant leurs écrits, pratiquant leurs leçons,
> Voulut même imiter jusqu'à leurs actions. . . .:

A.D.H.A., ms. 342.

[64] The poem opens:

> Je chante ce prélat dont la morale utile
> Nous trace vers le ciel un chemin plus facile,
> Qui, chassant les ennuis du lieu de son séjour,
> Ne se refuse pas les plaisirs de l'amour.

A.D.H.A., ms. 342. T. Gautier, born at the end of the eighteenth century, reported that the poem was generally credited to curé Rolland: *Histoire de la ville de Gap*, ii, 403.

[65] For biographical information, see Antoine de Vareilles-Sommières, *Les souvenirs et traditions de Sommières* (Poitiers, 1938), especially pp. 132–141.

[66] See below, Chapter X.

François-Henri de la Broüe de Vareilles, bishop of Gap from 1784 to 1791. (*Evêché de Gap*)

All of the bishops were from noble families, and some—Narbonne-Lara, Condorcet, Vareilles—were from among the most notable families in France. But none originated in the diocese itself and, after Pérouse, none originated in Dauphiné. Most were comparatively young, with an average age of forty-four years when they began their tenure as bishops. For each of them, Gap was the first appointment to episcopal rank. This mediocre benefice, with its seat of residence isolated in the Alps, was usually only a first step in an ascending career, until an individual could move on to a more lucrative and prestigious post elsewhere in the kingdom.[67]

The turnover was rapid indeed: an average of seven years per bishop. Several of the curés of the diocese in 1789 would have served under five or even six different bishops. When we take into account the inevitable interim period between the departure of one bishop and the taking of possession of the successor, we find the number of years of actual tenure reduced even further. Every bishop after Berger de Malissoles spent periods of time outside the diocese. Often there were good reasons for this. There were the temporal affairs of the diocese and the episcopal benefice to be defended in the courts of Paris, Grenoble, and Aix; and there were the meetings of the Clergy of France to prepare and attend. In an age when governmental and ecclesiastical administrations were still largely

---

[67] Bishop Vareilles was exceptionally frank when he described the bishopric of Gap to the Ecclesiastical Committee of the National Assembly in March 1790: "Une place aussi pénible et aussi peu rétribuée, n'a peut-être pas inspiré un grand attachement à ceux qui l'ont occupée. Le site de Gap n'est pas agréable; le climat en est très austère. Dans le temps où la faveur a pu influer sur le choix des évêques, ceux de Gap ont profité du crédit qu'ils pouvaient avoir pour se procurer des sièges plus désirables. Et ne peut-on pas même regarder ces translations comme autant de récompense d'une vie laborieuse passée dans un pays ingrat, et qui n'offre d'autres consolations que celles qu'on peut espérer de son ministère?": A.N., D XIX 24.

dependent on personal relations, it was difficult to avoid regular travel to Paris. The practical effect of this frequent non-residence was to augment greatly the authority of the bishops' delegated representatives in the diocese, the vicars-general.

The succession of new bishops brought a broad assortment of personalities and abilities to the seat of Gap. An anti-Jansenist was followed by a possible Jansenist sympathizer, a pious scholar by a wayward young nobleman. There could be little continuity in such a state of affairs. The curés of the diocese of Gap, as we shall see, genuinely longed for a close father-son relation with their prelate. But there could be little guidance or consolation from this kaleidoscope of young bishops with slight personal attachment to the diocese.

After the bishop, the most prestigious members of the secular clergy were the canons. There was, however, only one small corps of canons in the diocese, the cathedral chapter of Gap. Thirteen men sat in this chapter in 1790,[68] each ranked in a strictly preserved hierarchy of honor and precedence established by tradition and by the chapter's statutes. There were twelve canonries with their corresponding prebends numbered from one to twelve. There were also four "dignities" that were held as benefices with or without a canonry and whose possessors were given special responsibilities and financial advantages within the chapter. The first of the dignitaries was the dean, who presided over capitular assemblies; the second was the archdeacon, who served as second presiding officer; then came the provost, with various disciplinary functions; and finally the sacristan, who was treasurer and archivist of the chapter.[69] Unlike the bishops, the canons usually came from the diocese itself and often from the city of

---

68 Declarations of revenue of the canons in 1790: A.D.H.A., I Q I 108(1).

69 Guillaume, *Inventaire sommaire, série G*, IV, xii–xv.

Gap.[70] But, on occasion, the bishop would introduce a personal protégé or secretary into the capitular ranks.[71] Closely associated with, but distinct from, the canons were the twelve cathedral auxiliaries, the *semi-prebendaries* or *"bénéficiers,"* as they were most frequently called in Gap. These clergymen, who were not necessarily priests, assisted the canons and took part in most cathedral ceremonies, always in a position distinctly subordinate to that of the canons. Taken together, the corps of the cathedral clergy, canons, and *semi-prebendaries*, was known as the "university." The two co-curés of Gap always held semi-prebends, and were also to be included in the university.[72]

The revenues of the chapter, like the episcopal benefice of Gap, were modest compared to those in many other parts of the kingdom. The canons' individual incomes in 1790 ranged from about 900 to 4,100 *livres* per year, depending on the dignity and prebend held. But most were between 1,000 and 2,000 *livres*.[73] The revenues of the *bénéficiers* were much smaller: 400 to 800 *livres* per year.[74] Yet all of the cathedral clergy was in a particularly advantageous position to accumulate benefices not requiring residence.[75]

The canons, assisted by the *bénéficiers*, recited the canonical hours within the cathedral and generally assured the liturgical service and public prayer of the episcopal seat. They adorned the processions and feast days with the

---

[70] See below, Chapter II.

[71] This was the case of Isidore-François Robin from Paris, secretary of bishop Vareilles, named canon of Gap about 1789: A.D.H.A., I Q I 108.

[72] Guillaume, *Inventaire sommaire, série G*, IV, xiv–xv and v, v.

[73] Declarations of 1790, A.D.H.A., I Q I 108. Compare with the 3,000 to 12,000 *livres* earned by the canons of Lyon: Michel Peronnet, "Les problèmes du clergé dans la société de l'Ancien régime de 1770 à 1789" in Roland Mousnier, *Société française de 1770 à 1789*, 2 vols. (Paris, 1970), I, 42–43; and the "rather more than 3,000 *livres*" earned by the canons of Angers: John McManners, *French Ecclesiastical Society under the Ancien Régime, A Study of Angers in the Eighteenth Century* (Manchester, 1960), p. 58.

[74] A.D.H.A., I Q I 108.   [75] See below, Chapter IV.

pomp and circumstance that many churchmen considered indispensable for the dignity of the bishop's church. The canons were also to provide the bishop with counsel and assistance in the administration of the diocese. The extent to which they exercised such advisory functions depended on the personality and good graces of each bishop. But commonly the bishops did consult with the principal dignitaries of the chapter—if not with the entire corps—before taking decisions, particularly on spiritual or disciplinary questions.[76] It was also from among the cathedral canons that the prelate chose many of his principal administrative commissioners for the diocese, the vicars-general, the ecclesiastical judges, and the financial syndics.[77] The canons, serving as vicars-general, often assured the government of the diocese during the absences of the bishops. It was primarily with these men rather than with the prelate himself that the lower clergy had to deal in their day-to-day relations with the episcopal see.

In the Middle Ages, the regular clergy may have constituted a large part, perhaps even the majority, of the priests serving in the diocese. Numerous groups of monks had been sent out by the major religious orders of southeastern France to form small priories in the Alps and to insure the religious care of the populace.[78] But in the eighteenth century, all of these priories had long since disappeared or were falling in ruin. Only their titles and their revenues remained, beneficed lands and tithing rights now usually possessed by non-resident clergymen. In 1790 there were not more than four regular clergymen

[76] For example, bishop Vareilles consulted with the chapter before revising the ceremonies of the procession of Saint-Arey in Gap: A.D.H.A., G 992, ordinance of Mar. 15, 1788.

[77] For example, in 1764 three canons were among the six vicars-general named by the new bishop Narbonne-Lara. A canon was also named as ecclesiastical judge: A.D.H.A., G 818.

[78] *Histoire de la ville de Gap*, pp. 38–39. Already in the mid-sixteenth century, there were very few priors in residence in the parishes: see the pastoral visits of 1551 to 1553: A.D.H.A., G 1538–1542.

in the diocese per 10,000 individuals.[79] They represented only about 11 percent of the resident clergy.[80] The most dynamic of the local religious orders were the Carthusians of Durbon and the Capuchins of Gap.[81] The Carthusians, living in seclusion on their lands in the Bochaine, tending their herds and their forests and periodically firing up a small iron furnace,[82] were seldom seen except by the neighboring villagers. The Capuchins, on the contrary, through their widespread preaching activities, maintained an active presence in the diocese. Traveling in groups of two or three, they conducted numerous rural missions and series of Easter or Christmas sermons in every corner of the diocese.[83] But the other religious orders for men were in full decline. The regular Augustinian canons of La Baume-lès-Sisteron, scandal-ridden for decades, were forbidden to accept novices after 1762;[84] and proposals were being made before 1789 to suppress the Dominicans and the Cordeliers of Gap and the Trinitarians of La Motte-du-Caire, each of which had only two or three members.[85] There were also two feminine orders in the diocese: the Ursulines of Gap, active in the education of girls, and the

[79] Compare to the 9 regulars per 10,000 individuals in the Isère in 1790: Godel, pp. 58, 244; or the 6 to 8 per 10,000 in the diocese of Embrun: Tackett, "Le clergé de l'archidiocèse d'Embrun," *loc. cit.*, p. 186; or to the approximately 6 per 10,000 in the department of the Sarthe, in western France, in 1789: calculated from data in M. Giraud, *Essai sur l'histoire religieuse de la Sarthe de 1789 à l'an IV* (Paris, 1920), pp. 43–45; and Charles Girault, *Les biens d'église dans la Sarthe à la fin du XVIIIe siècle* (Laval, 1953), pp. 79–348.

[80] See above, note 50. In 1789, regular clergymen are known to have served as curés in only four parishes: Aulan, Barras, Manteyer, and Reilhanette: "Pouillé ou état général des bénéfices séculiers et réguliers du diocèse de Gap avant 1789," *BHA*, x (1891), pp. 114–165.

[81] In 1791, 14 Carthusians and 15 Capuchins were listed by departmental officials: see notes by Paul Guillaume: A.D.H.A., ms. 385.

[82] Léon, I, 63–64.

[83] The "Livre des archives du couvent des pères capucins de la ville et cité de Gap," describes these mission activities: A.D.H.A., 3 H² 1.

[84] A.D.H.A., G 2670, royal order dated March 1762.

[85] Both the bishop and the sub-delegate had proposed this: A.N., G⁸ 68, "6e Etat" dated Jan. 12, 1786; and Subdel.Gap-1784, pp. 85–87.

Sisters of St. Joseph, who had the important functions of administering the orphanage of Gap and the hospitals of Gap and Ribiers.

The parish clergy constituted approximately 80 percent of the clergymen of the diocese in 1790. Theirs was the task of providing direct cure of souls in the diocese's 213 parishes, the cellular units of the Catholic Church. The directors of the parishes were the 214 parish priests or "curés" (there were two "co-curés" in the parish of Gap).[86] For administrative purposes, the parishes were grouped together into twenty-five *"archiprêtrés"* or ecclesiastical cantons, each named after a principal town or village within the canton (see Figure D).[87] An "archpriest" was commissioned from the parish priests serving in each canton to serve as the director of his colleagues and as the administrative and pastoral link to the bishop.

The number of souls in the keep of each curé varied enormously from parish to parish: from fifty or less in the tiny villages of Valença and Montrond, to several thousand in the city of Gap. But in the larger parishes, the curés were assisted in their duties by approximately seventy auxiliary priests.[88] Most of the latter, called "vicaires" or "secondaries," were specially commissioned by the bishop for service in particular parishes. There were also a few chaplains and sacristans holding beneficed rather than commissioned posts who habitually assisted in pastoral care.[89] Significantly absent in the parishes were the large numbers of non-beneficed priests—the *habitués* or *prêtres libres*—so characteristic of certain western regions such as Brittany

---

[86] In English, *"curé"* would be translated as "vicar" and *"vicaire"* as "curate." To avoid confusion, the French terms will be used throughout this study.

[87] *Almanach général de la province de Dauphiné pour l'année 1789* (Grenoble, 1789), pp. 358–363.

[88] See above, note 50.

[89] For example, the sacristan of Ribiers, the chaplain of Notre-Dame de la Miséricorde in Tallard, and the chaplain of the Penitents of Volonne. In several parishes, the chaplain of the lay confraternity of the Penitents served as an auxiliary in parish duties.

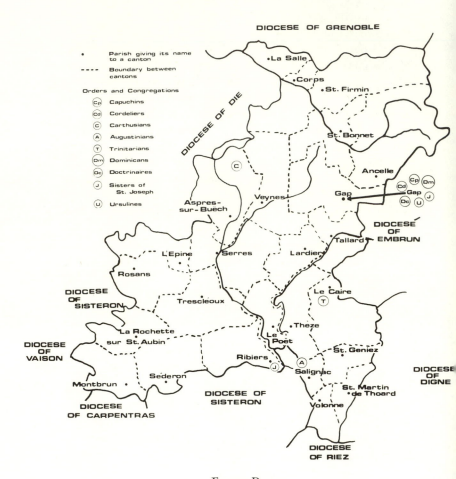

FIGURE D.
Ecclesiastical structures of the diocese of Gap in 1789: the ecclesiastical cantons

or Normandy.[90] In the parish of Gap, the two co-curés were aided by the curé of neighboring Saint-André—who no longer had a church of his own and who performed his functions in the hospital chapel—and by various of the cathedral semi-prebendaries who sometimes took temporary assignments in one or more of the eleven hamlets surrounding the town.[91] In the rural parishes of the diocese, an auxiliary priest was often permanently attached to a hamlet or group of hamlets removed from the central agglomeration. This was particularly necessary in the more mountainous regions, where an outlying settlement might be isolated from the rest of the parish by snow or swollen rivers for months at a time.[92] Thus it was unusual for a curé and a vicaire to work together regularly in the same church. The parish priest of the diocese of Gap was generally a solitary figure in the midst of his flock.

It is this group of individuals—the corps of parish clergy, men of God and village notables—that we propose to study in the following chapters.

[90] Charles Berthelot du Chesnay, "Le clergé diocésain français au XVIIIe siècle et les registres des insinuations ecclésiastiques," *RHMC,* x (1963), p. 248.

[91] See bishop Vareilles' "Observations sur les curés de Gap," Dec. 14, 1785: A.N., G^s 68 (Dossier Gap).

[92] In the parish of Orcières, one vicaire served in the hamlet of Prapic, another in Serre-Eyrauds, both isolated in winter. The chaplain of Saint-Jean-Baptiste also seems to have done service as an auxiliary.

PART ONE
A Career in the Clergy

CHAPTER II

Entry into the Clergy[1]

A decision to enter the clergy was not surrounded by any aura of mystery in eighteenth-century France. Whenever anyone thought to write on the subject, it was commonly assumed that the family, and particularly the father, "directed" the son into this career. Clergymen themselves made the same assumption. Much of the discussion within the General Assembly of the Clergy of France over the decline in clerical vocations at the end of the eighteenth century centered on the possible ways of persuading more fathers to "consecrate" their sons to the priesthood. But if the importance of the family in the decision to enter the clergy was generally agreed on, the motivation for the family's decision was greatly debated. Many members of the General Assembly argued that the primary cause of declining clerical recruitment was the insidious *"esprit philosophique"* that was undermining respect for religion and the priest. Others seemed to emphasize socio-economic factors. There were various suggestions for making a career in the clergy more attractive by increasing the security and financial advantage of the clergyman's position. Seminary scholarships and higher ecclesiastical salaries were recommended.[2] Henri Reymond, leader of the curés of Dauphiné in 1789, was participating in the same debate when he pleaded for old age pensions for priests

[1] This chapter is a revised version of my article, "Le recrutement du clergé dans le diocèse de Gap au XVIIIe siècle," *RHMC*, xx (1973), pp. 497–522. I wish to thank the *Revue d'histoire moderne et contemporaine* for granting permission to reprint this article.

[2] Michel Peronnet, "Les assemblées du clergé de France sous le règne de Louis XVI (1775–1788)," *Annales historiques de la Révolution française*, xxxiv (1962), p. 24.

"above all, so that fathers might be encouraged to intend their children for the pastoral profession."[3]

In this chapter, we shall examine the conditions under which a young man and his family made the decision for a career in the clergy and explore some of the possible factors affecting this decision. The principal sources for our study are the registers of ordinations. Before a man could assume the sacerdotal functions of the priesthood, there were a number of preparatory orders through which he must pass. The earliest rite and symbol of a commitment to the clerical life was the tonsure. By canon law this could take place any time after a boy's seventh birthday, although in eighteenth-century France it was rarely given before a boy was twelve. Sometime thereafter, the candidate was ordained to the four "minor orders"—porter, lector, exorcist, and acolyte—always given on the same day. The sub-diaconate, given only after the twenty-first birthday, was the first of the "sacred orders," and the theoretical point of no return. Once he had received this order, the cleric was always expected to appear in ecclesiastical dress. The next order, the diaconate, gave the cleric the right to baptize and to preach. Finally, sometime after his twenty-fourth birthday, an individual could be raised to the priesthood.[4] Bishops alone had the power to give tonsures and ordinations. If a man was ordained outside his home diocese, he was required to produce a letter of permission, a dimissorial letter, signed by his own bishop. The tonsures, ordinations, and dimissorial letters were all carefully set down in an episcopal register by the bishop's secretary and in a register of *insinuations ecclésiastiques* by a lay clerk. These registers, and certain related documents, make possible a statistical analysis of the particular kind of demographic flow constituted by entry into the clergy.

[3] *Cahier des curés de Dauphiné* (Lyon, 1789), p. 124.
[4] Pierre Durand de Maillane, *Dictionnaire de droit canonique et de pratique bénéficiale,* 5 vols. (Lyon, 1776), articles "âge," "ordres," "clerc"; and *Ord. Syn.,* I, 33, 201 and *passim.*

Trends in Recruitment during the Eighteenth Century

An exceptionally well-preserved series of ordination registers allows us to enumerate the entries into the priesthood in the diocese of Gap during the entire eighteenth century.[5] Plotted as a five-year moving mean (see Figure E), the curve of clerical recruitment reveals a general upward trend during the first part of the century, a decline in the 1730's, followed by a recovery in the 1740's and a peak about 1755; then there was an abrupt and severe decline after 1766 and a rebound prior to the Revolution to a level only slightly higher than at the beginning of the century. Given the present state of research, it is uncertain whether the curve for the first part of the century reflects trends in France as a whole or purely local tendencies. The rise in recruitment in the first three decades may be related to the vigorous efforts of the bishop Berger de Malissoles to increase the number of priests in his diocese.[6] For the second half of the century, however, we can identify a marked resemblance to the trends in other dioceses of France, such as Reims, Rouen, Autun, Rodez, and Grenoble:[7] a similar mid-century maximum followed

[5] A.D.H.A., G 899 and G 901–908 for the ordination registers. Before 1740, the dimissorial letters were inscribed only in the registers of the bishop's secretariat: A.D.H.A., G 811–812. After 1740, all dimissorial letters were included in the registers of ordinations. Only secular clergymen are considered in the following statistics. Regulars originating in the diocese were not systematically listed in the diocesan ordination registers (notably, when they were ordained outside the diocese), and their careers are consequently much more difficult to follow.

[6] Note, in particular, Malissoles' efforts to establish a *petit séminaire* in Tallard: A.D.H.A., G 952.

[7] Dominique Julia, "Le clergé paroissial dans le diocèse de Reims à la fin du XVIIIe siècle," *RHMC*, XIII (1966), p. 202; M. Join-Lambert, "La pratique religieuse dans le diocèse de Rouen de 1707 à 1789," *Annales de Normandie*, V (1955), pp. 35–36; A. D. Saône-et-Loire, G 818, G 824, G 826–836, G 886, 2 G 320–326, 2 G 339–343 (research in collaboration with D. Julia); A. D. Aveyron, 1 G 253–264; A.D.I., 4 G 329–355. There were, to be sure, other dioceses that did not follow this exact pattern.

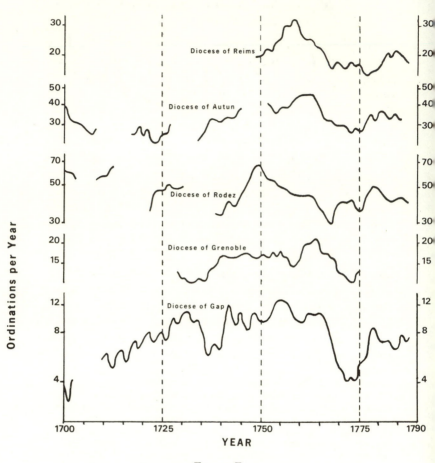

FIGURE E.
Ordinations to the priesthood in the diocese of Gap and in four
other dioceses (five-year moving means)

44

by a rapid decline, a similar partial recovery in the last decades before the Revolution. Doubtless this general decrease in the number of ordinations after 1760 was a factor inciting the Assembly General of the Clergy to undertake its inquiry into recruitment in 1775.[8]

The bishops of Gap drew up no such yearly statistics on sacerdotal vocations. Nevertheless, they were keenly aware of these general trends when they attempted to manipulate the "supply and demand" of priests for the parishes of the diocese.[9] By a careful study of the provisions of benefices, we find that an average of about nine new priests were required each year to fill the vacancies occasioned by the death or retirement of incumbent curés.[10] A comparison, then, with the recruitment curve would suggest that only toward mid-century, primarily between 1741 and 1765, could the diocese have been self-sufficient for its supply of curés.[11] It is not surprising that bishop Pérouse in 1760 should describe his inability to place an excess of priests,[12] or that a number of young clergymen should request formal permission during this period to leave the diocese of Gap and to seek employment elsewhere.[13] But from the bishops

8 Peronnet, *loc. cit.*

9 The bishops of Gap had the right of the direct nomination of more than 80 percent of the cures in the diocese: A.D.H.A., G 2328.

10 Based on the registers of the bishop's secretariat, 1779–1788: A.D.H.A., G 823–828. The provisions of benefices always mention the previous holder of a benefice and the reason for the vacancy: death, resignation *en cour de Rome*, etc. Since the number of curés and secondaries remained practically unchanged throughout the eighteenth century, the figure of nine should be valid for the entire period under consideration. These calculations do not take into account those cases, presumably rare, of the death or retirement of a priest who was only a vicaire.

11 It is to be noted that the great majority of priests originating in the diocese went into the parish clergy, about 93 percent for the period after 1751: statistics from a personal *fichier* and from the *fichier* by Paul Guillaume preserved in A.D.H.A., ms. 377.

12 Letter to the marquis De Moydans, Jan. 21, 1760: A.D.H.A., F 2468.

13 Numerous *exeats* were granted to priests between 1755 and 1765 "pour aller travailler dans un diocèse étranger": register of approbations: A.D.H.A., G 829.

at the end of the century, as from Berger de Malissoles at the beginning, we find the continual complaint of a "dearth of priests, insufficient to fill even the established and most necessary posts."[14] The decline in recruitment before the Revolution was probably felt most acutely when the bishops attempted to fill the posts of the vicaires, positions generally occupied by younger priests just beginning their careers. The vast majority of vicaires assigned between 1747 and 1762 came from the diocese of Gap itself.[15] But in the 1780's numerous newly ordained priests were being brought in from the diocese of Embrun to fill these positions, following a standing request from the bishop of Gap to the archbishop of Embrun.[16] To be sure, compared to certain other dioceses in France, the situation was far from critical. The diocese of Gap was nearly self-sufficient in priests for its parishes. Within the sector of the southern Alps, it might be seen as a middle ground between the diocese of Embrun, which produced a surplus to fill positions all over southeastern France,[17] and the diocese of Die, to the west, chronically undersupplied. The percentages of the parish clergy native to each diocese in 1789 are revealing: 99 percent for the diocese of Embrun, 83 percent for the diocese of Gap, 53 percent for the diocese of Die.[18]

14 The phrase is used by Maillé de la Tour-Landry in the register of the secretariat, A.D.H.A., G 823, entry of June 13, 1781. We find similar complaints by Malissoles in 1707: see A.D.H.A., G 952.

15 "Registres journaliers d'approbations et prorogations": A.D.H.A., G 829–830.

16 *Exeats* addressed to the diocese of Gap from the diocese of Embrun: A.D.H.A., G 897. See, in particular, the note attached by the archbishop's secretary to the *exeat* of Antoine Gérard: "Enfin, le seul prêtre que nous puissions vous envoyer, arriva hier au soir du fond du Queyras, sans que nous eussions pu lui faire savoir plus tôt qu'il y avait une place vacante dans le diocèse de Gap."

17 See my article, "Le clergé de l'archidiocèse d'Embrun à la fin de l'Ancien régime," *Annales du Midi*, LXXXVIII (1976), pp. 181–183.

18 For Gap and Embrun: A.D.H.A., ms. 399; supplemented by information kindly given to me by the abbé Adrien Loche for the Drôme, and by the abbé Jean Godel for the Isère. For the diocese of Die, Jacques Lovie, "La vie paroissiale dans le diocèse de Die à la fin de l'Ancien régime," *BD*, LXV (1935), p. 18.

Entry into the Clergy

The changes in ordination patterns in the diocese of Gap can be related, in part, to the perseverance through the clerical orders of those men receiving the tonsure (see Table 2). Between 1720 and 1760 the number of men

TABLE 2

Rate of Perseverance

	Number of Tonsured Clerics	Number of Clerics Who Became Priests	Rate of Perseverance to the Priesthood (percent)
1721–1730	127	74	58
1731–1740	130	80	62
1741–1750	116	99	85
1751–1760	133	94	71
1761–1770	74	51	69
1771–1780	87	52	60

tonsured per decade changed only slightly. But the proportion who actually continued into the priesthood rose from 58 percent in 1721–1730 to 85 percent in 1741–1750.[19] The high rate of perseverance for the clerics of the 1740's helps to explain the apogee in sacerdotal ordinations in the following decade. After 1760, however, the number of tonsured clerics dropped abruptly and the rate of perseverance declined as well. The decline in ordinations in the 1760's may also be related to the disruption in secondary education caused by the expulsion of the Jesuits. The secondary school in Embrun had traditionally trained numerous future priests for the diocese of Gap, and, after the departure of its Jesuit directors in 1763, the institution was thrown into a severe financial and organizational crisis.[20]

[19] Research in the diocese of Autun, in which Dominique Julia and I are collaborating, reveals a similar sharp increase in the rate of perseverance. In this diocese, the change took place about 40 to 50 years earlier than in the diocese of Gap.

[20] For the financial side of this crisis, see F. N. Nicolet, "Les biens et revenus du collège d'Embrun avant la Révolution," *BHA*, xi (1892),

But perhaps the most important factor to be related to the changing patterns of recruitment was the remarkable transformation in the geographic origins of the diocesan clergy. At the moment when a young man received his first tonsure, the names and residence of his parents were carefully noted in an ordinations register by an episcopal scribe. It is thus possible to ascertain the probable parish of birth of nearly all men entering the priesthood in the diocese after 1720.[21] In Table 3 we have calculated the recruitment to the priesthood in the various natural regions of the diocese in proportion to the population.[22] The same data are represented cartographically in Figures F and G. Clearly, there were a number of regions that provided relatively small numbers of clergymen throughout the century: notably the high-mountain regions of the Dévoluy and the Valgaudemar-Upper-Champsaur, and the two regions with the largest Protestant minorities, the Serrois and the Northern Baronnies. In fact, during the first half of the century a broad negative correlation seems to have existed throughout the diocese between clerical recruitment and the presence of Protestants (see Figures C and F).[23] In other

---

pp. 320–322. For the attempts to reorganize and "modernize" the curriculum—and the heated opposition to these attempts—see A.D.H.A., F 779 and A.C. Embrun, prov. 1199.

[21] Before this date, the secretary frequently neglected to include the parish of origin, noting only that the cleric was from "this diocese."

[22] For the province of Dauphiné, I have used the intendancy census reports of 1748: B.M.G., U 5210, printed in R. Vallentin du Cheylard, *Essai sur la population des taillabilités du Dauphiné* (Valence, 1912), pp. 165–202. This report lists the number of households per community. For the parishes in Provence, I have used the abbé Expilly's pioneering demographic study in his *Dictionnaire géographique, historique et politique des Gaules et de la France*, 6 vols. (Paris, 1762–1770), V, 925–968. In fact, Expilly gives the number of houses per community rather than the number of households. But, according to the *affouagement* of 1728, there was approximately the same number of houses and of households in the communities of the diocese within Upper Provence: A.D.B.A., C 59. The population figures for the two parishes within the Comtat-Venaissin have been taken from the pastoral visit of 1740: A.D.H.A., G 788.

[23] Was there not a "frontière de catholicité" operating here—the close proximity of a large Protestant population serving as a spur to

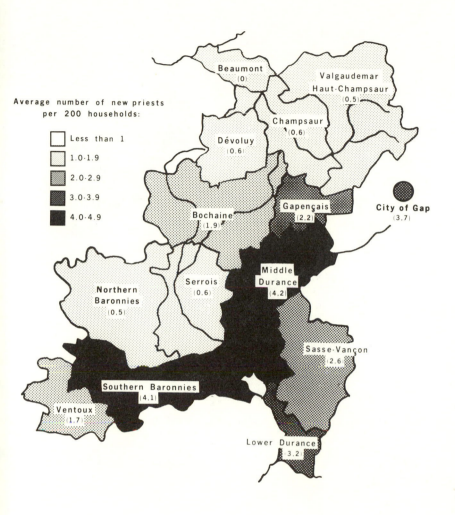

Average number of new priests
per 200 households:

Less than 1

1.0-1.9

2.0-2.9

3.0-3.9

4.0-4.9

Beaumont
(0)

Valgaudemar
Haut-Champsaur
(0.5)

Champsaur
(0.6)

Dévoluy
(0.6)

Gapençais
(2.2)

City of Gap
(3.7)

Bochaine
(1.9)

Middle
Durance
(4.2)

Serrois
(0.6)

Northern
Baronnies
(0.5)

Sasse-Vançon
2.6

Southern Baronnies
(4.1)

Ventoux
(1.7)

Lower Durance
3.2

FIGURE F.
Regional distributions of ordinations to the priesthood,
1721 to 1745

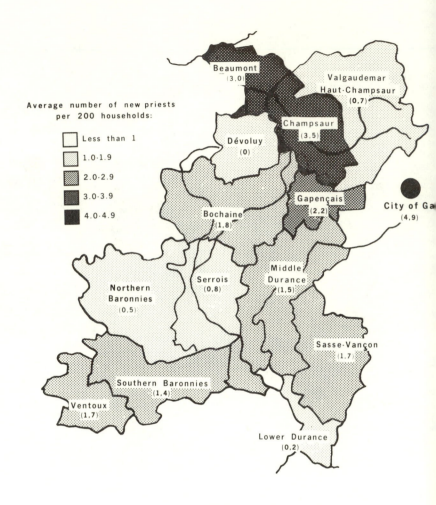

Average number of new priests
per 200 households:

☐ Less than 1
▨ 1.0-1.9
▨ 2.0-2.9
▨ 3.0-3.9
▧ 4.0-4.9

Beaumont
(3.0)

Valgaudemar
Haut-Champsaur
(0,7)

Champsaur
(3.5)

Dévoluy
(0)

Gapençais
(2,2)

City of Ga
(4,9)

Bochaine
(1,8)

Middle
Durance
(1,5)

Serrois
(0,8)

Northern
Baronnies
(0.5)

Sasse-Vançon
(1.7)

Southern Baronnies
(1,4)

Ventoux
(1,7)

Lower Durance
(0,2)

FIGURE G.
Regional distributions of ordinations to the priesthood,
1766 to 1790

TABLE 3

Recruitment to the Priesthood

	Population (Families)	PERIOD 1721–1745		PERIOD 1766–1790	
		Priests	Rate for 200 fam.	Priests	Rate for 200 fam.
Middle Durance	2977	63	4.2	22	1.5
Alpine Lower Durance	825	13	3.2	1	0.2
Sasse-Vançon	1173	15	2.6	10	1.7
Ventoux	688	6	1.7	6	1.7
Southern Baronnies	1432	29	4.1	10	1.4
Northern Baronnies	1682	4	0.5	4	0.5
Serroís	1233	4	0.6	5	0.8
Bochaine	1660	16	1.9	15	1.8
Dévoluy	362	1	0.6	0	0.0
Valgaudemar-Upper-Champsaur	828	2	0.5	3	0.7
Champsaur	1882	6	0.6	33	3.5
Beaumont	804	0	0.0	12	3.0
Gapençais (minus city of Gap)	447	5	2.2	5	2.2
City of Gap	1184	22	3.7	29	4.9
Total, diocese	17177	186	2.2	155	1.8
Total, *bourgs*	1874	45	4.8	16	1.7
Total, villages (minus Gap and *bourgs*)	14119	119	1.7	110	1.6

areas of the diocese, however, a dramatic shift occurred between the two periods, 1721–1745 and 1766–1790. During the early part of the century, the largest proportion of

the religious vitality of a neighboring Catholic region? This might well have been the case for the early eighteenth century between the Serrois, with almost 25 percent *nouveaux convertis,* and the Middle Durance, with almost no Protestants and the highest recruitment ratio in the diocese. At any rate, the "frontier effect" would no longer seem to have been operative in 1766–1790. See Pierre Chaunu, "Jansénisme et frontière de catholicité," *RH,* LXXXVI (1962), pp. 115–138; and "Une histoire religieuse sérielle," *RHMC,* XII (1965), pp. 5–34.

clergymen was coming from the south of the diocese, especially from the valley of the Durance and the Southern Baronnies. But in the decades before the Revolution, the recruitment ratio in the south had dropped precipitously to a level below that of the diocese as a whole. Simultaneously, the northern region of the Champsaur-Beaumont, an area of minimal recruitment in the earlier period, had become a veritable reservoir of priests by 1766–1790. Also of interest is the rapid decline in the number of priests originating in the medium-size towns or *"bourgs."*[24] The recruitment ratio for the villages, on the contrary, was stationary at a relatively low level, while the town of Gap remained a generally consistent source of new priests throughout the century.

Examining on a more refined scale the zones where the greatest changes occurred (see Figure H), we find that the pivotal period came just after mid-century, in 1751–1760 for the Drac and in the following decade for the Durance. It was obviously the influx of priests from both north and south during the decade 1751–1760 that produced the peak in the eighteenth-century recruitment curve. There was nothing gradual about the changes that took place; in each area it was a question of a sudden sharp increase or decrease. In the four towns of the Durance valley, however, a more gradual decline in vocations had already begun in the 1730's, thus anticipating by several decades the decline in the Durance valley as a whole.

Samples have also been taken in ordinations registers of the seventeenth and of the nineteenth centuries. In the seventeenth century, the greatest proportion of clerics came from the southern, "Provençal" sector of the diocese; in the nineteenth century, it was the Drac valley of Upper Dau-

---

24 For present purposes, a *"bourg"* has been defined as a community of more than 200 households, most of which were located in a central agglomeration: *i.e.*, Corps, Saint-Bonnet, Veynes, Serres, Tallard, Ribiers, Mison, and Volonne. Gap itself was considered to be a *ville*.

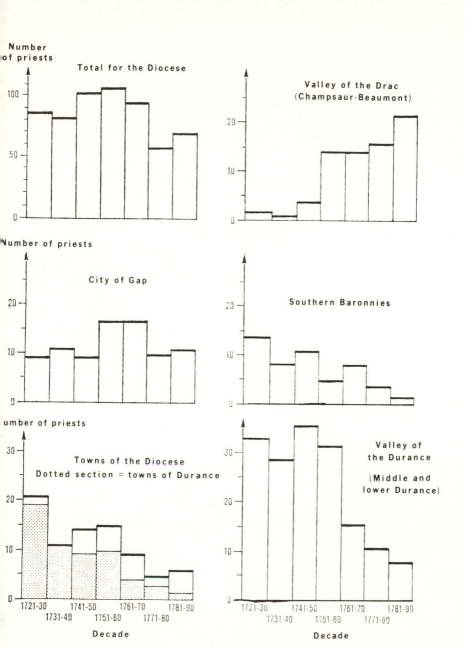

FIGURE H.
Ordinations to the priesthood by decade, 1721 to 1790

53

phiné that provided by far the largest contingents.[25] Thus
the period between 1750 and 1770 seems to have marked a
major turning point in the history of clerical recruitment
in the region during three centuries.

FAMILY ORIGINS OF THE CLERGY

Before a young man became a sub-deacon, he was required to give proof of a regular source of income that
would provide for his upkeep until he had obtained his
first benefice. For the great majority, approximately 90 percent of all sub-deacons ordained in the diocese after 1751,
this guaranteed income took the form of a "patrimony"
constituted for the future priest by his family. The notarized act involved, the "patrimonial title" as it was called,
provides valuable information about the social and
economic milieu from which the clergy originated.[26]

In general, the patrimonial title was a straightforward
legal document, rarely giving evidence of religious commitment.[27] It was not unlike a marriage contract insofar as

[25] The sample was made for tonsured clerics only. In the period
1640–1647 of 250 tonsured clerics for whom origins are known, 41
percent came from the Durance valley and 4 percent from the Champsaur-Beaumont: A.D.H.A., G 898. For the period 1841–1865, when the
Beaumont and the left bank of the Durance were no longer in the
diocese of Gap, 8 percent came from the Durance valley and 50 percent
from the Champsaur: register of ordinations, Archives de l'évêché de
Gap. Note also the statement by Bishop Bonabel concerning the religious vitality in the Hautes-Alpes in 1936: "le Champsaur et le Queyras
sont assez bien conservés, tandis que le sud du diocèse s'est converti au
socialisme": *RHEF*, (1936), 479.

[26] The ordinations register specifies the type of clerical title provided
for each subdeacon. In addition to those ordained *sub titulo patri-
monii*, a few were already in possession of a benefice and were therefore not required to establish a patrimony; they were ordained *sub
titulo beneficii*. Sources: A.D.H.A., G 877–880, register of *insinuations
ecclésiastiques*, 1751–1771; A.D.H.A., G 906–908, registers of ordinations,
1780–1790. Certain of the titles dating 1771–1780 have been located in
notary minutes by means of the *contrôle des actes*.

[27] There was usually only a formula phrase such as "pour seconder
les intentions pieuses de son fils." I found only one mention of the
"divine inspiration" that had moved a man's son from childhood to

it established the precise financial responsibilities between the contracting parties, the cleric and his family, and limited the future claims the former might make on the family fortune. With few exceptions the patrimony was provided by the father or by an elder brother, following the stated wishes of the father; and sometimes it was even written into the older brother's marriage contract. The evidence indicates that the clergy in the diocese of Gap was essentially a corps of younger sons.[28] The income involved usually consisted of a yearly pension of 100 *livres* to be paid by the donor and his heirs to the clergyman. Sometimes the pension was due only until the priest had obtained his first benefice; sometimes it was to be paid for life. Only rarely was there an actual donation of property that the priest might bequeath as he chose. In return for his pension, the cleric often renounced all claims on the family inheritance, an arrangement clearly advantageous for preserving the family fortune from division among too many younger sons.[29] The patrimonial titles also help to prove the existence of families of priests, just as there were families of notaries or carpenters or wig-makers. Uncles and nephews entering the clergy sometimes followed in succession through several generations.[30] Among the clergymen serving in 1790 who had originated in the diocese of Gap, nearly one in four had a brother in the priesthood.[31]

Primarily by means of the patrimonial titles, it has been

---

desire to become a priest: A.D.H.A., G 906, patrimonial title of Joseph Blanchard, May 20, 1784.

[28] A sample of the wills of priests' fathers has also been studied. In 16 such wills, located in notary minutes by means of the alphabetical tables for the *bureau* of Gap, I found only 2 or possibly 3 cases in which the oldest son entered the priesthood.

[29] In most of the same 16 wills of priests' fathers, the clergyman was, in fact, given nothing from the father's heritage beyond the clerical patrimony.

[30] *E.g.*, the Millon family of Chaillol had been furnishing priests for the diocese since at least the fifteenth century: notes by Paul Guillaume on the clergy of the diocese of Gap: A.D.H.A., ms. 377.

[31] Fifty-two of 227 (23 percent).

possible to ascertain the occupations of the families of 79 percent of all clerics obtaining the sub-diaconate between 1751 and 1790.[32] The percentages for the occupations of the heads of the priests' families are given in Figure I. Within this total group, it is important to distinguish those priests who would hold benefices without cure of souls—primarily the canons and priors—from those who would serve in the parish clergy. The former, only about seven percent of the total, apparently came entirely from families that we might classify as "notables": nobles, office-holders, members of the liberal professions, and those calling themselves "bourgeois" (a title normally assumed by individuals living off revenues from land rents and various other non-commercial investments). Well over half of those for whom professions are known were members of the nobility, and the great majority came from the town of Gap itself.[33] The parish clergy, on the other hand, came from a much broader spectrum of backgrounds: about one-fourth from the peasantry, over one-third from a merchant-artisan milieu, and only 37.5 percent from the group of "notables"—including no more than two percent from the nobility.[34] The Gap parish clergy thus appears to have been relatively similar in its social origins to the clergy of such

32 A special case is that group of sub-deacons for which a patrimonial title was found that did not specify the occupations of the father or brother (11 percent of the titles). The occupations of many of these families were later located in the *capitation* rolls; almost without exception, they were found to be among the peasant classes. This group has therefore been included in the category of *laboureurs*. On the use of the patrimonial titles, see Charles Berthelot du Chesnay, "Le clergé diocésain au XVIIIe siècle et les registres des insinuations ecclésiastiques," *RHMC*, x (1963), pp. 241–269.

33 Between 1751 and 1790, there were 22 priests originating in the diocese who seem not to have made a career in the parish clergy (of a total of 329 priests ordained). For these, the family origins were as follows: 10 nobles, 2 "bourgeois," 4 *officiers*, 1 doctor, 5 unknown.

34 Removing the clergy without cure of souls from the total group reduces the percentage of nobility to 2 percent. Otherwise, there is no important change in the percentages of the various categories as indicated in Figure I.

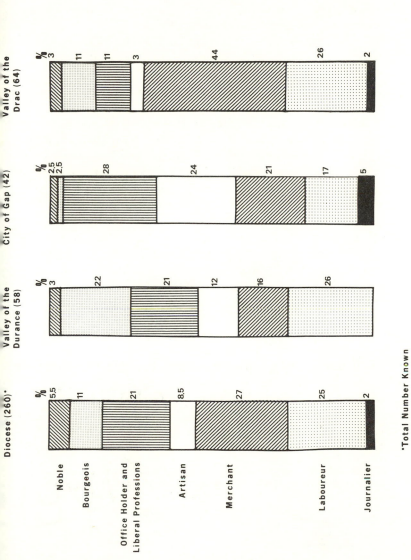

FIGURE I.

Social origins of priests ordained between 1751 and 1790

dioceses as Autun, Reims, and Le Mans. This is true despite the considerable geographic and socio-economic differences between Upper Dauphiné and these distant dioceses of central, northern, and western France.[35] Nevertheless, there were important regional differences in the occupational titles of priests' families within the diocese of Gap. In the valley of the Durance, the percentages were close to those for the diocese as a whole. Of particular note, however, was the large group of priests, 46 percent of the total, coming from families of notables. In contrast, only 25 percent of the priests from the valley of the Drac came from these milieux. For the Drac valley we are particularly puzzled by the large group, 44 percent, originating in "merchant" families. The meaning of this occupational description is not immediately clear. Within the Durance valley, the term presents few difficulties. Most of the merchants there used the term *"marchand-négociant"* or simply *"négociant"* and were therefore probably substantial wholesale merchants; other merchants appeared in the tax rolls as shopkeepers or artisan-shopkeepers.[36] The merchants of the Durance, then, although probably possessing widely varying incomes, seem generally to have been involved in town-based occupations. The "merchants" of the Drac appear to have been something different. Only two of those found added the word *"négociant."* And when we examine the tax rolls for the Champsaur, the title of "merchant" rarely appears, except in the town of Saint-Bonnet. We find rather a rural society consisting almost entirely of *laboureurs* and *journaliers*. In several instances, the merchant of the clerical title appears

[35] A. D. Saône-et-Loire, 2 G 330–343, data obtained in collaboration with Dominique Julia; Julia, "Le clergé paroissial dans le diocèse de Reims," p. 207; and data for the diocese of Le Mans, kindly shown to me by M. Alex Poyer. Due to the variations in the meaning of specific occupational titles from region to region, and the variations in the social groupings used by researchers, these comparisons must be made with some caution.

[36] In the rolls of the *capitation* and the *vingtième*, one was a *boulanger*, another a *vitrier*.

in the tax rolls as a *laboureur*—a title indicative of a relatively substantial, land-owning peasant.[37] The "merchants" of the Drac valley, then, were primarily agricultural merchants, and perhaps, above all, livestock merchants. Indeed, by contemporary accounts, it was the livestock trade —buying animals in the lowlands, fattening them on mountain pastures, and reselling them in Provence—that brought the greatest wealth to the Champsaur.[38]

These distinctions are important. For we now see that while about one-fourth of the priests originating in the Durance valley were from peasant families, almost two-thirds of those from the Drac valley were probably of rural origin, from peasant or peasant-merchant families. Thus, the shift of the principal centers of clerical recruitment that took place in the second half of the eighteenth century carried with it a shift in social origins as well. The "ruralization" of the clergy, which has been observed in studies of the nineteenth-century priest,[39] had begun considerably before the Revolution in the case of the Champsaur-Beaumont.

The family origins of men entering the priesthood can be further clarified as to economic position by reference to the *capitation* rolls. In Dauphiné this tax was assessed separately in each community by a group of locally elected notables and was to be based on the total income of each head of household.[40] For present purposes, we have relied

[37] This is the case, for example, of Claude Martin, father of Mathieu: *capitation* of Saint-Eusèbe of 1777, A.D.H.A., F 199. Men who proudly called themselves "merchants" on the occasion of a clerical title or a marriage contract might naturally use the less pretentious title of *laboureur* when it came time to be evaluated for taxes. Such examples serve to emphasize, once again, the fluidity of occupational titles under the Old Regime.

[38] See especially A. Farnaud, *Exposé des améliorations introduites depuis environ cinquante ans dans les diverses branches de l'économie rurale du département des Hautes-Alpes* (Gap, 1811), pp. 54–59.

[39] Dominique Julia, "La crise des vocations, essai d'analyse historique," *Les Etudes*, no. 326 (1967), pp. 249–251.

[40] The tax was to be levied "à proportion de leurs facultés, tant immobilières, que mobilières et industrielles": printed circular for the

primarily on the *capitation* of 1790. Administered by the Interim Commission of the Provincial Estates rather than by the intendant, this final *capitation* of the Old Regime was to be assessed in accordance with the reform principles established by the Estates of Romans.[41] The rolls of 1790 are especially valuable insofar as they include the former privileged classes who were to be taxed on the same basis as everyone else. [42]

In order to appraise the relative economic position of the priests' families within their respective villages, a percentile index of tax assessed has been calculated for each of the families in question. This index denotes the percentage of heads of household in the community who paid a tax lower than that of the priest's family. Obviously, it pertains to an individual's wealth only in the context of his own community. There might be a great difference in the absolute wealth of two men with the same index, one living in a small village and the other in the town of Gap.

In all, the tax rolls of thirty-three communities have been examined, representative of nearly every region of the diocese. They included the heads of the families of 39 percent of all priests ordained in the diocese from 1766 to

---

capitation of 1790: A.D.H.A., L 1235. Before 1790 the intendant had been less specific: ". . . suivant la connaissance que vous aurez des facultés de chaque habitant . . .": A.D.D., E 3232 (60), circular for *capitation* of 1760.

[41] For the report by Lacour d'Ambésieux on the *capitation* in Dauphiné presented to the Provincial Estates, see Jean Egret, *Les derniers Etats de Dauphiné. Romans (1788–1789)* (Grenoble, 1942), pp. 106–109. Among other reforms, it was suggested that individuals paying the same tax be grouped together on the rolls for easy verification by the public at large. This procedure was, in fact, made requisite for the rolls of 1790.

[42] Doubtless there were occasionally acts of favoritism in drawing up the rolls. In 1784, the sub-delegate of Gap, Delafont, drew attention to certain inequalities in the assessment of the *capitation*. But he further indicated that complaints about it were rare: "Mémoire sur l'état de la subdélégation de Gap en 1784," ed. Joseph Roman, *BHA*, XVIII (1899), pp. 67–68.

1790.[43] For the sake of comparison, we have also retrieved seven *capitation* rolls from the earlier part of the eighteenth century, and have thus located the families of 13 percent of the priests ordained between 1721 and 1745 (see Table 4).[44] The wealth indices of all of these families have been displayed graphically in Figure J.

TABLE 4

Economic Situation of the Families of Priests

(*Capitation* of 1790)

'ommunity	Priest	Year of Priesthood	Relative Paying Cap.	Profession	% Paying Lower Cap.
:habottes	Para	1790	father	bourgeois	99
	Rambaud	90	father	laboureur	93
	Allec	69	brother	laboureur	85
‣uissard	Rambaud	78	brother	laboureur	91
	Blanc	90	brother	marchand	91
t-Julien	Mazet	84	father	marchand	91
	Duserre	89	father	laboureur	83
	Robin	75	father	laboureur	72
t-Bonnet	Motte	66	father	bourgeois	99
	Ebrard	69, 80	brother	serrurier	51
	Brun-More	90	father	fournier	51
t-Eusèbe	Martin	72, 82	father	marchand	90
	Escalle	88	father	ménager	74
‚a Motte	Roux	85	brother	meunier	88
énévent	Grimaud	85	brother	?	88
	Davin	90	father	marchand	52
t-Laurent	Blanc	81	father	ménager	90
a Fare	Blache	85	father	marchand	88
	Manuel	87	father	laboureur	77

[43] A.D.H.A., L 499, L 1234, L 1388, for the rolls of communities in the Hautes-Alpes. Four communities situated in Provence have been included via the *capitation* of 1789 in order to broaden the sample: A.D.B.A., C 78.

[44] A.D.D., E 3279 (Montauban), E 3223 (Mévouillon), E 3177 (Lachau); A.C. preserved in A.D.H.A.: Tallard CC 95, Ribiers CC 25, Manteyer G 4; A.C. preserved in A.D.B.A.: Thèze CC "capitation." I wish to thank MM. Chomel, Playoust, and Renaudin, *directeurs des services d'archives* in the Isère, the Hautes-Alpes, and the Drôme, for their efforts to locate the earlier *capitation* rolls.

A Career in the Clergy

Community	Priest	Year of Priesthood	Relative Paying Cap.	Profession	% Paying Lower Cap
Le Noyer	Christophle	1781	father	laboureur	77
	Villar	87	father	greffier	78
Le Glaizil	Gautier	88	brother	bourgeois	99
	Sechier	87	father	négociant	92
Aspres/Corps	Manuel	89	father	marchand	96
	Calvet	88	father	marchand	63
St-Maurice	Galland	85	father	marchand	94
Gap	Jacques	77	father	marchand	97
	Escallier	82	father	avocat	94
	Rappellin	75	father	marchand	91
	Reynoard	80	brother	ménager	79
	Rolland	71, 80	father	maréchal	75
	Vallet	89	father	ménager	69
	Armand	83	father	perruquier	53
	Ubaud	89	brother	tapissier	53
	Reynier	74, 82	brother	perruquier	39
Rambaud	Moulin	90	father	marchand	40
Bâtie-Neuve	Meyssonier	88	father	journalier	25
Bâtie-Vieille	Boyer	87	father	négociant	79
La Roche	Mondet	85, 88	father	négociant	96
Veynes	Lesbros	85	father	marchand	69
Aspres/Veynes	Corréard	78	father	négociant	94
	Motte	67	brother	notaire	86
Serres	Chevandier	83	father	médecin	83
St-André/Boch.	Morgan	66	brother	notaire	94
	Robin	86, 90	brother	aubergiste	39
	Roux	90	father	négociant	87
L'Epine	Arnaud	88	father	journalier	40
St-André/Rosans	Charras	80	brother	ménager	91
Salérans	Gabriel	70	brother	notaire	99
La Saulce	Pellenc	87	brother	négociant	86
Ventavon	Brun	72	father	"maire"	95
Upaix	Clément	90	brother	ménager	94
Ribiers	Pellegrin	87	bro.-in-law	blanchier	60
Valernes*	Tourniaire	80	father	?	97
St-Geniez*	Dalmas	73	father	notaire	92
	Bernard	67	brother	lieut. de juge	92
	Bougeral	77	father	ménager	87
	Comte	86	father	maréchal	75
Curbans*	Davignon	71	brother	bourgeois	99

ommunity	Priest	Year of Priesthood	Relative Paying Cap.	Profession	% Paying Lower Cap.
lamensane*	Burle	1772	father	bourgeois	98
	Chardavon	90	father	ménager	80
		Capitations of 1710–1725			
anteyer	Chevalier	22	father	lieut.-châtelain	99
	Léautier	48	father	travailleur	75
achau	Camerle	30	father	maçon	37
	Francon	24	father	laboureur	97
	Salva	37	father	?	90
évouillon	Mourrenas	23	father	?	99
	Jullien	24	father	?	94
ontauban	Pascal	21	father	?	94
	Charras	30, 31	father	?	99
	Eysserie	36	father	?	87
ibiers	Arnaud	25	father	tailleur	52
	Bois	43	father	ménager	99
	Bouillet	22	father	cardeur	37
	Bois	43	father	procureur	85
	Evêque	26	father	cordonnier	77
	Jean	22	father	procureur	91
	Salva	31, 41	father	bourgeois	98
	Viguier	26, 37	father	travailleur	89
allard	Collombon	44	father	?	83
	Berne	38	father	?	92
	Augier	34	father	?	83
	Céas	37	father	ménager	67
hèze	Brochier	30	father	ménager	98
	Barou	41	father	cardeur	36

Capitation of 1789, Provence.

Despite the wide variety of occupations practiced by the priests' families, the great majority were clearly among the economic elite of their communities. To be sure, it was possible throughout the century for a man to attain the priesthood even if his parents were situated in the bottom half of the local economic scale. The bishops of Gap had long sought to enable more modest families to send their sons into the priesthood—notably, by means of financial assist-

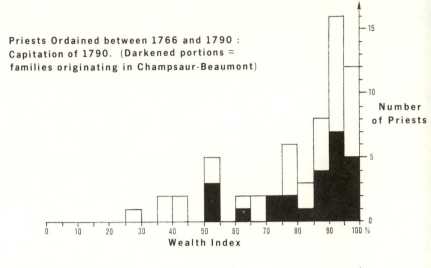

Priests Ordained between 1766 and 1790 :
Capitation of 1790. (Darkened portions =
families originating in Champsaur-Beaumont)

Number
of Priests

Wealth Index

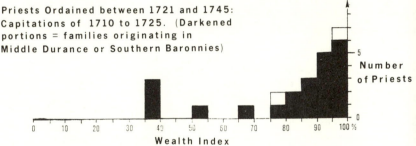

Priests Ordained between 1721 and 1745:
Capitations of 1710 to 1725. (Darkened
portions = families originating in
Middle Durance or Southern Baronnies)

Number
of Priests

Wealth Index

FIGURE J.

Economic situation of priests' families based on the *capitation* rolls

ance for the seminary—and apparently their efforts had
been somewhat successful.[45] But the principal fact remains:

[45] In 1707 bishop Malissoles was trying to establish a *petit séminaire,*
"en faveur de jeunes enfants pauvres qui voudront se destiner à l'état
ecclésiastique . . .": A.D.H.A., G 952, deliberations of the clergy of
Gap, Nov. 9, 1707. See also the letter from Tournu, sacristan of Gap,
mentioning bishop Jouffroy-Gonssans' efforts to "former des bourses
pour faire élever les pauvres ecclésiastiques": letter to Saint-Genis dated
Mar. 8, 1776: A.D.H.A., G 2088. See also below, Chapter III.

more than half of the priests' families were in the upper 15 percent, more than three-fourths in the upper 30 percent of taxpayers in their respective localities.

The sample for the earlier period is considerably smaller than that for the decades before the Revolution. Yet the general concordance in the profiles of family wealth for the two groups of priests leads us to suppose that the situation changed very little during the eighteenth century. There also seems to have been little economic difference between the families of priests originating in the principal centers of recruitment in the two periods, between the Middle Durance and the Southern Baronnies in 1721–1745 and the Champsaur in 1766–1790. The priests from the peasant milieu of the Drac, like the more specifically "bourgeois" priests of the Durance of the early part of the century, all seem to have come from families that ranked near the top of the local economic scale.

EXPLORATIONS OF INTERPRETATION

Thus, the geographic and socio-economic dichotomy, previously identified within the diocese of Gap, was also reflected in the regional variations in recruitment to the clergy. The century-long ordinations curve for the diocese as a whole masked the effects of certain opposite and apparently independent trends in the different zones of the diocese. The decline after 1760 in the southern "Provençal" regions was permanent; in the valley of the Durance there was never a sign of a rebound at the end of the century. On the contrary, in the northern valley of the Drac, recruitment, based in a milieu of prosperous peasants, seems to have been little perturbed in the 1760's, rising progressively after 1750 and, after the hiatus of the Revolution, continuing into the nineteenth and twentieth centuries.

A number of variables are probably to be related to this differential evolution of clerical recruitment. For the

A Career in the Clergy

valley of the Drac, the existence of a rapidly expanding population after mid-century has already been noted. Such a trend might well have been a factor in encouraging families to designate excess sons for careers in the clergy.[46] Further, the Champsaur had probably become the most prosperous area in the diocese at the end of the Old Regime. In addition to an important commerce in livestock, the region profited greatly from the grain trade with Lower Provence.[47] In fact, the rapid increase in vocations in the Champsaur-Beaumont after 1750 closely followed the upward turn of grain prices in Dauphiné in the 1740's. There can be no doubt that financial considerations—the major family expenditures required for the patrimonial title and the education of the cleric—weighed heavily in the decision to enter the priesthood.[48] It was precisely that milieu of peasant-merchants—that group which profited most from the trade in produce and livestock that was at the base of the Champsaur's prosperity—which provided such a large percentage of the priests from the Champsaur.[49] But, whatever the influence of economic and population trends on recruitment in the north, it is difficult to identify any corresponding relation in the south of the diocese. Population in the Durance basin may have risen

[46] See above, Chapter I. Due to the paucity of demographic research in Upper Dauphiné, we do not know if the elite families in the Drac region, from which most of the clergy originated, were growing as rapidly as the other families in that region.

[47] See Farnaud, pp. 54–59; also the memorandum by the subdelegate of Gap on the *cosse*, Feb. 28, 1787: Collect. Roman, LII.

[48] Between 1753 and 1763, Jean-Balthazar Marcellin, notary in Rémuzat, spent 1,304 *livres*, 13 *sous*—a substantial sum—for the education of his younger brother who was preparing for the clergy. This does not include the 2,000 *livres* in capital required for a 100 *livres* per year clerical title: "Etat de ce que j'ai fourni à mon frère": archives of the cure of Rémuzat, Fond Marcellin.

[49] Young men from peasant backgrounds in the Drac valley were also favored, as a group, for entry into the clergy by the apparently high masculine literacy rates in this region. Yet already, in the early part of the century, this rate had been higher than that in the Durance valley: see above. Chapter I, note 49.

more slowly, but there is no evidence of a demographic crisis after 1750. Grain prices increased in Provence as in Dauphiné, and although the southeast was not the most favored region of the diocese at the end of the century, neither does there seem to have been any severe economic decline.

For the southern portion of the diocese, there is increasing evidence that the changes in clerical recruitment were closely related to a broad transformation of religious attitudes. One cannot but be impressed by the close parallels between the ordination trends for the Durance valley within the diocese of Gap and the general evolution in Provence of certain manifestations of a "Baroque" religious culture examined by Michel Vovelle. Relying primarily on the clauses in wills, Vovelle devised a number of quantitative indices—such as the requests for requiem masses—for gauging collective religious mentality. Both the ordinations in the Durance and many of Vovelle's indices exhibit the same slight decline in the 1730's (perhaps related to the Jansenist controversy?), the same century-long peak near 1750, and the same abrupt collapse after 1760.[50] Significantly, the changes registered by the wills after mid-century were particularly dramatic among that group of non-agricultural commoners—artisans, town merchants, officeholders, and members of the liberal professions—that furnished the largest contingent of priests in the Durance valley.[51] It thus seems clear that the southern portion of the diocese of Gap, so closely related to Provence in its economic activities and community structures, partook of the same "major mutation of collective responses" identified for the Provençal sphere as a whole.[52]

Any such change in religious attitudes, spreading so rapidly from Lower Provence through the clustered-village society of the Durance basin, seems never to have

---

[50] Michel Vovelle, *Piété baroque et déchristianisation en Provence au XVIIIe siècle. Les attitudes devant la mort d'après les clauses des testaments* (Paris, 1973), especially pp. 265–300.
[51] *Ibid.*, pp. 133–139.   [52] *Ibid.*, p. 613.

penetrated the dispersed, hamlet communities of the northern zone of the diocese.[53] Unfortunately, for the valley of the Drac, we can call on no major research in religious mentality comparable to Vovelle's study. Yet one approach is open to us: the study of the foundations of devotional confraternities. In his research on the diocese of La Rochelle, Louis Pérouas found a definite correspondence between regions of heavier recruitment to the clergy and regions of heavy concentrations of rosary confraternities: a convergence of indices that enabled him to identify zones of relatively greater religious vitality.[54] A map of the rosary confraternities in the diocese of Gap for the late eighteenth century reveals the existence of these associations in almost all areas of the diocese—with the important exception of certain parishes in the Serrois and the Baronies containing large Protestant minorities. The critical factor here is the date of foundation. When the distinction is made between the confraternities founded in the seventeenth and those founded in the eighteenth century, a certain movement from south to north does seem to appear (see Figure K).[55] Above all, we note the particular concen-

[53] Charles Tilly's comments bearing on Southern Anjou in the eighteenth century are applicable here: ". . . it does seem that ideas, programs, and movements from outside reach all inhabitants of agglomerated villages more rapidly and uniformly, and in that way are more likely to incite a collective response . . . in such communities [than in hamlets and isolated farms]." *The Vendée* (2nd ed.; New York, 1967), p. 86.

[54] Louis Pérouas, "Le nombre des vocations sacerdotales, est-il un critère valable en sociologie religieuse historique aux XVIIe et XVIIIe siècles?" *Actes du 87e Congrès de sociétés savantes, Poitiers, 1962* (Paris, 1963), pp. 35–40.

[55] Among the principal sources: "registre général" of confraternities, 1695: A.D.H.A., G 939; pastoral visits of 1710–1713 and of 1740–1741: A.D.H.A., G 787–788; "registres d'approbations et prorogations," 1745–1779: A.D.H.A., G 829–830. The "registre général" of 1695, based on the written replies of the curés, does not include all the parishes in the diocese. This is the reason for the uncertainty as to the date of foundation in certain parishes. Foundations and "re-foundations" have been grouped together. The latter, relatively rare, apparently occurred when the original association had lost most of its following or had altogether disappeared. See also below, Chapter VIII.

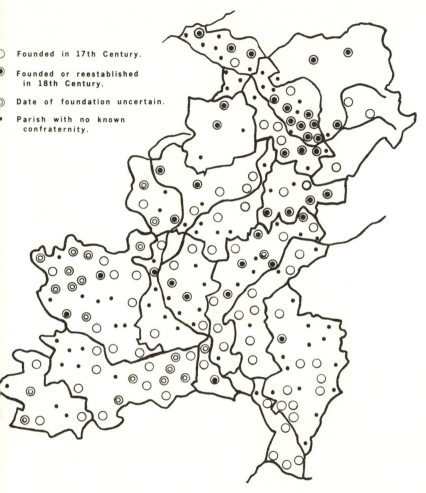

○ Founded in 17th Century.

◉ Founded or reestablished
   in 18th Century.

◑ Date of foundation uncertain.

• Parish with no known
   confraternity.

FIGURE K.
Regional distribution of Rosary confraternities

tration of eighteenth-century confraternities in the valley
of the Drac. Most of the latter had been created in the
first three or four decades of the century, approximately

one generation before parents in this region began directing their sons into the priesthood. Many of the foundations
had, in fact, been encouraged by bishop Berger de Malissoles as part of a series of revival missions carried out in
the region in collaboration with the Capuchins of Gap.[56]
Thus, whatever the importance of economic and demographic trends in fostering the increase of recruitment in
the Drac valley, we should not underestimate the influence
of a rise in religious fervor, a rise that would form a marked
contrast to the downward movement in the south.[57]

In conclusion, our consideration of recruitment patterns
in the diocese of Gap has served to suggest the multiplicity
of factors that might have been involved in the choice of
a career in the clergy. It seems undeniable that a large
measure of prosperity on the part of an individual's family
was a virtual prerequisite for making such a choice. It also
seems clear that, in the context of the eighteenth century,
the clergy was a professional option, like many others, from
which definite economic and social advantages might be
derived, both for the clergyman and his family. It is a common supposition—but a supposition that we have verified

[56] Missions were held throughout the diocese, but the Champsaur-
Beaumont seems to have been a favorite target for Malissoles during
the earlier years of his episcopacy, possibly because of the Protestant
population in the valley. Between 1707 and 1716, 17 of the 39 special
missions held in the diocese by the Capuchins (44 percent) took place
in the Drac basin. The records of the Capuchins also seem to indicate
a particular enthusiasm for these missions on the part of the Champsaur population: see the "Livre des archives du couvent des Pères
Capucins de la ville et cité de Gap": A.D.H.A., 3 H² 1.

[57] Research in the archives of the diocese of Grenoble reveals that
clerical vocations were also increasing in the Gresse, the Matheysine, the
Valbonnais, and the Oisans, the mountainous regions just to the north
of the diocese of Gap. The increases were far less dramatic than those
in the neighboring Champsaur-Beaumont: a 50 to 100 percent increase
during the century, compared to an increase of 450 percent in the
Champsaur. Throughout the century over 50 percent of all clergymen
of the diocese of Grenoble originated from the episcopal city itself.
These percentages are based on samples taken of the origins of tonsured
clerics during the two periods, 1727–1738 and 1776–1787: A.D.I., 4
G 329–334 and 4 G 349–354.

by means of the patrimonial titles—that sending a younger son into the Church helped to reduce future claims on a father's heritage and thus to keep the family fortune intact. Yet it would be a mistake to discount religious motivation. Our analysis has, in fact, suggested a strong correlation between recruitment to the clergy and religious fervor. Perhaps the "consecration" of a son to the priesthood, the "calling" to the priesthood, was not entirely absent after all.

CHAPTER III

The Education of the Parish Priest

It was one matter to determine a young man's vocation to the priesthood; it was another to form and prepare that vocation for active service in the clergy. The central experience in a clergyman's intellectual preparation was his seminary training. By the middle of the eighteenth century, virtually each diocese had a seminary and every future priest was required to spend time there. But the education of a parish priest was a process that began well before and continued long after his studies in the seminary.

Preparation Prior to the Seminary

Preparation prior to the seminary, as all pre-professional education in eighteenth-century France, was exceedingly diverse and unstructured. The lack of a standard, institutionalized school system required each family to improvise the schooling of its offspring in accordance with its financial means and geographic location. The problem was especially acute in Upper Dauphiné, where there was no university and only a small number of secondary schools. Certain families probably hired tutors or sent their sons to schools in Grenoble, the Rhône valley, or Provence.

In the diocese of Gap the local curé himself might play an important role in the earliest preparation of the future priest. A curé would take in a youth who had been tonsured to serve him in the parish as a kind of apprentice clergyman. The boy—the "little cleric," as he was called—would aid the priest both in religious ceremonies and in domestic life, in return for room and board and a small salary.[1]

---

[1] *Cahier des curés de Dauphiné* (Lyon, 1789), p. 114. The *petit clerc* was deemed particularly necessary for those curés—the majority—who

Boys in the city of Gap sometimes received their "apprenticeship" to the clergy while serving as choirboys and later cross-bearers in the cathedral.[2] The parish priest seems also to have served as a link in the local educational process between the parish day school and the secondary school. A young parishioner or relative who was preparing for the clergy—or for another profession demanding an advanced education—might spend a winter in the rectory to receive his elementary instruction in Latin.[3] Ideally, the boy would then be ready to enter an advanced grade in the secondary school, thus saving several years of board and tuition for his parents. Chaix, curé of Les Baux, for example, taught Cicero and Phaedrus to several little nephews and to the younger brothers of his friend Villars.[4] Joseph Marcellin, who was ordained a priest about 1790, had been sent by his father at age thirteen to serve and be tutored by an older cousin, the curé of Aouste.[5] Numerous future clergy-

---

had no vicaires. At the end of the Old Regime, curés were demanding financial aid from the tithe owners in order to pay for the *petits clercs*. Candy, curé of Aubessagne, requested this in 1772 in a declaration of revenue: A.D.H.A., G 2338; Bertrand, curé of Saint-Laurent-du-Cros made a similar complaint in 1780: *Mémoire à consulter et consultation pour les curés de la province du Dauphiné* (Paris, 1780), p. 103.

[2] For example, Louis Léautier was a cleric and *porte-croix* in the cathedral in 1790. He was then 19 years old and had been serving in the church for 7 years, first as choirboy: A.D.H.A., I Q I 108[1].

[3] Jean Faure-Duserre, departmental official and local poet, stressed this role of the curés in a report on education in the Hautes-Alpes in 1814: "Rapport au Conseil général des Hautes-Alpes," *AA*, II (1898), pp. 134–135. Faure himself, destined by his family to enter the clergy, had received his primary education from the curé of Chabottes in 1785: M. E. Gaillaud, "Notice biographique" in *Oeuvres choisies de Jean Faure-Duserre* (Gap, 1892), pp. 5–6. Ambroise Faure, a mathematician from La Plaine, was prepared for *collège* by several different curés: *BHA*, XXVIII (1908), p. 345.

[4] Letters from Dominique Chaix to Dominique Villars, especially those dated Nov. 7, 1773; Feb. 26 and Aug. 1, 1774; Feb. 10 and Mar. 4, 1775: B.M.G., R 10073.

[5] Letters from Brun, curé of Aouste, to Jean-Balthazar Marcellin, notary in Rémuzat, Aug. 16, 1777 and Aug. 30, 1779: Fond Marcellin, held in the cure of Rémuzat. The notary had earlier assisted his younger brother to become a priest by paying his board and room with the curé of Le Buis: expense record, 1753–1755: *ibid.*

men may have received their first training from a local curé in this way.

For their secondary education, most clergymen in the diocese probably attended either the municipal *collège* of Gap or the *collège* of Embrun.[6] The former was a modest institution that greatly suffered during the eighteenth century from frequent changes in its directors. Only after 1763, when the school was definitively confided to the Fathers of the Christian Doctrine, was there some continuity in the courses of studies. Yet even at the end of the century, professional teachers could be afforded only for the upper grades; most of the classes were put in the hands of students from the seminary.[7]

The *collège* of Embrun was perhaps the most widely known secondary school in Upper Dauphiné. It was said to have provided pre-seminary training for clergymen from all over the southern Alps. Until 1761, clerics attending this school would have received the traditional Jesuit education, concentrating on philosophy, rhetoric, history, geography, and the Latin classics.[8] After the expulsion of the Jesuits, the secular priests who assumed the direction of the school initiated a general modernization of the curriculum. The headmaster, Jean-Joseph Rossignol, wrote a plan of studies in which astronomy, surveying, botany, and physics were to be studied, in addition to philosophy. Students would take regular walks in the countryside and

[6] It has been impossible to find complete lists of students from either school. A few printed *"Exercices littéraires"* reveal future Gap priests in attendance at both schools. A few priests are also known to have attended the Jesuit *collège* in Grenoble. Others, from villages in the Baronnies, undoubtedly went to Avignon.

[7] F. N. Nicollet, "Le collège communal de Gap avant la Révolution," *Bulletin des sciences économiques et sociales du comité de travaux historiques et scientifiques,* 1895, pp. 10–24.

[8] Antoine Albert, *Histoire géographique, naturelle, ecclésiastique et civile du diocèse d'Embrun,* 2 vols. (Embrun, 1783–1786), II, 358–362. See also the unsigned report describing the *collège* addressed to the Revolutionary government in Paris, ca. 1791: A.D.H.A., F 779; also P. Delattre, "Embrun," article in *Les établissements des Jésuites en France depuis quatre siècles,* fasc. 6 (Wettern, Belgium, 1950), p. 339.

make butterfly collections.[9] The school's philosophy professor, the abbé Blanc, became a well-known amateur botanist in the region.[10] The ultimate effects of this new curriculum would be difficult to assess. But it is certain that many of the younger priests of the diocese of Gap in 1789 had been exposed to Newton, Franklin, and Buffon as well as to Ovid and Pliny.[11]

On the completion of their secondary studies, most clergymen seem to have gone directly into the seminary. There was no university in the diocese, nor in any of the adjoining dioceses, and prolonged studies at the universities of Avignon, Valence, or Aix could be very expensive. Nevertheless, some curés in the diocese of Gap are known to have possessed university degrees. University graduates were given preference for benefices becoming vacant during certain months of the year. It was thus in the interest of every graduate to have official notification of his diplomas communicated to the patrons of benefices and registered in the *insinuations ecclésiastiques*.[12] By referring to these documents and to certain other sources, we find only 27 parish priests in the diocese in 1789—13 percent of the total—in possession of such degrees.[13] This low per-

9 In spite of opposition from some of the faculty, Rossignol's plan was approved by the school governing board on Sept. 20, 1775. See A.D.H.A., F 779 and Jean-Joseph Rossignol, "Plan d'un cours de philosophie," *Collection complète des Oeuvres*, 6 vols. (Turin, 1823), v, 1–40.

10 On one occasion, Blanc had his students help prepare a butterfly collection for a scientist in Paris. See letters by curé Chaix to Dominique Villars, June 24, 1779 and Apr. 9, 1785: B.M.G., R 10073.

11 Rossignol, "Plan d'un cours de philosophie," pp. 22–26; also undated *mémoire* against this plan: A.D.H.A., F 779 (22).

12 Graduates were given priority for benefices becoming vacant through the death of the previous holder in the months of January, April, July, and October. The right of the graduate could not be maintained unless the degree had been insinuated in the diocese: see Pierre Durand de Maillane, *Dictionnaire de droit canonique et de pratique bénéficiale*, 5 vols. (3rd ed.; Lyon, 1776), article "Gradué."

13 I have gone systematically through the registers of *insinuations ecclésiastiques* for the diocese of Gap, preserved for the period 1751–1771: A.D.H.A., G 877–880. Certain of the original notifications made

centage of university educated curés was perhaps not untypical of many dioceses of France at the end of the Old Regime.[14]

The clerical tonsure, the first formal commitment to a life in the church, could be given at any time in a young man's course of studies. A sample has been taken of the parish clergy serving in 1790. Within this group, the ages at the first tonsure ranged from 12 to 28 years (see Figure L.1).[15] Apparently there were two periods at which the commitment to the clergy was most commonly decided—indicated by the two modes of the graph. The first was at age 18, the age at which many young men would have completed their secondary education. The second was between ages 20 and 22, probably after the completion of a

---

after 1771 are found in A.D.H.A., G 896 and G 1810. I have also examined the provisions of benefices from 1755 to 1789 in which the university degrees of the new benefice holders are often mentioned: A.D.H.A., G 814–828; and copies of the *nomination de grades* sent by the University of Valence between 1768 and 1789: A.D.D., D 41–44.

[14] At about the same period, less than 20 percent of the curés in a portion of the diocese of Le Mans, less than 10 percent in the diocese of Autun, and about 30 percent in the diocese of Tarbes seem to have possessed university degrees: Alex Poyer, Les curés de la Quinte du Mans au XVIIIe siècle (Mémoire de maîtrise, Université du Mans, 1974), p. 85; A.D. Saône-et-Loire, 2 G 340–341 and research in the archives of the universities of Paris and Dijon; and A. D. Hautes-Pyrénées, Series G, data given to me by Dominique Julia. Perhaps only in dioceses like Reims and Arles, in immediate proximity to universities (respectively, Reims and Avignon), might the proportion approach or surpass 50 percent: Dominique Julia, "Le clergé paroissial dans le diocèse de Reims," *RHMC*, XIII (1966), pp. 211–212; and Jean Roy, Le prêtre paroissial dans deux diocèses provençaux; Aix et Arles au XVIIIe siècle, société et religion (Thèse de troisième cycle, Université d'Aix-Marseilles I, 1975), p. 65.

[15] Birth dates of priests living during the Revolution have been obtained, for the Hautes-Alpes and Basses-Alpes, from A.D.H.A., L 1043–1047 and ms. 399; A.D.B.A., L 421 and L 430; and, for the Drôme and the Isère, from information kindly given to me by abbés Loche and Godel. The sample consists of all those parish clergymen living in 1790 for whom birthdates are known whose last names began with B, M, or P.

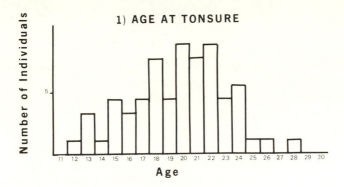

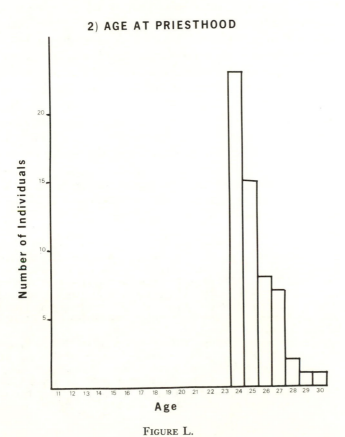

FIGURE L.

Age at the moment of the tonsure and the priesthood for a sample group of priests ordained in the second half of the eighteenth century

few years at the university. Men who obtained university diplomas sometimes waited until the requisite five years of study had been completed before receiving their tonsure.[16]

THE SEMINARY

Whatever the earlier educational experience, the preparatory careers of the clergymen of the diocese converged a few years before their twenty-fourth birthday with the entry into the seminary. It was here that the church attempted to put its stamp on its future servants and mold them into something resembling a uniform corps. Not all priests originating in the diocese attended the seminary of Gap. Bishop Berger de Malissoles had accepted the Jesuit seminary of Sainte-Garde in Avignon as a substitute. Throughout the eighteenth century, a few clergymen continued to frequent the seminaries of Avignon.[17] But the total number going outside the diocese for clerical training was probably small.[18]

At the seminary of Gap, the minimun course of studies was two years,[19] although many clerics seem to have spent four years or more.[20] It was usually during this period that

[16] Jean-François Villars and Dominique Mondet both graduated from the University of Valence in 1780 and were tonsured in 1782 at the ages of 23 and 21, respectively: A.D.H.A., G 1810 and G 906.

[17] *Mémoire* on the seminary of Gap by the canon De Pina, ca. 1740: A.D.H.A., G 2692. In the later eighteenth century, we find Etienne-François-Ignace Gruel of Lemps and François Charras of Saint-André-de-Rosans attending the seminary Saint-Charles of Avignon: A.D.H.A., G 879 and G 894.

[18] By studying the dimissorial letters given by the bishop of Gap for the sub-diaconate—an order generally given during the final year in the seminary—we can estimate the number of clerics attending a seminary outside Gap. Following this method, we would estimate that about 15 percent of all Gap priests went elsewhere to seminary, over 50 percent of the priests from the Baronnies, however, would seem to have attended other seminaries.

[19] Chaix to Villars, letter Sept. 4, 1782: B.M.G., R 10073. Dispensations might be given, however, to clergymen who had studied at the university: *ibid*.

[20] In 1749 and 1753 all of the deacons and sub-deacons—those next in line for the priesthood—had spent at least 3 years: A.D.H.A., G 2692.

a man was promoted by the bishop through the successive clerical orders: the four minor orders, the sub-diaconate, the diaconate, and the priesthood. The ordination to the priesthood, which marked the successful completion of the clerical training, almost always occurred between the twenty-fourth and the twenty-seventh birthday (see Figure L.2);[21] the "late vocation" was extremely rare.

The cost of a ten-month term, including meals and an individual room—"comfortable but hardly roomy"[22]—was 210 *livres*.[23] This was a substantial sum for the more modest families financing their sons in the clergy. But some clerics might earn their way by serving as schoolmasters in the *collège* attached to the seminary. There were also a few scholarships available—the *places fondées*—established by pious donors for clerics of poorer families.[24] As we have seen, "poor" clerics entering the priesthood in Gap were rare, but the recipients of the scholarship seem generally to have come from the least wealthy families.[25]

Since the first years of its foundation, at the end of the seventeenth century, the seminary had been directed by the Fathers of the Christian Doctrine. Gap was probably one of the Doctrinaires' less prosperous establishments,[26] and it was seemingly the younger members of the order who were sent to serve there. In 1790, the superior of the seminary, the oldest of the six Doctrinaires in Gap, was only

21 See above, note 15. The minimum age required for the priesthood was 24.

22 Anonymous *mémoire* of ca. 1791 concerning the seminary of Gap: A.D.H.A., L 1053.

23 E. Jacques, *Le séminaire de Gap, 1577–1789* (Gap, 1924), p. 30.

24 A.D.H.A., G 2692.

25 *Ibid.* Lists are preserved for the recipients of scholarships in 1749 and 1753–1758. Of the 22 for whom family professions are known, 20 were among the lower- or middle-class professions: artisan, peasant, or merchant; 2 were from families calling themselves "bourgeois."

26 About 1791 the net revenue of the seminary was said to be 1,800 *livres*: A.D.H.A., L 1053. Unfortunately, I was unable to consult the definitive study of the Doctrinaires: Jean de Viguier, *Une oeuvre d'éducation sous l'Ancien régime: les Pères de la Doctrine chrétienne en France et en Italie (1592–1792)* (Paris, 1975).

39.[27] Achard, curé of Serres, complained of the youth of the seminary directors in his *cahier de doléances* of 1789 and suggested that the bishop would do better to assign older experienced curés to train seminarians.[28] There were also persistent suspicions that the Doctrinaires had been tainted by Jansenism. Berger de Malissoles expressed serious misgivings as to the purity of their doctrine in 1720,[29] but twenty years later the vicar-general found the members of the congregation perfectly orthodox.[30] Both Malissoles and Condorcet were outspoken opponents of the Jansenists. After 1742, all priests serving in the diocese, including the directors of the seminary, were required to sign a register accepting the bull *Unigenitus*.[31] Moreover, the basic theological text used in the seminary of Gap, the *Théologie de Poitiers*, was extremely traditionalist and implicitly opposed to Jansenism.[32] There is no evidence that the diocesan clergy of Gap was ever strongly influenced by the Jansenist movement of the eighteenth century.[33]

[27] A.D.H.A., I Q I 78.

[28] "Cahier des curés," *AA*, XIII (1909), p. 203.

[29] See the letters addressed to Malissoles by the bishops of Nimes and Mende: A.D.H.A., G 1016.

[30] *Mémoire* by De Pina, *ca.* 1740: A.D.H.A., G 2692.

[31] A.D.H.A., G 969. Begun in 1742, the register was kept until at least 1771.

[32] A.D.H.A., G 2692. The *Théologie de Poitiers* was one of the most widespread texts used in French seminaries prior to the Revolution: see A. Dégert, *Histoire des séminaires français jusqu'à la Révolution*, 2 vols. (Paris, 1912), II, 237–243.

[33] E. Préclin, *Le Jansénisme du XVIIIe siècle et la Constitution civile du clergé* (Paris, 1929), maps opposite pp. 84 and 124. In an anonymous *mémoire* to the bishop on the moral status of the curés in *ca.* 1741, only three curés are accused of Jansenist tendencies; they are said to have been contaminated by Jansenists from other dioceses, Grenoble or Senez: A.D.H.A., G 2328. The Jansenist newspaper *Les nouvelles ecclésiastiques* indicated that there was no opposition among the clergy of the diocese to the anti-Jansenist measures taken by Condorcet: the bishop "y fait signer un horrible formulaire; n'y fait pas parler de lui parce qu'il n'y a point de réclamation pour la vérité": *Table raisonnée et alphabétique des nouvelles ecclésiastiques* (n.p., 1767), I, entry "Condorcet." No priests from the diocese of Gap appear in the extensive lists of those protesting the bull *Unigenitus* published by Nivelle,

In any case, the primary emphasis in the seminary was not on the religious sciences. It was, after all, a school for parish priests, not for theologians. Seminarians would be specifically warned against venturing into religious subtleties that might only arouse the idle curiosity of their parishioners. The common people needed milk, not solid food.[34] An indication of the theological grounding required of graduates of the seminary of Gap is given by ten canonical examinations preserved from the second half of the eighteenth century.[35] Administered by the professors of the seminary, commonly assisted by one or both of the curés of Gap, the tests were designed to gauge the preparation of priests named from outside the diocese or whose qualifications were, for other reasons, unknown to the bishop. They were not formalities, but serious examinations: about one-half of the candidates failed. The same kinds of questions were asked each time: above all, questions with direct bearing on the practical aspects of pastoral care. First, the candidate was drilled on the nature of the sacraments and the manner of administering them, particularly penance and the Eucharist. What were the basic parts of the sacraments? Could a priest refuse to administer them and, if so, to whom? There were several propositions concerning the hearing of confession, especially the problem of restitution. Then, in the realm of canon law, there were questions on usury and on marriage banns and the canonical impediments to marriage. More

---

La Constitution Unigenitus déférée à l'Eglise universelle, 3 vols. (Cologne, 1757). The only curés in Dauphiné found among these lists are 17 from the diocese of Grenoble, all signing as *appelants* in 1717: *ibid.,* vol. III, 206–208. See also Maurice Virieux, "Jansénisme et molinisme dans le clergé du diocèse de Grenoble au début du XVIIIe siècle," *RHEF,* LX (1974), pp. 297–319.

34 *Ord. syn.,* I, 168–169.

35 Of the 10, 8 are inscribed in the register of the secretariat: A.D.H.A., G 814–825; 2 others are in A.D.H.A., G 965. The dates of these examinations range between 1744 and 1783; they took place under 5 different bishops.

abstruse theological problems were rarely given. Only once was a candidate asked about the human and divine nature of Christ; only twice were there questions concerning grace. Many of the questions might have been taken from one of those basic theological primers—like Binfeld's *La théologie des pasteurs*[36]—and many of the answers could have been rote responses memorized from the same primer.

Seminary training was above all a psychological preparation, a spiritual retreat during which a man was to "leave this world." The seminarian's life was closely patterned after the schedule of the monastery. From the time he rose at five o'clock in the morning until the end of his day at nine o'clock at night, his hour-by-hour program was dominated by prayer, meditation, and spiritual exercise. Scripture was read during meals; daily exercises consisted in walking under the chestnut trees of the garden while reciting the rosary. Only three hours a day were spent in lessons: theology and Bible studies, lectures on preaching or on the duties of the curé.[37] It was generally agreed that the curé could teach his parishioners more effectively by example than by words. He was to be a moral and spiritual model for the community.[38] In the seminary, the behavior and attitudes of the aspiring clergyman were evaluated as closely as his intellectual development. In their grading comments the professors spoke of the character of their students as though it were a raw ore to be refined and forged into a Christian metal. A cleric who was gentle, affable, decent, and assiduous in his spiritual exercises was given great praise; another, who was turbulent, restless, and disobedient, still had a good deal of progress to make.[39]

During the dangerous months of summer vacation, when the seminarians were at home with their families, the village curés were to keep the young clerics under careful

---

[36] Dégert, II, 187–189, 216.   [37] Jacques, pp. 26–29.
[38] *Ord. syn.*, I, 31 and 202–203.
[39] "Catalogue de MM. les séminaristes, 1749": A.D.H.A., G 2692. Each seminarian is evaluated in terms of his "qualités" and development.

surveillance, to insure that they maintained an external bearing appropriate to their status as clergymen.[40] Participation in secular activities such as agriculture, appearance in public without a soutane, the use of coarse language, undue familiarity with women: all could be grounds for severe reprimand by the seminary directors. Dominique Chaix, curé of Les Baux, was deeply shocked when a young seminarian acquaintance was found to have been working on the farm: "It is indecent for those of our profession to perform heavy labor in the fields."[41] He commented on the entry into the seminary of his closest friend's brother: "He has only just left the world; now it is proper that he learn to bear the clergyman's burden. His knowledge and his ability can be tested in an [entry] examination; but the *esprit ecclésiastique*, so necessary for those of our profession is another matter altogether. . . ."[42] A primary goal of the seminary was to impress the clergyman with the set of pious virtues, the pattern of outward behavior, described by Chaix as the *esprit ecclésiastique*.

THE CANTONAL CONFERENCES

The architects of the Catholic Reformation in France had early realized that seminary training alone might not be sufficient to raise and maintain the moral and intellectual level of the parish clergy. Isolated in a remote village during a thirty- or forty-year career as curé, a priest could rapidly wear through the meager theological baggage and the moral fervor he brought with him from the seminary. Two principal measures had been taken to counter the dulling effects of prolonged isolation. First, there were periodic retreats to the seminary of small groups of clergymen for a week or so of spiritual exercises. Second, there

[40] Note the *Mandement et ordonnance de monseigneur l'évêque et prince de Grenoble portant règlement pour les clercs de son diocèse et aspirants aux ordres* (Grenoble, 1774).
[41] Letter to Villars, June 17, 1783: B.M.G., R 10073.
[42] Letter to Villars, Jan. 3, 1783.

were local associations of the parish clergy that met at regular intervals for religious reflection and discussions on questions of mutual interest.

For the eighteenth-century diocese of Gap, we have little information concerning the retreats, and it is impossible to determine whether they were pursued during the century as vigorously as in certain other French dioceses.[43] We know only that Berger de Malissoles, in his *Ordonnances synodales*, had made the seminary retreats voluntary,[44] although he had strongly encouraged them; and that bishop Condorcet, in 1745, was resolved to hold them at least once a year.[45]

But the associations of the parish clergy, first established in the diocese of Gap about 1686,[46] are known to have functioned throughout the eighteenth century.[47] In each of the ecclesiastical cantons, the archpriest was given the responsibility of organizing the periodic meetings of the "conferences," as they were called in the diocese. These conferences would assemble about once a month—except in winter—either in a single centrally located parish or in different parishes by rotation. All priests approved to hear confessions within the canton were required to attend unless excused for a valid reason. The meeting would last all day and would include prayer readings, debates on two predetermined subjects—one concerning piety and one concerning doctrine—and general discussions on any parish questions that might arise. The conclusions reached during

---

[43] *E.g.*, in the neighboring diocese of Embrun, all priests were required to make an 8-day retreat every 2 years: Albert, II, 457–458.

[44] *Ord. syn.*, I, 195–197.

[45] Printed letter from Condorcet to the parish clergy dated July 28, 1745: B.M.G., Vh 1095.

[46] Ruling of bishop Charles-Bénigne Hervé: A.D.H.A., G 925.

[47] When Bishop Pérouse renewed Malissoles' rulings on the cantonal conferences in 1759, he expressed dissatisfaction with the conferences in certain of the more remote regions of the diocese—particularly in the mountains of Provence—that were not meeting as regularly as they should. But he implied that the majority were functioning well: A.D.H.A., G 814, pp. 429–433.

the discussions were to be recorded in writing by the secretary and sent to the bishop.[48] The cantonal conferences also served an administrative function. They were the occasion for the delivery of pastoral letters or commissions from the bishop and for the distribution of the holy oil for extreme unction. The archpriest himself was to serve as a reporter, the "eyes and arms" of the bishop in the countryside, evaluating the performance of young priests, and corresponding with the bishop on particular problems concerning the canton.[49]

The conferences, then, were to continue and renew the seminary training of the parish clergy. It was hoped that the more learned of the curés, particularly those who had been to the university, would spread their learning and experience among those who were more poorly prepared.[50] Of equal importance—and the bishops stressed this again and again—the conferences were to create a sense of teamwork, of community among the parish clergy of a given region; "a pious society of thought and affection"[51] was the phrase used by Malissoles. Among other responsibilities, the clergymen of each canton were to look after one another during sickness and insure medical care to any curé or vicaire incapacitated by illness or accident. Whenever a member of a canton died, all of his colleagues were to dedicate special masses for the repose of his soul.[52]

By the second half of the eighteenth century, the cantonal meetings had become an established institution in the diocese of Gap. The conferences of Serres were said to have been lively and active;[53] those of Tallard were meeting regularly "according to the useful and venerable custom

48 *Ord. syn.*, I, 121–135; renewed by the pastoral letter of Nov. 19, 1759: A.D.H.A., G 814.
49 *Ibid.*, pp. 103–111.
50 *Ibid.*, p. 130.
51 *Ibid.*, p. 122.
52 *Lettre d'archiprêtré* of Barthélémy Chaine, Sept. 7, 1780: A.D.H.A., G 823.
53 Louis Jacques, "Histoire religieuse de Serres," ms. held in A.E. Gap, p. 93.

observed in this diocese."[54] The conference of Saint-Bonnet would travel to Gap as a group in 1774 in order to offer its respects to the newly appointed bishop, Jouffroy-Gonssans.[55] In a later chapter, we shall examine the cantonal conferences during the last decades of the Old Regime, as they became increasingly politicized and independent from episcopal authority.

AN INTELLECTUAL BIOGRAPHY: DOMINIQUE CHAIX

Outside the institutionalized studies pursued in the school, the seminary, and the cantonal conferences, the intellectual development of the parish priest is usually difficult to follow. An extensive search in the departmental archives has uncovered only two inventories of the books possessed by parish clergymen of the diocese.[56] In both instances, the priest's library was extremely rudimentary and scarcely transcended the immediate needs of his ministry: a bible, a breviary, or a diurnal; a few volumes of sermons; a multi-volume history of the world or a text on moral theology; and a work or two by such classical French religious writers as Massillon or Fénelon. We catch occasional glimpses, through correspondence or personal notes, of much broader interests on the part of certain parish priests. There was, for example, Jean-Michel Rolland, vicaire and then curé of Le Caire, a blacksmith's son who apparently owned several volumes of Voltaire and who prided himself on his literary talents. At various periods Rolland wrote a mock epic that ridiculed one of his bishops, a series of verses—in a Fragonardesque, Rococo style—dedicated to local noblemen and their wives, and a

---

[54] Procuration from the *archiprêtré* of Tallard, May 6, 1788: A.D.H.A., G 2366.

[55] Letter from curé Millon of Laye to the baron Des Preaux, Oct. 4, 1774: A.D.H.A., F 1346.

[56] Pellenc, vicaire of Gap, possessed 6 works in 1793: I Q I 290 (1); Marchon, curé of Le Noyer, possessed 9 works in 1748: A.D.H.A., F 2908. Both priests died while still relatively young.

pedantic dictionary of the "faulty expressions" used in the Alps.[57] There was Jean-Joseph Jean, curé of the isolated parish of Montjai in the Baronnies, who took up the study of canon and civil law to serve him in his interminable squabbles with neighboring clergymen and with his own parishioners, and who filled his letters with learned citations by noted lawyers of the age.[58] The most intellectually prominent of all the curés was undoubtedly François-Léon Réguis. Little is known of his life, but he was born in Barret-le-Bas in 1725 and he returned as curé of the parish between 1766 and 1773. It was during this period that he published a collection of model sermons, *La voix du pasteur*, which was widely read throughout France in the late eighteenth century.[58a]

For one curé of the diocese, however, a relatively detailed intellectual biography can be constructed: Dominique Chaix of Les Baux. Chaix's interests and activities are known to us, thanks to a series of 170 letters written over a period of twenty-seven years to his closest friend, Dominique Villars, doctor of medicine and botanist in Grenoble.[59] The letters are of special interest in that they

[57] Letters and manuscripts by Rolland: B.M.G., N 2471; *Dictionnaire des expressions vicieuses et des fautes de prononciation les plus communes dans les Hautes et Basses-Alpes, accompagnées de leurs corrections* (Gap, n.d.).

[58] Letters by Jean, 1785–1787: A.D.H.A., G 978, G 995, VII E Jarjayes 144. Jean cites or gives reference to Ferrière, Jousse, Denisart, Piales, Rousseau de la Combe, and Durand de Maillane, among others.

[58a] The first edition was published in Paris in 1766 and succeeding editions were being printed as late as 1855. Réguis was first named curé of Bonny in the diocese of Auxerre in 1758: A. D. Yonne, G 1740. He was named to Barret-le-Bas on Sept. 9, 1765: A.D.H.A., G 880. He followed bishop Condorcet to the diocese of Lisieux where he ended his career as curé of Notre-Dame-du-Hamel (named Jan. 4, 1773): Abbé Piel, *Inventaire historique des actes transcrits aux insinuations ecclésiastiques de l'ancien diocèse de Lisieux*, 5 vols. (Lisieux, 1895), v, 123–124. Réguis held a *licence* in theology. See also Bernard Groethuysen, *The Bourgeoisie, Catholicism vs. Capitalism in Eighteenth-Century France* (New York, 1968), p. 243 and *passim*.

[59] These letters are available to the public in the form of three volumes of transcriptions made by the former archivist of the Hautes-

give us insight into a whole network of friendships and correspondence of which Chaix was a member and central figure.

Dominique Chaix was born in 1730, a younger son of a family of sheep raisers in the mountains of the Bochaine.[60] After three years of Latin studies with a local curé, he entered the Jesuit secondary school in Grenoble, paying his way by serving as tutor to the oldest son of a family of parlementary magistrates.[61] He was ordained to the priesthood in 1754, but continued his studies at the university of Avignon in order to obtain a degree. In 1758 he was named to the cure of Les Baux, where he would serve for more than thirty years. This small parish in the mountains above the river Buëch provided a meager ecclesiastical revenue,[62] but the location was convenient for Chaix. It was only about ten miles from Gap, where the curé could walk to visit friends or colleagues and attend the quarterly fairs. He felt at home in the mountains not far from his birthplace, and he spoke with pleasure of his rustic life in a thatched-roof rectory far from the bustle of the town. But, most important, the reduced pastoral duties of Les Baux allowed him ample time to pursue his greatest passion in life, the study of botany.

Chaix was in his early twenties when one of the Sisters of Saint-Joseph in Gap first initiated him to the collection and classification of plants.[63] After instructing himself in the principles of Linnaeus, he began applying the Swedish

---

Alpes, Georges de Manteyer, from the original collection held by the family Gauthier-Villars: B.M.G., R 10073. The correspondence is preserved from July 26, 1772 to 15 Messidor VII (July 3, 1799). The letters are arranged in chronological order. They will be cited hereafter by date only. Chaix frequently wrote that Villars was the dearest friend he had in the world. See, for example, letter, Oct. 10, 1782.

[60] The biographical information which follows is mostly from Dominique Villars, "Notice historique sur Dominique Chaix," ed. Paul Guillaume, *BHA*, iii (1884), pp. 291–319; and from F. A. Allemand, *Dictionnaire biographique des Hautes-Alpes* (Gap, 1911), pp. 141–143.

[61] Letter, Mar. 12, 1785.   [62] See below, Chapter V.

[63] Villars, "Notice historique," p. 10.

philosopher's classification system to the flora of the Alps, and he undertook a complete catalogue of the vegetation of the Gapençais. It was a mutual interest in botany that formed the lifelong friendship between Chaix and Villars.[64] The two men pursued their studies with the enthusiasm of explorers of an unknown land. Each discovery brought a fever of study and correspondence until the species was properly named and classified. When Villars published his book on the plants of Dauphiné, he gave credit to Chaix for preparing the portion on the Gapençais.[65]

Chaix was in contact with professional and amateur botanists all over France. Among those mentioned in the letters to Villars were abbé Pourret of Narbonne, chevalier de Lamanon in Provence, Roux in Geneva, Thouin (head of the botanical gardens of Paris), and Liotard of Grenoble.[66] The letters also give us a glimpse of Chaix's intellectual acquaintances within the immediate area of Gap. On the map (Figure M) we have noted all those persons mentioned as being in contact with Chaix by correspondence, exchange of books, or personal visits involving non-ecclesiastical subjects. Most of these acquaintances were clergymen, primarily other curés, but a few lay notables were included as well—a doctor in Serres, a surgeon in La Roche, the sub-delegate of Gap. The network seems to have been centered in the ecclesiastical canton of Gap. The conferences would have been the occasion for regular meetings between the curé of Les Baux and his colleagues in the nearby parishes.[67]

---

[64] Villars was born in the Champsaur in Le Noyer and served there as doctor before becoming director of a hospital in Grenoble. Villars first met Chaix when he was a boy in Le Noyer and Chaix came to the village to preach a mission: see Villars, "Notice historique," 10.

[65] *Histoire naturelle des plantes de Dauphiné*, 3 vols. (Grenoble, 1786–1789), introduction.

[66] Letters, June 25, 1773; Apr. 30, 1781; Oct. 2, 1783; May 9, 1785; 18 Thermidor III: also, Chaix to Liottard, letters April 1 and November 23, 1770 and Sept. 25, 1773: B.M.G., N 2046.

[67] Chaix mentioned one such conference where he had talked with Villars' younger brother, the curé of La Bâtie-Vieille: letter, Apr. 27, 1787.

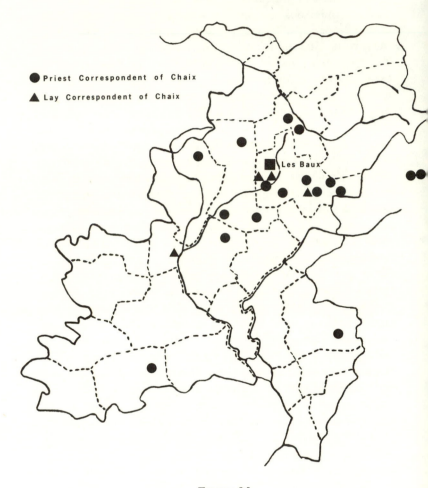

FIGURE M.
Intellectual acquaintances of Dominique Chaix, as mentioned in
his correspondence with Dominique Villars

The intellectual contacts took many forms. First, there
were the exchanges of seeds and plant specimens. Villars
and Chaix's friends in Paris sent him seeds of rare plants
from all over the world—from Palestine, the Cape of Good

Hope, Canada, Peru. These he carefully cultivated in pots or in a corner of the rectory vegetable garden.[68] Through his local correspondents, Chaix was also able to augment his collection of Alpine plants. Professor Blanc of Embrun, curé Gaillard in Provence, and curé Meyer in the Baronnies each sent Chaix specimens from the country near their parishes.

Occasionally, Chaix and his friends took botanical field trips together. He visited the Valgaudemar with curé Martin and Buis-les-Baronnies with Martin and the surgeon Serre.[69] Nearly every year Chaix made the difficult journey to the Carthusian monastery of Durbon. This was in part a spiritual pilgrimage. It was to "these holy monks" that he sent two of his young friends for a pious retreat not long before they entered the clergy.[70] But the monks were also interested in botany and chemistry. Chaix, Serre, and the doctor Chevandier might have passionate discussions with the Carthusians over recent discoveries in science.[71] Chaix also exchanged essays and literary compositions with his friends in the region. While attending Mardi Gras in Gap in 1779, the curé wrote a poem entitled *Florae Delphenensi carmen*. It was dedicated to Villars and it extolled the objects of their mutual study in the Alps. Chaix passed copies of the poem to various friends, to curé Cougourdan of Laye, curé Donnette of Saint-Etienne-en-Dévoluy, and others. Unfortunately, an unnamed individual began passing around a devastating critique on Chaix's Latin form and meter, an "overwhelmingly critical treatise" that did not even grant him "the benefit of Christian charity."[72]

Of particular interest are the informal book exchange

[68] Letters, Sept. 26, 1772 and Apr. 16, 1786.
[69] Letters, July 23, 1784 and June 17, 1787.
[70] Letter, June 30, 1778.
[71] Letters, Sept. 22, 1780 and Feb. 7, 1789. Dom Prieur and Dom Grangier showed a particular interest in botany: letters, May 9, 1785 and Mar. 21, 1789.
[72] Letters, Feb. 21, Mar. 30 and June 24, 1779. The original poem and the critique are in B.M.G., N 2783.

circuits in which Chaix participated. On one occasion, professor Blanc sent Chaix copies of three of Rossignol's essays. Chaix mailed them on to Villars and to the curé of Le Noyer, who forwarded them to the curé of Romette, who handed them to Escallier, curé of Gap, who returned them to Chaix.[73] Such book exchanges seem to have been common.[74] Books were expensive: two volumes of Linnaeus, for example, might cost 30 *livres*.[75] It was often only after Chaix had read a work that had been loaned to him, that he decided to order a copy for his own possession.[76]

We can reconstruct a part of Chaix's reading list by means of the letters to Villars: books or authors that Chaix discussed or that he asked his friend to purchase for him in Grenoble. The list is undoubtedly incomplete. But it includes precisely those works which Chaix felt noteworthy enough to be mentioned to his closest friend. Many were probably being passed around the intellectual circuit of which Chaix was a part.

Books dealing with botany constituted by far the largest group on the list. Chaix owned or had read works by all the great botanists of his day—Linnaeus, Jussieu, Lamarck, Haller, Buffon[77]—and he was familiar with a great number of lesser-known authors and their catalogues of plants from all parts of the world.[78] He studied many of the other scien-

[73] Letter, Oct. 5, 1781. The circuit is described since one of Rossignol's essays was lost while making the rounds and Chaix was trying to locate it.

[74] Another example: a book sent by Villars to Chaix was loaned to the monks of Durbon and then to an unnamed party: letter, Sept. 11, 1787. Generally, however, Chaix did not specify the names of those with whom he exchanged books.

[75] Letter, July 1, 1785.

[76] This was the case, for example, when Chaix asked Villars to buy him *L'institution divine des curés*: letter, Sept. 2, 1785.

[77] Letters, Apr. 19, 1782; Dec. 22, 1789; Dec. 29, 1786; Oct. 18, 1776; Mar. 29, 1787; see also the list of botany books which he possessed in the Year III (32 works): A.D.H.A., L 1007.

[78] See also Chaix's description of the development of botany in the eighteenth century in *Récit historique et moral sur la botanique* (Gap, 1793).

tific and pseudoscientific questions that were of such passionate interest to his contemporaries. There were books on Montgolfier's experiments with balloons, on the secrets of Mesmer, and on Villars' own research in medicine.[79] There was at least one travel book, *Voyage en Barbarie*, as well as a work on *La politique du Divan*.[80] He followed and supported the efforts to introduce science into the curriculum of the secondary schools. He read Rossignol's proposed reforms for the *collège* of Embrun. When a collector in Paris asked Chaix for specimens of Alpine butterflies, he forwarded the request to Embrun, with the suggestion that abbé Blanc's schoolboys take charge of the collection.[81] He also read and corresponded with the provincial newspaper, *Les affiches de Dauphiné*. He followed the debate in this newpaper on the problems of poverty in the countryside and submitted an essay on the subject to the academy of Grenoble in 1788.[82]

Books on religious subjects were mentioned less frequently than books on science and nature. There was a work on the Eucharist and another on the life and pastoral activities of bishop La Motte of Amiens.[83] In 1785, Chaix ordered a book by the Richerist theologian, Maultrot, *L'institution divine des curés*—a work with political significance for the struggle between curés and upper clergy.[84] In the following year he obtained a copy of *La théologie de Lyon*, recently authorized by the archbishop of Lyon for use in the seminary. Chaix thus confirmed in his own mind the rumors he had heard that this new theology was tainted with the errors of Jansenius.[85]

Chaix was certainly familiar with the writings of the philosophes, although only Voltaire and Buffon were men-

[79] Letter, Mar. 19, 1784.
[80] Letters, Mar. 3, 1792 and Mar. 19, 1784.
[81] See above, note 10.
[82] Letters, Feb. 19, 1782, Sept. 18, 1787, and May 27, 1788.
[83] Letters, Oct. 5, 1781; May 27, 1788.
[84] Letter, Sept. 2, 1785.
[85] Letters, Jan. 27 and Feb. 24, 1786.

tioned by name in the letters.[86] The ideas of these men left him profoundly disturbed. In general, the Christian religion was so fundamental to his view of the world that the hypotheses of Buffon struck him as mere "reveries, absurdities, contradictions." They seemed far less "reasonable" to him than the Christian view of the origins of life based on the irrefutable proof of Holy Scripture: "Only philosophers could talk such nonsense."[87] The philosophy of Liotard botanist and acquaintance of Rousseau, was "a monstrosity for religion and for humanity."[88] In Chaix's view, there was never any conflict between science and Catholicism, between reason and religion. Indeed, his personal observations of the inner structures of plant life seemed further evidence of the glory and wisdom of God. He admired the famous Catholic "modernizer," abbé Pluche, known for his teleological proofs of the existence of God. And he eagerly read other works by defenders of Christian orthodoxy, like Pelissier's *Voltaire parmi les ombres* and Nicolas Jamin's *Pensées théologiques relatives aux erreurs du temps*.[89] He vowed that he would memorize the latter as his credo against the irreligion of the age.[90] To his death in 1799, Chaix's faith in a personal God remained unshaken:

"The philosophers put forth sophistries embellished with eloquence; but when thoroughly studied, their reasoning establishes nothing. . . . Man without religion is not man; he cannot reason; he holds merely the highest position among the brute animals."[91]

"Without having profited from the most recent discoveries, the learned Pluche has reasoned as well as [the philosophers] and has always arrived at better conclusions. I admire the depth of [the philosophers'] learning, but I

86 Letters, Sept. 2, 1785 and Mar. 29, 1787.
87 Letter, Mar. 29, 1787.
88 Letter, Jan. 3, 1783.
89 Letters, Sept. 2, 1785 and June 17, 1783.
90 Letter, Oct. 2, 1783.
91 Letter, June 17, 1783.

abhor their proud and shameful obsessions. How I congratulate myself on my simplicity and insufficiency! What pleasure I take in my solitude and obscurity! I would consider myself wiser than they, if only I knew my origin and my end: *noverim te, Deum, noverim me.*"[92] Dominique Chaix was not a typical country curé in the diocese of Gap. Unlike the great majority of his colleagues, he had a university degree, and he was one of only two or three in the diocese who had written for publication. Nevertheless, his career illustrates the kind of intellectual life possible for any parish priest with an active and inquisitive mind. Both for his learning and his service as a priest, Chaix was known to his contemporaries as a model of the *bon curé* to be imitated by other parish clergymen. Curé Rolland described him as such and so did the sub-delegate, Delafont.[93] And as we have seen, Chaix was not alone in his intellectual endeavors. By means of the circle of friendships and correspondents to which he belonged, it was possible for books of considerable modernity to circulate between the parish priests. When the Revolution came to the mountains of Dauphiné, conditions were already set for a rapid dissemination of pamphlets and ideas.

[92] Letter, 19 Fructidor VI.

[93] Pierre-Joseph-Marie Delafont, "Mémoire sur l'état de la subdélégation de Gap en 1784," *BHA*, xviii (1899), pp. 73–93; Jean-Michel Rolland, "Précis de l'éloge de M. Chaix," in *Mélanges littéraires . . . de la société d'émulation des Hautes-Alpes* (Gap, 1807), p. 191.

CHAPTER IV

Career Patterns and the Benefice System

A primary goal for any individual pursuing a career in the secular clergy in eighteenth-century France was to attain a benefice. Several different meanings and social values were combined in the concept of a benefice. For theorists of canon law it was at once a spiritual function to be performed in the service of the church; the right to collect a revenue set aside for the performance of this function; and the revenue itself.[1] One may question the degree to which clergymen actually made these subtle distinctions between the spiritual and the temporal. In point of fact, while every benefice had a revenue, many—the "simple" benefices, such as most chapels and priories in the diocese of Gap—no longer required any function whatsoever. As the canonists indicated, property rights were conferred by a benefice. Once a clergyman had legally "taken possession" of a benefice, in a ceremony registered by a notary, there was little anyone could do to deprive him of it—unless he married or became extraordinarily unfit physically or morally to perform a required function.[2] He need resign only when he chose. Under certain circumstances, he could even select his successor. With its irrevocability and its

[1] See Pierre Durand de Maillane, *Dictionnaire de droit canonique et de pratique bénéficiale* (3rd ed.; Lyon, 1776), article "Bénéfice." Also, Louis Châtellier, "Société et bénéfices ecclésiastiques: le cas alsacien (1670–1730)," *RH*, CCXLIV (1970), pp. 75–98; and Charles Berthelot du Chesnay, "Le clergé diocésain au XVIIIe siècle et les registres des insinuations ecclésiastiques," *RHMC*, x (1963), pp. 241–269.

[2] Unless, of course, a benefice were contested by a second party legally provided with the same benefice or by a party claiming through "devolution" a benefice illegally collated. According to canon law, once a man had held a benefice uncontested for three years, his possession could no longer be challenged.

proprietary character, the benefice had much the same status within ecclesiastical society as the *office* within secular society.[3]

Each time a member of the clergy received a benefice, the essential documents concerning the nomination, collation, and taking of possession were inscribed in two different ecclesiastical registers. These registers allow us to follow the careers of clergymen with greater precision than is possible for many other professional groups in the society of the Old Regime.[4] In the present study of career patterns and the benefice system, two different perspectives have been taken. First, we have studied as a series all benefices collated between 1771 and 1789. Second, we have attempted to reconstruct the individual careers prior to 1789 of the 108 priests ordained between 1751 and 1760. In the sample of careers, 28 of the 108 never possessed benefices in the diocese of Gap. This was a decade of a surplus of priests, and many were undoubtedly forced to go else-

[3] A seventeenth-century scholar, the abbé Claude Fleury, specifically defined the benefice in these terms: "Un bénéfice est un office ecclésiastique, auquel est joint un certain revenu, en sorte qu'il n'en peut être séparé": *Institution du droit ecclésiastique de France*, 2 vols. (Paris, 1721), I, 360: cited in Châtellier, *loc. cit.*, p. 76.

[4] I have based my study on the registers of the secretariat of the bishop, 1755–1789: A.D.H.A., G 814–828. This information is duplicated and supplemented by the registers of *insinuations ecclésiastiques* complete through 1771 only: A.D.H.A., G 877–880. By means of these two series of registers, the archivist Paul Guillaume prepared an analysis of benefices held in the diocese (1) by individual: A.D.H.A., ms. 377; and (2) by parish: *Bénéfices et bénéficiers de l'ancien diocèse de Gap* (Gap, 1909), reproduced in *Inventaire sommaire, série G*, VI (Gap, 1909), pp. ix–cclxxvi; supplemented for parishes outside the *département* of the Hautes-Alpes by *Bénéfices et bénéficiers du Beaumont aux XVIe, XVIIe, et XVIIIe siècles* (Grenoble, 1896); *Bénéfices et bénéficiers . . . de l'archiprêtré de Provence . . .* (Digne, 1896); and *Bénéfices et bénéficiers . . . du Rosanais . . .* (Valence, 1895). I have also used Guillaume's analysis of the careers of the cathedral canons in the introductions to *Inventaire sommaire, série G*, IV and V (Gap, 1901 and 1904). Unfortunately, Guillaume's lists are incomplete, especially in the case of those parishes not contained in the present-day diocese of Gap, *i.e.*, the department of the Hautes-Alpes.

where to find positions.[5] Of the 80 who would eventually hold benefices in the diocese, 68 would serve in the parish clergy and 12 would serve in the cathedral chapter or only hold benefices without cure of souls.

APPRENTICESHIP: THE SECONDARY

Within a few weeks or months after their ordination to the priesthood, most young clergymen of the generation 1751–1760 who had chosen to stay in the diocese would be appointed to the post of "secondary" or "vicaire."[6] The secondary's status differed fundamentally from that of the curé in that he held a commissioned post rather than a benefice. His tenure could thus be revoked at any time, either by the bishop or by the curé under whom the secondary served.[7] In return for his services, the secondary was usually paid a fixed salary by a non-resident tithe owner or by the curé himself, depending on who controlled the revenues of the parish.[8] There were various degrees of secondaries with different degrees of responsibility. A newly ordained priest usually began as a vicaire living in

[5] See above, Chapter II. The priests who obtained posts outside the diocese are difficult to trace. By means of information given me by abbés Godel and Loche, however, several have been located in the regions of the Drôme and the Isère. Among those ordained between 1751 and 1760 were Pierre Chauvet, who became curé of Chichilianne (diocese of Grenoble); and Jean-Louis Oddon, who became curé of Tréminis-enTrièves (diocese of Die). Claude Callandre was curé of Pontaix (diocese of Die) before returning to the parish of Montmaur in his home diocese, fourteen years later.

[6] In the diocese of Gap, the word *"vicaire"* was generally used for a priest serving directly under a curé, while the word *"secondaire"* referred to the pro-curés and to the priests assigned to the annexes, as well as to the vicaires. The words were often used interchangeably and I will do likewise. Most of the generalizations concerning the secondaries in this section are based on a study of the commissions of secondaries inscribed in the registers of approbations: A.D.H.A., G 829–830.

[7] In rare instances, the secondary held a beneficed office, *e.g.*, in the parish of Mison.

[8] The amount of the vicaire's salary was established by royal edict. See above, Chapter V. The salary of the pro-curé was paid by the incumbent curé, whether or not he was a tithe owner.

the same village as the curé and serving under the direct supervision of the older priest. Later he could be promoted to a position of greater independence, such as the secondary of an annex or *"succursale,"* permanently assigned to an outlying hamlet within the jurisdiction of a parish; or the "pro-curé," a temporary replacement for a sick or aging curé. There was often a considerable degree of mobility during this apprenticeship stage in the clergyman's career, with many priests serving in several different parishes before obtaining a cure of their own.[9]

According to canon law, the curés had the right to choose their own vicaires, but this choice was to be controlled by the bishop from whom each prospective vicaire received his official commission,[10] and, in practice, most secondaries were probably assigned directly by the prelate. A curé might well prefer a young priest with whom he was acquainted and make his preference known to the bishop; but, with the shortage of new clergymen after 1765, it would have been difficult for the average parish priest to locate a candidate on his own initiative. Many vicaires had to be brought in by the bishop from the neighboring diocese of Embrun.[11] It was good policy for the bishop, whenever possible, to commission a priest born in the

[9] At least one third of the corps of vicaires in 1751 would change parishes at least once within five years, and some would serve in several: *e.g.,* Jean Long, who served in Saint-Etienne-en-Dévoluy (1751–1752), Valernes (1752–1755), Le Poët (Feb. 1755), Quet (after Aug. 1755): A.D.H.A., G 829–830. Everywhere in France, the mobility of the vicaires seems to have contrasted sharply with the stability of a priest's career once he had become a curé: see Philippe Loupès, "Le clergé paroissial du diocèse de Bordeaux d'après la grande enquête de 1772," *Annales du Midi,* LXXXIII (1971), pp. 17–19.

[10] See Durand de Maillane, article "Vicaire de paroisse." We have found no instances in which the parishioners themselves also had a formal voice in the choice of the vicaire, as apparently occurred in the province of Maine: Charles Girault, *Les biens d'église dans la Sarthe à la fin du XVIIIe siècle* (Laval, 1953), p. 69.

[11] See above, Chapter II. Abel, curé of Laborel, specifically suggested two candidates as vicaire for his parish in a letter to the bishop, Mar. 7, 1785. But he added, "Je m'en rapporte au choix qu'il vous plaira de faire": A.D.H.A., G 978.

region of the parish in which he was to serve.[12] A local priest might be accepted more readily by the parishioners, particularly when the priest's family was among the local social and economic elite. Such was the case, for example, of Gabriel Maximin, recommended by the archpriest of Tallard to serve as pro-curé of Piégut. Maximin's father was the "principal inhabitant" of Piégut, and for this reason, in the opinion of the archpriest, he would be better received in the village than any other priest.[13]

The time spent by a young man as vicaire was intended as a further training period following the theoretical studies of the seminary. In general, he was to share the pastoral duties of the parish with the curé, officiating at one of the masses on Sundays, and assisting in the various sacraments—for which he was to receive his fair share of the fees and offerings. If he resided in the same village as the curé, he was often given his board and room in the rectory itself, although the community might also provide him with a separate lodging elsewhere in the village.[14] In all his actions, the vicaire was to show complete obedience to the parish priest. He was, in effect, the secondary of the curé, and not the secondary of the parish. He would be carefully observed by the curé and the archpriest, and his performance would be evaluated in regular reports sent to the bishop.[15] Some vicaires in France bitterly complained of this position of subservience in which they were placed and of being treated by the curés as mere domestic servants.[16] But only two instances of open conflict between

12 A sampling of the commissions of vicaires would indicate that many were appointed either to the canton in which they were born or to a canton immediately adjoining it: A.D.H.A., G 829–830.

13 Letter to the bishop, Jan. 15, 1785: A.D.H.A., G 978.

14 Malissoles had specifically recommended that curé and vicaire lodge together "pour se maintenir dans l'union et la bonne correspondance . . . et pour se fortifier et s'animer réciproquement par leurs bons exemples." *Ord. syn.*, I, 198–199.

15 *Ord. syn.*, I, 197–198; and pastoral letter of bishop Pérouse, Nov. 12, 1756: A.D.H.A., G 814.

16 See Emile Sévestre, *L'organisation du clergé paroissial à la veille de la Révolution* (Paris, 1911), pp. 23–24.

parish priest and vicaire have been encountered in the diocese of Gap during the second half of the eighteenth century.[17] It was clearly in the younger priest's career interest to constrain his pride and independence, and show all due respect toward his immediate superior.

No clergyman in the diocese of Gap is known to have spent his entire career in the ranks of the vicaires—as sometimes seems to have occurred in Brittany.[18] The number of years before the first cure was obtained varied enormously. For the generation of 1751–1760, the average waiting period was about ten years, but it ranged in individual cases from as little as two to as long as thirty-three years (see Figure N). This wide variation depended in part on the personal abilities and aptitudes of the priests of the diocese, but it was also the result of the hazards and complexities of the search for a benefice.

Obtaining a Cure

The fountain and source of the great majority of the cures of the diocese of Gap—with *pleno jure* nomination of more than 80 percent—was the bishop himself.[19] This was perhaps a particularly high percentage, compared with other dioceses of eighteenth-century France. Only about 21 percent of the cures in the diocese of Le Mans, 6 percent in

---

[17] Jean, curé of Montjai vs. Escallier, his vicaire, 1787: A.D.H.A., G 978 and G 998; Bougerel, curé of Barret-le-Bas vs. Roux, his vicaire, 1790: A.D.H.A., G 978. Using the records of the ecclesiastical courts, Jacques Lovie found only one or two such disputes in the eighteenth-century diocese of Die: "La vie paroissiale dans le diocèse de Die à la fin de l'Ancien régime," *BD*, LXV (1935), p. 20.

[18] Armand Rébillon, *La situation économique du clergé à la veille de la Révolution dans les districts de Rennes, de Fougères et de Vitré* (Rennes, 1913), p. cii.

[19] Other than the bishop, who controlled at least 171 of 214 cures, the most important patrons were the Augustinian canons of Baume-lès-Sisteron (controlling 9 cures), the *collège* of Embrun (7), the prior of Beaumont (6), and the cathedral chapter (4). There were no lay patrons of cures in the diocese of Gap. These figures are derived from numerous sources, especially from A.D.H.A., G 2328 and from the collations of benefices in the register of the bishop's secretariat: A.D.H.A., G 814–828.

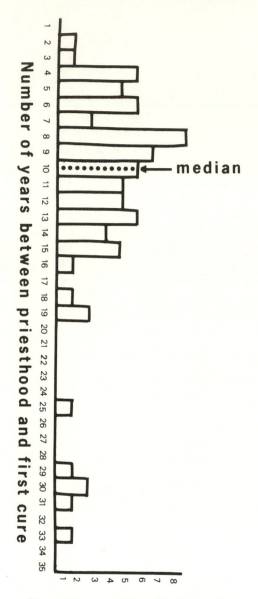

FIGURE N.

The period of apprenticeship: number of years between the ordination to the priesthood and the taking of possession of the first cure

the diocese of Reims, and 9 percent in the diocese of Chartres were in the hands of the respective bishops; the others were named by a broad assortment of chapters, monastic houses, or even lay patrons.[20] On occasion, the bishops of Gap seem to have tried to use their unusually extensive authority to fill vacant parishes on the basis of merit or seniority. This was one of the reasons for requesting the periodic progress reports on the vicaires from the archpriests and for drawing up lists of the corps of secondaries at a given date with the number of years that each had served at his post.[21] All efforts to rationalize the system of curé appointments were hindered by the constant changes and frequent non-residence of the bishops. During the intervals of the bishop's absence, benefices could be collated by the vicars-general. The latter were commonly cathedral canons who originated, as we have seen, from the local nobility and bourgeoisie of Gap. For such men, the temptations of playing favorites in the distribution of benefices were ever present. Good personal relations and a protector were inevitably important for rapid advancement within the parish clergy. Documents concerning this kind of patronage are not often preserved, but we do catch an occasional glimpse. In some cases, the protector might be another priest already established and respected in the diocese. Thus curé Chaix made several visits to Gap to put in a good word with a vicar-general on the behalf of Villars' brother. When a position opened up, Chaix felt confident that the young Villars would be named, despite the

[20] M. Giraud, *Essai sur l'histoire religieuse de la Sarthe de 1789 à l'an IV* (Paris, 1920), p. 75; Dominique Julia, "Le prêtre au XVIIIe siècle, la théologie et les institutions," *Recherches de science religieuse*, LVIII (1970), p. 525, n. 19; and Michel Vovelle, "Le chapitre cathédral de Chartres," *Actes du 85e congrès national de sociétés savantes. Chambéry-Annecy, 1960* (Paris, 1961), p. 241. Note, however, the high percentages of nominations held by the bishops of two other dioceses of southern Dauphiné: approximately 80 percent in the diocese of Valence, 86 percent in the diocese of Embrun: A.N., G⁸ 81 (Valence) and G⁸ 74 (Embrun).

[21] *E.g.*, the "Etat des secondaires" of *ca.* 1764: A.D.H.A., G 1109.

competition of one of the bishop's favorites, since Villars was both "well deserving" and "well protected."[22] A priest might also seek the help of one of the local nobles. Thus the marquis of Moydans wrote a series of letters to one of the vicars-general, his cousin, requesting the appointment to vacant posts of two priests originating in his region.[23] It was good policy for a bishop to take into account the recommendations of the seigneurial lord of a parish. After all, if a curé were to perform his functions effectively, it was important that he have the support of the local nobility.[24]

There were also a number of means by which a priest could effectively force an appointment in his favor from the bishop or the vicars-general. The most important of these procedures used to obtain cures in the diocese of Gap were the *expectative* of the university graduate, the *prévention* of the vice-legate of Avignon, and the resignation through the court of Rome.[25] All parishes vacating through the death of the previous holder during four months of the year—January, April, July, and October— were reserved by canon law to candidates with university degrees. A priest had only to serve official notice of his diplomas to the bishop—or to whichever ecclesiastic held the patronage of the benefice—and await his turn. Vacancies occurring in January and July were to be given by seniority; vacancies occurring in April and October could be given to any graduate chosen by the bishop or the patron of the benefice.[26] In addition, there were three

---

22 Letter dated Aug. 8, 1786: B.M.G., R 10073. Note also Jean-Michel Rolland's efforts to obtain a cure for his younger brother: letters written from the National Assembly in Paris to the mayor of Gap in early 1790: *AA*, xi (1907), pp. 47-53, 112-114.

23 Letters to Moydans from the vicar-general, La Villette, Dec. 17, 1773 and Sept. 10, 1777: A.D.H.A., F 2468.

24 The baron Des Preaux was making such recommendations to bishop Pérouse in 1759 for the cure of Laye—a parish in which he was seigneurial lord: letter from the bishop to Des Preaux, Feb. 26, 1759: A.D.H.A., F 1371.

25 There is no evidence that any cure was obtained through devolution or indult during the second half of the eighteenth century.

26 Durand de Maillane, article "Gradué."

parishes in the diocese for which university degrees were mandatory—the two co-cures of Gap and the cure of Volonne in Provence.[27] But if the use of a university degree was one of the quickest and surest means of obtaining the first parish, it was unusual in the diocese of Gap because only about 10 percent of the parish clergy possessed the required degrees.[28]

The second method of forcing an appointment was through the papal vice-legate of Avignon. Within the regions of Dauphiné and Provence[29] the vice-legate held the right—exercised only by the Pope in the other provinces of France—of providing vacant benefices that had not yet been collated by the bishop himself. There were many stories and rumors concerning the abuses of the *prévention*, of clergymen concealing the death of a previous benefice holder from the bishop in order to obtain a quick provision via Avignon, or of requests of provisions being made in advance of an impending death—the so-called *"course ambitieuse."*[30] Despite such stories and the frequent complaints of the bishops,[31] it was rare that a cure of the diocese of Gap changed hands through Avignon. Only seven instances have been found during the period 1771–1789, less than five percent of the collations.[32]

Much more common was the resignation made through

[27] *Ibid.*, article "Ville."

[28] Among the parish clergy ordained between 1751 and 1760, 9 are known to have been graduates. All 9 obtained their first cure in less than nine years after their ordination.

[29] Or, more precisely, within the *ecclesiastical* provinces of Aix, Arles, Avignon, Embrun, and Vienne.

[30] See Marcel Marion, *Dictionnaire des institutions de la France aux XVIIe et XVIIIe siècles* (Paris, 1923), pp. 45–48.

[31] The bishop Jouffroy-Gonssans claimed that such abuses took place in Provence and Dauphiné "chaque jour," and that they gave cause for many "mauvais sujets" among his parish clergy: letter to the agents-general in Paris, June 9, 1777: A.N., G⁸ 632 (97).

[32] The cures of Barras (Aug. 24, 1776), Valernes (Sept. 30, 1776), Châteaufort (Sept. 9, 1777), Châteaufort (July 13, 1779), Savoillan (Feb. 18, 1780), Saint-Martin-d'Argençon (Nov. 14, 1785), and Aspres-lès-Veynes (Sept. 11, 1786).

the papal court of Rome by which one clergyman resigned in favor of another. A curé and his chosen successor drew up and notarized an act of resignation that was sent to Rome via a special agent. If the curé were on the verge of retirement and had served in his parish for fifteen years, he could conceivably reserve himself a small pension to be paid by the individual accepting the resignation. When the papal provision was returned, the candidate presented the act to his bishop and requested a "visa." The bishop had the right to examine the candidate and to refuse the visa if the latter was found insufficiently prepared; but such a refusal could often be overruled through appeal to a higher ecclesiastical authority or to the Parlement of Dauphiné. Between 1779 and 1788 over one-fourth of all cures changed hands through resignations in Rome.[33] More than half of these took place at the moment when the older priest went into retirement and some may have included provisions for a pension.[34] The remaining resignations seem to have been made merely as a favor to a friend or relative and involved no particular commitment other than that the priest accepting the resignation would pay the legal fees involved.[35] On occasion, three or even four priests took part in a series of multiple resignations involving a reshuffling of several parishes.[36] It is not always possible for us to know

[33] Of 146 cures changing hands, 41 (28 percent) were through Rome. Note, however, that virtually no cures were provided in this way when Pérouse was bishop, 1756–1764. Compare with the diocese of Autun, where, between 1783 and 1787, 47 percent changed hands through Rome. In this diocese, however, a large percentage of the cures were not in the nomination of the bishop: A.D. Saône-et-Loire, 2 G 340–341.

[34] Twenty-four of 46 (52 percent). On the difficulties of obtaining such pensions in the diocese, see below, Chapter V.

[35] *E.g.*, the resignation of the cure of Lazer by Gaspar Bernard—newly named curé of Tallard—to Jean-Pierre Truphemus, vicaire of Lachau. No pension was involved in the notarized act, June 11, 1763: A.D.H.A., IE 6398.

[36] Thus, between July 1786 and Sept. 1788, Marin Isnard resigned the cure of Chardavon to Barthélémy Marcellin, who resigned the cure of Sigottier to Honoré Catellan, who resigned the cure of Roussieux to Joseph Rougon, who, himself, had been vicaire of Sigottier.

the precise relationship between the priests involved. Yet resignations between close relatives were less common than one might suppose. During the period 1779–1788 only about one-fifth seem to have taken place between brothers, first cousins, or uncle and nephew.[37] One-fourth were between a curé and his vicaire or pro-curé.[38]

The system by which the curés bypassed the authority of their bishop and co-opted their own successors was much decried by the leaders of the Gallican Church. But for those priests who were unable or unwilling to work the levers of patronage, a resignation through Rome or Avignon might be the only means of obtaining a benefice without an interminable wait among the ranks of vicaires. Such, at least, was the opinion of one eighteenth-century canonist:

"It would perhaps be dangerous to abolish the resignation [through Rome] unless it were replaced by a legitimate canonical method by which benefices might be obtained without protectors or cabals or intrigues. How many excellent candidates might never have found positions if personal friendships and kindness had not provided them this favor otherwise denied to them by ecclesiastical patrons and collators."[39]

Inevitably, cases arose in which two or more candidates received provisions to the same benefice by two or more different methods. When it was a question of one of the cathedral prebends, epic struggles could ensue between rival pretenders. All possible financial resources and family connections would be mobilized in lawsuits, intrigues, and arbitration which could draw out over several years.[40] But even a humble country parish with only a small fixed salary as revenue was considered desirable game in the benefice hunt.

In 1787, for example, both Jean-Baptiste Gabriel and

[37] Nine of 46.   [38] Eleven of 46.
[39] *Encyclopédie méthodique*, cited in Marion, p. 486.
[40] A very revealing series of letters between the brothers Tournu de Ventavon describes their efforts to obtain the sacristy of Gap for one of the two: A.D.H.A., VII E Jarjayes 155.

A Career in the Clergy

Antoine Borel laid claim to the cure of Saint-Jean-des-Vertus: Gabriel by virtue of a resignation in his favor from the previous curé, Pierre Meffre; Borel by virtue of his university degree.[41] Normally, a resignation through Rome took precedence over any other kind of appointment, but Borel, who had already resigned a previous benefice and who had no other ecclesiastical revenues, was not ready to yield so easily. He brought suit before the bailliage court of Grenoble, claiming that Gabriel's resignation had not been properly registered and that it was tainted with simony. It was common knowledge, Borel argued, that Meffre was offering his benefice to the highest bidder. Was it not suspicious that on the very day the resignation took place, Gabriel also purchased a plot of land from Meffre for twice its real value? Gabriel replied that the property value was enhanced because the land was so conveniently located near the rectory of Saint-Jean, and that if Meffre ever made a statement about auctioning his benefice, it had been long before and had had no bearing on the present resignation. In fact, the resignation was motivated purely by Meffre's feelings of affection for Gabriel. The outcome of the lengthy legal battles that ensued was apparently still pending at the beginning of the Revolution.

Perhaps even more revealing was the case involving François Marchon.[42] In 1768, the curé of Romette, Pierre de la Bastie, seventy-three years old and confined in bed by illness, resigned his benefice in favor of Marchon, a young priest of about twenty-eight. The resignation was sent to Rome via an agent in Aix and, as soon as it was admitted by the Pope, Marchon and his father, a doctor in Gap, appeared together before the three vicars-general to obtain the visa. The triumvirate split two to one against Marchon and refused the visa. Marchon's father, suspecting that the cure had in fact been promised to someone else,

---

[41] Complaints and legal briefs by the two parties: A.D.H.A., B 574.
[42] The legal briefs and appended documents dating from 1768 to 1773 are preserved in A.D.H.A., F 722.

and seeing that the sickness of the resigning priest was growing ever more dangerous, immediately set off on horseback—although it was the middle of winter—to plead his son's case before the bishop himself. The bishop, whom Marchon finally found in Riez, was scarcely more encouraging. At first he refused the visa outright because of a legal technicality; and then he offered to give the younger Marchon the next parish available if he would only retract his claims to Romette. At this point, Marchon, with the help of an older brother who was a lawyer in Gap, took his case before the Parlement of Dauphiné, where he easily won approval and an order to the bishop to collate the benefice. The bishop countered by requiring Marchon to submit to a canonical examination. The visa was again refused when Marchon was found to have an imperfect knowledge of Eucharistic dogma. Finally, after more wrangling and arbitration and intrigues—of which the details escape the records—Marchon obtained the collation of his benefice. The affair was far from over. In the meantime, La Bastie had died, and the vicars-general had immediately given the parish of Romette to their own favorite, a certain Jean Gaillard.[43] Gaillard now brought suit against Marchon, claiming that the resignation through Rome had been tainted, since Marchon's father had been La Bastie's doctor when the aged curé was on his deathbed. It was only in 1772, four years after the resignation had been made, that Marchon won the final appeal and was instated as peaceful possessor of the cure of Romette.

The case of François Marchon further illustrates the importance of personal relations in the pursuit of a benefice. Without the protection of the vicars-general and the bishop, a clergyman could expect considerable difficulty. Yet a

[43] It was by no means uncommon for the bishop or vicars-general to collate the same benefice to more than one contending party. In this way, they effectively washed their hands of the dispute and allowed the opposing parties to take their case before a civil court. The ultimate mark of the possession of a benefice was not the ecclesiastical collation but the notarized ceremony of the taking of possession.

great many obstacles could be overcome through the energetic assistance and support of one's family. Marchon was in a particularly advantageous position since his father was a notable of Gap and his brother a practicing lawyer with connections in the Parlement of Grenoble. He was thus able to secure his first cure within the relatively brief span of three and a half years after his ordination to the priesthood. A young priest whose family was not so well placed might expect to have much greater difficulties.

A reconstruction of clerical careers has, in fact, revealed a definite advantage in the benefice hunt for men originating in families of what we have termed "notables": nobles, "bourgeois," officeholders, and members of the liberal professions.[44] Of 48 priests ordained between 1751 and 1760 for whom family professions are known, 16 came from families of notables. Fourteen of these had obtained their first cure within nine years (sooner than the median of ten years for the total sample). Of the 32 coming from "non-notable" backgrounds—merchants, artisans, and *laboureurs*, for the most part—only 10 obtained their first cure within nine years. Equally revealing is the case of those priests who never secured benefices in the diocese and who left to seek posts elsewhere: 13 of 16 for whom family professions are known came from the same merchant, artisan, and *laboureur* milieux. It was decidedly more difficult for men from the lower levels of the social hierarchy to obtain their first benefices.

LATER ADVANCEMENT

The salient feature of a career in the parish clergy after the first cure had been obtained was its stability. Among the 68 priests ordained between 1751 and 1760 who became curés in the diocese, 40 remained in their first parish until their death or until they were ousted during the Revolu-

44 See above, Chapter II.

tion; and 60 of the 68 changed once at the most.[45] It was not unusual to find a priest serving forty or even fifty years in the same village.[46]

Changing parishes could be both expensive and risky. If one were depending only on the nomination of the bishop and had no resignation through Rome or Avignon, one might suddenly find oneself "out on the street," having resigned a previous cure and then being dislodged from the new cure by a competitor who had bypassed the bishop.[47] This was at least one of the reasons why many priests were allowed to hold the old and the new benefices simultaneously during a certain transitional period.[48] But many other curés, after the long efforts and waiting to secure the first benefice, were seemingly content to remain in their parish and enjoy the security of a guaranteed income and a *situation acquise*. Curé Chaix had a number of opportunities to move to benefices with a higher income and greater prestige, but, as he remarked several times to Villars, he had no ambitions beyond his small parish of Les Baux: "the mountains and the forests are my element."[49]

Various factors might have been involved in a curé's decision to change his parish. Many of the moves made by the priests ordained between 1751 and 1760 brought an increase in revenues. Usually this meant exchanging a bene-

[45] The remaining 8 changed twice. None within this sample changed more than twice.

[46] For example, Barthélémy Faure, curé of Châteauneuf-d'Oze, was named in 1739 and died in office in 1790. Jean-Baptiste Teissier, curé of Montclus, was named in 1742 and died in office in *ca.* 1792: Guillaume, *Clergé ancien et moderne*, pp. lviii and cxxxix.

[47] Letters from curé Pontian Brun to the vicar-general, Saint-Genis, Oct. 4 and 20, 1779: A.D.H.A., G 2092. Brun had been named to the parish of Eourres, but later heard rumors that someone else had already obtained it via Avignon.

[48] There are many examples of this in the register of the secretariat. *E.g.*, François Gaude, named to Furmeyer in Oct. 1786, resigned his previous cure of Oze only in May 1787: A.D.H.A., G 827. There was, of course, another good reason for holding two cures as long as possible: one could collect a double revenue during this period.

[49] Letter, Feb. 17, 1784: B.M.G., R 10073.

fice that paid only a fixed salary for one that gave a right to the tithes. Of equal importance were the changes that brought an individual closer to his parish of origin. Some priests were obviously willing to accept a decrease in revenues in order to be closer to their home village.[50] Other motives might also be involved. Curé Pontian Brun disliked the parish of Savournon because of its isolation—"a rugged country where letters can scarcely get through"[51]—and he requested that the vicar-general keep him in mind if another cure became available. Augustin Millon left the parish of Laye in order to take over the benefice of an elderly uncle and care for him in his retirement; he felt an obligation, since the uncle had helped to finance his training for the priesthood. But Millon also admitted a general antipathy for his present parishioners, who continually plotted against him and refused to obey him: "It seems that I can no longer bear fruit in this parish."[52] Certain parishes were considered undesirable because of a large Calvinist population that made life miserable for the curé,[53] and some of the Protestant parishes seem to have had an especially rapid turnover of curés.[54] Finally, a priest might wish to arrange a transfer at the end of his career to one of those cures with a decent income but a tiny population and hence reduced pastoral functions. He would "retire to some small parish," as one curé put it.[55]

In addition to changing cures, there were other ways in

[50] Of 36 changes in cures made by this group, 12 brought an increased revenue, 13 brought the individual closer to his home parish; 2 brought both; 9 brought neither.

[51] Letter to Saint-Genis, Apr. 20, 1778: A.D.H.A., G 2089.

[52] Letter from Millon to the baron Des Preaux, seigneur of Laye, May 27, 1780: A.D.H.A., F 1350.

[53] The parish of La Charce had more than 90 percent Protestants. See curé Robert's plea to be transferred from La Charce in a note attached to his declaration of revenue of Mar. 29, 1772: A.D.H.A., G 2337.

[54] Note, for example, the parish of Trescléoux, which had 9 curés between 1731 and the Revolution: Guillaume, *Clergé ancien et moderne*, p. ccl.

[55] Curé Joseph Pellenc, in a letter to Jean Pinchinet, Mar. 13, 1782: A.D.H.A., F 266.

which one might progress in a career in the parish clergy. First, there was the possibility of being named archpriest. The archpriests, like the vicaires, were commissioned in their posts and could thus be appointed and dismissed at will by the bishop. They were to be named on the basis of their learning and their personal qualities and they were frequently among the oldest members of their canton.[56] Thus, the promotion to the post of archpriest might crown a long career in the service of the diocese. Curés with university degrees, however, could receive this commission much earlier, even at the beginning of their careers.[57] The position carried considerable prestige and authority within the parish clergy, but apparently no financial benefits.[58]

Secondly, a curé might hope to increase his ecclesiastical revenues by obtaining additional benefices not requiring residence. There were approximately 200 "simple benefices" within the diocese, of which about seventy-five were priories and the rest were chapels.[59] They varied greatly in their revenues, although the chapels were generally of minor value—usually well under 100 *livres* per year—while the priories provided very substantial revenues of several hundred *livres*.[60] To a far greater extent than the cures, the simple benefices were obtained via the court of Rome or the vice-legate of Avignon: three out of four priories were secured in this way between 1771 and 1789.[61] A few parish priests were apparently quite successful in acquiring these

[56] I have used the *Almanach général de Dauphiné* (Grenoble, 1789), pp. 358–363 to identify the 25 archpriests in 1788. They ranged in ages from 46 to 73 years old, with an average of about 63.

[57] Alexandre Achard, curé of Serres, was named archpriest before Nov. 10, 1750, at the age of 35, and held the position for 40 years. Honoré Nicolas, curé of Ribiers, graduate of the University of Valence, was named archpriest Sept. 3, 1788 at the age of 27: A.D.H.A., G 828.

[58] See above, Chapter III.

[59] See Guillaume's introduction to *Inventaire sommaire, série G*, II (Gap, 1895), pp. viii–xv. Also the *pouillés* of 1729 and 1755: A.D.H.A., G 1107 and 1108.

[60] See the declarations of revenue of 1790–1791: A.D.H.A., I Q I 108 and I Q I 137.

[61] Twenty-four of 32.

kinds of benefices. François-Joseph Chabert, curé of La Saulce in 1790, had accumulated several chapels and the priory of Sigottier. He had thus more than doubled the income of his cure.[62] Yet, for the most part, the parish clergy of the diocese gained relatively little benefit from these sinecures. During the nineteen years before the Revolution, only about one-half of the chapels and one-tenth of the priories were given as benefices to those making careers in the parish clergy. Two-thirds of all simple benefices went to a relatively small group of the chapter clergy in Gap or to clergymen not even residing in the diocese (see Table

TABLE 5

Clergymen to Whom Simple Benefices
Were Collated, 1771–1789

	Parish Clergy	Chapter Clergy	Non-Diocesan Clergy	Total
Priories	3 (9%)	10 (31%)	19 (60%)	32 (100%)
Chapels	26 (46%)	20 (36%)	10 (18%)	56 (100%)
Total	29 (33%)	30 (34%)	29 (33%)	88 (100%)

5).[63] In 1789 the great majority of the curés of the diocese held no benefices other than their cures.[64]

Finally, a curé might hope to advance into the ranks of the canons. In Gap, as in other dioceses of France, there seems always to have been a certain degree of mobility be-

---

[62] Chabert, the younger son of a *négociant* in Gap, had a total net revenue in 1790 of 1,973 *livres* per year, one of the highest of all the curés of the diocese: A.D.H.A., I Q I 108. Note also that Chabert was one of the few curés who changed his parish frequently: he held four cures prior to the Revolution, each change bringing an increase in revenue.

[63] A few of the priories could be given only to regular clergymen.

[64] In the declarations of revenue of 1790, only a small minority of the curés reported additional benefices: A.D.H.A., I Q I 108 and I Q I 137.

tween the parish clergy and the chapter clergy.[65] Yet such mobility was clearly the exception rather than the rule and it was particularly limited in the diocese of Gap, where there were no collegiate chapters and only twelve prebends in the cathedral. Only three former curés are known to have become canons after 1750: Joseph-Bruno Tournu in 1752, Pompon-Benoît Delafont in 1763, and François Marchon in 1779.[66] In the diocese of Gap and probably in most dioceses in the kingdom, entry into the chapter clergy was largely restricted to a small social elite.[67] To be sure, there were no explicit requirements in the statutes of

[65] Thus, in the diocese of Autun, 13 of 48 new canons (27 percent) between 1705 and 1709 came from the parish clergy; between 1783 and 1787, 10 of 61 (16 percent) came from the parish clergy: A.D. Saône-et-Loire, 2 G 319–320 and 2 G 340–341 (research in collaboration with Dominique Julia). In the future department of the Moselle, 24 of 71 canons in 1790 (34 percent) are known to have done some service in the parish clergy: data from Jean Eich, *Les prêtres mosellans pendant la Révolution*, 2 vols. (Metz, 1959–1964).

[66] There is not a single example of a canon entering the parish clergy. It was not uncommon for a canon to receive a collation of a cure, but in every case he held it for only a matter of weeks and almost certainly never took possession. This was probably simply a means of enabling a canon to collect a portion of the revenues of the cure until a serious candidate could be found and instated. For example, Pompon Gautier, vicar-general of Gap, held the cure of Saint-Eusèbe from June to July 1788: A.D.H.A., G 823. Occasionally, a younger canon would serve as a temporary "pro-curé" for a few weeks. Ignace de Cazeneuve, future constitutional bishop, was pro-curé of Volonne from December 1784 to March 1785: undated letter from Cazeneuve to bishop Vareilles, A.D.H.A., G 975.

[67] In the diocese of Le Mans for the period 1759 to 1789, 76 percent of the new canons who were native to the diocese originated in the nobility, officeholding families, or families calling themselves "bourgeois": data kindly given me by M. Alex Poyer. In the diocese of Autun between 1783 and 1787, 71 percent of the new canons came from these milieux: A.D. Saône-et-Loire, 2 G 340–341 (research with D. Julia). In the future department of the Moselle, 80 percent of those for whom origins are known came from these milieux: data from Eich, *op. cit.* In each region, the remaining percentage came almost entirely from town merchant families. Canons from artisan or peasant milieux seem to have been extremely rare.

the Gap chapter concerning family origins.[68] But the canons had the right to bring in new members by co-optation[69] and, in practice, their choice went primarily to priests originating in families of the nobility and the officeholding bourgeoisie; and most commonly, to priests from the city of Gap itself.[70] Of the three curés who became canons after 1750, Tournu was a nobleman's son, Delafont was related to the local sub-delegate, and Marchon, as we have seen, belonged to a powerful and ambitious family of notables in Gap. For the most part, members of the chapter clergy advanced through a career that was largely distinct and separate from the career in the parish clergy. It was a career that commonly led from the semi-prebend[71] through the various ranks of canons to positions of administrative responsibility in the diocese such as ecclesiastical judge or vicar-general. Only rarely did it include positions involving pastoral care and the cure of souls, the central preoccupation of the men in the parish clergy.

Once a man had become a curé in the diocese of Gap, he had entered a virtual *cul-de-sac* in his ecclesiastical career.

[68] Twenty-one chapters in France allowed entry only to members of the nobility: Michel Peronnet, "Les problèmes du clergé dans la société de l'Ancien régime de 1770 à 1789" in Roland Mousnier, *Société française de 1770 à 1789*, 2 vols. (Paris, 1970), I, 42.

[69] The canons as a corps held the right of collating all prebends; see the *pouillé* of the end of the eighteenth century: *BHA*, X (1891), pp. 116–117. A great many prebends were resigned directly from one clergyman to another via the court of Rome. This was a relatively expensive procedure: an additional reason why priests from families of the upper bourgeoisie and nobility were at an advantage for entering the chapter.

[70] See above, Chapter II. There were also a few canons originating from outside the diocese; for these, I have no information on social origins.

[71] The semi-prebend was the one benefice at which the chapter career and the parish career sometimes overlapped. Most men who obtained semi-prebends either remained in this post for life or used it as a stepping stone for entering the chapter. There was also a small number of curés who began their careers with such a benefice. A few of the semi-prebends apparently served to provide financial aid to poorer clerics and were accepted as substitutes for the patrimonial title.

There was little possibility of obtaining a cathedral prebend and only slight hope of accumulating simple benefices. The principal dignities and sinecures of the diocese, the principal positions of prestige and importance, were usually reserved for the sons of the Gapençais nobility and upper bourgeoisie; and the average curé did not originate in these milieux. It is difficult to say whether the blocking of clerical careers to talent and seniority was, in itself, a major source of grievance. As we have seen, many parish priests—even so capable a clergyman as Dominique Chaix—were apparently content to remain in their first parish and enjoy the stability and security, the considerable prestige within the village society that accrued to the position of curé. Yet, whatever a curé's appreciation of the social realities of the clerical career, he was invariably sensitive to the economic realities. Thus, before attempting a conclusion, we must examine the economic position a man might attain in the course of a career in the parish clergy.

CHAPTER V

Economic Situation of the Parish Priest

The primary sources of revenue for most clergymen in eighteenth-century France were the tithes and the bene-ficed lands or glebe. But both the absolute value and the mode of exploitation of these revenues varied considerably from region to region. A significant proportion of the ec-clesiastical wealth of the kingdom seems to have been con-centrated in northern and western France, particularly in the Parisian Basin, Normandy, Picardy, and Champagne. The clergy of Dauphiné, on the contrary, was relatively dis-favored economically.[1] A more restricted yield from the land in the Alps, a mean tithe rate that was lower than the overall French average (about 5 percent of agricultural and pastoral production, compared to 7 to 8 percent nation-ally),[2] and extremely reduced ecclesiastical land holdings: all contributed to the relative poverty of the clergy of this

[1] Jacques de Font-Réaulx has calculated the total declared value of Church revenues in fourteenth-century France as a function of the surface area of the various dioceses. He estimates an overall value of 6 *livres* 12 *sous* per square kilometer for the kingdom as a whole. The corresponding values for four dioceses in Dauphiné ranged from 3 *livres* 6 *sous* in the diocese of Vienne to about 1 *livre* in the diocese of Die. At the same time, the relative wealth of the diocese of Paris was 35 *livres* 10 *sous* per square kilometer. In general, well over half of the ecclesiastical wealth of the kingdom was contained in the three ecclesiastical provinces of Reims, Sens, and Rouen. The broad distri-bution of revenues probably did not change significantly through the end of the Old Regime. See Font-Réaulx, "Les pouillés de la province de Vienne," *BD*, LXIX (1943), pp. 30–31; and "La structure comparée d'un diocèse," *RHEF*, XXXVI (1950), pp. 184–185.

[2] P. Gagnol, *La dîme ecclésiastique en France au XVIIIe siècle* (Paris, 1910), p. 150, sets the average tithe rate as 1/23 for the Isère, 1/23 for the Drôme, and 1/17 for the Hautes-Alpes; he estimates an average rate for the kingdom at about 1/15. There was, however, an enormous variation from parish to parish. Marcel Marion, *Dictionnaire des institutions de la France aux XVIIe et XVIIIe siècles* (Paris, 1923), p. 174, estimates an average of about 1/13 for the kingdom.

province. Thus, in the northern portion of the diocese of Gap, less than 1 percent of the land was owned by the Church—less than ½ of 1 percent, if the parish of Gap itself is excluded.[3] For the kingdom as a whole, the corresponding average was probably 6 to 10 percent, rising as high as 20 to 40 percent in certain regions of northern France.[4]

Some clergymen in Dauphiné were far more disadvantaged than others. Due to the particular manner in which ecclesiastical revenues were distributed, the burden of the Church's poverty fell on the parish clergy. In most of the dioceses of eastern Languedoc, Provence, and Dauphiné, from 60 to over 90 percent of the curés did not have the right to collect the tithes and exploit the glebe directly.[5]

[3] Calculations based on the surveys made primarily in 1790–1791 of Church land to be sold in the district of Gap: A.D.H.A., I Q I 112–113. For conversions from Old-Regime measurements to hectares, I used Paul Aimès, *Anciennes mesures des Hautes-Alpes* (Gap, 1965). The Church holdings in individual parishes varied from over 10 percent of the land in Romette and almost 5 percent in Gap to considerably less than o.1 percent in several parishes. In the district as a whole, o.75 percent of the land was owned by the Church (o.45 percent if Gap is excluded). *Cf.* to the average of 1.79 percent Church land in eight parishes in the Haut-Grésivaudan, diocese of Grenoble: cited in Georges Lefebvre, "Répartition de la propriété et de l'exploitation foncières à la fin de l'Ancien régime," in *Etudes sur la Révolution française* (Paris, 1963), p. 305. Time limitations disallowed the lengthy research and calculations required for the study of Church property in other areas of the diocese.

[4] *Ibid.*, pp. 285–286.

[5] Calculated from figures reported to the General Assembly of the Clergy in 1760: A.N., G8 499–516, printed in Claude Léouzon Le Duc, "La fortune du clergé sous l'Ancien régime," *Journal des économistes,* 4e série, xv (July-Sept. 1881), pp. 228–230. There were the following percentages of congruists in the seven dioceses of Dauphiné in 1755: Vienne, 93 percent; Valence, 41 percent; Die, 61 percent; Saint-Paul-les-Trois-Châteaux, 74 percent; Embrun, 80 percent; Grenoble, 92 percent; Gap, 68 percent. The percentages changed somewhat following the edict of May 1768, which raised the *portion congrue*, but allowed the *gros-décimateurs* to abandon the tithes to the curés if they so chose. This source does not provide data for the dioceses outside the authority of the Clergy of France: *e.g.*, Lorraine, Franche-Comté, Hainaut, Roussillon.

The parish revenues were possessed most often by clergymen who had no pastoral functions in the parish and who usually did not reside there. The tithe-owner—the *"gros-décimateur,"* as he was called—paid only a fixed salary or *"portion congrue"* to the resident curé. The predominance of salaried parish priests in the southeast formed a sharp contrast to the situation in most other regions of France—despite the impression given by many historians. On the whole, only about one-third of the curés in the kingdom were salaried, and in wide areas of the north and the west the "congruists" represented from 25 percent to as little as 5 percent of the corps of the diocesan parish priests.

An appreciation of these characteristic economic structures of the Church in Dauphiné is essential not only for our understanding of the material condition of the Gap diocesan clergy, but also for our later analysis of the position of the curés in lay and ecclesiastical society.

Ecclesiastical Revenues: Prior-Curés and Congruist Curés

At mid-century, the ecclesiastical revenues in some two-thirds of the parishes of the diocese of Gap were controlled by non-resident clergymen or corps of clergymen.[6] The bishop was sole or co-owner of the tithes of 14 parishes, the cathedral chapter in 12, the Order of Malta in 7, the regular canons of La Baume-lès-Sisteron in 5, and the Carthusians of Durbon in 1. The tithes of a few other curés were controlled by religious corps and institutions located outside the diocese.[7] Far more important were the approximately

---

[6] *Pouillé* of 1755: A.D.H.A., G 1108. In 1755 there were 146 curés with the *portion congrue*, 68 (32 percent) with all or part of the tithes. In 1789 there were 131 congruists (61 percent) and 83 tithe-owning curés (39 percent): see the roll of the *décime* of 1789: A.D.H.A., G 2492; and the *pouillé* of *ca.* 1785: *BHA*, x (1891), pp. 113–165.

[7] The *collège* of Embrun (6), the chapter of Sisteron (1), Saint-André d'Avignon (3), Saint Jean-de-Jérusalem of Avignon (1), the chapel of Notre-Dame-des-Doms of Avignon (3), and the Abbé Saint-Ruf of Valence (1).

63 priors who held all or part of the tithes in 94 parishes as simple sinecures. The term "prior" harked back to a period in the Middle Ages when many of the parishes were actually manned by small groups of regular clergymen; but by the eighteenth century most of the priories had been secularized or put *in commendam*. The majority of the priors—as we have seen in the previous chapter—were not members of the clergy of Gap and had probably never even set foot in the diocese. They were absentee landlords of ecclesiastical possessions, exploiting the tithes and glebe by means of benefice farmers and collecting the revenues as a kind of rent.

There were so many parishes in which a prior held the tithes that the word was also used locally as a synonym for "tithe owner." The 32 percent of the curés in the diocese who controlled all or part of the tithes themselves were known as "prior-curés" or simply "priors."[8] There were prior-curés in virtually every region of the diocese although they were in the minority in all but two of the ecclesiastical cantons before 1768 (see Figure O).[9] Most seem to have exploited their benefices directly with the help of one or two hired laborers.[10] Thus Antoine Millon, curé of Saint-Michel-de-Chaillol, took on one servant each year from May to November to cultivate the glebe and to collect the parish tithes.[11] But even when a priest leased his rights to the tithes and beneficed lands, he usually demanded that

[8] *Almanach général de la province de Dauphiné* (Grenoble, 1789), p. 373. In Dauphiné the title of "prior-curé" did *not* mean that a regular clergyman held the cure—as "prior-curé" did imply in certain regions of France.

[9] The cantons of L'Epine (3 congruists and 5 prior-curés) and of Trescléoux (5 congruists and 6 prior-curés). After 1768, the prior-curés were also in the majority in the cantons of Thoard, La Rochette-du-Buis, and Saint-Firmin.

[10] At the beginning of the Revolution, 30 of 48 prior-curés whose mode of exploitation is known collected their portion of the crops without the intermediary of a tithe farmer: A.D.H.A., L 1024, I Q I 108 and I Q I 137.

[11] Declaration of revenue, 1772: A.D.H.A., G. 2338.

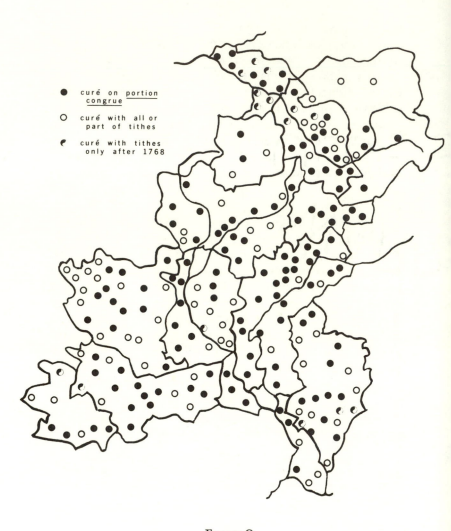

curé on portion
congrue

○ curé with all or
part of tithes

☾ curé with tithes
only after 1768

FIGURE O.
Congruist curés and prior-curés, second half of the eighteenth
century

a portion of the lease be paid in kind, leaving him enough for his personal needs and perhaps even a little for sale as well. Curé Davignon, for example, leased the tithes and a portion of the glebe of Saint-Pierre-de-Chaillol for four years at 300 *livres* per year plus two *setiers* of barley, two *setiers* of oats, and fodder for a horse and a goat. He kept two gardens and a small plot of land belonging to the rectory for his personal use.[12] All of the prior-curés would have been closely bound to the agricultural interests and market activities of the rural communities in which they lived. Many were veritable priest-farmers, cultivating crops and raising livestock on their beneficed lands and selling their produce at the local fairs in much the same manner as their parishioners.

With a few exceptions, the parish glebe was only a minor source of revenue for the prior-curés, and commonly there was no glebe at all.[13] As for the tithes, an extraordinary particularism reigned. The rates, the items taxed, the manner of collection, and the overall value all differed from one community to another. The tithes were levied everywhere on grain, and frequently on wine, lambs, hemp, and vegetables as well.[14] In France, however, there were no "personal tithes," tithes paid on income from rent, commerce, or industry. The grain tithes might be paid in sheaves on the field, in grain on the threshing floor, or in bags in the granary. The rates could vary from as much as 14 percent to as little as 2 percent of the total production, depending on the item and on the parish or the section of the parish involved. Generally speaking, the portion of grain levied was somewhat smaller in the north, in the Champsaur and the Val-

12 Lease dated May 23, 1771, attached to declaration of revenue: A.D.H.A., G. 2338.

13 For example, the parish of Monêtier-d'Ambel: declaration of revenue, 1772: A.D.H.A., G 2337. See also J. Bermond, "Etude sur la dîme et les biens ecclésiastiques dans l'ancien diocèse de Gap," *BHA*, XLVI (1928), p. 268.

14 The tithes on items other than grain, the *menues dîmes*, were generally more limited in Dauphiné than in many other French provinces: Gagnol, p. 39.

gaudemar, and somewhat greater in the south, particularly in the Provençal zones of the left bank of the Durance (see Figure P).[15]

During the second half of the eighteenth century, the annual income of the prior-curés' benefices would have changed considerably from year to year following the rapid fluctuations in agricultural prices. We can obtain a good estimate of their total value at the end of the Old Regime by means of the declarations of revenue of 1790–1791.[16] The net incomes—subtracting the costs of exploitation, the upkeep of the church, and the salary of the vicaire —ranged from less than 300 to nearly 2,600 *livres* per year. The median was between 700 and 800 *livres* and the great majority were under 1,000 *livres* (see Figure Q).

For the remaining two-thirds of the curés and for all of the secondaries, the basic salary attached to the pastoral services was established by royal edict. Until 1768 it was set at 300 *livres* per year to be paid quarterly by the tithe owner or the tithe farmer. It was raised to 500 *livres* in 1768 and to 700 *livres* in 1786. In the meantime, the vicaires' salary was raised progressively from 150 to 350 *livres* per year.[17] In general, this salary seems always to have been paid in money. There is no evidence of any curé receiving a *portion congrue* in kind—a *"gros"*—as was frequently

[15] See Bermond, *loc.cit.*, pp. 257–267; and Paul Guillaume, "Quotité des dîmes en Gapençais en 1791," *AA*, XIII (1909), pp. 212–215. For the portion of the diocese in Provence, see the minutes of the *affouagement* of 1728 for the *vigueries* of Digne and Sisteron: A.D.B.A., C 57 and C 59.

[16] A.D.H.A., I Q I 108 and 137; A.D.I., L 604–624; A.D.D., L 87–89. I have not located the declarations of revenue for the *département* of the Basses-Alpes. The declarations of 1790–1791 are the single most reliable source for ecclesiastical revenues in the eighteenth century. The statements of priests were to be accompanied by leases or other proof of accuracy and were verified by both the village notables and the departmental administration. The declarations of revenue sent to the clergy of France during the eighteenth century were primarily for the purposes of tax assessment and were notoriously undervalued.

[17] Marion, pp. 445–446.

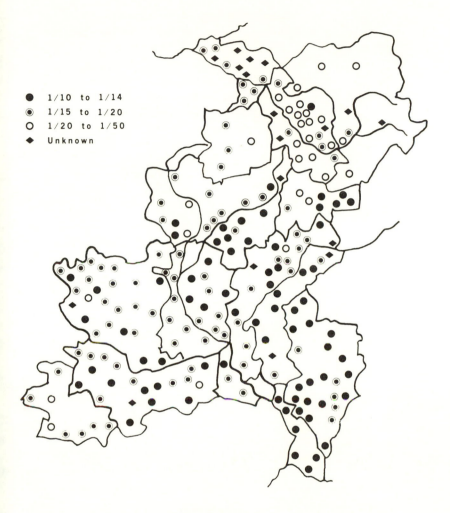

FIGURE P.
Portion of the grain crop paid in tithes (by parish)

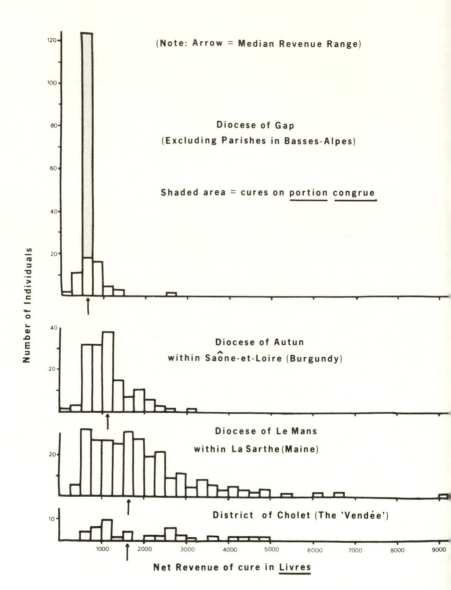

FIGURE Q.

Net incomes of the parish clergy in 1790 in the diocese of Gap (with comparisons for three other regions in France)

the case in dioceses of northern France. Formerly, some of the congruist curés had held small portions of beneficed lands and the tithes on newly cleared lands, but this was all to be ceded to the *gros-décimateurs* following the edict of May 1768. At best, they maintained only a small vegetable garden attached to the rectory—and some were denied even this.[18] As the curés themselves commonly phrased it in their declarations of revenue, they were entirely "reduced to the simple *congrue*."[19]

With the rise in prices after 1740, all of the congruists found their incomes being progressively eroded. This was the specific reason behind the government's decisions to raise the fixed salary. How the real value of the curé's income evolved during the last decades of the eighteenth century can be indicated by stating it as a function of current wheat prices in the market of Gap (see Figure R).[20] Grain was probably one of the basic elements in the priest's diet, and its cost can serve as a general gauge of the overall cost of living.[21] Clearly, in the last thirty-five years of the Old Regime, the curés' real income rose very generally with each increase of the *portion congrue*. The average value in the three years after 1786 was greater than many of the curés could have remembered. Yet the salient factor throughout this period was the instability of the salary occasioned by the violent oscillations of market prices. The gains of 1768 were largely annulled in the following years by soaring prices; the relative prosperity about 1777 was soon followed by a new period of price increase. On the eve of the Revolution, the curés' salary of 700 *livres* would have nearly equalled the median revenue of the prior-

18 The curé of Saint-Bonnet, for example; see the declarations of revenue of 1772: A.D.H.A., G 2337–2339.

19 *Ibid.*

20 The prices used here are the averages for the months of May and November of each year as reported by the sub-delegates of Gap: A.D.I., II C 52–62. The series begins in 1755.

21 The government itself used the price of wheat in the market of Paris as a basis for setting the *portion congrue*.

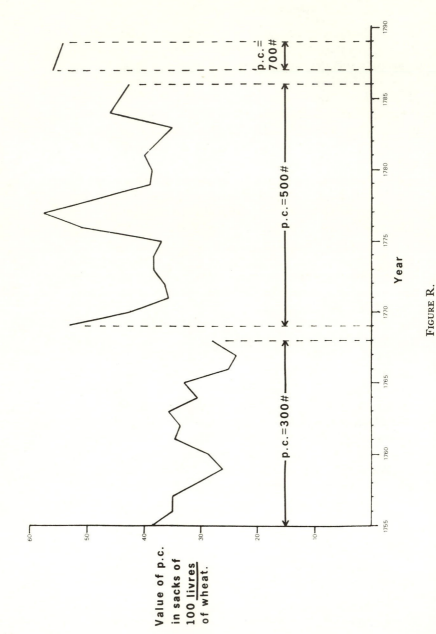

FIGURE R.

Value of the *portion congrue* after 1755 in terms of the price of wheat at the market of Gap

curés.[22] But the prior-curés were sellers of produce rather than buyers, and could expect to break even or even profit from the rapidly changing prices. The salaried curés could only hope that the royal government would continue to favor their cause and make successive readjustments in their fixed minimum income to match the evolving economic situation. They knew that every proposed readjustment would meet with the determined opposition of the tithe-owning upper clergy. The uncontrolled fluctuations of the revenues of nearly three-fourths of the parish clergy, curés and secondaries, inevitably generated a mood of anxiety and insecurity within this corps.

OTHER ECCLESIASTICAL BENEFITS

In addition to his cure, every parish priest had revenues and benefits by virtue of his functions and privileges as a priest. Both the curé and the vicaire were to be provided free lodging by the community. The occasional descriptions we find of the country rectories reveal small but comfortable houses with one or two bedrooms, a study, a kitchen, a servant's room, a wine cellar, and a grain attic. Often there was a barn and a vegetable garden attached to the house.[23] The community was not required to provide the curé with furniture for the rectory, nor with a horse and stable—except in large parishes such as Gap, where there were outlying hamlets that could not conveniently be reached on foot.[24]

As members of a privileged order, all clergymen were

22 The median revenue of about 750 *livres* per year for the prior-curés in 1790 was the equivalent of 61 one-hundred-*livre* sacks of wheat in the market of Gap in May 1790.

23 See the description of repairs to be made on the *maison curiale* of Sigoyer-sur-Tallard, dated Dec. 16, 1783: Collect. Roman, LII; also the description of the *maison curiale* of Le Noyer, *ca.* 1794: A.D.H.A., I Q I 291.

24 See the letters from D'Ormesson, intendant of finances, to Delaporte, intendant of Dauphiné, Mar. 25, 1750 and Feb. 14, 1752: Collect. Roman, LII.

exempt from such royal taxes as the *vingtième, capitation,* and *gabelle.* In Dauphiné, however, priests were subject to the *taille* on all their personal possessions and on all beneficed lands given to the Church since 1635.[25] Moreover, all parish clergymen—whether they were tithe owners or salaried—paid the ecclesiastical tax owed to the Clergy of France, the *décime.* In 1789, most of the congruists found their salary reduced by nearly 13 percent in payment of this tax.[26]

There were also certain incidental revenues, known collectively as the *casuel,* that members of the parish clergy could expect to receive.[27] These revenues included the voluntary offerings given at various times of the year, whether in the form of money, personal gifts to the priest, or pieces of candle wax for lighting the church. They also included the surplice fees, the honorariums paid to the clergyman by the parishioners on the occasion of baptisms, marriages, burials or other ceremonies requiring the presence of a priest. Set rates for these fees were published by the bishops of Gap. In 1762, for example, a curé could charge one *livre* 16 *sous* for publishing marriage banns; 14 *sous* for a high mass, whether votive, for a burial, or for the repose of the dead; and 5 *sous* for registering a baptism, marriage, or burial. Some of the fees could be raised for the rich or for the citizens of Gap, and all were to be lowered for the poor. Whenever the community provided the paper for the parish registers, the priest was forbidden to ask dues for inscribing vital statistics.[28] Thus the actual

25 Pierre Durand de Maillane, *Dictionnaire de droit canonique et de pratique bénéficiale,* 5 vols. (Lyon, 1776), articles "Immunités" and "Taille." Dauphiné was a *pays de taille réelle.*

26 On the *décime* roll of 1789, most curés on the *portion congrue* paid a tax of 88 *livres,* 3 *sous* on their revenue of 700 *livres*; the prior-curés generally paid a lower percentage: A.D.H.A., G 2492.

27 See Philippe Loupès, "Le casuel dans le diocèse de Bordeaux aux XVIIe et XVIIIe siècles," *RHEF,* LVII (1972), pp. 19–52.

28 See the printed instructions concerning the *casuel* issued by bishop Pérouse, May 10, 1762: A.D.H.A., G 966. Also *Ord. Syn.,* I, 185–188.

revenues from the surplice fees depended not only on the population and wealth of the parish, but also on the priest's personal definition of "rich" and "poor" and on his willingness to demand these "just dues" even in the face of widespread resentment and bitterness on the part of his flock.[29] On the basis of a questionnaire sent to the parishes in 1785, bishop Vareilles reported a *casuel* of 300 *livres* per year for each of the curés of Gap, about 50 to 100 *livres* in each of the other towns of the diocese, but only six to 30 *livres* per year in most of the villages—the smallest amounts being in the Protestant parishes of the Serrois and the Bochaine.[30] To these sums could be added the income from the perpetual foundations that existed in many parishes: small yearly pensions established for the parish priests in return for periodic requiem masses. The foundations reported by the communities in 1789 averaged only about 20 *livres* per year per parish.[31] In sum, the revenues from the incidental fees and the foundations, although varying greatly from parish to parish, could have brought only minor supplements to the incomes of the great majority of the curés.

NON-ECCLESIASTICAL REVENUES

A clergyman's total revenues were not necessarily confined to his ecclesiastical income. Every priest who was not a member of a regular order had full rights of buying and selling land and of inheriting or bequeathing property. Seminary training and synodal ordinances set strict standards against involvement in commerce, lending money at a profit, leasing land for exploitation, or participation in

[29] See below, Chapter VII.
[30] Report to the agents-general, Jan. 12, 1786: A.N., G⁸ 68 (Gap). Vareilles' circular was dated Oct. 19, 1785.
[31] Declarations of revenue of 1789: A.D.H.A., L 1024. The foundations reported ranged from six to 150 *livres* per year. Several curés claimed to have no foundations whatsoever.

family business.[32] Yet it was difficult to draw a sharp line in such matters. After all, one-third of the parish priests of the diocese received all or part of their ecclesiastical revenues in the form of produce and livestock, commodities that had to be sold at the fairs or bartered for other goods and services—and, naturally, at the best possible rates. Whatever their convictions and desire to remain aloof from "the world," the very nature of their ecclesiastical patrimony held them closely bound to the market place. For certain curés, the involvement in financial affairs and agriculture went well beyond the exploitation of the tithes. A few seem to have been important creditors in their communities. Often it was only a question of small loans at no interest. But the wills of the parish clergy also give evidence of substantial loans, fully notarized, involving life annuities or other forms of hidden interest.[33] A few parish priests, like Joseph Pellenc of Montbrand, associated themselves with local bourgeois as joint farmers of seigneurial or ecclesiastical lands in their parish.[34] Others, such as Augustin Millon of Laye and Jean-François Mévouilhon of Manteyer, served actively as the business agents of the absentee lords of the village.[35] One curé, Jean-Louis Borel of Saint-Genis, was in partnership with his brother-in-law for the exploitation of a lead mine.[36]

[32] *Ord. Syn.*, pp. 58–60, 77–78.

[33] Of 45 wills by parish clergymen of the diocese of Gap written after 1750, 12 gave evidence of such debts owed to the curé.

[34] Letter from Pellenc to Jean Pinchinat, Mar. 13, 1782: A.D.H.A., F 266. However, the curé retired from the association after he changed to another parish; he found that it was not fitting for a curé to be a *fermier* outside his own parish. Curé Millon of Laye considered taking a *ferme* of lands owned by the non-resident lord: see his letter to the baron Des Preaux, Mar. 6, 1779: A.D.H.A., F 1350. A few curés leased local beneficed lands belonging to non-resident tithe owners: see leases in A.D.H.A., G 2420.

[35] Letters from Millon to Des Preaux, Apr. 10, 1772 to June 6, 1780: A.D.H.A., F 1344–1350; from Mévouilhon to Pinet de Manteyer, Aug. 4, 1777 to Nov. 4, 1787: A.D.I., 14 J 212. See below, Chapter VI.

[36] Letters by the intendant and the sub-delegate of Gap, dated May 19 and June 9, 1789; Jan. 9, Mar. 9, and Apr. 20, 1790: Collect. Roman, LI.

Such examples, taken from various sources, immediately draw our attention. We should like to know how typical they were and, more broadly, the nature and extent of the private fortunes of the curés. Unfortunately, two of the most effective sources of information on individual fortunes —marriage contracts and Old-Regime tax rolls—are not applicable to the clerical order. But we can attempt a systematic study of the curés' private wealth in landed property, by means of the alphabetical tables to the *contrôle* of notarized acts and the *centième denier*. These tables, kept by the registry offices (*bureaux d'enregistrement*), contain tabular summaries of all acts of a certain category—sales, leases, wills, etc.—notarized or passed by private agreement within the circumscription of each office over a period of several decades. They were established primarily to assist the government clerks in verifying the payment of the *centième denier*, a tax due on all transfers of landed property or buildings except by lineal succession, marriage contract, or certain kinds of donations.[37] By scanning the column in these tables giving the professions of the parties involved, we can rapidly identify all of the acts of this kind in which priests took part, as well as the inheritance declarations made by their heirs. For present purposes, we have focused our attention specifically on the priests serving within the jurisdiction of the registry office of Gap, a region approximately coinciding with the ecclesiastical canton of Gap and the natural region of the Gapençais.[38] A greater number and variety of tables are preserved for this office than for any other in the diocese.

[37] See Claude-Joseph de Ferrière, *Dictionnaire de droit et de pratique* (new ed.; Paris, 1755), article "Centième denier." On the *bureaux d'enregistrement* and their registers, see Jacques de Font-Réaulx, introduction to *Répertoire numérique de la série II C, Archives départementales de la Drôme* (Valence, 1941), pp. 17–23; also Michel Vovelle, "Problèmes méthodologiques posés par l'utilisation des sources de l'enregistrement dans une étude de structure sociale," *Bulletin de la section d'histoire moderne et contemporaine*, fasc. 3 (1961), pp. 49–106.
[38] The circumscription also included a few parishes in the diocese of Embrun.

We have also examined the tables available for three of the surrounding registry offices—in Veynes, Tallard, and Saint-Bonnet—for cases in which a priest went to a notary outside the jurisdiction of Gap.[39]

In the first place, the alphabetical tables enable us to obtain the declarations of the value of the landed estate of certain priests.[40] Since priests had no lineal descendants— or none they cared to admit—such declarations were always required for the *centième denier* on their inheritances. The estimations given by the heirs are probably not to be taken at face value; it was natural to try to underrate the value of property on which a tax was to be paid. Yet they can provide us with an indication of the relative distribution of the priests' fortunes. We have represented in Figure S the declarations made to the registry office of Gap of the estates of sixteen curés deceased between 1769 and 1793. A few of the curés are seen to spread out across the scale with estates worth several thousand *livres*: Gaspar Reynier, curé of Saint-André-de-Gap (15,000); Joseph-Balthazar Amyer, curé of Valserres (9,000); Pierre Ricard, curé of Rabou (8,000). Yet most are grouped together near the bottom of the scale, half with less than 1,000 *livres* and two with negative declarations. Two of those under the median were curés of Gap: Claude Thomé and Gaspar Bonthoux.

It is difficult to compare the value of the estates of these curés with those of the lay society in general. Before

---

[39] A.D.H.A., 2 C 728ter, *mutations en ligne collatérale*, 1741–1791; II Q CVIII 84[1], *baux laïques*, 1753-an XI; II Q CVIII 81[2], *nouveaux possesseurs*, 1778–1791; 2 C 728 and II Q CVIII 80[1], *mutations de toutes manières*, 1772–1793; 2 C 714–716 and II Q CVIII 72[1] and 72[2], *testaments*, 1753–1807; II Q CVIII 79, *donations*, 1761-an II. Also, for the *bureau* of Veynes, A.D.H.A., II Q CXXIII 8[2], 10[1], 12[1], 15[2], 16[2]; for the *bureau* of Tallard, A.D.H.A., 2 C 1511–1512 and 2 C 721; and for the *bureau* of Saint-Bonnet, A.D.H.A., II Q CXVIII 13[1] and 13[2].

[40] In some cases, I have found the inheritance declarations in the tables of *mutations en ligne collatérale*; in other cases, I have had to make use of the registers of the *centième denier*. The latter are preserved in A.D.H.A., 2 C 664–703.

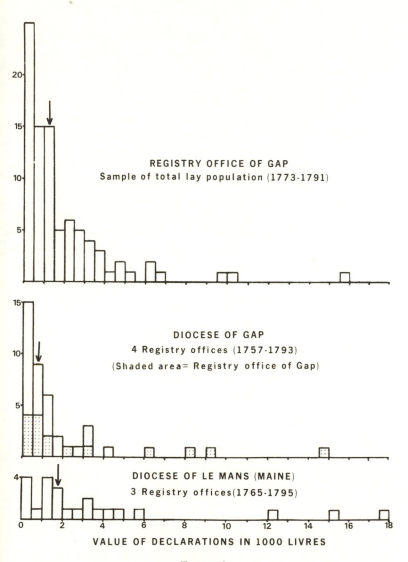

FIGURE S.

The landed estates of priests in the diocese of Gap based on the inheritance declarations by their heirs for the *centième denier* (with comparisons for a sample of the lay population and for priests in the diocese of Le Mans). Arrows indicate median range

the Revolution, no tax was paid on inheritances passed to lineal heirs and thus, in many cases, no declarations were ever made. But a comparison with a sample of those lay individuals in the region leaving inheritances to collateral heirs would suggest that the distribution of landed wealth of the parish priests may have closely paralleled the distribution for the society in general.[41] Curés Reynier, Amyer, and Ricard would have bequeathed estates equal to those of the wealthier members of the society. Yet the majority were clustered at the lower end of the scale, with landed possessions of approximately the same value as those left by the agricultural laborers in the community.[42] We have also taken note of the inheritance declarations of parish priests in the registry offices of Saint-Bonnet, Veynes, and Ribiers—in the regions of the Champsaur, the Bochaine, and the Middle Durance, respectively. The situation for the curés in these regions seems to have been similar: the majority left estates of under 1,000 *livres*, and several left no propertied inheritance whatsoever.[43] None, however, rose as high on the scale as in the region of Gap.

It is conceivable that some of the priests could have given away a part of their possessions shortly before their death, perhaps as marriage gifts to relatives. Yet any gifts involving property should be inscribed in the tables of eventual

[41] The sample taken from A.D.H.A., 2 C 728ter, includes all laymen within the jurisdiction of the registry office of Gap whose last name began with "A," deceased between 1773 and 1791. This curve might be skewed to the left, for there is no guarantee, in a region of Roman law such as Dauphiné, that a few of these successions were not split between a direct heir and a collateral heir. In such a case, only the part of the estate bequeathed to the latter would appear on the graph.

[42] The median for the *journaliers* was between 250 and 750 *livres*. The median for the *laboureurs* was between 2,750 and 3,250 *livres*. There is not a large enough number of the other professional categories within the sample to permit the identification of medians.

[43] For Saint-Bonnet, I have used the alphabetical tables of wills, A.D.H.A., II Q CXVIII 13¹–13² as a guide to the registers of the *centième denier*, 2 C 1255–1270; for Ribiers, the tables of wills, A.D.H.A., 2 C 1089, and the registers of the *centième denier*, 2 C 1078–1085. For Veynes, I have used the tables of *mutations en ligne collatérale*, 1755–1810: A.D.H.A., II Q CXIII 10¹.

donations for the registry office of Gap[44] or in the judicial insinuations of donations *inter vivos* for the bailliage of Gap.[45] An analysis of these registers has in fact revealed only one such case among those curés situated on our graph.[46] Moreover, by means of the alphabetical tables we can also hope to identify most of the notarized or private acts, involving the lease or transfer of property by parish priests of the region of Gap, that were passed during the last twenty or thirty years of the Old Regime. We thus obtain a general idea of the curés' possession and exploitation of property during their lifetime.[47] The findings from these tables seem to confirm the evidence of the inheritance declarations. Clearly, a few of the curés held extensive property and seemed actively engaged in exploiting their lands and increasing their holdings. The same curés with high inheritance declarations appear most frequently in these kinds of acts. Gaspar Reynier, a nobleman's son, possessed a large estate in the community of Reynier as well as land in the area of Gap. Pierre Ricard possessed several pieces of farm land, grazing pastures, and vineyards near his parish of Rabou. We know from other sources that he participated in the sheep trade, and that he had even been appointed to supervise the bishop's personal flocks.[48]

[44] A.D.H.A., II Q CVIII 79. These tables include donations that take effect only after the death of the donor.

[45] Preserved from 1731 to 1789; A.D.H.A., B 48–105, analyzed in detail by Paul Guillaume, *Inventaire sommaire, séries A, B, et C* (Gap, 1887).

[46] Jean-Baptiste Allard, for whom a negative declaration was given by his heir, had donated his half of a farm to his niece in a marriage contract fifteen years before his death: A.D.H.A., B 81.

[47] I have considered all the priests who served between 1770 and 1790 in the following parishes: Gap, Romette, La Rochette, Rambaud, La Bâtie-Neuve, La Bâtie-Vieille, Saint-André-de-Gap, Neffes, Château-vieux, Jarjayes, Valserres, Rabou, Les Baux, La Roche-des-Arnauds, and the two annexes of Gap, Chaudun and La Freyssinouse.

[48] Letters of the sub-delegate, Delafont, to the intendant, dated May 6 and Aug. 5, 1788, as cited in Camille Queyrel, "Un modèle de l'administration éclairée, Pierre Delafont et Pierre-Joseph-Marie Delafont, derniers subdélégués de Gap" (D.E.S., Université de Grenoble, 1933), pp. 84–88.

Joseph-Balthazar Amyer was in retirement during most of the period under consideration; but his great-nephew, Jean-Joseph Jacques, who received the cure and part of the fortune of his uncle, was buying, selling, and leasing property all over the Gap basin. Jacques was the son of one of the richest wholesale merchants in Gap[49] and he seemed to carry the family profession into the priesthood. Yet this type of enterprising curé-landholder was seemingly the exception in the region of Gap. Most of the parish priests in the area appear only rarely in the tables, buying, selling, or leasing small plots of land or vineyards or perhaps a house in their parish. A number of the curés, about one-half of those serving between 1770 and the Revolution, never figure at all in the tables.[50] Such was the case of Gaspar Bonthoux and Augustin Escallier, co-curés of Gap, and of Dominique Chaix of Les Baux.

We have not attempted a comprehensive study of curé wealth and economic activities in other regions of the diocese. But the evidence of the property tax rolls drawn up during the Revolutionary period in the districts of Gap and Serres leads us to the same general conclusions.[51] The *contribution foncière*, first levied in 1791, was to be paid by all landowners, including the previously privileged classes, on the net revenue from their property.[52] Within the districts of Gap and Serres seven curés—including Jean-Joseph Jacques and Pierre Ricard—are found among the wealthier landholders of the local society, paying a tax higher than three-fourths of the taxpayers of the communities in which the land was located, and, in a few in-

[49] Paul Jacques, who had a wealth index of 97 percent in the capitation roll of 1790.

[50] Of 26 curés or pro-curés considered, 12 did not appear at all.

[51] Rolls of the *contribution foncière*, district of Serres, 1791: A.D.H.A., L 1391; *matrices de rôles* of the *contribution foncière*, district of Gap, 1792 (the 1791 rolls have not been located): A.D.H.A., L 563. Within the two districts, the rolls for the town of Gap and for the cantons of Ribiers, Laragne, and Aspres-sur-Buëch have not been located.

[52] See Jacques Godechot, *Les institutions de la France sous la Révolution et l'Empire* (2nd ed.; Paris, 1968), pp. 164–166.

stances, owning land in more than one community.[53] Another 26 curés paid small to average taxes in relation to the rest of the community: greater than about one-fifth to three-fifths of the community. The remaining 60 curés living in the villages for which tax rolls are preserved paid nothing at all or only a very small tax, indicative perhaps of a tiny vineyard or meadow or the rectory garden.

All of the evidence seems to indicate the same general picture of the personal fortunes of the parish clergy. Land was not, of course, the only element in an individual's total assets; yet in the overwhelmingly rural society of the diocese of Gap, it was invariably the single most important form of wealth. It seems clear that most of the parish priests—at least within the province of Dauphiné—possessed relatively little landed property in their own right. To be sure, there were a few like Jean-Joseph Jacques and Pierre Ricard, unusually favored by family inheritance, and with an inclination for business that allowed them to amass substantial fortunes. But these were apparently the exceptions. Most of the curés had, in fact, been required to renounce all claims to their family's inheritance in exchange for the patrimonial title. This patrimony usually took the form of a fixed pension of 100 *livres*, frequently lasting only a few years until a benefice was obtained, and always subject to diminution in its real value through rising prices. With nothing but this meager family assistance and the mediocre salary of the *portion congrue*, the average curé could scarcely hope to accumulate any sizable capital, even if he so desired. For the majority of the parish priests in the region of Gap, personal non-ecclesiastical possessions prob-

---

[53] The seven large landholders were Ricard of Rabou (holding land in La Roche, La Freyssinouse, and Sigoyer), Jacques of Serres (Jarjayes, Manteyer, and Serres), Brun of Le Bersac (Le Bersac), Callandre of Eyguians (Eyguians), Amayon of Le Poët (Le Poët), Faure of Saint-Jean-de-Montorcier (La Rochette), and Bonafoux of Quet (Jarjayes). Note that part of the land owned by Brun in Le Bersac and Jacques in Serres was former Church land purchased in 1791: see the lists of purchasers of ecclesiastical land by Paul Guillaume: A.D.H.A., ms, 385.

ably provided only a small supplement to the benefice and the other ecclesiastical revenues.

It is not often that we are able to glimpse the financial situation, the standard of living, of this "average" parish priest. He rarely appeared in the notary records; his inheritance declaration, small or negative, tells us little of the nature of his possessions. But for one such curé, Dominique Chaix, we do have unusually good sources of information. Chaix seems never to have had much financial assistance from his family. His older brother, Joseph, was the heir of all their father's property, and the future priest was required to relinquish his rights to the family fortune when he received his patrimonial title. His pension of 100 *livres* per year lasted only five years, until he had received the parish of Les Baux.[54] This benefice gave him rights to the tithes, but the total value was approximately equal to the *portion congrue* before 1786.[55] As with many of his fellow curés, this one parish—along with a small *casuel* and a few foundations—was the sole source of ecclesiastical revenue. When Chaix occasionally referred to his economic condition during the long correspondence with Villars, the description is of a modest, if not a genuinely difficult, situation.[56] The loans he made to his parishioners and the small marriage gifts to his nieces sometimes put a serious burden on his personal budget;[57] and on occasion he was forced to beg a neighboring curé to share some foundation masses with him, so that he would have enough money for the winter.[58] When Villars sent Chaix a small "stipendium" for masses, the curé thanked him: "You are aware that my

[54] A.D.H.A., G 878, entry for Nov. 26, 1753; and G 815, entry for Sept. 11, 1758.

[55] The declared net value in 1791 was 473 *livres* per year.

[56] It is to be remembered that Villars was Chaix's closest friend and confidant. There is no evidence and no reason to believe that Chaix ever exaggerated his economic difficulties.

[57] *Etat de succession*: A.D.H.A., F 676. Chaix's dowry gifts to his five nieces were 100 to 200 *livres* each. On Chaix's loans to parishioners, see below, Chapter VI.

[58] B.M.G., R 10073, letter, Mar. 27, 1780.

small parish can scarcely provide for me."[59] Chaix might also spend several months making collections of Alpine plants to be sold to amateur collectors for a little money for himself and for the upkeep of the parish church.[60] He did not have a horse and went everywhere on foot.[61] At the time of his death, he owned no land and his small thatched-roof rectory contained books and furnishings that were sold for 358 *livres*.[62]

THE PROBLEM OF OLD AGE

The paucity of the priest's personal fortune helps to explain one of the most difficult problems in the career of a curé in Dauphiné: his old age. Unlike many other benefices, the cure of souls in a parish required a continuous and often arduous function. When a man grew too feeble or sick to perform these functions, he might even be put under strong pressures by the bishop or by the villagers to retire or find a replacement.[63] For those without sufficient personal possessions to provide an independent income, retirement might bring real economic hardship. The pro-curé, the temporary substitute, was to be in the pay of the titular curé; he had to be given three-fifths of the *portion congrue* and all rights to the *casuel*:[64] a considerable burden on the revenues of a congruist curé in the diocese of Gap. There was also the possibility of resigning one's benefice in favor of a younger priest in return for an

---

[59] *Ibid.*, letter, Feb. 10, 1776.
[60] *Ibid.*, letters, Sept. 2, 1785 and Oct. 30, 1788.
[61] Chaix even went to Grenoble and back on foot: *Ibid.*, letter, June 20, 1786.
[62] A.D.H.A., F 676.
[63] *E.g.*, the consuls of Chardavon sent a letter to the bishop, Sept. 18, 1786, asking that their curé, Marin Isnard, be forced to employ a pro-curé. Isnard was about 68 years old (ordained to the priesthood in 1743: A.D.H.A., G 903) and had been sick and incapable of serving the parish for six months: A.D.H.A., G 977.
[64] Edict of May 1768, art. XV: see Durand de Maillane, article "Portion congrue."

annual pension. But royal edict required that the priest receiving the resignation be left with at least the equivalent of the *portion congrue*; in effect then, it was usually not feasible for a salaried curé to reserve himself a pension.[65] Otherwise, the curé might hope to find a niece or nephew who would care for him in his old age, either out of kindness or in return for the curé's eventual inheritance.[66] Perhaps the most common course was simply to stay on in one's functions as best as one could and not retire at all. Many priests clung to their posts well into their sixties or seventies. The provisions of benefices indicate that almost two-thirds of the curés died while still holding their cures.[67]

The need for assistance to elderly priests was one of the most long-standing demands presented by the curés of the diocese to the upper clergy.[68] It was only in 1777 that the bishops of Gap were granted permission to tax all benefice holders an extra six *deniers* per *livre* in order to establish a fund for the aged.[69] Thereafter, 50 to 150 *livres* were allotted to five or six clergymen each year to help pay a procuré or to compensate for the older priest's ecclesiastical taxes.[70] To many curés, this token pension fund seemed wholly insufficient to meet their needs. The curé-archpriest

---

[65] *Ibid.*

[66] I have found two testaments made by priests in favor of the nephews with whom they were living in retirement: Jean Arnoux: A.D.H.A., 1 E 735, act Oct. 9, 1787; and Antoine Chevalier, ex-curé of Orcières: A.D.H.A., 1 E 2132, act May 31, 1776. Occasionally, a priest would obtain a retirement pension for himself in return for a marriage gift to a relative. Such was the case of Jean-Louis Martel, curé of Saint-Pierre-d'Avez: A.D.H.A., B 93.

[67] Between 1779 and 1788, 58 vacancies occurred through the death of the incumbent curé, 31 through his retirement: A.D.H.A., G 822–828.

[68] At the synod of Sept. 1, 1700, a contingent of curés had asked the bishop to establish a home for the care of aged curés "lorsqu'ils sont tombés dans un estat de caducité ou infirmité telle qu'ils ne peuvent plus servir, ni gagnier leur vie, et que, d'ailleurs, ils n'ont pas de biens patrimoniaux pour survenir à leurs nécessités. . . .": A.D.H.A., G 2358.

[69] Letter from bishop Jouffroy-Gonssans to the agents-general, Feb. 24, 1777: A.N., G⁸ 632 (97).

[70] Deliberations of the clergy of Gap, 1784–1790: A.D.H.A., G 2361.

of Serres, Alexandre Achard, expressed particular bitterness on this score in his *cahier de doléances* of 1789.[71] When other servants of the state are given retirement pensions after a certain age, why, he asked, are the curés alone forgotten? "The high price of food and the meagerness of the curés' revenues have made it impossible for them to save up for times of want; . . . what resources will they have for an age at which their needs begin to multiply?"[72] If they ask for a pro-curé, they must pay for him themselves. And if they resign their benefice in someone's favor, can they even reserve themselves a pension? In recent years, three curés of his own canton had passed through the "pathetic experience" of old age. One had to auction his furniture in order to pay his ecclesiastical taxes. Another, dying in misery, received nothing but two *louis* from the bishop. Cannot some of the Church's great wealth be shared with the servants of the parishes in their sickness and old age?[73] After all, the tithe owners have grown rich through the high prices of grain, grain that the curés are forced to buy. "Is it not a return to the days when Saint Paul could lament that some were without the basic necessities while others were overwhelmed with abundance?"[74]

Achard himself was seventy-four years old when he wrote this statement. He would die at his post the following year.[75] The grievances he expressed seem to have been widespread.[76] The plight of the parish priest at the end of his career was particularly revealing of the fundamental injustices in the distribution of the Church's wealth.

[71] *AA*, XIII (1909), 202–212. The document preserved seems to have been a first draft. It is unsigned, but all internal evidence would indicate that the author was, in fact, the curé of Serres.

[72] *Ibid.*, p. 205.   [73] *Ibid.*, pp. 205–206.   [74] *Ibid.*, p. 210.

[75] A.D.H.A., ms. 399.

[76] See also the *Cahier de doléances* of the clergy of the sénéchaussée of Sisteron (which included the Provençal portion of the diocese of Gap): *Archives parlementaires*, III, 362; and the *Cahier des curés de Dauphiné*, pp. 124–126, 128–139, 131–132. In the *cahiers de doléances* of the curés of the diocese of Auxerre, the demand for aid for aged priests was the most common of all grievances: Charles Porée, *Cahiers des curés et des communautés ecclésiastiques du bailliage d'Auxerre* (Auxerre, 1927), *passim*.

GENERAL EVALUATION:
A CAREER IN THE PARISH CLERGY

On the eve of the Revolution, the average country parish priest in the diocese of Gap could count on little income beyond the benefice of his cure. Rare were the curés who obtained additional simple benefices, chapels or priories; even more unusual were those who advanced into the ranks of the canons. The revenues from the *casuel* and from parish foundations were meager and would scarcely have sufficed to pay the clerical taxes; and supplemental incomes from personal possessions were usually of minor support. In 1789 more than nine-tenths of the curés of the diocese had total ecclesiastical incomes of under 1,000 *livres* per year, while the median range was between 500 and 750 *livres* per year (see Figure R).

It would be difficult to compare the curé's revenues with the income of the layman. The latter, after all, had also to support a family, maintain a house, and pay numerous taxes, expenses not normally incurred by the clergyman. The curé, on the other hand, had the additional financial burden of providing food and money to the parish poor—a service that, as we shall see, was basic to his role in the rural community. It can be noted, however, that the agricultural day laborer—the single most common occupation in the diocese—might earn an average of about one *livre* per day and perhaps 150 to 200 *livres* per year.[77] A chief bailliage magistrate—among the highest-ranking commoners in the local society—might receive 2,100 *livres* annually for his professional services alone.[78]

For the small numbers of priests originating in more

[77] See the replies by local notables in 1801 concerning workers' salaries prior to the Revolution: Paul Guillaume, ed., "Situation économique des Hautes-Alpes en 1801," *BHA*, XXXI (1913), pp. 166–197, 226–252; XXXII (1914), pp. 23–48. The day wages varied from as little as 10 *sous* to as much as one *livre* 10 *sous* depending on the season and the region. See also Georges Lefebvre, *Etudes orléanaises, Tome I, Contribution à l'étude des structures sociales à la fin du XVIIIe siècle* (Paris, 1962), p. 76.

[78] Philip Dawson, *Provincial Magistrates and Revolutionary Politics in France, 1789–1795* (Cambridge, 1972), pp. 81–82.

modest peasant or artisan families, a permanent position with an income of 500 to 750 *livres* might represent a significant advance from the life style they had experienced in their youth. For the more typical priests in the diocese, originating in relatively wealthier family milieux, a career in the parish clergy might even appear as a step downward —at least in purely economic terms. To be sure, such a career could still conceivably contribute to the upward social mobility of the cleric's family.[79] We have seen that in establishing a son with a guaranteed income and in insuring that the son would produce no heirs, the family helped to preserve its fortune from excessive division. At the end of their lives, virtually all of the curés returned their estates— modest though they might be—to members of their family, most commonly to a brother or a nephew.[80] There were numerous other services priests might render to their relatives: furnishing small loans or information about good investments in or near the parish; or serving as a general protector in finding a job, in staving off the tax collector.[81] The curé who took in his sisters and nieces as housekeepers until he could provide them with dowries and husbands—chosen from among his parishioners—was a virtual institution in Upper Dauphiné; so too was the curé who provided a free education to his nephews and then located protectors to establish them in a career.[82]

[79] The lengthy genealogical analysis—via family wills, marriage contracts, etc.—necessary for a quantitative study of inter-generational social mobility would not have been feasible, given the limitations of archival sources and research time.

[80] Of 45 wills located of parish clergymen serving in the diocese of Gap after 1750, 41 established close relatives as the universal heirs, and 31 returned the estate to close male heirs: a brother or a nephew. The wills were located in notary minutes by means of the alphabetical tables of wills for the registry offices of Gap, Tallard, Saint-Bonnet, Veynes, Upaix, Ribiers, and Rosans.

[81] A particularly good source of data concerning these kinds of curé services is the collection of letters written to Pinet de Manteyer, a principal tax collector in Gap: A.D.I., series 14 J.

[82] Dominique Chaix, for example, had an endless stream of nieces and nephews passing through his household: see especially his letters to Villars dated Mar. 4, 1775; Apr. 30, 1781; and July 28, Oct. 10, Dec. 12, and Dec. 29, 1786: B.M.G., R 10073.

In comparison with the revenues earned by their colleagues in other areas of France, the curés' incomes in the diocese of Gap seemed particularly modest. In Lorraine, for example, within the future department of the Moselle, the average net income of the curés was certainly greater than 1,000 *livres* per year in 1790; in Southern Burgundy, the median fell between 1,000 and 1,250 *livres*; and in both Upper Maine and the Mauges of Southern Anjou, it was between 1,500 and 1,750 *livres*, almost triple the median range in the diocese of Gap (see Figure Q).[83] Moreover, there was apparently an approximate correlation between the average ecclesiastical revenue of a group of curés and the average amount of personal capital the curés were able to accumulate in the course of their careers. A small sample of inheritance declarations by heirs of parish priests in Maine (see Figure S) and in Southern Burgundy suggests propertied wealth of measurably greater value than that held by the Gap parish clergy.[84]

But if the average yearly revenues were considerably greater for the curés of northern and western France, so too was the total range of incomes: often spanning the entire scale from as low as 300 to as high as 8,000 *livres*. Certain parish priests received only the *portion congrue* or less, but a great many others earned revenues that were even su-

[83] Jean Eich, *Histoire religieuse de la Moselle pendant la Révolution. Première partie. Dès le début à l'établissement de l'église constitutionnelle* (Metz, 1964), pp. 44–45: only the gross revenues are given, disallowing direct comparisons. Also A. D. Saône-et-Loire, 1 L 8/107, 110, 112, 113, 116; A. D. Sarthe, L 339–350, 353, 568; and A. D. Maine-et-Loire, 16 Q 80–83, printed in Marcel Faucheux, *L'insurrection vendéenne de 1793, aspects économiques et sociaux* (Paris, 1964), pp. 86–87.

[84] Data for Maine taken from the alphabetical tables of wills for the registry offices of Brulon, Montfort, and Sablé: A.D. Sarthe, II C 682, 2303, 3092. The median range of declarations was between 1,500 and 2,000 *livres*—compared to a median of between 500 and 1,000 *livres* in the diocese of Gap. A sample of 48 inheritance declarations for priests' estates in Southern Burgundy gave a median range of between 1,000 and 1,500 *livres*: registry offices of Autun, Bourbon-Lancy, and Paray (1739–1780): A.D. Saône-et-Loire, C 1043, 1047, 1220, and C Supplement (1928), 132–133.

perior to those of the local canons. In fact, the traditional distinction between the Lower Clergy and the Middle or Upper Clergy was of only limited value for differentiating economic levels within the ecclesiastical corps of many northern and western dioceses. Armand Rébillon, writing of the clergy in Lower Brittany, found the principal split between an "ecclesiastical bourgeoisie" of priors, canons, and tithe-owning curés, on the one hand, and an "ecclesiastical proletariat" of congruist curés and vicaires, on the other.[85] In the diocese of Gap, however, the same modest income was shared by virtually the entire corps of parish priests, an income distinctly inferior to that of the Cathedral canons—or to that of the lay bourgeoisie. This broad homogeneity of revenues would be, as we shall see, an important factor in the politicization and sense of unity of the clergy of Dauphiné prior to the Revolution. And while the great majority of the curés in Lorraine, Burgundy, Maine, Anjou, and Lower Brittany were tithe owners, two out of three in the diocese of Gap received only the fixed salary of the *portion congrue*, continually fluctuating in its real value during the long periods of unstable prices. In terms of their ecclesiastical revenues, the economic situation of the curés of Dauphiné was decidedly less than prosperous.

[85] *La situation économique du clergé à la veille de la Révolution dans les districts de Rennes, de Fougères et de Vitré* (Rennes, 1913), p. cxxi. Charles Tilly, in *The Vendée* (2nd ed.; New York, 1967), p. 105, states that the curés' "net incomes were in the same range as those of the country bourgeoisie."

PART TWO
Priest and Parish

CHAPTER VI

The Curés in Society: A Local Elite

When a new clergyman first arrived in a parish, he possessed qualities that would permanently distinguish him from the parishioners with whom he was to live and work. Typically, he had originated in one of the wealthiest families in his home town or village. His education in a secondary school and the seminary—and perhaps even in the university—was vastly superior to that of most of the other rural inhabitants. The assured revenues accruing to his benefice, while less than in many other regions of France, would still be greater than the income of the majority of his flock; and his rank and title as priest insured his membership in the most honorific order of society, with distinctive legal and fiscal privileges. These advantages alone might have earned for the clergyman the status of "notable."[1] Yet the full reality of the parish priest's position would emerge only from the powers he would wield and the functions he would perform in the village society. In fact, both as man of God and as local dignitary, he would play an elite role: an authority within the community and a mediator to the worlds, natural and supernatural, beyond the community.[2]

The present chapter will explore this dual nature of the

[1] By a nineteenth-century definition—largely valid for the Old Regime as well—a notable was one "qui occupe un rang considérable," and thus one who merits "égard" or "estime" which "vient de l'effet que nos qualités personnelles, notre crédit, nos richesses, nos places, font sur les autres": E. Littré, *Dictionnaire de la langue française* (Paris, 1863), vol. I, pt. 1, p. 751 and vol. II, pt. 1, p. 749.

[2] Elite roles have been defined as those which are "authorities within and spokesmen and agents without": Suzanne Keller, "Elites," *The International Encyclopedia of the Social Sciences* (n.p., 1968), vol. V, 26. Charles Tilly defines elite roles within the peasant community as those which most fully participate both in the norms and activities pervading the whole society and in those which are strictly localized: *The Vendée* (2nd ed.; New York, 1967), pp. 59–60.

parish priest's functions. The two succeeding chapters will focus on the patterns of conflict and competition that frequently marked the relations between priest and parish.[3]

THE MAN OF GOD

In the diocese of Gap, as everywhere in the Catholic realm, the parish clergyman was first and foremost a director of souls, the essential link within the rural world between man and the supernatural, man and his salvation. He and he alone could operate the requisite sacrificial rite of the Eucharist, one of the central mysteries of the Catholic faith. He had prime responsibilities in the initiation of the young to the cult through catechism. His powers were paramount in the rites of passage: baptism, marriage, and burial.[4] His role as guardian of the parish register (in which these rites were recorded in writing—a power denied to many of his parishioners) symbolized his supremacy in this domain. His position was further reinforced by his control of the parish bells, which marked off with great emotional force the hours of work and of worship, the processions, the feast days of the liturgical year, the passing events of life and of death.

The curé and vicaire were, to be sure, not the only priests with whom the villagers might have contact. It was common for a neighboring clergyman to serve as visiting priest

[3] On the basic functions of the curé of the Old Regime, see especially Albert Babeau, *Le village sous l'ancien régime* (3rd ed.; Paris, 1882), pp. 115–165; and Pierre de Vaissière, *Curés de campagne de l'ancienne France* (Paris, 1933) and "L'état social des curés de campagne au XVIIIe siècle," *RHEF*, XIX (1933), pp. 23–53. The present and the two following chapters will situate the parish clergy within the specific structures and contexts of the diocese of Gap and the province of Dauphiné.

[4] One might also include the *relevailles* or "churching" of women, a ritual purification of new mothers several days or weeks after they had given birth. This was not a sacrament and was not recorded in the parish register, but it held a very great importance in the peasant community: see Arnold Van Gennep, *Le folklore des Hautes-Alpes*, 2 vols. (Paris, 1946–1948), I, 1ᵉ partie.

when the parish's own curé was called away on personal or professional business.[5] Several of the larger communities were also able to pay a visiting preacher, regular or secular, to give special series of sermons before Christmas or Easter. Periodically, most parishes were visited by a "mission," a kind of week-long country revival meeting led by a team of two or three Capuchins or Dominicans.[6] Nevertheless, through their intimate day-to-day presence within the village, the parish priest and the vicaire were by far the most important representatives of the Church among the people. Canon law and episcopal ordinances held curé and vicaire to strict residence within their assigned parish.[7] Neither was to leave for longer than a short period without special permission from the bishop. Through his continual presence, through his control of the confessional and the parish register, the parish clergyman was to obtain as complete knowledge as possible of every family and of every individual in his keeping. No priest, other than the bishop himself, was allowed to hear the confession of a parishioner within the parish without the approval of the curé. At least once a year, accompanied by his vicaire or some "irreproachable person," the curé was to visit all the houses in the parish and make an "état des âmes," a list of the inhabitants and their servants, with annotations as to the principal moral irregularities and actual or potential sins.[8] Nothing was to escape the watchful eye of the parish priest.

This status as director of souls was of primary importance in the curé's image of his role in society. Metaphors of parenthood and guardianship permeated his references to the lay population of the parish. Thus, for François-Léon Réguis, curé of Barret-le-Bas, the parish priest was the father of his children, a mother hen warming her chicks under her wing, an eagle teaching his young to fly, a shepherd grazing his flock. Only the curé's spiritual authority,

[5] Register of approbations, 1745–1777: A.D.H.A., G 829–830.
[6] *Ibid.*
[7] *Ord. syn.*, I, 139–140.　　　　[8] *Ord. syn.*, I, 181–183.

deriving directly from Jesus Christ, should be of concern to his parishioners. Whether rich or poor, of good family or of the dregs of the lower classes, of saintly or dishonorable conduct, all curés must be treated with reverence and respect. "All is good, all is of value, all is pleasing from the lips of this good father, lifting up his voice in the midst of his children."[9]

This paternalistic attitude of the curé toward his parishioners had been greatly encouraged and strengthened by the Church itself. Prior to the late seventeenth century, many parish priests, in their clothing, life style, and relations with women, had been scarcely distinguishable from the average layman.[10] When in 1672–1673 the bishop of Grenoble, Le Camus, visited parishes in the Oisans, Matheysine and Valbonnais—regions immediately adjoining the Champsaur-Beaumont—he was appalled to find curés deeply involved in peasant activities, drinking, gambling, living with "wives" and children, and generally ignorant of many of their religious duties.[11] Although descriptions of the seventeenth-century parish clergy of Gap are somewhat lacking in detail, conditions there were probably similar.[12] But the seminary movement and the creation of the cantonal conferences, begun by the bishops of Gap at the end of the seventeenth century, would be critical in the formation of a new kind of parish clergyman.[13] Henceforward,

[9] *La voix des pasteurs* (Lyon, 1855), I, 249–250, and 262–264, and II, 73. In the preface to the first edition (Paris, 1766), Réguis said that the sermons in the first volume were essentially identical to those he delivered from the pulpit. Réguis served in Barret-le-Bas from 1766 to 1773.

[10] See the article by Dominique Julia, "Le prêtre au XVIIIe siècle," *Recherches de science religieuse*, LVIII (1970), pp. 521–534.

[11] Jacques Solé, "La crise morale du clergé du diocèse de Grenoble au début de l'épiscopat de Le Camus," in *Le cardinal des montagnes, Etienne Le Camus, évêque de Grenoble (1671–1707). Actes du Colloque Le Camus, Grenoble, 1971* (Grenoble, 1974), pp. 179–209.

[12] See especially the visits of the archpriests in 1686: A.D.H.A., G 786.

[13] See above, Chapter III.

in the diocese of Gap and throughout the kingdom, the parish priest was to be trained and drilled not only in the basic sciences of his profession, but also in the external demeanor he was to exhibit as continual affirmation of his status as a servant of God, as a man distinguished from the common of men. He must always appear in a cassock, never with gloves or bright-colored stockings or a wig (unless for health reasons as attested by a medical certificate). He was to eat with laymen as seldom as possible and to avoid inns and popular festivals. He must never indulge in gambling or hunting or excesses of strong drink. Above all, he should avoid undue contact with women; he must never engage a housekeeper younger than the "canonical age" of fifty; he should never imagine himself stronger than Samson or David.[14] In every way possible he must prove to his parishioners that he had, indeed, left "the world."

As we shall see, in the course of the eighteenth century, there would be a number of subtle modifications in the rules and in the standards of conduct for the parish clergy. But the essential elements of the pastoral reforms would remain. The priest was to be a man aloof and apart from the rest of men, the exemplar, the moral teacher and leader of the community. Perhaps for no other profession in society were the norms of behavior, the conception of one's self and of one's position in regard to others, so consciously taught and institutionalized.

THE VILLAGE NOTABLE

Beyond his religious functions, the parish clergyman played a significant role in the secular sphere of village life. Not only did he serve as keeper of the parish register, but he held the delegated right of overseeing the schoolteacher, and not uncommonly performed the functions of teacher himself.[15] Until he was forbidden to do so by royal letters

---

[14] *Ord. syn.*, I, 31–60.   [15] See above, Chapter III.

patent in 1770, he also had the power of receiving the last will and testament of any member of his parish.[16] The extent of the parish priests' participation in communal assemblies is difficult to determine, since the curés are almost never mentioned in the official minutes kept in the village archives.[17] Yet we know indirectly that some of them took an active part in deliberations. Curé Jean-Joseph Jean admitted his influence on decisions in the village of Montjai.[18] Allard, curé of Rambaud, was active in convincing the local assembly to repair the road to Gap: "I can't put myself at the head of the workers, since that is not fitting to my profession," but he did everything else he could to organize the effort.[19] Other priests, perhaps the only villagers with sufficient writing ability, are found serving as community secretaries.[20] Many were also members of the committees that drew up the villages' tax rolls. At least twenty-one curés in parishes of the future department of the Hautes-Alpes would sign the *capitation* rolls of 1789–

[16] *Lettres patentes*, registered by the Parlement of Dauphiné, July 11, 1770: *Recueil Giroud*, xxv, no. 69. This right was apparently held by the parish clergy in many provinces of France: Babeau, p. 146. In the region of Ribiers, the curés accepted testaments in approximately five percent of the cases: see the alphabetical tables of wills for the registry office of Ribiers: A.D.H.A., II C 1089. The curés were required to give the minutes of these testaments to an apostolic notary within eight days: Louis de Héricourt, *Les loix ecclésiastiques dans leur ordre naturel* (Paris, 1766), p. 94.

[17] In sharp contrast to the situation in areas of western France, such as southern Anjou, where the records give proof that the curés "almost always attended, and were rarely silent": Charles Tilly, "Civil Constitution and Counter-Revolution in Southern Anjou," *French Historical Studies*, I (1959), p. 175.

[18] Letter to Tournu, prior of Montjai, May 20, 1773: A.D.H.A., VII E Jarjayes 145; letter to the bishop, Aug. 8, 1785: A.D.H.A., G 978.

[19] Letter to Pinet de Manteyer, May 27, 1772: A.D.I., 14 J 226.

[20] At least two curés, Amat of Agnielles and Nicolas of Pomet, are known to have written the replies of their villages to the intermediary commission of the Estates of Dauphiné: Paul Guillaume, ed., *Recueil des réponses faites par les communautés de l'élection de Gap au questionnaire envoyé par la Commission intermédiaire des Etats du Dauphiné* (Paris, 1908).

1790, sometimes with the additional title of "notable," or "secretary."[21] Certain curés were probably asked on an informal basis to assist in the complex calculations involved in the distribution of the *tailles* and the *vingtième* and to serve as scribes in writing up the rolls.[22]

But perhaps the most important role taken by the curé in community affairs was in charity and poor relief. Since the early days of the Church, the poor had traditionally been one of the special concerns of the clergy. The curé was thought to be particularly well-qualified to determine which families and individuals within the parish were genuinely deserving of charitable assistance. By law the parish priest was to be a member of the governing board of the hospitals for sick poor people and soldiers.[23] In every parish, even those—the majority—which had no established hospitals, he worked in conjunction with the community officers in drawing up rolls for the *vingt-quatrième*, the portion of the tithes set aside throughout Dauphiné for feeding the poor;[24] and he participated in or was wholly responsible for the *greniers d'abondance* (public granaries) that loaned out reserves of grain during periods of want.[25]

[21] A.D.H.A., L 499, L 1234, L 1388. The sub-delegate, Delafont, wrote in 1784 that many curés were on the *capitation* committees: Joseph Roman, ed., "Mémoire sur l'état de la subdélégation de Gap en 1784," *BHA*, XVIII (1899), p. 67.

[22] D'Eyglun, curé of Ballon, was asked by the consuls and *auditeurs* of the community to attend a tax-assessment meeting on Feb. 21, 1758 "pour leur aider à en faire un juste examen." We learn this only because the curé became involved in a suit arising out of the meeting: A.D.H.A., G 2668.

[23] Royal declaration of Dec. 12, 1698, reprinted in Héricourt, p. 655. Hospitals are known to have existed in the following parishes of the diocese of Gap: Gap (two: Sainte-Claire and La Charité), Tallard, Rosans, Ribiers, Serres, Corps, Saint-Bonnet, L'Escale, Orpierre, Veynes, Ventavon, and La Roche-des-Arnauds.

[24] See the decision of the Parlement of Dauphiné, Aug. 26, 1774: *Recueil Giroud*, XXVI, no. 23; also the question concerning the *vingt-quatrième* in Guillaume, *Recueil des réponses*.

[25] For a description of the *greniers d'abondance* in the Hautes-Alpes, see Pierre-Antoine Farnaud, *Exposé sur les améliorations introduites depuis environ cinquante ans dans les diverses branches de l'économie rurale du département des Hautes-Alpes* (Gap, 1811), pp. 111–114.

He performed similar tasks whenever money or food was available for the poor from individual or community donations.

Over and above their institutional responsibilities in charity, many curés came to identify themselves personally with the plight of the poor in their parishes. Curé Millon of Laye often wrote to the seigneurial lord, Baron Des Preaux, for assistance to the parish poor: "Because of my status as curé and of the affection which you have shown for me . . . I have often had occasion to ask you for generosity toward the needy of my parish."[26] Dominique Chaix, in his letters to Villars, frequently wrote with great sympathy for the suffering of the poor. Chaix was especially incensed by the rumors of grain hoarders who would "suffocate the indigent through excessively high prices for [wheat]": "May God have mercy on His poor people."[27] Perhaps every curé—like Chaix or Martin of Saint-Michel-de-Chaillol—had a box full of IOU's scrawled on little scraps of paper: small charitable "loans" to parishioners at no interest that were never paid and probably never expected to be paid.[28] Few parish priests were prepared to follow Malissole's synodal ordinances to the letter and share all their revenues with "the other poor in Jesus Christ."[29] Yet widows and orphans, the poor and the oppressed, commonly found donations in the curés' wills.[30] Some parish

26 Letter to Des Preaux, Nov. 19, 1779: A.D.H.A., F 1350.

27 Letters, June 21, 1785 and Feb. 20, 1790: B.M.G., R 10073.

28 See Martin's personal papers: A.D.H.A., F 1443. At his death, Chaix had a stack of unpaid promises dating back over thirty years and totaling 1,373 *livres*: A.D.H.A., F 676. The brothers Sandre, serving in the diocese of Embrun, left dozens of such promises when they emigrated to Italy; most were to parishioners and all were without interest: A.D.H.A., I Q I 291.

29 *Ord. syn.*, I, 248–249.

30 Of 45 testaments examined, 27 parish clergymen specifically set aside money for the parish poor—sometimes for the poor of all the parishes in which they had served during their career. Several others gave money to other designated charities, such as hospitals or orphanages.

clergymen even took an active part in the general debate at the end of the Old Regime on the reform and improvement of relief for the poor.[31] Pellegrin, vicaire of Ribiers, was apparently a primary instigator of reforms in the poor hospital of his parish.[32] Albert, curé of Seynes, wrote against closing up the indigent in buildings when they might be better helped directly in their homes.[33] And Chaix, in an essay submitted to the academy of Grenoble, seems to have suggested that a portion of the Church's wealth be set aside as a means of suppressing begging.[34] On the eve of the Revolution, this role as "defender of the poor" had become part and parcel of the curé's self image.

In a number of capacities the parish clergy served as an important link between the local rural society and the policies and culture of the urban world and the national state. Although most of the village dwellers of the diocese of Gap could understand French, they generally could neither speak it nor write it, and they necessarily relied on a small educated elite—the curé, the notary, or the local seigneurial lord—to translate between their Provençal dialect and the national language.[35] The curé was also one of the few villagers with access to a broad network of friends and acquaintances outside the local community. Virtually every priest had lived in Gap and many had spent time in the surrounding cities of Grenoble, Valence, or Aix. They all had

[31] See Jean-Pierre Gutton, *La société et les pauvres. L'exemple de la généralité de Lyon, 1534–1789* (Paris, 1971), pp. 428–429.

[32] A.D.H.A., F 1004.

[33] *Histoire géographique, naturelle, ecclésiastique et civile du diocèse d'Embrun*, 2 vols. (Embrun, 1783–1786), II, 415.

[34] He first mentions the composition of this essay in a letter to Villars, Apr. 29, 1788. Indications as to some of its contents are in the letter of Dec. 22, 1789: B.M.G., R 10073.

[35] Albert, I, 93, observed that the peasants were usually unable to speak French, although all understood it. Unlike many regions of France, the curés used French in sermons and catechism. See also the response of curé Jean-Michel Rolland to the Abbé Grégoire's survey of *patois* in France: B.N., Nouv. aquis., F 2798 f. 99, *verso*, indicated to me by Dominique Julia.

well-established contacts through the church administration and their fellow curés. Many had further influence by virtue of blood ties with various notable families in the area.[36] The curé was often the first to whom a villager might go to seek assistance and a letter of recommendation for finding a job in the city. Dominique Chaix wrote to Villars in Grenoble in behalf of young men seeking positions as servants, apprentice printers, or schoolteachers; and he was instrumental in enabling Jean-Joseph Serre—later a deputy to the Convention—to become a surgeon.[37] Pinet de Manteyer, a rich tax official in Gap, received many similar requests from curés asking positions for worthy parishioners.[38] A letter from the priest might also be sought for protection in a judicial suit or to voice a complaint against unjust tax treatment. Mauduëch, curé of Eourres, defended a young parishioner allegedly ill-treated by a "triumvirate" of village notables in an affair concerning the *tailles*.[39] And Chaix solicited assistance for parishioners indicted before the sovereign courts in Grenoble.[40] On occasion, the parish priest might even take the part of marriage broker. He had an institutional role in the preliminary arrangements of all marriages, investigating possible impediments to the union between two individuals, and publishing the banns on three successive Sundays. His broad circle of acquaintances could make him an ideal go-between for bringing together suitable parties. Annotations and comments on the requests of

---

[36] See above, Chapter II.

[37] Letters dated June 8, 1778; Dec. 17, 1779; May 27, July 15 and 30, 1785; Sept. 12, 1786: B.M.G., R 10073.

[38] *E.g.*, letters from Allard, curé of Rambaud, Apr. 30, 1775; and from Bonnet, curé of Rambaud, Nov. 3, 1780: A.D.I., 14 J 226.

[39] Letters to Pinet de Manteyer, Jan. 4 and Nov. 27, 1782: A.D.I., 14 J 172. Pinet seems to have received a number of such letters from curés on behalf of illiterate parishioners: see also, *e.g.*, the letter by the curé of Eygliers in favor of the widow Bonnardel, Sept. 27, 1776: *ibid.*

[40] Letters to Villars, Feb. 19, 1782; Feb. 7 and 21, 1789: B.M.G., R 10073.

dispensations addressed to the bishop would suggest the important role played by some curés.[41] Whenever disaster struck the parish, the curé could be expected to take the initiative in obtaining outside assistance. Curé Amat approached first the sub-delegate and then the Marquis du Langon to seek relief for the homeless after Agnielles had been nearly destroyed by fire in 1774.[42] The parish priest of La Motte-en-Champsaur sought and obtained aid from the bishop in 1788 when the village was decimated by disease.[43]

In the later part of the eighteenth century, some of the curés who were best informed through newspapers or correspondence began acting as the veritable tutors of their parishes in technological and scientific innovation. Albert of Seynes had undertaken the cultivation of his beneficed lands on a hillside by using stone retaining walls and terrace plowing. As he had hoped, the neighboring peasants soon began following his lead, thus reportedly increasing their grain harvests.[44] Davignon, curé of Chaillol, had gone to considerable expense to build a reservoir and irrigation system for his beneficed lands, developments that were ideally to serve as models for the rest of the community.[45] Chaix invented a new method of exterminating gophers that he showed to his parishioners and proudly submitted for publication in the Grenoble newspaper.[46] Chaix was also sought out by the local peasants for medical assistance to

[41] See the series of requests and inquests for dispensations, 1784–1790: A.D.H.A., G 1064–1076. In 1760, curé Pons of Ancelle was serving as go-between for a man in Gap in his bid of marriage to one of Pons' parishioners: letter to Jean Marchon, June 28, 1760: A.D.H.A., F 696.

[42] Camille Queyrel, "Un modèle de l'administration éclairée, Pierre Delafont et Pierre-Joseph-Marie Delafont, derniers subdélégués de Gap" (D.E.S., Univ. de Grenoble, 1933), pp. 189–190.

[43] Letters from the curé to the bishop, May 1 and Sept. 17, 1788: A.D.H.A., G 986.

[44] Albert, I, 85–86.

[45] Declaration of revenue, June 12, 1772: A.D.H.A., G 2338.

[46] Letter to Villars, Sept. 18, 1787: B.M.G., R 10073.

the sick. After bleeding the patient or trying other home remedies he would write to Villars for his advice.[47] In 1786, with Villars' guidance, he began administering the first smallpox inoculations ever given in the parish.[48] Doctors and surgeons were rare in the countryside of Dauphiné and the curés may have served as prime sources of medical assistance for many rural dwellers.[49]

Fully aware of the pivotal position occupied by the parish priest within the village, the lay authorities attempted to use him as a means of communication with the rural inhabitants. There is evidence that the curés were the preferred local agents of many non-resident noblemen. Baron Des Preaux, lord of Laye and Valserres, corresponded for nearly ten years with the curé of Laye, Augustin Millon.[50] Millon regularly reported on all manner of items of interest to the baron: on the weather and the state of the crops, on the management or mismanagement of the baron's estates by the *fermiers*, on encroachments by the royal courts on the baron's seigneurial jurisdiction.[51] Because of the "limited knowledge and ability" of the lay population of the village, the curé was asked to take full charge of the re-division of the seigneurial domains.[52] He was also the supervisor of the construction of a chateau and an inn the baron was having built in the parish: he hired and paid the workers for this purpose, and rode all over the Champsaur to barter for building material.[53] Curés Mévouilhon of Man-

[47] Letters to Villars, Sept. 16 and 26, 1779; Apr. 19, 1782; Jan. 7, 1785; Dec. 5, 1786; Nov. 28, 1790: B.M.G., R 10073.

[48] Letters, June 20 and July 28, 1786.

[49] Mévouilhon, curé of Manteyer, requested a special "boîte de remèdes" from Pinet de Manteyer in Gap so that he would be "à portée de rendre service au voisinage": letter, July 5, 1787: A.D.I., 14 J 212. On the shortage of doctors, see Guillaume, *Recueil des réponses*, question number 3.

[50] Much of the correspondence has been lost, but 46 letters are preserved from Millon to Des Preaux between Apr. 10, 1772 and June 10, 1780: A.D.H.A., F 1344–1347 and F 1350.

[51] *E.g.*, letters July 3, 1773; Apr. 10, 1772; Dec. 12, 1779.

[52] Letter, Mar. 15, 1780.

[53] *Passim* in correspondence.

teyer and Allard of Rambaud performed similar reporting and overseeing functions for Pinet de Manteyer for lands held by this nobleman in their respective parishes.[54]

In the second half of the eighteenth century, the royal bureaucracy also attempted to use the curés for gathering and propagating information in the countryside. Turgot's celebrated effort to convert the Limousin parish clergy into a corps of government functionaries was probably imitated by many other intendants in France—including those of Dauphiné.[55] In fact, the government's attempts were often thwarted by the bishops, who feared, not without reason, that the bureaucracy might preempt the curés' loyalties to the detriment of the ecclesiastical hierarchy. The bishops could point to the edict of April 1695, which explicitly prohibited the publication of laws and judicial decisions from the pulpit.[56] Thus when Delafont, the sub-delegate of Gap, asked the curés to initiate the people during the Sunday services in the use of smallpox vaccinations (a year after Chaix had begun doing so independently), bishop Vareilles forbade his curés to comply in any way.[57] Moreover, not all curés were prepared to give their undivided allegiance to the crown's administrators. Millon described his dilemma when he was asked by the intendant to report on the parish's grain production and income in 1773. He decided to understate the actual values, fearing that the parish taxes might be raised if the reality were known. The intendant was "a superior to whom we owe obedience; and yet I fear

[54] Letters to Pinet from Mévouilhon, May 7, 1783 to July 5, 1787: A.D.I., 14 J 212; from Allard, May 8, 1770 to Nov. 19, 1776: A.D.I., 14 J 226.

[55] See Douglas Dakin, *Turgot and the Ancien Régime in France* (London, 1939), esp. pp. 58–60 and 97–98; also Queyrel, cited above.

[56] Article 32, reprinted in Héricourt, p. 531.

[57] Letters from Caze de la Bove, intendant, to Delafont, June 10, 1787; and from Delafont to Caze de la Bove, July 25, 1787: A.D.H.A., Collect. Roman, L. *Cf.* the efforts of the agents-general to prevent the intendant of Bordeaux from using the curés to disseminate methods of combatting an animal epidemic: letter, intendant to agents-general Nov. 2, 1776: A.N., G8* 2631, f. 75.

causing problems for my parishioners if I tell the truth."[58]
Despite these difficulties, most curés would continue to
lend the government valuable assistance in obtaining demographic data, in verifying the state of the economy, in assisting cartographic surveys, and in various other ways.[59]
Many seem to have cooperated, at least in an unofficial
capacity, by passing on information and instructions
through informal conversation outside the Church. In this
way, Chaix received ordinances from the intendant, sent to
him personally via Villars, which he promised to spread
to his acquaintances.[60] Sub-delegate Delafont used informal
letters to curés and other notables to suggest a new method
for wintering livestock,[61] and he called on curé Pierre Ricard
of Rabou to take charge of an experimental herd of Spanish
sheep sent to Gap by the intendant in 1788.[62]

In one area of concern, the ecclesiastical hierarchy fully
concurred with the use of the parish priests by the royal
bureaucracy: civil obedience and submission to authority.
It had always been one of the clergyman's tasks to buttress
the stability of the social order. Curé Réguis described the
ideal Christian state in one of his sermons: "The upper
classes will be just, modest, kindly, considerate, benevolent;
the lower classes will be submissive, obedient, charitable,
and unselfish; all of the poor will be hard-working and content."[63] In preaching submission, are not the ministers of
the Church "the most necessary and precious corps in the
state?"[64] Clearly, the parish clergymen themselves were

[58] Letter to Des Preaux, Nov. 17, 1773: A.D.H.A., F 1346.
[59] *E.g.*, the abbé Expilly worked in cooperation with the intendants
to obtain demographic data from the curés in 1764: Edmond Esmonin,
"L'abbé Expilly et ses travaux de statistique" in *Etudes sur la France
des XVIIe et XVIIIe siècles* (Paris, 1964), pp. 272–313; Cassini had
circulars sent to the curés to obtain information for his famous maps:
the originals are preserved in the *cartothèque* of the Institut géographique national; note also the economic survey of the intendant
described by curé Millon, previous note.
[60] Letter to Villars, Feb. 19, 1782: B.M.G., R 10073.
[61] Queyrel, pp. 94–95.   [62] *Ibid.*, pp. 84–88.
[63] Réguis, I, 121.   [64] *Ibid.*, II, 313.

among those "superiors" within the society to whom the people must be obedient and submissive.

To some administrators, the parish priests seemed the ideal agents for quelling popular riots and public discontent. After the grain riots of 1775, Turgot sent an appeal to all the curés of France to help calm the people and assure them of the government's efforts and concern.[65] There can be no doubt that most curés followed such instructions with the greatest sense of responsibility. Curé Achard of Serres, for example, proudly reported in 1789 that he and his colleagues in the canton had always taught submission to one's "masters" and that there had been no riots or rebellions in his region in recent memory.[66]

Indeed, the authority and prestige of the curé as village notable would be particularly manifest in a moment of community crisis and disorder such as the Great Fear of 1789. Everywhere in Dauphiné the parish clergy was reported to have played a major part in quieting the panic and organizing the public in defense against the "brigands."[67] The curé and vicaire of Ribiers were the first to step forward and contribute to the creation of a citizens' militia.[68] The curé of Saint-Marcellin was asked to represent the municipality of Veynes in requesting troops and ammunition from the provincial authorities in Grenoble.[69] When a messenger arrived in Saint-Maurice-en-Valgaudemar with news of an approaching "army," he went first to the rectory to seek out the curé, Alexandre Ruynat-Gournier. The curé immediately had the tocsin rung on the

[65] Dated May 9, 1775: *Oeuvres de Turgot et documents le concernant,* ed. Gustave Schelle, 5 vols. (Paris, 1912–1923), IV, 436–442.

[66] "Cahier de doléances des curés du diocèse de Gap," *AA,* XIII (1909), pp. 210–211.

[67] *Cahier des curés de Dauphiné* (Lyon, 1789), pp. 89–90. On Aug. 9 the sub-delegate of Gap sent a royal letter to be read by all the curés in the region in order to help to pacify the populace: letter from Delafont to the count de Durfort, Aug. 19, 1789: A.D.H.A., Collect. Roman, LI.

[68] Deliberations of Aug. 9, 1789: A. C. Ribiers, BB 37.

[69] Deliberations of Aug. 7, 1789: A. C. Veynes, BB 32.

church bells. The priest and the chatelain then met in the rectory with the villagers as they arrived to organize a defense and to set up a guard at the bridge. The *ad hoc* committee was also notified of the latest rumors about troop movements through a letter from the curé of neighboring Saint-Firmin.[70] In numerous communities, the parish clergymen were appointed members of the committees of public safety established to confront the emergency, sitting together with the mayors, the judges, the lawyers, and the other principal notables of the village communities.[71]

TOWARD A NEW SELF-DEFINITION: THE BON CURÉ

During the second half of the eighteenth century, a new model, a new style of parish priest, was emerging in the diocese of Gap and perhaps in France generally, a model in which particular stress was placed on the curé's status as village notable. To be sure, the earlier model, the Catholic-Reformation priest envisioned by bishops such as Berger de Malissoles and Le Camus, would not be entirely supplanted. The seminary movement of the seventeenth century would remain a major watershed for the eighteenth- and even the nineteenth-century curés, well-trained and educated, fully confident of their importance and distinctiveness in the parish community. The most blatant moral shortcomings of the seventeenth-century curés would largely disappear. There are few known instances of gambling or excessive drinking among the diocesan clergy of Gap after mid-century; relatively rare are the cases of priests accused of using physical violence or of succumbing

---

[70] Documents printed in *AA*, XIII (1909), pp. 122–129.
[71] Sources cited above for Saint-Maurice, Veynes, and Ribiers; also A. C. Gap, BB 76–77; A. C. Montmaur, BB 19; unfortunately, most of the community deliberations of 1789 have been lost. Georges Lefebvre, in *La Grande peur de 1789* (2nd ed.; Paris, 1970), p. 175, notes the role of the French curés in spreading the news of the arriving "brigands."

to sexual temptations.[72] Indeed, one has the impression that the curés were viewing the world with a puritanical eye, rigidly disapproving of all of the self-indulgences that they themselves were denied. The most serious accusations heard before the ecclesiastical court of Gap between 1774 and 1778 concerned priests who had failed to pay small debts.[73]

Yet the bishops' reform efforts had perhaps never entirely succeeded in the principal goal of extracting the parish priests from "the world," of setting a premium on their spiritual and pastoral functions. If they no longer gambled or took part in public games, certain curés were involved in agricultural or even financial enterprises. If they no longer frequented taverns and popular festivals with the common people, they might well be seen at receptions or dinner parties in the company of more eminent laymen. Curés Mévouilhon, Millon, Chaix, and Allard are all known to have entertained or to have been entertained on occasion by neighboring nobles or other notables.[74] There are also indications that hunting and the wearing of wigs, two of the symbols of notable status in the village,[75] were making a quiet reappearance among the parish clergy

---

[72] See the following chapter.

[73] Register of the *officialité*: A.D.H.A., G 2669. This is the only register preserved. Using a much longer series of *officialité* registers, Jacques Lovie came to much the same conclusion for the diocese of Die: "La vie paroissiale dans le diocèse de Die à la fin de l'Ancien régime," *BD*, LXV, no. 269 (1936), pp. 277–282.

[74] Mévouilhon made several mentions of dinner parties he had had; at one, Pinet de Manteyer and the La Flotte family were both invited to dine with him: letters to Pinet, May 7 and 10, 1783: A.D.I., 14 J 212. Millon often invited the baron Des Preaux to visit him; in 1773, he, his two brothers in the priesthood, and the curés of Château-d'Ancelle and La Bâtie-Vieille, all planned to spend some time at the baron's chateau in Valserres: letters, July 3 and Sept. 7, 1773: A.D.H.A., F 1345. In 1776, Allard invited Pinet for dinner and a cup of coffee after the meal: letter to Pinet, July 23, 1776: A.D.I., 14 J 226.

[75] Stendhal wrote of his grandfather, a doctor in Grenoble, "l'opinion publique de 1760 lui déclara impérieusement que s'il ne prenait pas perruque, personne n'aurait confiance en lui": *Vie de Henry Brulard* (Paris, 1949), p. 59.

—despite earlier interdictions by the bishops. In 1765, Jean-Joseph Jean, vicaire of Brantes at the time, asked the bishop for permission to go hunting occasionally "by way of recreation"; he said that several priests of the diocese had assured him that the prohibition on priests' hunting was no longer in force.[76] In 1772, curé Millon begged Des Preaux to intercede with the bishop on his behalf so that he might be allowed to hunt: "It's not that I'm thinking of overindulging, for I've carried a gun scarcely three times this season. But human nature is always more inclined toward what is forbidden."[77] There is no way of knowing how many parish priests wore wigs. But it is of interest that, beginning in the mid 1750's, an increasing number of priests were claiming baldness or head diseases, which required them to ask and obtain permission to wear wigs.[78] In two cases of assaults on parish clergymen, witnesses observed that the priests were struck so hard that they lost their wigs.[79]

Perhaps, in creating a greater social and cultural distance between priest and parishioner, in cultivating the priest's sense of identity and moral authority, the seminary movement had actually broadened the potentialities of his elite status in the secular affairs of the village. We have examined the important role played by the curé in the village government, in charity, and as a general link to the outside world. In addition to their duties of pastoral care, parish priests were taking increasing responsibilities in the physical and economic well-being of their parishioners.

---

[76] Letter to the bishop, Feb. 26, 1765: A.D.H.A., G 970.

[77] Letter, Aug. 22, 1772: A.D.H.A., F 1344. Note also that when the abbés Brun and Bonthoux were taken to court for shooting birds in 1783, they were attacked less for the hunting itself than for allowing their dogs to trample a wheat field and for pushing a peasant when he threw rocks at the dogs to chase them away: A.D.H.A., B 574.

[78] Register of approbations: A.D.H.A., G 829–830. Thirteen permissions were granted between 1756 and 1761. Only one was granted between 1745 and 1756.

[79] Cases involving Salva, *sacristain* in Ribiers, 1759: A.D.H.A., B 554; and Martin, curé of Lemps, 1758: *dossier judiciaire* deposited in the rectory of Rémuzat.

Many were ready and willing to cooperate with the royal bureaucracy as mediators between the king and the people. Social realities often diverge from literary types. Yet there was a definite resemblance between this new style of parish priest and the *"bon prêtre"* or *"bon curé"* popularized and glorified by so many eighteenth-century writers from the Abbé de Saint-Pierre through Voltaire, Rousseau, and Bernardin de Saint-Pierre.[80] While few curés could have subscribed to the deism or blatant utilitarianism of Téotime or the Vicaire Savoyard, they could not but be flattered by the widely circulating literature extolling the virtues of the *bon curé* as the key agent of the king, tutor of society, servant of Enlightenment in the countryside. "The philosophes admitted," wrote curé Jean-Michel Rolland, "that no man on earth is more useful and respectable than a *bon curé*. Such praise is all the more remarkable since it was dictated less by instinctive sympathy [for the curé] than by the logic of the unvarnished truth."[81] The image of an idealized *bon curé*, unjustly treated by the elite of the Church, would be used to great effect during the politicization of the parish clergy of Dauphiné at the end of the Ancien Régime.[82]

[80] See Pierre Sage, *Le bon prêtre dans la littérature française* (Lille and Geneva, 1951); and William H. Williams, "Voltaire and the Utility of the Lower Clergy," *Studies in Voltaire and the Eighteenth Century*, LVIII (1967), pp. 1,869–1,891.

[81] "Précis de l'éloge de M. Chaix, botaniste, rédigé d'après une notice composée par M. Villars," in *Mélanges littéraires . . . de la société d'émulation des Hautes-Alpes* (Gap, 1807), pp. 190–191.

[82] See below, Chapter IX.

CHAPTER VII

Patterns of Community Rivalry

Important though his functions were in the local society, the curé did not always enjoy an easy existence there. Among the limited number of individuals constituting the parish, confronting one another year after year in the intense concerns of earning a living and raising a family, competition and conflict were endemic; rumor and gossip, suspicion and criticism, envy and fear of envy, were all common fare. Few curés could avoid occasional antagonisms with their parishioners: whether as conflicts of interest, personality clashes, or rivalries based on institutional functions or social status. What is more, the curé was in most instances a foreigner, an outsider whose success in grafting himself into the social tissue often depended not only on his own ability but on the group psychology of the village itself.

The study of the patterns of conflict between priest and parish, in the present and in the following chapters, is based on two principal series of documents. First, all records preserved for the second half of the eighteenth century from the bailliage courts of Gap and Le Buis-les-Baronnies have been examined for cases, both civil and criminal, involving clergymen.[1] The bailliage courts were

---

[1] A.D.H.A., B 543–579 (1750–1790); and A.D.D., B 2185–2196 and B 2201–2214 (1775–1790). Neither of these series is complete. Efforts to determine the number of cases missing have not been successful. When a case was appealed to the Parlement of Dauphiné, the entire dossier was usually forwarded to Grenoble. This would explain many of the missing dossiers. Some of the missing records have been recovered in a wide variety of archives. A few have been found in the ecclesiastical archives (series G) or in the private archives of lawyers (series F). I have also examined that small portion (perhaps five percent) of the judicial dossiers of the archives of the Parlement of Dauphiné that have thus far been classified (A.D.I., series B, *procès criminels*). If a

the lowest secular courts in which ecclesiastics would normally appear.[2] Following a centuries-long erosion of the authority of the ecclesiastical courts, the civil magistrates had acquired direct jurisdiction in disputes involving the tithes, possession of benefices, sacrilege, the activities of the Protestant population, debts and reparations claimed by priests, and all manner of verbal and physical violence between clergymen and laymen.[3] A total of 71 such cases have been analyzed, all initiated between 1750 and 1790. Of these, 39 (55 percent) were disputes between resident priests and lay individuals.[4] Second, we have examined the series of episcopal inquests, ordinances, and related correspondence preserved intact for the tenure of the bishop La Broüe de Vareilles, 1784 to 1790.[5] This series contains approximately 250 dossiers, including the requests and com-

---

printed brief was made for a case before the Parlement, I was sometimes able to locate it in the collection of *factums* in the B.M.G. Finally, efforts were sometimes made by the agents-general of the clergy to have cases removed to the king's council. Records of a few of these have been found in the A.N. (series G[8]).

The combined jurisdictions of the bailliage courts of Gap and Le Buis constituted about 75 percent of the territory of the diocese. I have generally limited research to those cases originating in the jurisdiction of the Parlement of Dauphiné.

[2] Philip Dawson, *Provincial Magistrates and Revolutionary Politics in France, 1789–1795* (Cambridge, Massachusetts, 1972), pp. 52–53. There were some types of cases, however, where priests appeared first before a seigneurial judge and then appealed the decision to the bailliage. A suit between a clergyman and an entire community would go directly before the Parlement of Dauphiné.

[3] By the eighteenth century the competence of the ecclesiastical jurisdiction was limited to purely spiritual questions—ecclesiastical discipline, the sacraments, religious vows, etc.—and to certain questions of marriage: see Marcel Marion, *Dictionnaire des institutions de la France aux XVIIe et XVIIIe siècles* (Paris, 1923), article "justice ecclésiastique," pp. 321–322; also Norman Ravitch, *Sword and Mitre: Government and Episcopate in France and England in the Age of Aristocracy* (The Hague, 1966), pp. 24–34.

[4] The others involved non-parish clergy or entire communities, or were between two or more clergymen.

[5] A.D.H.A., G 973–975, G 977–993, and G 995–996; G 988–993 are the actual registers of ordinances rendered by the bishop.

plaints of priests and laymen addressed to the bishop, the official inquiries made by appointed clerical commissioners, and the ensuing decisions taken by the bishop. These two basic sources have been complemented, whenever possible and appropriate, by registers of pastoral visits, correspondence of the sub-delegates of Gap, minutes of community deliberations, several series of correspondence from individual curés, and a wide variety of other documents. A strictly quantitative analysis of these sources would be of dubious value, given the nature and the state of preservation of the documents involved.[6] The series of episcopal inquests covers a period of only six years, and necessarily reflects the priorities and concerns of a single bishop. As for the analysis of court records, the dossiers preserved represent only a fraction of an undetermined total number of cases heard before the bailliages. In particular, those cases appealed from the bailliages to the Parlement have usually not been recovered. Two statistical facts are, nevertheless, worthy of note. First, in lawsuits between resident priests and laymen, the clergyman's antagonist was, in over half the cases, a member of the village elite: a nobleman, bourgeois, notary, community official, or wealthy wholesale merchant (*négociant*).[7] Second, the single most common subjects of litigation between laymen and the Church were problems involving the tithes.[8]

---

[6] It is particularly regrettable that our data proved too heterogeneous for the study of possible regional variations in priest-and-parish relations. How might the differences in community structures, in masculine literacy rates, in apparent religious piety and vitality have affected such relations in the Drac Valley as compared to the Durance Valley? All efforts to identify regional distinctions gave ultimately inconclusive results.

[7] In 35 cases the professions of the antagonists are known, and 19 fall within the 5 categories mentioned.

[8] Of the 71 cases involving priests, 13 directly concerned the tithes; 7 others concerned responsibilities incumbent on the tithe owner. Not included in these 71 cases are numerous others that involved the tithes but that were pursued by lay tithe farmers rather than by clergymen.

The relations between the parish clergy and the nobility in the diocese of Gap were always somewhat ambiguous. The curé, as we have seen, could serve as an important intermediary between the lord and his subjects, both as a source of information and as an agent to carry out his orders. In return, the lord could offer valuable protection and assistance to the parish clergy serving on his fiefs. The baron Des Preaux performed numerous services for curé Millon, from sending up wine and *pâté* for the curé's dinner or lending him the latest newspaper, to protecting him from a cabal of parishioners organized against him.[9] Millon could secretly report a misdemeanor committed by a parishioner who was subject to the seigneurial court, and then ask that the fines levied for the crime be paid to the curé himself to help enlarge the parish church.[10] In a similar manner, Pinet de Manteyer assisted the curé of Manteyer in collecting debts owed to him and in selling his produce from the tithes and the glebe.[11]

But especially in those parishes where the lord resided locally,[12] priests could feel galled and humiliated by the nobles' demands for special ceremonial prerogatives and distinctions—the so-called "honors of the Church"—in the course of religious services.[13] Such a clash, between curé Masse of Jarjayes and the local seigneur, Jean-Antoine Reynier, grew into a *cause célèbre* in Dauphiné and was a type example of the rivalries over honorific rights occurring between nobles and parish priests throughout the

[9] Millon to Des Preaux, letters, July 3 and Aug. 28, 1772, and Mar. 13 and May 27, 1780: A.D.H.A., F 1344 and F 1350.

[10] Millon to Des Preaux, letter, Apr. 10, 1772: A.D.H.A., F 1344.

[11] Letters from curé Mévouilhon to Pinet, undated and Nov. 24, 1787: A.D.I., 14 J 212.

[12] According to the sub-delegate, Delafont, most of the nobility of the sub-delegation of Gap lived on their lands and was "peu riche mais honorable": "Mémoire sur l'état de la subdélégation de Gap en 1784," *BHA*, XVIII (1899), pp. 88–93.

[13] See Pierre de Vaissière, *Curés de campagne de l'ancienne France* (Paris, 1933), pp. 291–303.

kingdom.[14] In 1762 Reynier had a special pew built for himself and his family beside the main altar. He then pressed the curé to administer holy water to the noble family before it was given to the rest of the congregation and to use the aspergillum rather than a mere "vague sprinkling without any form of distinction." The curé refused, pointing to a passage in the Synodal Ordinances that specifically forbade the use of the aspergillum. Bishop Pérouse firmly backed his curé, but the following bishop, Narbonne-Lara—who "never refuses anything to a noble," as one curé put it[15]—declined to take sides in the matter, thus opening the way for Reynier's appeal to the Parlement of Dauphiné. The lord of Jarjayes won his case, and the curé was ordered not only to use the aspergillum with all due distinction but also to offer a special swing of the censer to the seigneur and his family. Reynier had the court's decision formally heralded to the sound of a trumpet on the church steps of Jarjayes and Tallard and threatened to have it read all over the province.

Such arrogant affirmations of the nobility's authority stirred a profound bitterness in many curés—of whom 98 percent were themselves commoners. To whom did the church belong, to the parish and to God, or to the nobility? The plight of the curé of Jarjayes incited the immediate commiseration of other parish priests in Dauphiné. Amyer, curé of Valserres and "syndic" of the curés of the diocese of Gap, protested to the agents-general of the Clergy of France against the court's decision, so "humiliating for the pastoral ministry." He expressed the fear that the Parlement was using the case to set a precedent.[16] Curés from the diocese of Grenoble likewise complained against

---

14 See the arguments of the two sides and the decision of Parlement, July 28, 1770: *Recueil Giroud*, xxv, no. 80; also the letter from Amyer, curé of Valserres and syndic, to the agents-general, Nov. 8, 1770: A.N., G⁸ 632 (dossier Gap).

15 Millon, curé of Laye, to the baron Des Preaux, Aug. 22, 1772: A.D.H.A., F 1344.

16 Letter cited above.

the Parlement's ruling and "the humiliations that tend only to debase the curé, to the detriment of religion."[17] But the agents-general and the bishops, who were all nobles themselves, showed only token sympathy for the problems of curé Masse. The parish clergy of Dauphiné was simply reminded of the deference which it owed to all the local nobility.[18]

THE CURÉS AND THE LAY NOTABLES; THE NOTARY AND THE SCHOOLMASTER

In the daily functions of his ministry, the curé was frequently confronted with the physical presence of the lay notables. Judges, lawyers, notaries, "bourgeois," and town officials marched directly before or behind the priest in most of the parish processions. The same group of individuals ardently competed with one another for the possession of family pews at the front of the parish church as close as possible to the altar and pulpit. An eminent pew location was one of the most important status symbols of the village dignitary.[19] From such strategic vantage points, they could impress not only the congregation but the priest himself by their imperious presence. Some had no qualms about shouting comments and observations to the curé in the middle of the Sunday service.[20] The curé was, as we have seen, a notable in his own right, exercising or attempting to

---

[17] Letter to agents-general, ca. 1770: A.N., G⁸ 634 (dossier Grenoble).

[18] Agents-general to Amyer, Nov. 1770: A.N., G⁸* 2605, no. 463.

[19] The notability of the private pew holders is attested by the applications to the bishop to obtain or renew rights for church pews. Between 1746 and 1754, 29 such requests were granted to individuals. Of those for whom professions were given, there were 4 nobles, 3 notaries, 2 judges, 1 apothecary, 1 surgeon, 1 "bourgeois", and 1 merchant: A.D.H.A., G 829. Disputes over pew positions were not uncommon: *e.g.*, between Gaspar Bernard and the *marguillier* Dou in Tallard in 1765: A.D.H.A., G 966; between the notory Allemand and the prior, Amat, in Saint-André-de-Rosans in 1780: A.D.H.A., B 572.

[20] Abel, notary, and his son in Châteauneuf-de-Chabre interrupted the curé from their pew just next to the altar on at least two occasions: see below.

exercise powers that encroached on the domain of secular affairs. The church itself was a central stage on which many of the inevitable rivalries of authority between lay and ecclesiastical elites could be played out before the eyes of the assembled congregation.[21]

In the predominantly agricultural society of the diocese of Gap, where the social structure was relatively simple and rural industry was of little importance,[22] the curé's arch-rival may well have been the notary. The priest and the notary were usually the two best-educated persons in the village community. Both held powers—spiritual on the one hand, temporal on the other—indispensable to the rural inhabitants. Each possessed a kind of omniscience of village affairs—the curé from his confessional, the notary from his register of minutes—that put them in natural positions of leadership or of coercive dominance. Sometimes the notary also served as a village official or chatelain. The potential for friction was further accentuated in Dauphiné as long as the parish priest preserved the power of receiving the wills of the "poor"—which could mean anyone wishing to avoid payment of the notary's fee.

Seething rivalries between priest and notary are frequently evidenced in the records. In their reports to the bishop in 1707, two curés specifically complained of "cabals" engineered by the notary.[23] Jean-Joseph Jean, serving in Brantes in 1765, accused the notary Clément of leading a similar "cabal," attempting to force Jean to leave the

21 *E.g.*, the dispute between the curé and the notary in Châteauneuf-de-Chabre: *ibid.*; the insult against the abbé Martin led by the wife of the chatelain of Montmorin on Mar. 16, 1760: A.D.H.A., F 1450; the dispute between the notary and the prior in Saint-André-de-Rosans on Christmas Day, 1780: A.D.H.A., B 572.

22 In the Mauges of Southern Anjou, an ambitious manufacturing and commercial bourgeoisie was one of the principal rivals to the parish priest's authority: Charles Tilly, *The Vendée* (2nd ed.; New York, 1967), pp. 111–112. This type of bourgeoisie—whose greatest source of revenues came from rural domestic industry—was scarcely present in most of the diocese of Gap.

23 Curé of Lardier: A.D.H.A., G 1100; curé of Valserres: A.D.H.A., G 1104.

parish.[24] The notary of Saint-André-de-Rosans was involved in a series of altercations with the priors of the parish.[25] It is often difficult to determine the precise cause and nature of these quarrels. In two cases, however, the documents permit a deeper sounding of some of the underlying grievances and motives.

A whole range of issues set curé Jean-Joseph Julien of Châteauneuf-de-Chabre against Dominique Abel, notary, *procureur*, and tax collector, one of the richest bourgeois and principal notables of the parish.[26] First there was the question of the choice of officers for the women's confraternity of the Rosary. In 1766, the curé encouraged the previous officers to co-opt their own replacements, but Abel retorted—interrupting the Sunday service to make his point —that only the lay notables could choose these officers, and that the election must take place in the village hall, not in the curé's house. In addition, Abel was the leader of the opposition against making extensive repairs on the rectory. He was accused by Julien of breaking down the rectory door on one occasion in order to make an inspection. Abel also attacked the curé for making himself the "absolute master" of village poor relief.[27] Julien was said to have drawn up the *vingt-quatrième* rolls without consulting the lay officials and to have placed one of those officials on the rolls in order to keep his support. Julien replied that the poor rolls had previously been dictated by Abel, who distributed much of the money to his supporters and friends. Beneath these specific squabbles, an underlying competition for authority was at stake. Abel decried Julien's "pontificate" over the parish;[28] the curé denounced the notary's dicta-

24 *Mémoire* written by Jean, ca. 1765: A.D.H.A., G 970.

25 Allemand vs. Jean-Antoine Amat, 1750: A.D.H.A., B 544; Allemand vs. Etienne-Ignace Amat, 1780: A.D.H.A., B 572.

26 Letters from Abel to vicar-general, Nov. 18, 1766 and Apr. 12, 1767; and from Julien to vicar-general, Oct. 24, 1766: A.D.H.A., G 2668. Also, from Abel to the bishop of Gap, June 17, 1767; and from Julien to the bishop, July 9, 1767: A.D.H.A., G 967.

27 Letter, June 17, 1767.   28 Letter, Nov. 18, 1766.

torial pressure on the poorer peasants who "tremble at the
very name of 'Abel.' "[29] Abel felt that the curé was even
encroaching on his own professional domain, giving advice
to local inhabitants and performing functions that were
properly the concern of the *procureur*.[30] The curé had
also used his sermons to direct the moral opprobrium of
the parish against Abel, accusing him—unjustly, according
to the notary—of usury in his role as tax collector.[31]

A similar rivalry occurred between Etienne Morgan,
notary and tax collector in Saint-Julien-en-Bochaine, and
the parish priest, Marc Blanc.[32] The immediate cause for
the suit was Morgan's insult of Blanc in the village square
of Saint-Julien after the curé had opposed Morgan's marriage to the daughter of a rich *fermier* (Morgan was
seventy-two years old at the time). The two had been in
disputes ever since Blanc was named to the parish. First
the curé had opposed Morgan's use of the *corvée* in order
to build a dike. Then he had admonished him for billeting
soldiers with the villagers to force them to pay their
taxes. The notary was incensed that a young priest from
Gap, an outsider, should try to tell him what to do. Blanc,
on the other hand, announced it as common knowledge that Morgan was "the enemy of priests and of the
Church."[33] Morgan was especially bitter that the curé
should attempt to meddle in the notary's own profession.
Blanc had even prevented people from going to Morgan for
their marriage contracts, offering to make all legal arrangements himself. "Nowadays," he declared, "priests want to
get their hands in everything and make themselves up as
lawyers, attorneys, and notaries."[34]

Unlike the notary, the schoolmaster was not commonly
a rival to the parish priest in the eighteenth-century diocese

[29] Letter, July 9, 1767.
[30] Letter, Nov. 18, 1766.   [31] Letter, Apr. 12, 1767.
[32] Suit initiated June 10, 1760: A.D.H.A., F 1494.
[33] *Ibid.*: deposition of Charles Evêque, June 13, 1760.
[34] *Ibid.*: Morgan's statement under interrogation, June 19, 1760.

of Gap. The edict of 1695 had given the curé and the bishop broad powers of granting and revoking the commission of the parish schoolteacher.[35] For the teacher was responsible for instruction not only of elementary reading and writing, but also of "the principles of religion and of Christian doctrine."[36] It seems, too, that most schoolmasters in the region were itinerant, outsiders serving in different parishes or hamlets each year and only for a period of a few months during the winter season.[37]

Yet the two known instances of conflict between priest and schoolteacher are worthy of note.[38] Both cases occurred in the 1780's and, in both, the teacher was reproached, above all, for his free-thinking, his "epicurean" or "libertine" attitudes. In the two instances, the teacher was able to remain in the parish—according to the curé—only because he was backed by a few village notables as the "instrument" of their irreligion. Perhaps the classic nineteenth-century rivalry between curé and schoolmaster had already begun in some parishes at the end of the Old Regime.

THE CURÉ AND THE COMMUNITY

Many of the same notables who faced the curés from the front rows of the parish church also served the village in official capacities as mayors, *consuls*, or other community authorities. The participation of the parish priest in community government is, as we have seen, difficult to document. But there were two areas of joint concern in which

[35] Marion, article "enseignement primaire," pp. 205–208. Many commissions given to schoolteachers were inscribed in the register of approbations: A.D.H.A., G 829–830.

[36] Ordinance by bishop Pérouse, Jan. 18, 1760: A.D.H.A., G 814.

[37] See especially Aristide Albert, *Le maître d'école briançonnais* (Grenoble, 1874).

[38] Curé Charras vs. Roux, teacher in Lachau: letter, curé to bishop, Jan. 7, 1788: A.D.H.A., G 995; curé Garnier vs. Meylian, teacher in L'Escale: letters and *mémoires* by curé and village officials, 1785–1788: A.D.H.A., G 981–982.

curé and community officials were invariably brought together: in poor relief, and in church and religious expenditures.

In 1789, the *cahier de doléances* of the curés of Dauphiné
would express the fear that many parish clergymen were
being maneuvered out of their rightful positions in hospital
administration and local poor relief.[39] Such complaints may
well substantiate the conclusions of certain historians
concerning the laicization of poor relief at the end of the
eighteenth century and a movement away from Christian
charity toward a more modern concept of *bienfaisance*.[40]
But if confrontations of this order perhaps existed in Provence and Lower Dauphiné, there is little indication of
rivalries over the control of charity in the diocese of Gap.
The only known lay-ecclesiastical conflict concerning the
administration of poor relief was that occurring in
Châteauneuf-de-Chabre.[41] Most lay authorities seem to
have tolerated and even cooperated with the curés, at least
as long as the latter did not attempt to dominate decisions.
Everywhere, the parish clergy was admitted to the committees that established the rolls of the needy and distributed
alms, thus carefully complying with the royal edicts on
these matters.[42] Sometimes the curé was even formally
invited to attend meetings of the village council when questions of charity were to be debated.[43] While priest and parish

[39] *Le cahier des curés du Dauphiné* (Lyon, 1789), pp. 127, 150–151:
see below, Chapter X.

[40] See, especially, Michel Vovelle, *Piété baroque et déchristianisation
en Provence au XVIIIe siècle* (Paris, 1973), pp. 229–264. Also, Jean-
Pierre Gutton, *La société et les pauvres. L'exemple de la généralité de
Lyon, 1534–1789* (Paris, 1971), pp. 419–437.

[41] See above.

[42] See the reply to question number 22 in Paul Guillaume, ed.,
*Recueil des réponses faites par les communautés de l'élection de Gap
au questionnaire envoyé par la Commission intermédiaire des Etats de
Dauphiné* (Paris, 1908).

[43] When the city officials of Tallard noticed that there was a question concerning poor relief on the questionnaire sent them by the
Interim Commission of Dauphiné, they immediately invited the curé
to attend the meeting: *ibid.*, p. 546.

shared responsibilities in the governing of hospitals, it was often the curé who performed the bulk of the actual administration. When Alexandre Achard, curé of Serres, complained of abuses in the town's poor relief, he was eventually given authority to direct the reform of the entire system.[44] In Serres, Tallard, Saint-Bonnet, and Ribiers the parish priest was given the title of "director" or "rector" of the hospital;[45] and Gaspar Bonthoux, co-curé of Gap, served in the key position of treasurer of Sainte-Claire's hospital.[46] At least within the diocese of Gap, the curé's self-image as defender of the poor seems generally to have been accepted by his parishioners, notable and non-notable alike.

The various problems of parish finances could present serious difficulties for priest and community relations. According to the Edict of April 1695, all expenses for the maintenance of the choir, bell tower, and altar were to be incurred by the tithe owner; but the community was to pay for the nave of the church, the rectory, and the parish cemetery.[47] Most villages allotted a small yearly sum out of local taxes for the requisite upkeep.[48] But whenever ecclesiastical orders were given for more costly repairs, community officials might react with extraordinary outrage and indignation, and employ every tactic at their disposal to prove the futility of the repairs or, at least, to delay their execution. Occasionally, the bishop was forced to lay a gen-

[44] Louis Jacques, "Histoire religieuse de Serres," ms. deposited in A.E. Gap, p. 91.

[45] Jacques, p. 91; account books of the hospital of Saint-Bonnet, 1746–1750: A.D.H.A., 5 H Supplement 1; reply of Tallard to the questionnaire of 1789: Guillaume, *Recueil des réponses*, p. 551; A. C. Ribiers, *BB* 37, deliberations of Jan. 1, 1788 (the curé was co-rector along with the chatelain and the outgoing councilman).

[46] *Comptes-rendus* by Bonthoux, 1774–1783: A.D.H.A., H Supplement 576–577.

[47] Article 22: *Recueil général des anciennes lois françaises, depuis l'an 420 jusqu'à la Révolution de 1789*, ed. François-André Isambert et al., 29 vols. (Paris, 1821–1833), xx, 249.

[48] Several of the communities give complete local budgets in their replies to the Interim Commission in 1789: Guillaume, *Recueil des réponses*.

eral interdict on a parish church or cemetery before the parishioners would respond to his demands.[49]

No problem was apt to draw the more vigorous involvement of the parish priest himself than the repair or reconstruction of his own rectory. It probably seemed normal for a curé to desire some measure of comfort and convenience for a house in which he was to spend thirty or forty years of his life. Millon, curé of Laye, also felt that a decent and comfortable rectory was requisite to his station in life; for did not a curé's home serve a public function as a "refuge for shelter and relief . . . to all kinds of people of every position?"[50] He painted a dismal picture of his own dilapidated house, which could not even keep out the wind and the snow. He was ready to use every friend and protector he could muster and brave the hostility of his parishioners in order to obtain the desired improvements.[51] The curé of Sigoyer, Jean Guichard, admitted that his efforts to have a new rectory purchased had brought an enormous storm of protest and that there were pressures to force him out of the parish altogether. But then how could a curé reside in a house where the rain leaked in?[52]

Disputes also arose over the question of the parish cemetery. In the years following 1784, bishop Vareilles placed interdicts on a number of cemeteries because they were not properly enclosed by walls. Several of the curés were enlisted by the parishioners to write letters requesting

[49] *E.g.*, interdicts on the parish churches of Arzeliers, ordinance of Feb. 14, 1746; of Chabestan, Jan. 2, 1750; of Quet-en-Beaumont, May 1, 1751: A.D.H.A., G 829.

[50] Letters, Millon to baron Des Preaux, Dec. 7 and 9, 1774: A.D.H.A., F 1347.

[51] *Ibid.* Millon wrote several letters to Des Preaux and to the sub-delegate arguing his case. The community sent a representative to Gap and even to Grenoble in an attempt to block the curé's efforts.

[52] Letters from Guichard to the sub-delegate, May 14, June 29, and Aug. 20, 1771: A.D.H.A., Collect. Roman, XLVI. See also, *e.g.*, complaints and requests by Masse of Jarjayes: letter from sub-delegate, June 18, 1786: A.D.H.A., Collect. Roman, LII; by Davignon of Chabottonnes: letter, Oct. 5, 1786: A.D.H.A., G 977; by Julien of Châteauneuf-de-Chabre, Nov. 18, 1766: A.D.H.A., G 2668.

reprieves.[53] In a few cases, the curés themselves received the brunt of the community's anger after the priests attempted to enforce the interdictions.[54] In 1788 and 1789, the necessity of finding a new site for the cemetery of Ribiers split the entire community into two factions, one backing the *consuls'* solution and the other backing the curé's solution. Young curé Nicolas, later to play a prominent role in the Revolution, fully involved himself in village politics in order to win over a majority to his side.[55]

Other aspects of parish finances were somewhat different in Dauphiné from those in most other regions of France because of the virtual non-existence of the *fabrique*. The *fabrique* was the independently endowed parish treasury established to provide certain key items necessary for the mass, especially the *"menues fournitures"* such as oil and candles for lighting, bread and wine for communion, the washing of the sacred linen, and the "little cleric."[56] A great many parishes in Dauphiné had no such institutions. This fact, often reported by the bishops of the province,[57] is attested to by the inventories of the parish treasuries made during the Revolution. Thus, only 8 of 58 communities in the district of Gap would report the existence of endowed lands belonging to a parish *fabrique*.[58] At the

[53] *E.g.*, requests by Vincent, curé of Monêtier-d'Ambel, 1786; by Bertrand, curé of Saint-Laurent-du-Cros, 1786: A.D.H.A., G 974.

[54] *E.g.*, request by the community of Rabou to the bishop, *ca.* 1789: A.D.H.A., G 985. The curé "n'a voulu que jeter du trouble et l'alarme dans sa paroisse. . . ."

[55] Copy of a letter from Nicolas to the Parlement of Dauphiné, 1789: A.D.H.A., G 984; community deliberations, Jan. 6, 1788 through July 10, 1789: A. C. Ribiers, *BB* 37. See also below, Chapter XI.

[56] On the *"petit clerc,"* see above, Chapter III.

[57] *E.g.*, see the "Observations préliminaires relatives aux portions congrues," by bishop La Broüe de Vareilles, Nov. 1, 1785: A.N., G⁸ 68 (dossier Gap). See also the decision of the Parlement of Dauphiné, July 24, 1781, "qui juge plusieurs questions relatives aux obligations des décimateurs envers les églises paroissiales qui n'ont point de fonds de fabrique": *Recueil Giroud*, xxvi, no. 16.

[58] Replies by the community officials to the District of Gap, Year III (1794–1795): A.D.H.A., I Q I 110.

same period, every parish in the department of the Sarthe (the Old-Regime diocese of Le Mans, for the most part) had a permanent *fabrique* and 419 of 440 held endowed lands.[59] In the parishes of Dauphiné which had no treasuries of their own, the expenses of the mass were assumed not by the community, but by the tithe-owners: the non-resident "priors" or the prior-curé as the case might be. A royal declaration of 1747 and various interpretive decisions of the Parlement of Dauphiné required the tithe owners to pay the congruists a fixed yearly sum for this purpose.[60]

Since there was no parish treasury, there was no need for lay treasurers to take charge of the funds. The evidence is not entirely conclusive, but it would seem that in most parishes of the diocese of Gap, the office of parish church warden, or *marguillier,* did not exist as such. Church wardens are never mentioned in the minutes of the bishops' pastoral visits; and the various registers, which the church wardens would normally have kept, are not to be found in the communal or departmental archives.[61] Most of the duties the church wardens performed in other regions of France—such as obtaining the preacher for Easter, or appointing a village bell ringer—seem to have been fulfilled in the diocese of Gap by the regular community officials or

[59] Charles Girault, *Les biens d'église dans la Sarthe à la fin du XVIIIe siècle* (Laval, 1953), pp. 64 and 70.

[60] See the royal declaration of Oct. 16, 1747: *Recueil Giroud,* XXII, no. 44; and the decision of the Parlement of Dauphiné, Feb. 16, 1751: *Recueil Giroud,* XXIII, no. 3. The fixed fee was first set at 15 *livres* and later raised to 40 *livres*: see *Recueil Giroud,* XXVI, no. 116.

[61] I have found records or mention of church wardens in only a few of the towns or villages of the Durance Valley, in the south of the diocese: "*marguilliers*" are referred to in requests for establishing private pews in Vitrolles and Vilhosc: entries of Feb. 15 and Oct. 10, 1747: A.D.H.A., G 829. The "*marguilliers*" of Tallard are mentioned in a letter from curé Bernard to the bishop, Mar. 11, 1765: A.D.H.A., G 966. There were also apparently no *fabriques* in most parishes of Provence and, in many cases, no *marguilliers*: Jean Roy, *Le prêtre paroissial dans deux diocèses provençaux: Aix et Arles au XVIIIe siècle, société et religion* (Thèse de troisième cycle, Université d'Aix-Marseilles I, 1975), pp. 102–104.

by the curé himself.[62] Thus, many curés would never have been exposed to the lay parish officials, who, in other regions of France, were among the most dangerous institutional rivals to their authority.[63]

The Problems of the *Casuel* and the Tithes

Perhaps the most common sources of conflict between priest and parish were the revenues paid by the parishioners to the curé himself. During his pastoral visits bishop Pérouse found that the *casuel* gave rise to endless wrangling in certain parishes.[64] Many people paid only grudgingly and only after a certain amount of bargaining with the curés. Some priests, on the other hand, even required payment for administering the sacraments—when only offerings freely given should be accepted—or threatened not to perform their services at all if fees were not paid in advance. Others were reported to have issued certificates allowing parishioners to move to other parishes only after being paid in advance for all the services that might eventually have been rendered—marriage banns, churching, burial, etc.—had the individuals remained in the home parish. Such mercenary activities on the part of the parish clergy were clearly exceptional; Pérouse was careful to stress the attitude of Christian charity shown in this matter by most of his curés. Yet the *casuel* would continue to cause

[62] The *marguilliers* in some provinces also had authority over the upkeep of the church, rectory, and cemetery, which, in the diocese of Gap—as we have seen—were in the charge of the community officials. See Daniel Jousse, *Traité du gouvernement spirituel et temporel des paroisses* (Paris, 1769), pp. 113–115.

[63] For the problems between the curé and the *marguilliers* see Gérard Bouchard, *Le village immobile: Senneley-en-Sologne au XVIIIe siècle* (Paris, 1972), pp. 216–223; Albert Babeau, *Le village sous l'Ancien régime* (3rd ed.; Paris, 1882), pp. 131–143; Vaissière, pp. 272–279; John McManners, *French Ecclesiastical Society under the Ancien Régime* (Manchester, 1960), pp. 151–162.

[64] Pastoral letter, May 10, 1762: A.D.H.A., G 816. On the nature of the *casuel*, see above, Chapter V.

irritation and bad feelings until it was abolished at the time
of the Revolution. In 1789, the villagers would complain
against this "unjust institution that forces the parishioners
to pay twice for the same service. . . ."[65] But clergymen
themselves were only too sensitive to the hostility engendered by these fees, which were, as one group of curés put
it, "a disgrace for the minister and the ministry . . . an
impediment to the work of God, destroying the parishioners' confidence in their curés."[66] Even before the Revolution, many parish priests would demand that the *casuel*
be suppressed.[67]

If the *casuel* was a source of irritation, the tithes could
be a fundamental barrier to good relations between clergymen and lay society. For the Church in the diocese of Gap,
the tithes constituted by far the greatest single source of
income. For the peasant, they represented an annual loss
of some two to ten percent of their total revenues from
agriculture and livestock. It is not surprising, then, that
questions involving the tithes formed the single most important grounds for suits between parishioners and the
Church.[68]

There were, to be sure, relatively few attempts to avoid
paying the tithes altogether. The man who simply harvested
his crop without notifying the prior-curé,[69] and the peasant
who lived in one parish and furtively cultivated an isolated
plot in another without paying the tithes,[70] were apparently

[65] *I.e.*, they had already paid the tithes for the curé's services: "Observations sur la dîme" by the community of Upaix: A.D.I., III C 34.
See also Montmorin's protest against the *casuel*: Guillaume, *Recueil
des réponses*, p. 286.

[66] "Mémoire des curés du diocèse de Gap," *ca.* 1765: A.N., G⁸*
2523, no. 408.

[67] *Ibid.*; several curés made such demands to bishop Vareilles: "Etat
des curés à portion congrue," Jan. 12, 1786: A.N., G⁸ 68 (dossier Gap);
see also the *cahier des doléances* of the curé of Serres: *AA*, XIII (1909),
209; and the *Cahier des curés de Dauphiné* (Lyon, 1789), p. 113.

[68] See above, note 8.

[69] Curé François Bellon of Verclause vs. Etienne Gaillard, 1777:
A.D.D., B 2201.

[70] Curé Antoine Abert of Sorbiers vs. Antoine Richaud of Montjai,
1755: A.D.H.A., B 550.

isolated cases. It is unlikely that many eighteenth-century peasants ever put into question the basic principle of the tithes, especially insofar as the latter were actually used to pay their pastor.[71] But there were numerous allegations of cheating on the full payment of the tithes: slipping a part of the wheat into the barn before the collector arrived, or arranging for the tithe owner's sheaves to be smaller and of poorer quality.[72] And there were ample possibilities of legal haggling over the practices of tithe collection, the rates, the items to be taxed, and the stage during the harvest when the tax was to be levied. From 1774, one community after another won suits in the Parlement of Dauphiné allowing them to change the mode of tithe collection, effectively diminishing the tithers' portion of the crop.[73]

In all problems concerning the tithes, the prior-curés and the salaried curés were in fundamentally different positions with regards to their parishioners. There was always a considerable potential for friction between a tithe-owning parish priest and his flock, even if the great majority of

[71] George V. Taylor found demands for abolishing the tithes in the *cahiers de doléances* of only five percent of the 428 parishes and *bourgs* in his sample: "Revolutionary and Non-revolutionary Content in the *Cahiers* of 1789: an Interim Report," *French Historical Studies*, VII (1972), p. 499, table 5. See also Paul Bois, *Paysans de l'ouest* (abridged ed.; Paris, 1971), p. 308; and Henri Marion, *La dîme ecclésiastique en France au XVIIIe siècle et sa suppression* (Bordeaux, 1912), pp. 194–214.

[72] *E.g.*, curé Mévouilhon of Manteyer vs. Antoine Clément, *ménager*, 1764: A.D.H.A., B 554; curé Bois of Saléon vs. Jean Gondre, 1775: A.D.H.A., B 566; tithe farmer Jean Ricou-Réalon of Orcières vs. Jean Meizel, 1783: A.D.H.A., B 574.

[73] An ordinance of Parlement, Dec. 1780, allowed the community of Chabottes to have wheat tithes collected on the fields before the sheaves were brought together in stacks (*gerbiers*). This meant that the tithe farmer had to travel all over the parish to collect his duties. If the farmer did not arrive after a few hours' advance notice, a peasant could gather up his share of the sheafs and simply leave the tithes on the field. Verification of the tithes was consequently far more difficult. (For this reason, the community of Chabottes was accused by the tithe farmer of systematic tithe fraud in 1782: A.D.H.A., B 573.) Similar rulings seem to have been made in favor of the communities of Aspremont (1775), Forest-Saint-Julien (1782), and Saint-Laurent-du-Cros (1784): notice by bishop Vareilles to agents-general, 1786: A.N., G⁸ 68 (dossier Gap).

the people accepted the principle of the Church's dues. Some curés felt that they must be ever vigilant and suspicious of their parishioners, ready to pursue them in court if necessary to avoid establishing precedents that could eventually diminish their tithes.[74] A defensive, possessive attitude was engendered that was hardly propitious for a genial relationship with the people. Thus, a terrible feud between Arnoux, curé of Les Infournas, and a peasant family, in which the priest allegedly beat a pregnant woman, all stemmed from Arnoux's suspicions that the family was cheating on their vegetable tithes.[75] On occasion, the parish priest became locked in legal struggles with the entire parish, as when the prior-curés of Laragne and Arzeliers were sued by the officials of their respective communities over whether the tithes were to be collected in sheaves or on the threshing floor and whether hemp was a tithable item.[76] Perhaps even more frequent were disputes over certain secondary responsibilities impinging on a curé tithe owner: the upkeep of the choir and bell tower of the church, the furnishing of the *vingt-quatrième*, or the salary of a vicaire. The curé of Laborel battled with the parish for more than twenty-five years over his refusal to pay a vicaire for certain of the outlying hamlets.[77]

The situation of the salaried parish priest was altogether different. It was not he, but the *fermier* of the non-resident tithe owner who appeared before the peasant at harvest time to collect the Church's portion of the crops. The curé himself was effectively aloof from the animosities and litiga-

[74] *E.g.*, the complaint by Abert, prior-curé of Sorbiers against Antoine Richaud, 1755: A.D.H.A., B 550.

[75] Jean-Jacques Davin, *ménager* vs. Arnoux, 1770: A.D.H.A., B 562.

[76] *Mémoire* to agents-general, *ca.* 1783: A.N., G⁸* 2728; and *Consultations, vu les pièces du procès des consuls et communautés d'Arzeliers et Laragne contre les sieurs prieurs-curés des paroisses d'Arzeliers et Laragne* (Grenoble, 1782).

[77] Letters by François Abel, curé, to the bishop or vicar-general, *ca.* Aug. 1765, Sept. 26 and Oct. 8, 1765: A.D.H.A., G 966; letter, Mar. 7, 1785: A.D.H.A., G 978; three *mémoires* to the agents-general, June-July 1780: A.N., G⁸* 2537, nos. 830, 832, 834.

tion this tax might incite within the parish. In fact, the logical outcome was to bring priest and parish closer together, united against a common adversary, the non-resident "prior." The congruist curé's natural antagonist in matters of church finances was not the parish but the tithe owner. The latter was responsible not only for the salaries of curé and secondary, but also for the maintenance of the sacred ornaments, the upkeep of portions of the church, and the *menues fournitures* whenever the parish had no *fabrique*. On occasion, curé and parish might even work together in joint law suits concerning these questions. The curés of both Saint-Pierre-d'Avez and Montjai would act in close cooperation with their respective communities in forcing the priors to provide certain sacred vases and vestments;[78] the curé and community of La Motte-en-Champsaur did likewise in an attempt to obtain money for a parish vicaire.[79] The congruist curé of Chabottes even went so far as to support the community in its efforts to diminish the amount of the crop paid in tithes.[80] In Dauphiné the exceptionally large proportion of salaried curés—as compared to most other areas of France—may actually have lessened the potentialities of conflict between priest and parish.

Popular Revolts against the Curé

Most of the problems we have just examined arose, in reality, as conflicts between the parish priest and other

[78] *Mémoire pour la communauté de Montjai contre M. Tournu, prieur majeur* (Grenoble, 1782): see below, Chapter IX; Jean-Louis Martel, curé of Saint-Pierre-d'Avez vs. Sandilleau, commander of Joucas and prior, 1786: A.D.H.A., B 576.

[79] Letters by curé Joseph Borelly and the community of La Motte to the bishop of Gap, Dec. 2, 1787, May 26 and Sept. 17, 1788: A.D.H.A., G 986.

[80] Antoine Brochier, tithe farmer vs. Chabottes, deposition by Jean-Baptiste Léautier, April 13, 1782: A.D.H.A., B 573. Curé Peauroy was reported to have said that "en donnant une petite gerbe pour la dîme, on remplissait son obligation."

local notables. Even the disputes over the tithes or church repairs were often pushed most energetically by a few dignitaries, large landowners themselves for whom a great deal more was at stake than for the common peasant.[81] The net effect of such disputes on the priest's position in the community seems difficult to assess and may have been slight. But occasionally one encounters instances of the hostility and dissatisfaction of a broad segment of the parish toward the curé. Complaints against Martin, curé of Lemps, were so numerous and widespread that the bishop was obliged to call him in for a personal interrogation.[82] The people of Chabottonnes, under the threat of a *monitoire*—excommunication for failure to reveal the truth to an ecclesiastical commissioner—manifested a deep dislike, even hatred, for their prior-curé, François Avon.[83] Prior-curé Rappellin of Barret-le-Bas was attacked by eleven heads of household, who claimed they represented many more.[84] Large-scale protests have also been found against prior-curé Abel of Laborel and Escallier, vicaire of Montjai.[85]

In cases such as these, a veritable revolt of the parishioners could arise against the curé. All the dictums about the sanctity of the priest's person and his divinely ordained mission were pushed aside, and strong pressures were brought to bear to force the priest to resign his cure and leave the parish. Court suits or appeals to episcopal authority were not the only tactics that might be used. Some peo-

---

[81] The leaders of the suit concerning the tithes in Chabottes were reportedly "les plus riches et les plus en place": complaint by Antoine Brochier, tithe farmer, Apr. 6, 1782: A.D.H.A., B 573.

[82] Register of the secretariat of the bishops, Dec. 29, 1758: A.D.H.A., G 814.

[83] Suit between François Avon and unknown parties, 1774–1775: A.D.H.A., B 565.

[84] Complaint addressed to the bishop, *ca.* April 1785: A.D.H.A., G 974.

[85] Letters from Abel to the bishop, Sept. 26 and Oct. 8, 1765: A.D.H.A., G 966; complaint by Vaucluse (hamlet of Montjai) addressed to the bishop, Aug. 8, 1787: A.D.H.A., G 978.

ple expressed their discontent through passive resistance, refusing to confess to the curé in question, or attending mass but declining to participate in the liturgy.[86] Others resorted to open violence. Abel and Avon found the crops on their glebe cut down.[87] Martin was physically attacked and beaten by two men in the courtyard of the priory.[88] It was also possible and very effective to incite the parish children to riot against the curé, shouting insults or throwing stones. The latter technique was apparently used in forcing the resignation of the curé of Salérans and was threatened against Rappellin.[89]

The precise origins of popular revolts of this kind are often difficult to ascertain, for there was usually an accumulation of grievances from many different individuals. Some kinds of financial problems usually came into play. Martin was accused of overcharging for the *casuel*. Rappellin was said to pay too little for the *vingt-quatrième*; and both curés reportedly kept parish money—designated for repairs or decorations—for their personal use. Avon was continually bringing law suits against the people of the village, "ruining his parishioners in debts."[90] Yet the most vehement complaints seemed to concern certain moral failings on the part of the priests: physical violence, anger and vindictiveness, the use of foul language, or improprieties with women. Martin frequently swore in public, insulted, badgered, and beat his parishioners, including the children. (The curé admitted beating the children, but only

[86] Martin, curé of Bruis, vs. several individuals in Montmorin (where Martin was serving as a temporary replacement), 1760: A.D.H.A., F 1450.

[87] Abel to bishop, Oct. 8, 1765: A.D.H.A., G 966; Avon vs. unknown, 1774–1775: A.D.H.A., B 565.

[88] *Procureur du roi* vs. unknown, 1758: *dossier judiciaire* held in the rectory of Rémuzat.

[89] Personal reply of Joseph Moulet, May 25, 1784: A.D.H.A., G 974. The problems between the curé of Salérans and his parishioners are also recounted in book III of the *Landriade*: A.D.H.A., ms. 342.

[90] In 1756–1758 he was involved in suits with Joseph Julien and Joseph Faure-Perrin concerning a boundary dispute: A.D.H.A., B 551.

during catechism and when they deserved it.) Escallier not only cursed and quarreled with everyone, but was sometimes seen cutting wood or hauling hay, activities unfitting to the status of a priest. Rappellin and Avon were accused of similar irascibility, violence and anger improper for a curé. All four were found to be much too familiar with the women of the parish. Escallier, Martin, and Rappellin were accused of wrongdoings with their servant women. Avon was less interested in the children than in the children's mothers, while Rappellin amused the village women by playing his fiddle on the porch at night (as a prelude to enticing them into the barn, or so certain husbands believed).[91] There was probably no area in which the parishioners exercised a more critical scrutiny over their curé than in his relations with women. His sexual purity was considered to be part and parcel of his religious holiness. The village men were perhaps particularly sensitive on this score and fearful of the fascination that such purity might have for the women.

Of course, in all of these cases it is sometimes difficult to distinguish fact from rumor and hearsay. Yet it seems clear that the parishioners, no less than the bishops themselves, had a firm idea of the *esprit ecclésiastique*, the moral standards that an individual in the role of curé should meet. Even the common man had a clear preconception of what a good curé should be, and the transgression or suspected transgression of such standards could be a prime justification for revolting against him.

On the whole, the instances of parish uprisings were probably relatively rare. It is significant that the people of the Champsaur, in their depositions, found that Avon was "not a curé like the other curés," and they compared him unfavorably with parish priests in the valley on whom they could rely (the *"curés de confiance"*).[92] But the five or six cases examined here do illustrate the potential pressure

91 See cases cited above.
92 Case cited above, depositions of, *e.g.*, Madeleine Chabre, Catherine Lagier, Augustin Escallier.

the parishioners could exert on the curé whenever, for any reason, they disapproved of his actions and he lost their confidence. In the following chapter, we shall examine the influence the laymen could wield over their parish priests in the sphere of religion itself.

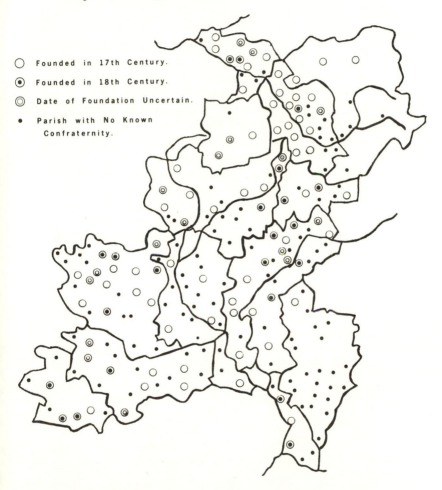

○ Founded in 17th Century.

◉ Founded in 18th Century.

◎ Date of Foundation Uncertain.

● Parish with No Known Confraternity.

FIGURE T.

Regional distribution of confraternities of the Penitents

CHAPTER VIII

Patterns of Religious Rivalry

LAY CONFRATERNITIES

The basic unit of lay participation within the Church was the parish. Every Catholic, by virtue of his baptism or present residence, was a member of such a unit and was required by the laws of the Church—and sometimes of the State—to fulfill a minimum of religious rites in the presence and through the mediation of the priests attached to that parish.[1] At least since the Middle Ages, the Church had also encouraged the formation within the parish of associations of laymen desirous of expressing religious devotion beyond the basic requirements. The confraternities or sodalities, as the associations were called, were to bring together a lay religious elite of the village in the practice of various pious exercises and in the execution of charitable good works for fellow members and for the community at large. The confraternities could thus help to channel the villagers' natural social inclinations toward the service of religion and the Church.[2]

In the eighteenth-century diocese of Gap, there was a broad assortment of lay confraternities with which the

---

[1] As a bare minimum, every parishioner was to confess and take communion once a year, at Easter, and participate in the various Christian rites of passage, from baptism to extreme unction. On the legal requirements of practicing Catholicism see Gabriel Le Bras, "L'obligation juridique de pratiquer la religion chrétienne sous l'Ancien régime," in *Etudes de sociologie religieuse*, 2 vols. (Paris, 1955–1956), I, 25–26.

[2] The most useful works on confraternities under the Old Regime are Gabriel Le Bras, "Les confréries chrétiennes, problèmes et propositions," *Revue historique de droit français et étranger*, 4e série, XIX–XX (1940–1941), pp. 310–363; and Maurice Agulhon, *Pénitents et Francs-Maçons de l'ancienne Provence (Essai sur la sociabilité méridionale)* (Paris, 1968).

parish clergy might come into contact. Various episcopal registers indicate the existence toward mid-century of at least 343, situated in 164—or 77 percent—of the parishes of the diocese.[3] Inevitably, some of these associations were far more active than others. But if the degree of vitality and activity is usually impossible to measure, it is interesting to note that at least 90 were founded in the eighteenth century, including 16 after 1749.[4]

As for their ostensible objectives, 45 confraternities were dedicated to devotion of the Virgin, the Holy Spirit, the Trinity, or specific saints in the celestial hierarchy.[5] Another 59 were organized around particular devotional rites, such as the Blessed Sacrament, the Souls in Purgatory, or the Sacred Heart.[6] There were also at least 4 professional confraternities—all in Gap—closely associated with guilds[7]

[3] Principal sources: the "registre général" of confraternities, 1695: A.D.H.A., G 939; pastoral visits of 1710–1713 and 1740–1741: A.D.H.A., G 787–788; register of approbations, 1745–1779: A.D.H.A., G 829–830; and various isolated references in A.D.H.A., series G.

[4] Thus of the 291 for which the approximate dates of foundation are known, 31 percent were founded in the eighteenth century. Among these were 23 confraternities of Penitents, 37 dedicated to the Rosary, 13 to the Blessed Sacrament, 5 to the Sacred Heart, 3 to Saint Joseph, and 9 to various other saints or rites. The latest foundations in the century were in 1764 for the Penitents (Reilhanette), 1765 for the Rosary (Saint-Genis), and 1789 for the Sacred Heart (Savournon and La Chapelle-en-Valgaudemar). In fact, the impetus to found new confraternities may have continued longer in the diocese of Gap than in many other regions of France: *cf.* Le Bras, "Les confréries chrétiennes," pp. 329–330.

[5] Holy Spirit (two confraternities), Holy Trinity (2), Holy Family (1), Notre Dame (4—not including those dedicated to the Rosary), Saint Joseph (12), Sainte Monique (1), Sainte Barbe (3), Sainte Anne (4), Sainte Claire (1), Saint Sébastien (2), Saint Jean-Baptiste (1), Saint Jacques (1), Saint Blaise et Saint Eloy (5), Saint Antoine (2), Saint Laurent (1), Saint Fabien (1), Saint Grégoire (1), Saint Pancrace (1).

[6] Blessed Sacrament (41 confraternities), Tiers-Ordre (6), Sacred Heart (5), Souls in Purgatory (3), Scapular (3), Immaculate Conception (1).

[7] Sainte Luce (tailors and shoemakers), Saints Cosme and Damien (surgeons), Notre-Dame-de-l'Assomption (spinners and weavers), Saint Joseph (carpenters and masons). A few others may have existed in the

and 12 associations designed for service to the poor.[8] The majority of these groups are known to us as scarcely more than names in registers: little can be determined of their activities or membership. Two, however, are somewhat better documented: the confraternities of the Rosary and of the Penitents. These were the most widespread—there were at least 129 confraternities of the Rosary, 96 of the Penitents (see Figures K and T)—and probably the most highly organized of the religious groupings, and they were forces to be reckoned with by the majority of the curés of the diocese.

The confraternities of the Rosary seem always to have been primarily organizations for women. The members were 63 percent women in the Rosary of Ribiers, 81 percent in the Rosary of Barcillonnette at the beginning of the century, and in both the proportion of men seems to have decreased in the course of the century.[9] The requirements of active membership were uncomplicated, well suited for the largely illiterate women of the peasant communities. All were expected to attend the special prayer sessions dedicated to the Virgin throughout the year, and to recite the Rosary in unison before the altar specifically consecrated to that effect within the parish church. Confraternity masses might also be held if there was enough money in the treasury to pay a priest. If all the regulations were followed, a member could hope to participate in the special

---

larger *bourgs*, but have not been specifically identified. All professional confraternities were abolished by the edict of February 1776.

[8] La charité or Dames de la charité (9 confraternities) and La miséricorde or Dames de la miséricorde (3).

[9] A. C. Ribiers, GG 9–10: approximately 41 of 65 members were women in 1702; the percentage would appear to have been higher in the 1760's, although no complete list is available for that period. A. C. Barcillonnette, GG 1: 96 of 118 members were women in 1727; only one male parishioner was admitted between 1760 and 1777. The feminine dominance in Serres is confirmed by Louis Jacques, *Les confréries de Serres*, ms. in A.E. Gap. For the diocese of Die, see Jacques Lovie, "La vie paroissiale dans le diocèse de Die à la fin de l'Ancien régime," *BD*, LXIV, no. 257 (1933), pp. 32–38.

indulgences issued by the Pope. In addition to the purely devotional activities, the members marched together as a group in processions, proudly displaying their confraternity's banner—if they had been able to afford one. A few of the members were usually chosen to care for the altar and to add decorations for feast day assemblies. Charitable functions may also have been attached to some of the confraternities: thus two of the officers in Serres were named *dames de charité*. None of the Rosary confraternities, however, seems to have been wealthy. The account books show budgets of only 10 or 20 *livres* per year coming from membership dues, offerings, or small legacies. Their few possessions consisted of the vestments and chalice that their chaplain was to use and perhaps a processional banner.[10]

While the Rosary confraternity existed in many regions of France,[11] the confraternity of the Penitents was a phenomenon typical of southern France and the Mediterranean regions.[12] Dressed in their ceremonial costumes—long white robes and pointed sack-like hoods with holes cut for the eyes—the Penitents were one of the most picturesque elements of parish life in the diocese. While the Rosary was an organization primarily for women, the Penitents comprised the most common masculine religious association. To be sure, women could be admitted as members; their numbers were even on the increase in certain of the societies in the later eighteenth century:[13] the sexual dichotomy between the Rosary and the Penitents was never clear-cut.

10 See previous note.

11 *E.g.*, in the diocese of La Rochelle: Louis Pérouas, *Le diocèse de La Rochelle de 1648 à 1724: sociologie et pastorale* (Paris, 1964), map p. 501; in the diocese of Paris, Jeanne Ferté, *La vie religieuse dans les campagnes parisiennes (1622–1695)* (Paris, 1962), p. 75.

12 Agulhon, p. 87.

13 No women appeared in the Penitents of Bruis until 1732, fourteen years after the foundation: A. C. Bruis, GG 1. There were no women among the Penitents of Chauvac between 1721 and 1768, but from 1768 to 1789, 20 of 32 new members were women: "livre ou catalogue des Pénitents blancs": A. E. Valence, O 18.

Yet women were always a minority and they seem generally to have been excluded from voting, from officeholding, and from wearing the confraternity's ceremonial garb.[14] Although the socio-economic status of the members is usually difficult to determine, the Penitents of Serres, Neffes, and Châteauvieux-de-Tallard appear to have represented virtually all professions and all but the very poorest members of the parish.[15] But in each of these three confraternities and in the Penitents of Gap, the local notables—community officials, officeholders, professional men—formed an important contingent.[16]

The avowed goal of the Penitents was to do penance, through prayer and supplication, for the transgressions of men against God, and thus to obtain special indulgences for Purgatory. The members met every Sunday morning and on all the major feast days to say their offices, usually just prior to the parish mass. They also took their place in all of the parish processions, especially those on Holy Thursday and on the feast days of the Virgin. In addition, the entire confraternity was to meet and to provide ceremonial pomp at the death of any of its members. They accompanied the curé as he carried extreme unction and the Viaticum through the village to a member's home. At the

[14] Registers of Penitents: A. C. Châteauvieux, GG 1; A. C. Neffes, GG 3; A. C. Bruis, GG 4; A. E. Valence, O 18 (Chauvac); A. E. Gap, *liasse* on Penitents of Gap; statutes of Penitents of Reilhanette, ca. 1764: A.D.H.A., G 966.

[15] Jacques, cited above. In Châteauvieux and Neffes, the members and officers of the Penitents have been located on the *capitation* rolls of 1790: A.D.H.A., L 499 and L 1234. All the rural professions—from *journalier* to artisan to officeholder—were represented. The taxes paid ranged from well below the average to nearly the highest in the communities.

[16] *Ibid.*; also A. E. Gap, *liasse* on Penitents. On the list of the Penitents of Gap paying dues in 1781, one finds the names of many of the notaries, lawyers, and wealthy merchants of the city. We have not attempted, in the context of the present study, a careful statistical approach to test the validity for the Hautes-Alpes of Agulhon's thesis, *i.e.*, that the notables were deserting the Penitents at the end of the eighteenth century. But one has the impression that the thesis does not hold in Gap.

funeral itself, they marched in their ghostly apparel, torches lit, drums beating, carrying the corpse face-upward on a plank. Commonly, even the families of non-members would pay the Penitents to provide a baroque orchestration for the burial of a loved one, so that they had virtually assumed the function of a village burial society. It was perhaps in this role that they were best known to the rural community as a whole.[17]

For centuries, certain of the religious sodalities had posed threats to the clergy by their independent and unruly conduct.[18] But within the diocese of Gap, the differences in the membership and the activities of the Rosary and the Penitents put the two confraternities in distinctly different relations with the local parish clergy. The ladies of the Rosary seem always to have been under the close tutelage of the curés. In Serres, Barcillonnette, Ribiers, and probably in most of the other confraternities, the parish priest served as director, chaplain, and secretary of the Rosary.[19] Many of the women assisted the curé in the simple but necessary tasks of sweeping out the church and adding decorations. Perhaps, like the ladies of charity in Malijai, they also served the curé in a vigilante role, informing him of sexual misconduct or other "scandal" in the parish.[20] The Rosary confraternities were, in fact, strongly encouraged by the clergy throughout the eighteenth century. Malissoles had urged all curés to aid their foundation in the parishes and had often taken part in their establishment during his pastoral visits.[21] The curés seem to have readily followed their bishop's lead well into the century,

[17] Arnold Van Gennep, *Le folklore des Hautes-Alpes*, 2 vols. (Paris, 1946–1948), I, 175–180; Agulhon, pp. 86–123; Lovie, *BD*, no. 260, pp. 169–183; statutes of Penitents of Reilhanette: A.D.H.A., G 966.

[18] Le Bras, "Les confréries chrétiennes," pp. 351–352.

[19] Jacques, cited above; A. C. Barcillonnette, GG 1; A. C. Ribiers, GG 9–10.

[20] Statutes of "Les dames de la charité et miséricorde" of Malijai, 1738: A.D.H.A., G 960.

[21] *Ord. syn.*, I, 246–247; A.D.H.A., G 987, f. 10, 21–23.

influencing their parishioners to embellish chapels and to send in official requests for confraternities.[22] In general, disputes between the parish priest and the Rosary confraternity were extremely rare.[23]

The potentialities for conflict between the priest and the Penitents were always present. Dominated by men, including many of the leading village notables, the association wielded considerable emotional authority by virtue of its social and folkloric functions in the community. The Penitents' chapel was usually quite distinct from the parish church, whether in the tribune at one end of the church or in an entirely separate building elsewhere in the village.[24] Several of the confraternities, especially in the south of the diocese, possessed independent incomes from land or rents.[25] Some even had their private chaplains.[26] Throughout the eighteenth century, the curés would complain against Penitents who attempted to escape their authority. The members refused to consult the curé on their budget and expenditures or before admitting new individuals to the brotherhood.[27] They insisted on holding proces-

[22] See the requests by curés for founding Rosary confraternities in Charbillac, Sept. 9, 1747; in Nibles, Oct. 10, 1749; in Savoillan, Oct. 12, 1750: A.D.H.A., G 829.

[23] We have found only one such conflict, concerning the right to name the woman director of the Rosary of Châteauneuf-de-Chabre: but this seems to have been primarily a dispute between the curé and the village notables, who themselves claimed the right of nomination (see above, Chapter VII), A.D.H.A., G 2668.

[24] As a rule, the separate chapels were most common in the south of the diocese (*e.g.*, in Lachau, Barret-le-Bas, Ballons, Ventavon, Tallard, Salignac, La Rochette-sur-Saint-Auban, Plaisians, Montbrand, and Ribiers) and the tribune chapels were most common in the north (*e.g.*, in Aspres-sur-Buëch, Manteyer, Saint-Laurent-en-Beaumont, Saint-Michel-en-Beaumont, La Salle-en-Beaumont, Corps, Le Noyer, La Fare, Montmaur, and Saint-Bonnet): A.D.H.A., G 788, G 790, G 829–830, G 953, G 984.

[25] *E.g.*, this was the case of the Penitents of Lardier, Jarjayes, and La Saulce: declarations of the confraternities of the District of Gap in the Year II (1793–1794): A.D.H.A., I Q I 111.

[26] *E.g.*, in Ribiers and Salignac.

[27] Complaints by the curé of Ribeyret in 1707: A.D.H.A., G 1101; by the curé of Salignac in 1754: A.D.H.A., G 829, f. 31; by the curé

sions and ceremonies after dark, when pious services might easily degenerate into open scandal.[28] But most galling, from the curé's point of view, the Penitents seemed to be establishing a kind of parallel religious cult, separate from and in competition with the regular parish mass. After attending their own offices, they neglected the curé's services or, worse yet, wandered off to the cabaret to drink during mass.[29] In some parishes where the Penitents had their own chaplain, even non-members flocked in to attend the confraternity's shorter mass, where no sermon was given, thus drawing away a large portion of the parish at the expense of the curé. Curé Albert's comment must have reflected the feelings of many parish priests in the diocese of Gap: ". . . while the Penitents' chapel is filled with people, all hurrying to sing a few psalms and hear a low mass, the principal parish church is deserted."[30]

Most curés, like Albert himself, had probably resigned themselves to the continued existence of the Penitents as a necessary evil.[31] They might, it was reasoned, serve a useful purpose in the conversion of the Protestants.[32] Tronquet, curé of Sahune, summarized his position in the journal which he kept: "To be sure, the confraternities are a source of considerable difficulty for a curé. From the very first they want to lord it over him, and if he should try prudently to indicate the abuses which so often slip into their activities, he must meekly and charitably swallow the

---

of Vaumeilh in 1772: A.D.H.A., G 2339. There were several general complaints by the curés in the "états des paroisses" of 1707: A.D.H.A., G 1098–1104 (*e.g.*, the curés of Valernes and Ribeyret).

[28] Curé of Ribeyret in 1707: A.D.H.A., G 1101; curé of L'Escale in 1787: A.D.H.A., G 981.

[29] Curé of Ribeyret: A.D.H.A., G 1101; curé of Lemps in 1737: A. C. Lemps, Parish Register, entry of Mar. 30, 1773.

[30] Antoine Albert, *Histoire géographique, naturelle, ecclésiastique, et civile du diocèse d'Embrun*, 2 vols. (Embrun, 1783–1786), II, 474. See also bishop Berger de Malissoles' comments in *Ord. syn.*, I, 179–180, and 242–250.

[31] Albert, II, 473–474.

[32] Curé of Montmorin in 1740: A.D.H.A., G 964.

little mortifications which are given to him in return. Nevertheless, the confraternities must be recognized as necessary and even useful for the spiritual and temporal welfare and the good government of the parish."[33] By 1789, amid growing political aspirations on the part of the parish clergy, many curés would come to view the Penitents with far less patience and forbearance, and some would eventually demand their complete suppression.[34]

PROCESSIONS

Throughout the history of the Church, the procession had played an important part in Christian ceremonial and pageantry, punctuating the liturgical year with solemn manifestations of group piety. Each year, in every parish of the diocese of Gap—and in France generally—the curé was expected to lead the people in a wide variety of processions. Some included only a portion of the parishioners, like those organized by the Penitents or Rosary confraternities; most welcomed the participation of all the inhabitants, even the children. The processions to the chapels of Notre-Dame-de-Paris in Saint-Jacques-en-Valgaudemar and Notre-Dame-du-Laus near La Bâtie-Neuve were veritable pilgrimages, drawing crowds from all over the diocese.[35] In addition to those processional days (such as Palm Sunday, Rogations, Corpus Christi, and Assumption) celebrated everywhere in Christendom, each parish had its own tradition of local processions. L'Escale had at least seven in

---

[33] "Mémorial" written *ca.* 1728: A.D.D., XXVII G 1. Sahune was in an enclave of the diocese of Sisteron, immediately adjoining the diocese of Gap.

[34] See below, Chapter X.

[35] See the pastoral visit to Saint-Jacques, May 22, 1772: A.D.H.A., G 790; also, the mention of a procession to Notre-Dame-du-Laus by the confraternity of the Immaculate Conception in Gap: episcopal ordinance, Feb. 26, 1754: A.D.H.A., G 829. The chapel of Le Laus, immediately adjacent to La Bâtie-Neuve, was actually in the territory of the diocese of Embrun.

addition to those prescribed in the ritual of the diocese.
Other parishes probably had far more than this.[36] The
routes taken by the marching congregations varied greatly,
depending on the parish and the occasion: around the
church, around the entire village, or out across the
countryside to a neighboring chapel or rural cross. The
longer processions often made a number of stops along the
way at various chapels, and deserted villages or cemeteries
where the people might pay their respects to the dead.[37]
Of special interest in the region of the southern French
Alps were those—usually occurring in late spring or early
summer—referred to by Van Gennep as "high-mountain
processions." The entire parish marched for several hours
over meadow and stream to one of the highest points in
the territory of the village, there often to be met by neighboring parishes arriving from the other side of the mountain. After the respective curés had pronounced their bless-
ings on the flocks, the lakes, and the pastures, everyone sat
down for a community picnic.[38] Such was the procession
of Aspremont to Lake Sagne on May 3 for the purification
of the waters and the health of the animals;[39] or the trek
to the chapel of Saint Joseph on "an extremely high moun-

[36] Joseph-Marie Maurel, *Histoire de l'Escale* (Forcalquier, 1893), p.
167. We have found no eighteenth-century source listing all the processions of the diocese by parish.

[37] The procession of Saint Jean in the parish of Saint-André-de-
Rosans stopped at a former cemetery to sing prayers for the dead:
Charles Bermond, "Saint-André-de-Rosans," *Quinzaine religieuse du
diocèse de Gap* (1926), p. 43; the parish of La Saulce did likewise during a procession to the mountain of Sainte-Croix: declaration of church
lands, Sept. 20, 1790: A.D.H.A., I Q I 107; there was a procession from
La Plaine to a spot in the middle of a field to commemorate the dead
of a village destroyed by an unknown disaster at an unknown date:
Van Gennep, I, 356–358.

[38] Van Gennep, I, 317–356. The late nineteenth-century descriptions
used by Van Gennep have been corroborated, for the most part, by
seventeenth, eighteenth, and early nineteenth-century documents.

[39] F. Allemand, "Notice sur les sources minérales, les fonts saints, et
les fonts bénits dans les Hautes-Alpes," *BHA*, XXIII (1904), p. 225.

taintop" by the people of Volonne, La Pérusse, and other parishes;[40] or the processions by Valserres and Remollon, carrying the relics of Saint Maurice to a holy well at the top of a mountain on the second feast of Pentecost.[41]

Prior to any such procession, the curé was carefully to instruct his parishioners on the religious significance of the event, stressing the solemnity of the occasion and the need to avoid all superstitious practices.[42] But, clearly, the spiritual meaning was but one dimension of the procession for the eighteenth-century rural villager. The close connection between many of the processions and the agricultural or pastoral cycles is apparent. Whatever the theological subtleties employed, it was difficult for the common peasant to distinguish an ecclesiastical benediction from a magical curative or prophylactic rite. The processions are thus to be set in the context of a broader network of folklore, magic, and popular religion of which the Christian cult was only one aspect.[43] There was also an obvious recreational function attached to the processions. They were one of the few means of allaying the monotony, escaping the drudgery of agricultural concerns. To believe the various episcopal ordinances, the secular festivities accompanying the longer processions sometimes fell entirely out of hand. A holiday atmosphere reigned, with drinking and dancing and stragglers of different sexes disappearing into the brush.[44]

Finally, the parish processions held important symbolic social meaning. They were tangible representations of the parish society's conception of itself.[45] The entire village was marching together as a unit, an event that, as Gérard Bou-

---

[40] Pastoral visit to La Pérusse, Oct. 3, 1761: A.D.H.A., G 790; also, episcopal ordinance of June 11, 1754: A.D.H.A., G 829.

[41] Bishop's ordinance, May 4, 1786: A.D.H.A., G 974; also Van Gennep, I, 341–342.

[42] *Ord. syn.*, I, 278–287.

[43] See the following section of the present chapter.

[44] *Ord. syn.*, I, 278–287; ordinance of Mar. 15, 1788: A.D.H.A., G 992; ordinance of Feb. 22, 1748: A.D.H.A., G 829.

[45] See William A. Christian, *Person and God in a Spanish Valley* (New York, 1972), p. 70.

chard has suggested, perhaps helped to reinforce the cohesiveness and solidarity of the village society.[46] It also
frequently served as a representation of the status hierarchy existing in the parish. Everyone, dressed in his finest
apparel, suggestive of his rank or profession, took his place
in an order of march exactly prescribed by ordinance or
tradition. Thus in the Corpus Christi procession in Veynes,
the curé came first, carrying the Blessed Sacrament and
walking under a white canopy carried by the mayor and the
four councilmen; then came the other clergymen, followed
in turn by the local nobility, the officeholders, and the rest
of the parishioners grouped by confraternity, sex, and age.
One year, the members of the local confraternity of the
Blessed Sacrament had claimed the right to accompany the
curé and the Host by virtue of their religious position. But
the Veynes notables refused to allow "that kind of people"
to walk ahead of them in the procession.[47] In the city of Gap,
the procession of the patron Saint Arey was even more complex, with the bishop, the cathedral canons, the religious
congregations, and the various guilds also included.[48] The
procession might therefore be the perfect occasion for anyone with ambitious social pretensions to make his move.
When one of the noblemen tried this at the Veynes Corpus
Christi proceedings, suddenly moving one step ahead of his
"co-seigneur" counterpart, the procession degenerated into
a pushing and shouting match in the very center of the
church.[49] Such confrontations were probably not uncommon, and every curé had to be prepared for verbal or physical battles over precedence in the midst of supposedly
solemn ceremonies.[50]

[46] Gérard Bouchard, *Le village immobile, Sennely-en-Sologne au
XVIIIe siècle* (Paris, 1972), p. 306.
[47] Suit between D'Aiguebelle and De La Villette, 1754: A.D.H.A.,
B 549.
[48] Episcopal ordinance, Mar. 15, 1788: A.D.H.A., G 992.
[49] A.D.H.A., B 549.
[50] *Ord. syn.*, i, 278–287. Note also the confrontation between Jean,
vicaire of Brantes, and the village notary when the former tried to
assume the lead of the procession of the Blessed Sacrament: A.D.H.A.,
G 970.

During the second half of the eighteenth century in the diocese of Gap and in other dioceses in France, certain bishops began trying to limit or altogether abolish many of the parish processions. Some, it was felt, were no longer attended by a large enough group of participants. This was the principal reason given for the suspension of the procession of the Blessed Sacrament, which formerly circled the entire city of Gap on the Sunday after the Nativity of the Virgin. Despite the vigorous efforts of the curés, the procession "instead of being a ceremony for the edification of the parish has become something of a scandal by its lack of attendance."[51] There were characteristic popularity cycles through which most processions passed, from the initial enthusiasm at their creation to a gradual decline in interest on the part of later generations.[52] There was also the perennial problem of lay misconduct and "scandal" and general lack of seriousness during the processions. The rural and high-mountain processions were the special target of criticism in this regard. In 1754 the bishop tried to limit the number celebrated in L'Escale and probably in other parishes,[53] and eventually Bishop Jouffroy-Gonssans put a general interdiction on saying mass in country chapels, effectively sabotaging many of the rural processions.[54] Finally,

[51] Ordinances of bishop, Nov. 8 and Dec. 12, 1787: A.D.H.A., G 991.

[52] In 1707, Berger de Malissoles noted that "il n'arrive que trop souvent que les peuples dans leurs besoins pressants ont recours à Dieu et font des voeux d'aller en procession, et après quelques années ils oublient entièrement leurs voeux et y laissent aller leurs prêtres sans les y accompagner": *Ord. syn.*, I, 284. Christian, pp. 50–80, noted similar long-term historical cycles in the popularity of processions to different shrines in northern Spain.

[53] Maurel, p. 167.

[54] Requests by the curés of Valserres and Clamensane to the bishop, 1786: A.D.H.A., G 974. Jouffroy's ordinances have been lost, but they were perhaps similar to the ordinance he published in 1788, as bishop of Le Mans, confining all processions to the boundaries of the parish and limiting them to a maximum duration of one hour: A. D. Sarthe, 2 J 104 (Girault). Bishop Hay de Bonteville seems to have forbidden all high-mountain processions in the diocese of Grenoble in the 1780's: Pierre Grimaud, L'état des esprits en Dauphiné et la question religieuse

some ecclesiastical notables were coming to the conclusion that it was beyond the dignity of bishops, canons, or other clergymen to go marching through the countryside in full priestly attire. Thus, when bishop Vareilles modified Gap's yearly procession of Saint Arey from a rural to an intra-city event, he declared that "it is without precedent that an entire cathedral chapter, led by its bishop . . . should march in procession over paths like these to a little, isolated chapel in the middle of the countryside."[55] The regular canons of La Baume-lès-Sisteron seem to have followed a similar line of reasoning in abolishing a monthly procession in their parish.[56]

The various arguments used by the clergy were unconvincing to the lay parishioners, who vigorously protested the suppression of their processions and who perhaps, after all, had a very different conception of the meaning of religious ceremony and dignity than that of the elite of the Church. The notables of Gap were furious against the bishop for tampering with the procession of Saint Arey, one of the great social events of the year. When the bishop refused to change his ordinance, the municipal officers vowed to boycott the ceremony altogether.[57] Numerous complaints and petitions were also received at the episcopal palace from villages demanding that the rural or high-mountain processions be reestablished and appealing to the "immemorial tradition" on which the processions were based.[58]

à la fin de l'Ancien régime (D.E.S., Univ. of Aix-Marseilles, 1959), pp. 14–15.

[55] Ordinance of Mar. 15, 1788: A.D.H.A., G 992. The goal of the procession was changed from the rural chapel of Saint Arey to the chapel of the Capuchins at the edge of the city.

[56] Curé Grimaud to the bishop, letter, May 30, 1785: A.D.H.A., G 975. The canons claimed the paths they had to follow were too "difficiles."

[57] Deliberations of Mar. 3 and 24, 1788: A. C. Gap, BB 82.

[58] Letter from the community of Barras to the bishop, May 18, 1786: A.D.H.A., G 985. See also letters to the bishop from Valserres and Clamensane in 1786: A.D.H.A., G 974; and from Grimaud of La Baume-lès-Sisteron, May 30, 1785: A.D.H.A., G 975.

There is evidence that in other villages the bishops' interdictions were simply ignored and the processions continued as usual.[59] The position of the curés with regard to the processions was ambiguous. They too were wary of religious manifestations degenerating into popular festivals, and they were eager to have all such events kept under the strict discipline of the clergy. Yet many were not adverse to processions in general. Such ceremonies served, in fact, to spotlight their own special position in the society: marching at the forefront as leader of the flock. Confronted with the outrage of their parishioners, many curés were quick to come to the defense of the suppressed processions. They emphasized to the bishop the importance of the processions in the religious life of the people and the fact that the local devotional ceremony attracted many neighboring villagers.[60] Curé Grimaud complained bitterly that the discontinuing of one traditional procession "makes the people grumble and dampens their piety."[61] Curé Gassendi of Barras (later a deputy to the Estates General) asked that his high-mountain procession be reinstated in its traditional form "in order to revive and augment the piety of the faithful."[62]

At least one curé, however, Henri Reymond of La Bâtie-Neuve, seemed fully to accept the bishops' efforts to "purify" the processions.[63] The second year after he arrived in the parish, he had the bishop abolish an Assumption procession. He then brought pressure to have the high-mountain procession to Notre-Dame-de-Tournefort suppressed. This chapel, he argued, was a mere "hovel," indecent for the

---

[59] Maurel, p. 167.

[60] Letter from the community of Barras to the bishop (signed and undoubtedly written by curé Gassendi), May 18, 1786: A.D.H.A., G 985; Jacques, curé of Valserres, to the bishop, 1786: A.D.H.A., G 974.

[61] Letter to the bishop, May 30, 1785: A.D.H.A., G 975.

[62] A.D.H.A., G 974.

[63] Ms. transcriptions by Jules Chérias of documents in A. C. La Bâtie-Neuve: A.D.H.A., ms. 85. This curé is not to be confused with another Henri Reymond, curé in Vienne, who will be discussed in the following chapter.

mysteries of the Church. He also claimed that popular attendance had declined. In 1776 he found an excuse not even to appear at the procession, leaving only a tonsured cleric to lead the lay participants. The curé's actions led to a heated quarrel with several of the villagers, especially with the Penitents, who seemed to be the principal organizers of the procession. The latter attacked the curé for the "scandal" and "insult" he had committed against the community. In 1789, thinking back on a number of difficulties he had had with his parishioners, including the problem of the procession, Reymond would bitterly complain against the "fury of the fanatical common people" in La Bâtie-Neuve that neither he nor the bishop was able to control.[64]

FOLKLORE AND POPULAR RELIGION

In their relations with both the confraternities and the processional activities of the parish, the curés came to grips with powerful social realities that could not be ignored or lightly brushed aside. The right to wear the Penitent's "sack," the privilege of a front-ranking position in a parish procession, were integrally related to the community's system of symbols of status and esteem, a domain into which the Church could not easily enter, whatever the religious justification for doing so. At the same time, the parish priest was confronting a whole world of customs and magico-religious beliefs sustained not by theological doctrine but by local tradition: a sub-Christian, or perhaps pre-Christian culture or folklore[65] that was constantly influencing the forms of Catholic worship. This "folklorization" of the Catholic religion, as Jean Delumeau has described it,[66] is difficult

---

[64] Notes on declaration of revenue, *ca.* 1789: A.D.H.A., L 1024.

[65] Van Gennep, p. 30, argues that folkloric beliefs were largely independent from the official religion. In a given region, such beliefs and practices might exist almost unchanged in predominantly Catholic and in predominantly Protestant villages.

[66] *Le Catholicisme entre Luther et Voltaire* (Paris, 1971), pp. 243–248. See also Keith Thomas, *Religion and the Decline of Magic* (New York, 1971), esp. pp. 25–50.

to document in the eighteenth-century diocese of Gap. We catch only occasional glimpses of a body of practices and beliefs that were clearly of paramount importance in the popular mind, but that were seldom reflected on or described by the literate.

In the diocese of Gap, as everywhere in Christendom, there were dozens of local saints, relics, sacred springs with special efficacy against the ailments, fears, and miseries that plagued the individual or the community. The relics of Saint Gregory in Tallard could cure a child of fear, the church bells of Montmaur were useful against rabies, and many different sicknesses could be allayed by putting one's head through a hole in the wall of the Penitents' chapel in L'Escale.[67] Relief from drought was sought in L'Epine through a procession to the spring of Notre Dame and the ritual washing of the basin by a nude virgin.[68] If an infant died at birth, it might be revived, at least long enough to be baptised, by pilgrimages to the chapels of Notre Dame in Ribiers or in La Fare.[69] Parish priests themselves were said to have particular magical powers to drive off thunderstorms or to put out fires through the recitation of special prayers.[70] On the feast of Saint Antoine, the curés were expected to bless bread or salt for the animals to preserve them from disease; during Rogations they might be asked to bless small wooden crosses to be planted in the newly sown fields for the protection and fertility of the crops.[71]

For most of the major liturgical cycles and rites there were parallel folkloric cycles and celebrations. The Lent-

[67] Van Gennep, II, 108–118; pastoral visit to L'Escale, Oct. 29, 1772: A.D.H.A., G 790.

[68] Van Gennep, II, 38–43.

[69] Jean-Charles-François Ladoucette, *Histoire, antiquités, usages, dialectes des Hautes-Alpes* (1st ed.; Paris, 1820), pp. 144–145; F. Allemand, "Notice sur les sources," p. 210.

[70] Van Gennep, II, 60 and 99.

[71] Van Gennep, I, 364 and 229–231. Curé Millon of Laye mentioned blessing the lands and the crops of his villagers in letters to Des Preaux, Apr. 10, 1772 and May 4, 1780: A.D.H.A., F 1344 and F 1350.

en cycle was inseparably linked to the popular festivities of Carnival and Mardi Gras. The feast day of a parish's patron saint was always accompanied by the profane celebrations known in the diocese as *"vogues."* The rites of passage performed by the Church—baptism, churching, marriage, funerals—were all embellished by a rich tradition of popular ceremonies and superstitions. Many of the parallel folkloric activities were organized and presided over by the associations of unmarried men, known as "abbeys." It was usually the abbey and its leader, the "abbot," that organized the carnival and the *vogue*, which led the festivities at marriages, and which engineered the raucous ceremonies of public condemnation known as "charivaris."[72] One such charivari in Laragne in 1765, ridiculing a tailor named Joseph Philipon, who had allegedly been beaten by his wife, seemed to make a parody of certain orthodox church ceremonies. Effigies of Joseph and his wife were carried through town in a cart to the music of violins and various cacophonous instruments. The effigies were solemnly condemned in front of the house of the curé, and then taken elsewhere to be shot and burned. As they were buried, a rite was performed, with the words "asperges, asperges," as though holy water was being sprinkled on the graves. A few days later, on Ash Wednesday, one of the youthful participants put ashes from the cremated effigies on his forehead in imitation of the church ceremony at the beginning of Lent.[73]

Whatever the tolerance of some curés for the folk customs of their parishioners, the curé of Laragne could never have condoned this kind of affront to established religion. There are, in fact, many other examples of confrontations between the parish priests and the popular religious culture

[72] The abbey of Serres was still flourishing in 1764: see Van Gennep, I, 70–76 and 167–168. See also Natalie Z. Davis, "The Reasons of Misrule: Youth Groups and Charivaris in Sixteenth-Century France," *Past and Present*, no. 50 (Feb. 1971), pp. 41–75.
[73] Trial against several individuals in Laragne heard before the *bailliage* court of Gap: A.D.H.A., B 551.

of their flocks, confrontations that were probably taking place throughout France and throughout much of Christendom in the eighteenth century.[74] Curé Maurel of Ribiers attempted to suppress the local pilgrimages to the sacred spring of Notre Dame for the reviving of unbaptised children.[75] Albert of Seynes and many of his curé colleagues had tried for years to overcome the demands made by their parishioners to exorcise threatening thunder or hailstorms. The priests were virtually forced to have the church bells rung and to recite ritual prayers at the doorsteps: "If the priest performing this rite is unfortunate enough to fail to stop the hail from falling in the countryside, the vulgar, uneducated common people pin the blame on the priest himself. They say that he has insufficient grace to be obeyed by the winds and the storms."[76] Although Albert accepted a possible "scientific" rationale—that the movement of the bells helped to circulate the air and to chase the clouds away—he was clearly impatient with the superstitious attitude of the people.[77]

An especially dramatic instance of the power of popular beliefs to control the priest was the riot in 1759 against Jean Salva, a chaplain in Ribiers.[78] At the beginning of

---

[74] The disapproval of the French bishops for the popular festivities intertwined with Christianity dates back at least to the late seventeenth century: see Dominique Julia, "La réforme posttridentine en France d'après les procès-verbaux de visites pastorales: ordre et résistances," in *La società religiosa nell'età moderna. Atti del Convegno studi de storia sociale e religiosa, Capaccio-Paestum, 18–21 maggio 1972* (Naples, 1973), pp. 384–397; and Delumeau, pp. 256–261.

[75] Ladoucette, pp. 144–145.

[76] Albert, I, 18–19. During a pastoral visit to Claret, Sept. 8, 1759, the bishop forbade all weather exorcisms except those specifically contained in the ritual: A.D.H.A., G 789.

[77] Albert, I, 18–19; Ladoucette (3rd ed.; Paris, 1848), p. 594, said that if priests were unsuccessful against the weather, the *"vindicte publique"* could force them to resign from the parish. Similar beliefs in the power of the church bells were held in other parts of France: see Albert Babeau, *Le village sous l'Ancien régime* (3rd ed.; Paris, 1882), p. 117.

[78] Inquest and proceedings before the *bailliage* of Gap: A.D.H.A., B 554.

Sunday mass, Salva stepped to the pulpit with the intention of pronouncing a *monitoire*, a formal summons for everyone to testify to the curé any facts known concerning a recent crime—with a threat of automatic excommunication for anyone who failed to do so. Immediately a group of women began screaming and threatening the priest. They eventually attacked him at the altar, where he tried to retreat, ripping his soutane, tearing off his wig, apparently beating him with the processional crosses broken up for that purpose. On investigation, the women involved were found to be peasants and wives of artisans, all illiterate. Their principal motive seems to have been their superstitious fear of the effects of a *monitoire* on the village: "it would hurt the ripening of the harvest and cause hail and thunderstorms"; "a *monitoire* causes misfortune on a country . . . and brings down hail, windstorms, and the total loss of the crops."[79]

Objections by curés to their parishioners' profane celebrations of religious holidays were a prevailing theme throughout the eighteenth century in the diocese of Gap. In 1707 the curé of Chabottes complained about the bonfire dances that took place in the Champsaur on Shrove Sunday (during Carnival) and the first Sunday of Lent. "Bacchanalia," and "various remnants of paganism," he called them, during which young men, "yelling and screaming like madmen," tried to jump over the bonfires to help to promote the crops and to protect themselves from illness.[80] The worst abuses were attributed to the influence of Chabottes' *abbaye de Malgouvert*. Despite the curés' appeals, these *feux de joie* were still active in Chabottes and

---

[79] Statements by Jean Meygret and Marie Giraud: *ibid.* Perhaps clergymen themselves had previously contributed to the growth of such superstitions. There were reports of curés who threatened that anyone not giving information commanded by a *monitoire* could be changed into a werewolf: Babeau, p. 126.

[80] "Etat de paroisse": A.D.H.A., G 1099. The same customs were observed by Ladoucette for the late eighteenth and early nineteenth centuries: (3rd ed.), pp. 579–580. See also Van Gennep, I, 205–209.

the Champsaur in the early nineteenth century.[81] In the 1760's François-Léon Réguis, curé of Barret-le-Bas, would consecrate one of his most energetic sermons to the excesses of Carnival. He too considered the popular festival to be a pagan remnant, "the triumph of Hell and the shame of Christianity": "As if they grew tired of being and appearing as Christians, they want to lay aside the character of the rational, Christian man and take on the character of pagans and animals."[82] Whether Réguis' sermons were successful cannot be said, but his neighbor, Abel of Laborel, met the solid opposition of his parish when he tried to suppress a local festival known as the *"joyes de la Saint-Raphaël"*— described by the curé as a "source of scandal" in the parish. The curé's actions helped foment a long and heated quarrel between priest and parish.[83]

Doubtless many curés were willing to tolerate the modes of religious expression of the villagers, at least in their more innocuous manifestations. They were well aware of the danger of losing the confidence of their flocks if they tampered too much with the traditional local beliefs and practices. Yet there is often evidence of a confrontation between two religious cultures: between the religion of the curé—and thus the religion of the seminary, the religion of the city—on the one hand, and the religion of the rural parishioners, on the other. A priest might view this conflict in terms of the traditional categories: it was a struggle between the Church and the World, between the City of God and the works of the Devil. He could also condemn the madness, the irrationality, the fanaticism[84] of the popular religious and magico-religious activities of his

81 Van Gennep, I, 71.
82 *La voix du pasteur, discours familiers d'un curé pour tous les dimanches de l'année* (Lyon, 1855), I, 148–156.
83 Abel to the vicar-general, letter, Oct. 8, 1765: A.D.H.A., G 966. The curé was accused of being a "zélé outré." There were, however, other elements in the dispute between Abel and his parishioners: see above, Chapter VII.
84 See previous section of this chapter.

parishioners. Some of the parish priests had clearly come under the influence of those eighteenth-century French theologians and apologists who were advocating a "rational" religion.[85] The curés could also look to the actions and ideals of their own bishops: to those prelates, for example, who sought to abolish the "superstitious" rural processions; or to Pierre-Annet de Pérouse, who made a learned study of the saints worshipped locally and who ousted a number of them from the diocesan breviary as being apocryphal—much to the unhappiness of the lay population.[86]

The efforts of the curés and of the clergy in general to purify the local cult of its folkloric elements were to be largely unsuccessful. Many of the same beliefs and practices would continue to exist in the Alps of Dauphiné well into the nineteenth and even the early twentieth centuries.

THE CURÉ AND THE PROTESTANTS

An entirely different set of problems and frustrations was posed to many parish priests by the existence of the Protestant population within the diocese.[87] In the first years after the Revocation of the Edict of Nantes, the clergy had still nourished the hope of bringing the heretics back into the Catholic fold. Bishop Berger de Malissoles had made a supreme effort in the early eighteenth century through

[85] Note, for example, curé Chaix's admiration for the writings of the Catholic "modernizer," the abbé Pluche: see above, Chapter III.

[86] Pérouse was known locally as the "dénicheurs de saints." On the furor of protest caused by Pérouse's actions, see Théodore Gautier, *Histoire de la ville de Gap et du Gapençais*, 2 vols. (Gap. 1910), II, 382–384, 394.

[87] On the Protestants in Dauphiné during the eighteenth century, see, especially, Eugène Arnaud, *Histoire des Protestants du Dauphiné aux XVIe, XVIIe, et XVIIIe siècles*, 3 vols. (Paris, 1875–1876); Paul F. Geisendorf, "Recherches sur les conséquences démographiques de la révocation de l'édit de Nantes en Dauphiné," *CH*, VI (1961), 245–264; and Grimaud, cited above. The present section is concerned with the Protestants only in their relations with the parish clergy.

pastoral visits, missions, and letters to his curés.[88] But the attempts made by the bishop and his parish clergy were of little avail. *"Induratum est cor,"* wrote one discouraged curé in 1707.[89] Most of the "newly converted" did not even accomplish the minimal Catholic duty of confession and communion at Easter time.[90] The curés' efforts toward indoctrinating the children in catechism brought meager results: "usually they simply follow the example and inclination of their mothers and fathers."[91] The parish priests were especially discouraged and disheartened when the Calvinists refused to accept the last rites of the Church at the moment of death. Tronquet described the pains he would take with a dying Protestant: ". . . having proven my sympathy for him in his illness, [I] gently depict the danger which he is running, the soul which [I must] save, Eternity which is drawing near."[92] Only too often, the individual's death was kept secret by the family and he was buried in profane ground: "these are sad moments for a curé."[93]

By the middle of the eighteenth century, the Protestants were in the majority in only three parishes: La Charce, Trescléoux, and Sainte-Euphémie.[94] Here they could make life genuinely miserable for the curé, balking at paying the tithes—or paying them to a Calvinist pastor—and refusing to cooperate in any way with the Catholic Church.[95] La

[88] *Ord. syn.,* I, 5–12. On the changes in the Protestant population during the century, see above, Chapter I.
[89] "Etat de paroisse" by the curé of La Roche-sur-le-Buis: A.D.H.A., G 1101.
[90] The "états des paroisses" of 1707 list the number of *nouveaux convertis* in the parish who "do their Catholic duty": A.D.H.A., G 1098–1104; similar lists were made in 1734 and are preserved for some parishes: A.D.H.A., G 1037.
[91] "Etat de paroisse" by the curé of Séderon, 1707: A.D.H.A., G 1103.
[92] "Mémorial" of Bernardin Tronquet: A.D.D., XXVII G 1, f. 143–144.
[93] Notes by Tronquet in the parish register of Sahune concerning the death of a fourteen-year-old girl: transcribed by the abbé Lucien Van Damme and kindly loaned to me.
[94] Their populations were, respectively, 89, 78, and 82 percent Protestant.
[95] Notes in declaration of revenue by Robert, curé of La Charce: Mar. 29, 1772: A.D.H.A., G 2337.

Charce, with nearly ninety percent Protestants, was an especially hopeless case, and in 1786 bishop Vareilles suggested that it be abandoned altogether by the Catholic clergy.[96] Elsewhere, with the non-Catholics constituting only small but tenacious minorities, the clergy and the Protestants were forced to accept each other's existence with various degrees of suspicion or resignation.

Perhaps the greatest bone of contention in the relations between the curés and the Protestants was the question of marriage.[97] By law, the parish priest alone had authority over the sacrament of marriage for his parishioners. He also had control of the parish register by which acts of marriage were given legal validity. Thus, the very juridical existence of the Protestant family—the legitimacy of its children, its inheritance rights—was dependent on the parish priest. Many curés were particularly bitter over the Protestants' attitude toward the sacrament of marriage. Most had had experiences with Calvinist couples who went through the motions of sincere conversion, but who were never again seen in church once their wedding had been performed.[98] Even the normally mild and patient Tronquet of Sahune grew angry on this score: "What happens after all of the trouble which the pastor has taken for them? Once they are married, these seemingly faithless, perjurious, and sacrilegious people cease coming to church . . . and fall back into their previous state: in this way, they deride God, the Church, and their pastor, to the general scandal of the population."[99] Other Protestants escaped the curé's authority altogether, seeking the benediction of a clandestine

96 Comments sent to the agents-general Jan. 1, 1786: A.N., G⁸ 68 (dossier Gap), "5ᵉ état." The curé of La Charce "souvent ne peut pas dire la messe, à défaut de pouvoir trouver quelqu'un qui veuille la lui servir."

97 See Emile G. Léonard, *La question du mariage civil et les protestants français au XVIIIe siècle* (Aix, 1942); and David D. Bien, "Catholic Magistrates and Protestant Marriage in the French Enlightenment," *French Historical Studies*, II (1961–1962), 409–429.

98 "Etats des paroisses" of La Roche-sur-le-Buis, Sainte-Euphémie, and Séderon: respectively, A.D.H.A., G 1101, G 1102, G 1103.

99 Notes in parish register of Sahune, 1739.

itinerant pastor to marry "in the desert," or traveling to Geneva, or even accepting a purely civil marriage after a marriage contract had been drawn up by a notary.[100] Any child born to such a marriage was invariably recorded by the curé in the parish register as illegitimate.

Whenever the curés were able to obtain the backing of royal authority, they were ready and willing to see their Protestant parishioners indicted or even imprisoned in order to break up unsanctioned marriages. Several such cases appeared before the bailliage court of Gap in 1754–1755.[101] The local parish priest usually took a prominent role in the proceedings, leading a citizens' committee to the home of the offender and testifying as to the "scandal" in the parish caused by the illegitimate marriage.[102] Significantly, the Catholic lay witnesses never mentioned the word "scandal" in their own testimony. When the Calvinist Jacques Eymeric of La Baume-des-Arnauds was confronted with the law against his recent marriage outside the Church, he replied "that he thought that only the curés forbade such marriages."[103]

In the course of the century, the government grew increasingly lenient toward the French Calvinist population, and by 1757 it had permanently discarded a policy of overt repression.[104] Yet in the diocese of Gap and in many

100 Abbé Achard, "Histoire religieuse de Trescléoux," *BHA*, xxxv (1917), pp. 315–322; Grimaud, pp. 26–31; Gautier, ii, 300.

101 Against Paul Roux and his wife of Montbrand: A.D.H.A., B 549; against Jacques Gondard and his wife of Trescléoux: *ibid.*; against Jacques Eymeric, Pierre Evêque, and Jean Evêque and their wives of La Baume-des-Arnauds: A.D.H.A., B 550; against Joseph and François Nicolas-Pralong of Méreuil and Jean Romme of Orpierre and their wives: A.D.I., series B "Parlement," *procès criminel* no. 2215.

102 Testimony of Antoine Garcin, curé of Méreuil: A.D.I., series B, "Parlement," *procès criminel* no. 2215; of Claude Imbard, procuré of Montbrand: A.D.H.A., B 549; *procès-verbal* of the *confrontation* led by curé Rollin of La Baume-des-Arnauds: A.D.H.A., B 550.

103 A.D.H.A., B 550.

104 Burdette Poland, *French Protestantism and the French Revolution. A Study in Church and State, Thought and Religion, 1685–1815* (Princeton, 1957), p. 62.

other regions of France, the parish clergy continued to stand as a bulwark against the liberalization of the policies toward non-Catholics, thus acting in opposition to the wishes of the Parlement, the local royal officials, and even of their own bishops. When Jacques Vacher and Pierre Fourés were imprisoned for being married outside France by a Protestant pastor, the royal minister in charge of Protestant affairs, the count de Saint-Florentin, put pressure on the bishop of Gap to have the marriages quietly rehabilitated.[105] But the curés of the two wives involved refused to compromise their standards or cooperate with the bishop: "Am I thus expected to reinstate this woman [wrote the curé of Chabottes] without sufficient proof that she is morally in a state of grace? Can I give her a certificate stating that she is a Catholic and still not betray my ministry? No, I will not do it! The accommodation which you request of me will depend entirely on this woman's good faith. . . ."[106] A similar affair occurred in Montélimar in 1782. A curé refused to publish the marriage banns of a Protestant couple even when ordered to do so by the Parlement of Dauphiné. The bishop of Valence stressed the impossibility of obtaining the cooperation of the curés in such matters, given their training and preparation: ". . . we would have to send off our young priests to study in Geneva; because in our seminaries, the only doctrine taught is that one must never consent to the voluntary profanation of a sacrament."[107] In Dauphiné, and in many areas of late eighteenth-century France, the attitude of the curés was among the principal obstacles to the royal government's and the Parlement's *de facto* policy of toleration.[108]

---

[105] Grimaud, pp. 26–31.

[106] Letter to the vicar-general, Oct. 5, 1757: A.D.I., IV G 7, cited in Grimaud, pp. 81–82. Eventually, the two wives had to go to Grenoble where they made an unusually innocuous profession of faith.

[107] Letter to Miromesnil, July 10, 1782: A.N., G⁸* 2631, f. 439.

[108] Poland, pp. 65–67.

CONCLUSION

In our analysis of the relations between priest and parish, in this and in the previous two chapters, we have necessarily confined our observations to the diocese of Gap. Many of the same patterns of interaction were undoubtedly to be observed throughout eighteenth-century France. Everywhere in the kingdom the parish clergy exercised a powerful influence over the rural population. In their role as protectors of the poor and the downtrodden, in their efforts to promote respect for civil authority, the curés of the post-Catholic Reformation period may even have been a factor in the disappearance of the great peasant revolts so characteristic of the seventeenth century.[109] Perhaps also, as principal agents for propagating new agricultural techniques and "enlightened" attitudes toward problem solving, they contributed to a slow rise in the rural standard of living at the end of the Old Regime. Yet throughout the kingdom, the parish clergy invariably encountered many of the same rivals and obstacles to their authority. Conflicts between curés and noble lords, curés and lay notables, curés and Protestants, constituted an element of local folklore and gossip from Normandy to Provence. Widespread, too, was the influence of the laity over the forms of religious expression. In their dealings with the confraternities, with the processions, with the whole gamut of semi-Christian rituals and traditions, the pastors of the French flock had also to be followers if they hoped to maintain their influence over the fold.

Nevertheless, certain peculiarities in the economic structures of the Church in the southeast placed the curés of Dauphiné in a significantly different position in relation to their parishioners. Thus, the institution of the parish treasury, a major point of friction between clergy and laity in other regions of France, was apparently non-existent in

[109] Emmanuel Le Roy Ladurie, "Révoltes et contestations rurales en France de 1675 à 1788," *Annales E.S.C.*, xxix (1974), p. 9.

most of the villages of the diocese of Gap. Even more important was the large proportion of parish clergymen in Dauphiné—and the southeast generally—who had been disassociated from direct involvement in the Church's wealth. The congruist curés were effectively detached from the endless quarrels over the payment of the tithes and the responsibilities of the tithe owners—the most important category of litigation between clergymen and laymen in Upper Dauphiné. All the animosities engendered by the tithes were ultimately directed, not against the curés but against the unseen outsiders, the non-resident "priors," who carried away the ecclesiastical taxes without any contribution to the pastoral or economic welfare of the community. As early as in 1762, bishop Pérouse had complained of the "widespread ignorance among the common people," leading them to believe that all the tithes should be paid by right directly to the parish priest.[110] In this respect, then, priest and parish in Dauphiné found themselves drawn closer together, mutually disadvantaged by the same ecclesiastical institution, united against the same common adversary, the absentee tithe owner. Many of these distinctions take on further significance as we turn to examine the politicization of the Dauphiné parish clergy in the years before the French Revolution.

[110] Pastoral letter, May 10, 1762: A.D.H.A., G 816.

PART THREE
The Revolt of the Parish Priests

CHAPTER IX

Politicization of the Parish Clergy

THE BROTHERHOOD OF CURÉS

In the eyes of bishop Malissoles, the parish priests of the diocese were naturally bound together as part of the same pastoral family, the same spiritual community. But membership in a single ecclesiastical unit was only one, and perhaps the least important, element in the *esprit de corps* of the curés of the diocese of Gap. A social as well as a spiritual logic informed the "pious society of thought and affection."[1] Group ties were favored by the common backgrounds and common experiences of the curés. Most, as we have seen, originated in the diocese of Gap itself. To be sure, the occupational milieux of their respective families were diverse; but the majority of these families were among the wealthiest commoners in their villages. Many of the priests may have known one another from youth. All would have had similar educational experiences, shaped primarily by their seminary training; and most could expect to remain within a single general career pattern. Once installed in a parish, the majority of the curés would receive identical salaries for their services, the *portion congrue*.

The prevalence within the diocese of the congruist curés was of the greatest importance in promoting group awareness. Whatever their previous background or training, all congruists shared the same mediocrity of income, the same anxiety in the face of inflation. Mutual commiseration was a major impetus to unity. The salaried clergy also had a common antagonist, a "natural adversary"[2] within the ecclesiastical society: the non-resident tithe owners. The in-

[1] See above, Chapter III.
[2] The phrase is used by Henri Reymond, curé in Vienne, in a letter to Necker dated Sept. 30, 1788: A.N., B^a 74 (7).

justice was obvious to every congruist curé: he performed the pastoral functions, all of the toil for the Church, yet the bulk of the ecclesiastical revenues went to an outside landlord, who held the benefice as a sinecure. The antagonism was further exacerbated by the social distinction commonly existing between curé and prior. The priorships were usually held by priests originating in the nobility or the upper bourgeoisie and were thus out of reach for most of the curés.

The bishop was also a tithe owner, and for this reason conflicts inevitably arose between him and the congruist curés. But the greatest difficulty in the relations between parish priest and prelate in Dauphiné and in France generally was more complex. In the course of the eighteenth century, a growing percentage of the bishops originated in the highest levels of the sword nobility, in contrast to the parish priests, who were virtually all commoners.[3] Even more important was an increasing pastoral distance between the head of the diocese and his parish clergy. Many bishops of the seventeenth and early eighteenth centuries, like Berger de Malissoles in the diocese of Gap, had worked in close personal contact and cooperation with their curés through diocesan synods, pastoral visits, and cantonal conferences. The majority at the end of the century, like La Broüe de Vareilles, never held synods, showed little interest in the conferences, except as administrative organs, and were frequently absent from the diocese. The Catholic Reformation bishop was increasingly replaced by a kind of episcopal-seigneurial lord, reigning over his diocese from his episcopal palace and judiciously administrating his temporals. All the same, the bishop was never the curé's "nat-

[3] Virtually all the French bishops were nobles from the period of Louis XIV to the end of the Old Regime. In the course of the eighteenth century, increasing percentages were coming from the sword nobility, decreasing percentages from the robe and officeholding nobilities: Norman Ravitch, *Sword and Mitre: Government and Episcopate in France and England in the Age of Aristocracy* (The Hague, 1966), pp. 69–74.

ural adversary" in the diocese of Gap. Eighteenth-century Jansenism—a source of such acrimony between prelates and curés in some areas of France—had never taken hold in Upper Dauphiné. Each new bishop, as he arrived in Gap, was probably given the benefit of a doubt. Thus Bonthoux and Escallier, co-curés of Gap, were ready to entrust a bitter ten-year dispute with the cathedral chapter to the arbitration of the newly consecrated bishop Vareilles.[4] Whatever the curés' hatred or cynicism toward individual bishops, there persisted a deep-seated filial attachment to the ideal bishop and to the conception of the episcopal ministry. Curé Chaix showed the greatest admiration for the pious bishop of Amiens, La Motte—though as he read La Motte's biography, he was moved to sad reflections on the actual status of leadership in many of the dioceses of France: "If only the Church had among its ministers more pastors fashioned on a similar mold, irreligion would be silenced, heresy would be defeated, and piety would triumph. . . . Pray God that He may multiply such pastors for the care of His flock."[5]

In regard to the lay population, the curés' collective self-image was determined, as we have seen, by their dual elite status both as leaders of the religious cult and as community notables. The indoctrination of the seminary, the *"bon curé"* literature of many of the philosophes, and the efforts of the royal bureaucracy to use the curés as local civil servants, combined to give the parish priests an exceptionally high opinion of their own importance in the village society. The cohesiveness of the parish clergy was further strengthened by common problems and patterns of relations with their parishioners. Thus, by virtue of their institutional and pastoral functions, all parish priests probably viewed themselves as the friends and allies of the village poor. As the consecrated leaders of the people in the

---

[4] They would later regret this decision. Vareilles' "compromise" was a victory for the canons: A.D.H.A., G 1930 and G 1938.

[5] Chaix to Villars, letter dated May 27, 1788: B.M.G., R 10073.

paths of righteousness, however, the curés were in constant conflict with the "ungodly" residing in the community: the tavern keepers, the prostitutes, the gamblers, the Protestants. They were also commonly in competition with the lay confraternities of the Penitents. As village notables, the curés found themselves drawn into bitter rivalries of authority with other local dignitaries, of which the seigneurial lords and the notaries were perhaps the most important. Nevertheless, the fact that most curés in Dauphiné were on the *portion congrue* helped to bring the priests and their parishioners closer together.[6]

Common backgrounds and training, common problems and experiences within the lay and the ecclesiastical societies, all promoted a natural feeling of brotherhood among the curés. Some of these factors were general for all French parish priests in the eighteenth century. Others, particularly the widespread equality of revenues and the alienation of so many curés from the vested interests of the Church, were characteristic of conditions in southeastern France.

For many of the curés, dispossessed by their families of all inheritance, usually separated from their home villages, trained to remain aloof from the lay parishioners, the corps of parish clergy formed a substitute family and the closest circle of friendship. We have seen that Dominique Chaix's chain of intellectual associates consisted above all of neighboring parish priests. There was, in addition, a solid institutional structure for curé association: the local cantonal conferences. The loyalty among the curés of the same canton is revealed in their wills. One, and often several members of the conference, usually appeared at a priest's bedside as he dictated his testament to the notary.[7] On occasion, the priest would specify that the clergy of his canton was to be charged with all the masses celebrated during

---

[6] See above, Chapters VI through VIII.

[7] In 34 of 45 wills of parish clergymen of the diocese of Gap, one or more neighboring priests signed as witnesses.

and following his funeral services.[8] When any parish priest in the diocese died, all other parish clergymen were to say special requiem masses in his honor: "so that each priest can be assured . . . that the charity of his colleagues will compensate for what an unfeeling family might well refuse him."[9]

Both canon law and royal decree strictly forbade assemblies or associations of the parish clergy without the express permission or convocation of a clerical superior.[10] But in the later part of the eighteenth century, the brotherhood of curés became increasingly organized for unsanctioned group action in response to a series of economic and ecclesiastical grievances. As we turn our attention to this politicization of the parish priests, we must broaden the context of our study and follow the train of events in the province of Dauphiné and in France as a whole.

CURÉS AND TITHE OWNERS IN EIGHTEENTH-CENTURY DAUPHINÉ

Loose associations of the parish clergy had existed in Dauphiné since at least the seventeenth century. As early as 1635, the curés of the dioceses of Valence and Die are said to have jointly appealed to the king for the redress of grievances; and in 1664 an individual calling himself the "syndic for the curés of the province of Dauphiné" had appeared before the Parlement in Grenoble. The problems

---

[8] *E.g.*, François Meyer, curé and archpriest of Tallard in his will dated Apr. 10, 1761: A.D.H.A., E 2121.

[9] Antoine Albert, *Histoire géographique, naturelle, ecclésiastique, et civile du diocèse d'Embrun,* 2 vols. (Embrun, 1783–1786), I, 458. The situation was certainly similar in the diocese of Gap. It was the archpriest's duty to notify the entire diocese of a clergyman's death so that masses could be performed by all the parish clergy; see, for example, the *lettre d'archiprêtré* of Barthélémy Chaine, Sept. 7, 1780: A.D.H.A., G 823.

[10] Pierre Durand de Maillane, *Dictionnaire de droit canonique et de pratique bénéficiale,* 5 vols. (Lyon, 1776), articles "Assemblées illicites" and "Associations illicites."

caused by the *portion congrue* were the central issues. The tithe owners, it was argued, were living in wealth and luxury, but rising prices made the parish priests' salary of 150 *livres* insufficient for the "decency" requisite to their position. The situation was especially unjust since the priors had no function and were "useless" to the Church, while the curés were, by their services, essential members of the hierarchy.[11] Many of the same arguments would later be used in the eighteenth century.

The edict of January 1686, raising the *congrue* to 300 *livres* per year, seems to have quieted the unrest temporarily. But by the 1760's, rising prices had once again rendered the congruist's situation precarious, and the curés of the province were organizing anew. In 1765 the parish priests of the Grésivaudan—the valley of the Isère to the east and west of Grenoble—solicited statements of grievances from the curés of all the dioceses of Upper Dauphiné, including the diocese of Gap, in order to prepare a joint memorandum on the *portion congrue* for presentation to the General Assembly of the Clergy of France.[12] The curés were probably encouraged to meet in their cantonal conferences in order to draw up such statements.[13] Despite a royal order of 1765 banning all publications by groups of the parish clergy and reprimanding the illegal associations,[14] the curés continued their group efforts and their inter-diocesan correspondence. The bishop of Grenoble complained in 1767 of the "numerous and frequent" private

[11] *Requête du syndic des curés de la province de Dauphiné* (n.p., 1664).

[12] See the *"mémoire"* by the curés of the canton of Vif, *ca.* 1765: A.N., G^8* 2524, f. 97–100. The curés of the Grésivaudan were said to have already sent a statement of grievances to the General Assembly of the Clergy in 1760. An *arrêt du conseil du roi* of Sept. 1762 had banned a pamphlet on the *portion congrue* published by these curés in that year: A.N., G^8* 2524, f. 113–114.

[13] This was the procedure followed by the curés of the canton of Vif.

[14] *Arrêt du conseil du roi,* Nov. 16, 1765: see Durand de Maillane, article "Associations illicites."

assemblies of the curés of the province. Plans were afoot for a unilateral declaration by the Parlement of Dauphiné raising the curés' salary by 200 *livres* in all areas in its jurisdiction.[15] Only the royal edict of May 1768, increasing the *congrue* in the entire kingdom, brought a halt to this movement of protest.

The curés of the diocese of Gap may have associated with their colleagues in the rest of the province. The extent of their participation is uncertain. A statement written by the curés of the diocese about 1765 reveals the sentiments of at least one segment of the parish clergy.[16] As in the seventeenth century, the principal demand was for the improvement of their financial situation. The curés' utility to the Church was again compared to the parasitic existence of the non-resident priors: as Saint Paul had written, those who do not work should not eat. The protest now went beyond the question of the clerical salary. There was also an implicit demand for aid to elderly priests and for the suppression of the *casuel*, the "disgrace of the minister." A complaint was voiced against the unfair taxation levied on the curés' income by the clerical tax assessment board, the *bureau diocésain*. Finally, there was the theme of the curé as defender of the poor; improving the priest's financial situation would enable him to care more effectively for sick and impoverished parishioners.

The situation of the curés in the diocese of Gap and in Dauphiné generally was considerably changed by the edict of May 1768. This edict was the product of a series of compromises within the General Assembly of the Clergy of France. It left no one entirely satisfied and, in fact, had the effect of further polarizing the fundamental differ-

---

[15] *Mémoire* to the agents-general, Sept. 23, 1767: A.N., G⁸* 2524, f. 95–96.
[16] A.N., G⁸* 2523, no. 408. The *mémoire* is addressed to an unnamed "Monseigneur," apparently a royal authority in Versailles. It is to be dated after 1764 (there is a mention of bishop Pérouse's death) and before the edict of 1768. Perhaps it was written in 1765 at the instigation of the curés of the Grésivaudan.

ences in the province between the parish priests and the tithe owners. The curés' basic demand was now granted: the *portion congrue* was raised by 200 *livres*. Their salary was specifically set as a function of the price of grain and the king reserved the right to readjust it in the future if prices should rise significantly.[17] In return, the congruist curés had to relinquish to the tithe owners all of the beneficed lands and tithes on newly cleared lands that many had held as supplements to their salary prior to the edict. In addition, any *gros décimateur* could abandon the tithes and lands to the parish priest, if he so chose. Several former congruists in the Champsaur-Beaumont were now left with a revenue in tithes worth considerably less than the new *portion congrue*.[18] The text of the edict was sometimes ambiguous, susceptible of being interpreted by each side in its own best interest.[19] The law had scarcely been enacted when the tithe owners of Dauphiné, who had also organized to protect their interests, took the offensive in attacking certain clauses and demanding that the text be construed to their own advantage.[20] Much of the turmoil during the following twenty years between curés and priors arose out of the inadequacies and ambiguities of this edict.

The curés of the diocese of Gap would continue to protest the injustices of their ecclesiastical revenues. But two other long-standing difficulties were aggravated by the edict of 1768: first, the tithe owners' responsibilities for certain church expenses; second, clerical taxation.

THE PROBLEM OF PARISH FURNISHINGS

Everywhere in France the tithe owners were responsible for the upkeep of the choir of the parish church and for the

[17] Articles I, II, III. The edict is printed in Durand de Maillane, article "Portion congrue."

[18] Above, Chapter V, Figure P.

[19] Durand de Maillane, article "Portion congrue."

[20] Letter from the agents-general to the bishop of Grenoble, Aug. 31, 1768: A.N., G⁸* 2598, no. 436.

ornaments, vestments, and scared vessels used at the main altar. These basic expenses were further increased in Dauphiné by an institutional peculiarity: the paucity or non-existence of the parish treasuries. In accordance with various decisions of the Parlement of Dauphiné, the tithe owners were held accountable for all of the *menues fournitures* necessary for the celebration of mass, wherever a parish had no *fabrique*.[21] When the Parlement registered the edict of 1768, it carefully specified that Dauphiné's customs concerning the furnishings for the mass were not to be altered in any way.[22] Yet the edict itself clearly stated that the tithe owners could *not* be held for supplementary expenses, even if the parish treasury were insufficient.[23] Consequently, throughout the province, the tithe owners began ignoring the Parlement's restrictions and abruptly ceased payment for the extra expenditures.[24] Some priors used the clause in the edict as a pretext for eluding their responsibilities in the upkeep of the ornaments and sacred vessels as well.

This turn of events left the congruist parish priest in an especially difficult position. He now had a choice: either to pay for the necessary items out of his own pocket or—perhaps even more disagreeable—to demand that his parishioners undertake the expenses through local taxation. The added financial burden was only part of the problem. The miserly attitude of the tithe owners was a personal affront to the dignity and position of the parish priest. It was symbolic of the priors' general disregard for the direct servants of the Church among the people. These purely

21 On the *fabrique* and *menues fournitures*, see Chapter VII.

22 Restrictions added when the edict was registered on July 14, 1768: see *Recueil Giroud*, xxv, no. 45.

23 Article V: Durand de Maillane, article "Portion congrue."

24 In the name of the tithe owners of Dauphiné, the bishop of Grenoble protested the Parlement's restrictions on the edict of 1768. The agents-general promised to do all in their power to oppose the Parlement and protect the tithe owners: letter to the bishop of Gap, July 26, 1768: A.N., G⁸* 2598.

"temporal" pretensions seemed to work to the detriment of religion itself. Many of the curés were certainly sincere when they argued that damaged vessels or ornaments might render the holy sacraments inefficacious.[25] In any case, for the eighteenth-century clergyman, the splendor and the external brilliance of the sacred service was an essential element in the propagation of the faith. The curé could appeal to the bishop's own statement that it was one of the pastor's principal functions to maintain "the neatness and embellishment of the church and everything that contributed to the decency and splendor of the external ceremony."[26]

Most of the curés could do nothing in this predicament but patiently write to the tithe owners, or perhaps seek an ordinance from the bishop[27]—who was, however, a tithe owner himself, meticulously administering his own temporals. Litigation in the civil courts was long and expensive, beyond the financial possibilities of many priests. But occasionally such suits were brought to court. In 1780, Alexandre Achard, curé and archpriest of Serres, profited from his nephew's acceptance as a lawyer in Grenoble to make an appeal to the Parlement.[28] The prior of Serres, who was none other than the bishop of Grasse, had refused since 1768 to pay for oil, candles, the little cleric, and the other *menues fournitures* required for the mass. In addition to the legal arguments based on the previous decisions of the Parlement, Achard aimed attacks against the very institution of the non-resident tithe owners: those men whose

---

[25] Letter of Rollin, curé of La Bâtie-Montsaléon, to the chapter of Gap, *décimateur* of the parish, June 28, 1772: A.D.H.A., G. 2086.

[26] Bishop Vareilles in the summary of his pastoral visit of 1788: A.D.H.A., G 792, f. 37.

[27] Letters from the curés of Le Plan-du-Bourg, Savournon, and La Bâtie-Montsaléon, to their *décimateur*, the chapter of Gap: A.D.H.A., G 2086 and G 2166.

[28] *Mémoire pour sieur Alexandre Achard, archiprêtre et curé de Serres* (Grenoble, 1780). Achard's nephew was Alexandre Achard de Germane.

"duties are too few to take up the leisure of existing and looking after the preservation of their revenues. . . ." "A man who is enjoying the pleasures of opulence cannot conceive that others might lack the basic necessities."[29]

Of even greater interest was the case involving Jean-Joseph Jean, curé of Montjai. The prior of Montjai, canon in Gap and member of the Gapençais nobility,[30] had systematically ignored Jean's pleas for a new missal, dais, four-cornered cap, and black cope. Jean engaged the whole community of Montjai to back him in his claims by uniting his personal grievances with the village's longstanding complaints against the same prior over the question of the tithe collection.[31] The curé may also have resorted to coercion, refusing to perform the Lenten services unless the community helped him to obtain a new cope—necessary for those services.[32] Jean and his lawyer—Achard's nephew once again—cleverly pictured the curé and the peasants as mutually oppressed by the same absentee parasite: "The tiller of the soil . . . has all the difficulties imaginable: though master of the soil, he is scarcely able to profit from it"; and later: "One must carefully distinguish the privileged and indolent corps of priors from the sound and respectable group of pastors who . . . work, edify, console, and relieve the misfortunate."[33] The prior argued that the Parlement had no jurisdiction in these affairs of the Church. Jean replied that the bishop himself ignored or conveniently misplaced all of his letters of protest. The Parlement was now invited to step in for the protection

---

[29] *Ibid.*, p. 3. The outcome of the suit is unknown.

[30] Joseph-Bruno Tournu, sacristan of the chapter of Gap. The Tournu family held the *seigneurie* of Ventavon.

[31] *Mémoire pour la communauté de Montjai contre M. Tournu, prieur-majeur* (Grenoble, 1782).

[32] Jean admitted using this technique on a previous occasion in order to obtain new vestments: ". . . on ne peut rien obtenir des prieurs qu'à la pointe de l'épée . . .": letter from Jean to Tournu, Nov. 9, 1785: A.D.H.A., VII E Jarjayes 143.

[33] *Mémoire pour la communauté de Montjai*, p. 2.

of religion against the bishops and canons who were mis-handling its affairs.[34] Curé Jean was doubtless serious in all of these arguments, which, however, were carefully worded to win the sympathy of the Parlementary magistrates. But purer religious motives were inextricably linked to a deep bitterness and envy against the aristocratic tithe owner: "A prior or a canon [he wrote in a letter to the tithe owner] must of necessity be sumptuously clothed in order to attract the veneration of the people; but it is of little importance that a curé step to the altar with an ugly, worn, and frazzled vestment which makes him an object of scorn, and which even brings scorn for the religion of which he is the minister: such are the ideas which hold fashion among the priors. It is fortunate for the honor of religion that the sovereign courts have the author-ity to provide for the needs of the parishes."[35]

The legal briefs of both Jean and Achard were printed in Grenoble and probably read by curés all over the province. The second bone of contention raised by the edict of 1768 had an even more far-reaching effect on the forging of curé unity and political association: the question of clerical taxation.

Clerical Taxation and the Politicization of the Cantonal Conferences

Following the raising of the curés' salary, an interpretive decree of July 7, 1768 authorized the diocesan tax boards to redistribute the *décimes* in each diocese in proportion to the changes in revenue of the various benefice holders.[36]

---

[34] "Forcer les décimateurs à remplir leurs engagements, ce n'est pas empiéter sur la juridiction de l'église, c'est réellement la protéger. Quelle manière plus sûre de soutenir la religion, que de faire observer ses lois, et d'empêcher que ses ministres ne la déshonorent par des procédés contraires à son esprit": *Ibid.*, p. 18.

[35] Letter to Tournu cited above, note 32.

[36] Durand de Maillane, article "Décime."

The tax board of the diocese of Gap, entirely controlled by clergymen who were themselves absentee tithe owners,[37] did not hesitate to lower their own taxes and to more than triple the taxes of the congruist curés. With a salary increased from 300 to 500 *livres*, the curés suddenly found their *décime* raised from an average of about 20 *livres* to an average of about 71 *livres* per year.[38] The curés had long suspected the tax board of favoring the tithe owners, and now all their suspicions seemed to be confirmed. The congruists were especially indignant because they were convinced that the tithe owners undervalued their benefices in their tax declarations. The income of the majority of the curés was, however, public knowledge, established by royal edict. The declarations of revenue of 1772 reveal widespread bitterness towards these taxes, and skepticism of the possibility of receiving fair treatment from the tax board.[39] Several curés accused their priors of giving false declarations or of concealing their true incomes through secret arrangements with the tithe farmers.[40] The new taxes had "roused even the most indifferent to revolt,"[41] and the declarations of revenues, ostensibly designed to equalize taxation, were seen as "perfectly useless."[42]

It was under these circumstances that the curés of the diocese began organizing to obtain fairer representation on the tax board. As in most dioceses of France,[43] the curés'

---

[37] The members of the tax board prior to 1770 were the bishop, two canons, two priors, one monk of Durbon, the syndic of the clergy (usually another canon), and one curé: A.D.H.A., G 2360.

[38] Rolls of the *décime*, 1766 to 1777: A.D.H.A., G 2485. In 1767, the salaried curés paid between 18 and 20 *livres*; in 1769, they paid between 52 and 86 *livres*.

[39] A.D.H.A., G 2337–2339.

[40] *E.g.*, the curé of Venterol: A.D.H.A., G 2339; and the curé of Lachau: G 2338.

[41] The curé of Venterol: A.D.H.A., G 2339.

[42] The curé of Saint-Bonnet: *ibid.*

[43] In 1770 the agents-general undertook an inquiry into the activities and composition of the *bureaux diocésains* in France. In a sample which I made of 21 dioceses, there were only 4 (Beauvais, Poitiers,

single representative in this body was chosen by the board itself. Legally, this representative did not even need to be a curé, and in practice he was in a position of complete subservience to the other members of the board. Inspired by a victory of the parish priests of the diocese of Grenoble in 1764,[44] the Gap curés began demanding two representatives instead of one, both to be chosen by the curés themselves in elections organized by ecclesiastical canton.[45] They admitted that there was no precedent in the diocese for such elections—as there had been in the diocese of Grenoble. Instead, they argued that they now paid over half of the diocesan taxes; and they invoked the common-law dictum that a representative must be chosen by those whom he represents.[46] If the bishop refused to grant their request, the curés promised an appeal to the Parlement. The threatened appeal was never made. The intervention of the *procureur-général* of the Parlement was probably decisive for the eventual victory of the curés of Gap. In a letter dated March 1769, the *procureur-général* explained the Parlement's belief that any such corps should have the exclusive privilege of electing its own deputies. And he warned the bishop: ". . . we are in a period of agitation in which it would be best to avoid all scandal. . . . No power can prevent your curés from lodging an appeal with the Parlement if they believe that the tax board has refused them justice; and it would undoubtedly be disagreeable if, before a formal audience and in a printed brief, they

---

Senez, and Grenoble) in which the curés elected their own representatives. In the other 17, representatives of the curés were chosen by the tax board itself or by the bishop: A.N., G^8 30.

[44] The curés of Grenoble won this right through an appeal to the Parlement of Dauphiné: Henri Reymond, *Droits des curés et des paroisses considérés sous leur double rapport spirituel et temporel* (Paris, 1776), p. 283.

[45] Letter from bishop Narbonne-Lara to the agents-general, Nov. 22, 1768: A.N., G^8 632 (Gap): and the reply of Dec. 12, 1768: A.N., G^{8*} 2598, no. 610.

[46] Letter from Narbonne-Lara cited above.

criticized everything that the board had done and forced it to give an explanation of its tax assessments. . . ."[47]

The success of the curés of the diocese—two elected representatives began attending the tax board in November 1770[48]—was of the greatest significance. To be sure, the two curé deputies were still outnumbered on the *bureau diocésain* by the non-resident tithe owners, and complaints would continue concerning tax assessments.[49] But, more important, the cantonal conferences had now been legally instituted as political as well as pastoral bodies. Each time a new deputy was to be elected—generally every three years—each of the conferences would meet to choose an elector. The twenty-five electors would then assemble in Gap in the presence of the bishop to elect the curé deputies.[50] The electors were also, in fact, given mandates to bring specific grievances from their canton to the attention of the bishop. For example, in 1786, the conference of Le Caire instructed their elector to make special complaints concerning the *décime*; and the canton of Thoard asked their deputy to take all appropriate steps with both the bishop and the agents-general in Paris to effect a just augmentation of their *portion congrue*.[51] In 1788 the elector of the canton of Tallard was instructed to beg assistance for a curé who was sick and without resources.[52] The cantonal elections may also have served as the training ground for the future curé political leaders of the Revolution. Both priests of the diocese who were ultimately

[47] Letter, Mar. 2, 1769: B.M.G., Q 4 (1), f. 315, cited by Jean Egret, *Le Parlement de Dauphiné et les affaires publiques dans la seconde moitié du XVIIIe siècle*, 2 vols. (Grenoble, 1942), II, 98.

[48] Register of deliberations of the *bureau diocésain*: A.D.H.A., G 2360.

[49] Thus, Garnier, curé of L'Escale, wrote to the bishop on Apr. 13, 1788: "L'inégale imposition des décimes fait crier avec raison tous les curés qui sont surchargés . . .": A.D.H.A., G 981.

[50] Minutes of the secondary elections in Gap are inscribed in the registers of the bishop's secretariat: A.D.H.A., G 820–828. The first such election was held Sept. 26, 1770.

[51] Procurations dated *ca.* Apr. 1786: A.D.H.A., G 2365.

[52] Procuration of May 6, 1788: A.D.H.A., G 2366.

elected to the Estates General, Jean-Michel Rolland and Jean-Gaspar Gassendi, had begun their political careers before 1789 as the elected representatives of their cantons.[53]

In the various encounters between parish priest and prior in the later half of the eighteenth century, the role played by the Parlement of Dauphiné can scarcely be overestimated. The protection given by the court was a primary source of encouragement for group action, an incitement to take the offensive. Curé Jean had given full recognition of the Parlement's good graces in his letter to the prior of Montjai. But the sovereign court was necessarily only a passive ally. It could accept cases for review involving the curés, and favor them in its decisions or in its remonstrances against royal edicts that affected their status. It did not and could not provide the curés with active leadership. In any case, the real motives of the Grenoble magistrates remain unclear and may well have been mixed. Perhaps they felt genuine sympathy for the plight of the parish priest. There may also have been jealousy and animosity toward the wealthy, land-holding clergy who had the most to lose from the curés' victories. Or the coalition with the parish priests may simply have been another ploy on the part of the Parlement in the age-old struggle for jurisdiction between the royal courts and the upper clergy.[54]

It is difficult to identify any central leadership for the curés' activities prior to the 1770's. The various forms of protest described above were primarily reactions sparked by specific economic grievances. Except for the elections in the cantonal conferences, the curé associations and the inter-diocesan organization were sporadic and improvised in response to individual problems and crises. However, in

[53] Gassendi was elected successively in 1780, 1783, 1786, and 1788. Rolland was elected by five different cantons in 1788: A.D.H.A., G 2362–2363 and G 2365–2366.

[54] The bishops of France had long expressed concern over a possible coalition between the Parlements and the parish clergy: for example, during the General Assembly of the Clergy in 1730: see Ravitch, p. 45.

the last two decades of the Old Regime, a leader emerged from among the curés of Dauphiné, a leader who succeeded in enveloping the curés' concrete grievances in a powerful theological-ethical ideology.

HENRI REYMOND

Henri Reymond was born in 1737 in the city of Vienne. After a preparation at the local Jesuit secondary school, he went to Valence for seminary training with the Sulpicians and to obtain a university degree. He returned to his native city in 1763 to become professor of philosophy in the new secondary school that had replaced that of the Jesuits.[55] He seems early to have had contact with the writings of Montesquieu, Voltaire, and the economist Mirabeau, as well as with the *Encyclopédie*.[56] The first of his numerous confrontations with the upper clergy came about 1770, at the moment of his nomination by the archbishop to the parish of Saint-Georges of Vienne. The nomination was contested by the chapter Saint-Pierre-Saint-Chef, and Reymond appealed to the Parlement in Grenoble. In these circumstances, he began an independent study of canon law. Pleading as his own lawyer, he easily won his case.[57] Immediately thereafter, he came into conflict with the archbishop himself when he rejected the latter's appointment of a vicaire for the parish of Saint-Georges. Again he pleaded and won in the Parlement.[58]

During his early battles with the upper clergy Reymond assembled the ideas that would appear in his book, *Droits des curés*, published in 1776. The work had an immediate

[55] See Reymond's brief autobiography: "Notice biographique de Monseigneur Reymond, évêque de Dijon," *Chronique religieuse*, IV (1820), 365.

[56] Edmond Préclin, *Les Jansénistes du XVIIIe siècle et la Constitution civile du clergé. Le développement du richérisme. Sa propagation dans le bas-clergé: 1713–1791* (Paris, 1929), pp. 400–401.

[57] Reymond, "Notice biographique," pp. 365–366.

[58] Reymond, *Droits des curés*, pp. 72–73 and footnote.

and far-reaching influence in France, and its appearance has been said to mark the beginning of a "revolt of the curés" in the years prior to the French Revolution.[59] Yet it was written above all in response to the immediate and specific problems of the curés of Dauphiné. For example, Reymond's sharp dichotomy between the curé, on the one hand, and the tithe owner, on the other, would have been far less applicable for most dioceses outside southeastern France.[60] The work was at once a handbook of all the grievances voiced in the province for the previous fifteen or twenty years and a theological and legal justification for these grievances.

Throughout Reymond's book, the curés—the "essential ministers" of the Catholic religion—were compared with the "largely useless benefice holders," the priors and the canons.[61] Whenever a curé dies, "it is a flock that has lost its shepherd, a body its head, a child its father." But if a prior or even a whole monastery of monks were to die, what difference would it make for religion?[62] All the well-known complaints of the curés were elaborated and justified. It is only by abuse that the tithes no longer belong to the curés.[63] The tithe owners should at least be required to pay for the lighting and the upkeep of the churches and for the *menues fournitures*.[64] The *casuel* should be abolished.[65] The burden of clerical taxes should be alleviated for the curés, who should also have the right to elect their own deputies to the tax assessment boards.[66]

Reymond supported these economic grievances with learned arguments establishing the fundamental position that the curés occupied, or should occupy, within the Church. He relied heavily on the theological position known as Richerism. During the first half of the eighteenth

[59] Préclin, p. 403.
[60] Reymond himself makes this clear: "Notice biographique," p. 366.
[61] *Droit des curés*, pp. 271–272.   [62] *Ibid.*, pp. 26–27.
[63] *Ibid.*, p. 153.   [64] *Ibid.*, pp. 194–236.
[65] *Ibid.*, pp. 168–190.   [66] *Ibid.*, pp. 240–287.

century, the Richerist tenets had been developed primarily by the Jansenist *appelants* who were attempting to justify their refusal of the bull *Unigenitus,* imposed by the Pope and by most of the upper clergy in France. Reymond would entirely purge Richerism of its Jansenist components.[67]

The curés, so the Richerist theory went, were the direct successors of the seventy-two disciples of Christ, just as the bishops were the successors of the twelve apostles. The Pope, the bishop, and the curés were, therefore, the sole ministers of divine institution within the Church. The abbots, priors, and canons were only the inventions of man, superimposed through the ages on the basic ecclesiastical hierarchy.[68] How unjust it was that these purely extraneous elements now claimed dominance over the curés in the administration of the dioceses and in the assessment of taxes! How unjust that they should have usurped the control of the patrimony of the parishes at the expense of the curés! The curé, in fact, should have ordinary jurisdiction in his parish, as the bishop had in his diocese. He alone should grant permission to other priests to preach or to hear confession in the parish.[69] He alone should be able to choose his vicaires—although the bishop had the authority to approve this choice.[70]

Along with this theological justification for the curés' authority, Reymond developed a social and political justification. The curé of Vienne had undoubtedly been influenced by the *"bon curé"* of the philosophes. He also appealed to the policies of the French government itself. The *Droits des curés* was written while Turgot was in power, and the comptroller general's policy of collaboration with the parish priests was well-known to Reymond.[71] The

[67] Préclin, p. 402.
[68] *Droits des curés,* part I, article I.
[69] *Ibid.,* p. 46.   [70] *Ibid.,* p. 56.
[71] "On ne doute pas que sous ce nouveau règne, qui s'annonce si bien, on ne s'attache à donner au ministère pastoral une plus grande étendue": *Droits des curés,* p. 38.

curés, after all, were "the perfect citizens," and love of the *patrie* was one of their foremost convictions.[72] Indeed, "the people's happiness" was the very objective of the curés' ministry.[73] The parish priest was the ideal agent for contact between an enlightened government and the rural population. He was the government's natural ally in the organization of poor relief and hospitals.[74] He was the guardian of morality in the countryside against popular sedition on the one hand and irreligion on the other.[75] An underlying theme throughout the tract was the necessity of protecting Catholicism from the indifference and irreligion of the age. And what better way of promoting the "progress of religion"[76] than by restoring the Church to its primitive purity and reinstating the curé to a position of authority?

We do not know how many curés in Dauphiné actually read Reymond's book.[77] Its essential message was, however, widely disseminated in the course of the numerous suits and legal struggles pursued by Reymond in the 1770's and 1780's. The curé of Saint-Georges invariably identified his personal warfare against bishops, canons, and priors with the cause of parish priests in general. He sought, not without success, to initiate test cases for defining the jurisdiction of the Parlement of Dauphiné in various questions concerning the Church. He also began an active corre-

[72] *Ibid.*, pp. 146–147.

[73] *Ibid.*, p. 35.   [74] *Ibid.*, pp. 35–36.

[75] Reymond notes Turgot's instructions to the curés during the bread riots of 1775: *ibid.*, p. 38.

[76] The phrase is used specifically in the argument for abolishing the *casuel: ibid.*, p. 184.

[77] The *Droits des curés* was banned through the influence of the agents-general: see the declarations of the Parlement of Dauphiné, Aug. 21 and 23, 1779: A.D.H.A., G 2403. Nevertheless, the book soon passed into a third edition, and pirated editions began circulating all over the kingdom: Reymond, "Notice biographique," p. 367; and *Analyse des principes constitutifs des deux puissances* (Vienne and Embrun, 1791), p. 47. Curé Dominique Chaix did not mention the works of Reymond in his correspondence with Villars, although he did mention reading a book by the Richerist theologian, Maultrot: letter to Villars, Sept. 2, 1785: B.M.G., R 10073.

spondence with parish priests all over the province, soliciting information about local conditions and encouraging priests to meet in associations in order to back his efforts. As the archbishop Le Franc de Pompignan put it, Reymond had declared himself the "Don Quixote" of the curés.[78] In 1773 Reymond was leading a movement to obtain the right for the curés of the diocese of Vienne to elect their own representatives to the diocesan tax board.[79] Using the recent victories of the curés in the dioceses of Gap and Grenoble as precedents, he took his case before the Parlement. A decision by the court in the curés' favor was annulled by a declaration of the king's council, obtained through the influence of the agents-general.[80] A few years later, Reymond had organized the support of five other dioceses of the province and presented a joint plea directly to the king's council.[81] Reymond and the curés of Vienne finally succeeded in their efforts in 1786, and the curé of Saint-Georges himself began serving as one of the two representatives on the tax board.[82]

Simultaneously, the curé of Vienne initiated a suit against his own tithe owner, the Chapter Saint-Pierre-Saint-Chef, over the *menues fournitures* that the non-resident tithe owners were refusing to curés throughout the province. Once again, he personally pleaded his case in the Parlement, profiting from the occasion to make an eloquent appeal for the disinherited of the Gallican Church. Not only

[78] Letter to the agents-general, Jan. 10, 1781: A.N., G⁸ 661 (Vienne).

[79] Reymond is mentioned by name as having raised the "standard of revolt" among the curés. He had written letters to all the curés of the diocese, asking for their approval and requesting contributions for the legal fees involved: letter from the archbishop of Vienne to the agents-general: June 6, 1773: A.N., G⁸ 661 (Vienne).

[80] *Ibid.*; also, letter from the agents-general to Le Fèvre d'Ormesson, *intendant des finances*, June 27, 1773: A.N., G⁸* 2608, no. 199; and *Droits des curés*, pp. 284–286.

[81] Request presented to the king's council by the curés of the dioceses of Vienne, Embrun, Grenoble, Valence, Die, and Gap, *ca.* 1779: A.N., G⁸* 2544, no. 323.

[82] See the account books of the tax board of the diocese of Vienne: A.D.I., 1 G 36.

did Reymond win his case, but his speech and the court's decision were published and circulated throughout the province to serve as a precedent in all future contestations.[83]

In 1779 Reymond joined in an offensive for a new increase in the *portion congrue*. The initiative seems to have come from the curés of Provence, who in January of 1779 had obtained permission from the Parlement of Aix to elect a syndic to present their grievances to the king.[84] Thereafter, the curés of each of six dioceses in Dauphiné— Vienne, Grenoble, Gap, Embrun, Valence, and Die— obtained the authority of the sovereign court in Grenoble to assemble before local magistrates, to the exclusion of the bishops, and to deliberate on the problem of the *portion congrue*.[85] As one of the chosen syndics of the curés, Reymond seems to have sent questionnaires to a large number of curés in the province, soliciting information concerning the failure of the tithe owners to meet their responsibilities in the parishes. We do not know the preamble that Reymond attached to this circular, but the questions alone would have encouraged the parish priests to appraise

[83] Decision of the Parlement of Dauphiné, July 24, 1781: *Recueil Giroud*, XXVI, no. 116. Curé Jean seemed to invoke Reymond's victory as a precedent in his own suit against the tithe owner of Montjai: see above.

[84] Decree of the Parlement of Provence, Jan. 26, 1779; see letter from the agents-general to the archbishop of Avignon, Apr. 22, 1779: A.N., G⁸* 2616, no. 341. Also Reymond, "Notice biographique," pp. 368–369.

[85] Ordinances of the Parlement of Dauphiné, Apr., June, and Aug., 1779: see the request of the curés of Dauphiné to the king's council: A.N., G⁸* 2544, no. 323. The curés of Grenoble actually assembled on Apr. 27, 1779 before the *vibailli* of the Grésivaudan: A.N., G⁸* 2826, f. 460–463. Those of Vienne met July 1, 1779 before the *vibailli* of Viennois: *Mémoire à consulter et consultation pour les curés de la province du Dauphiné* (Paris, 1780), pp. 94–97. I have not been able to document the meetings of the curés in the other four dioceses. Reymond was described as the prime instigator of the assemblies in Gap, Embrun, Valence, and Die. The curés of Grenoble would seem to have remained more independent of Reymond's influence: A.N., G⁸* 2826, f. 460–463.

critically the inadequacies of the existing economic structures of the Church.[86]

Reymond and Hélie, curé of Saint-Hugues of Grenoble,
were chosen to go to Paris and present appeals to the king
and to the Assembly General of the Clergy. Reymond had
personal interviews with Necker—director of finance at
the time[87]—and he published a broad attack on the edict of
1768 in a *Mémoire à consulter*, approved by several of the
leading Richerist canonists of Paris.[88]

The organized efforts of the curés of Dauphiné and of
Provence may well have had an influence on the declaration
of 1786, which raised the *portion congrue* to 700 *livres*. But
the illegal curé associations and the apparent coalition between curés and Parlement also incited the firm opposition
of the upper clergy. The archbishop of Vienne, Le Franc
de Pompignan, and the two agents-general put all possible
pressure on the government to bring a halt to this "approaching revolution."[89] A royal declaration of March 9,
1782 reaffirmed the previous interdictions against unsanctioned curé associations.[90] The Parlement of Dauphiné,
alone among the Parlements of France, seems never to have
registered this declaration.[91]

In any case, the harm had already been done. The newly
appointed bishop of Gap, La Broüe de Vareilles, was ap-

[86] Seven responses to the questionnaire are reproduced as an annex
to the *Mémoire à consulter*, pp. 100–108. Included is the response of
Joseph Bertrand, curé of Saint-Laurent-du-Cros in the Champsaur.
Reymond claimed that these seven responses were only a small sample
of the documents held in the archives of the curés: *ibid.*, p. 94.

[87] Reymond recalls this fact in a letter to Necker (unsigned but in
Reymond's handwriting), Sept. 30, 1788: A.N., Bª 74 (7).

[88] Page 93; five of those signing—Maultrot, Camus, Jabineau, Blonde,
and Agier—were Richerists and/or Jansenists: Préclin, p. 404.

[89] Agents-general to De Beaumont, Apr. 10, 1781: A.N., Gˢ* 2620,
no. 439.

[90] *Recueil général des anciennes lois françaises*, XXVII, 167.

[91] Charles-Louis Chassin, *Les cahiers des curés* (Paris, 1882), p. 110;
also Joseph-Marie Maurel, *Histoire religieuse du département des
Basses-Alpes pendant la Révolution* (Digne, 1902), pp. 11–12.

palled by the lack of subordination on the part of his curés and "the manner of independence in which they live." He found that their declarations of revenue of 1783 were marked by a "spirit of impatience and revolt."[92] In 1787 he received a letter from curé Jean of Montjai that could only have confirmed him in his opinion. While hardly remarkable for the rigor of its logic, the letter was revealing of the extent to which this spirit of revolt had permeated the thinking of a country parish priest: ". . . the rules of subordination [wrote the curé] do not make the bishop a sovereign, nor the curé a mere clerk bound to the will of the bishop and obedient to his every whim. . . . True subordination consists in entire but enlightened submission, in sincere obedience regulated by equity, by reason, and by the sacred canons. Whenever a superior diverges from the dictates of reason, equity, and the rules of the church, then legitimate subordination consists in obeying not the ordinance of the superior but the ordinance of the law."[93]

Under the leadership of Henri Reymond, curés all over Dauphiné had grown accustomed to acting independently of their bishops and had formed associations among themselves for a broad attack on existing Church structures. In three of the dioceses of the province—Gap, Grenoble, and Vienne—the parish clergy had legally established their right to meet in their cantonal conferences for the election of representatives to the diocesan tax boards. Most important, the curés of Dauphiné had come into possession of a coherent theological and ecclesiological doctrine for the expression of their dissatisfaction.

[92] "Mémoire de Monseigneur l'évêque de Gap relativement aux portions congrues," Dec. 29, 1784: A.N., G⁸ 68 (Gap).

[93] Jean was arguing in favor of a curé's rights over an annex church within his parish: letter, June 1, 1787: A.D.H.A., G 995.

CHAPTER X

The Pre-Revolution in Dauphiné

THE PARISH CLERGY AND THE THIRD ESTATE

It was a curious coincidence that the province of Dauphiné, which was to become "the admiration, the model for the rest of the kingdom"[1] in the political revolution of 1789, had also given birth to a revolt of the curés that would serve, in a sense, as a model for the parish clergy of France. "The curés of the kingdom . . . already owe a great deal to their colleagues in Dauphiné": so stated a memorandum signed in 1788 by a large group of curés from Lyonnais, Forez, Languedoc, Auvergne, and Provence.[2] To be sure, during the second half of the eighteenth century, conflict between lower and upper clergy was in evidence in numerous French dioceses.[3] The ostensible causes of this agitation varied widely from one region to another: disputes over clerical taxation, conflicts involving distinctions of dignity

---

[1] *Histoire de la Révolution de 1789 et de l'établissement d'une constitution en France, par deux amis de la liberté* (1790), p. 86, cited in Jean Egret, *Les derniers Etats de Dauphiné, Romans (1788–1789)*, p. 53. In a letter to his mother in Nov. 1788, Barnave called Dauphiné the "consulting lawyer" of France: cited in *ibid.*, p. 58.

[2] Mémoire published at the end of Reymond's anonymous pamphlet, *Mémoire pour les curés de France relativement à la convocation des Etats généraux* (Avignon, 1788), cited in Chassin, pp. 110–111.

[3] The general question of curé unrest in late eighteenth-century France has been treated by a number of authors, notably Edmond Préclin, *Les Jansénistes du XVIIIe siècle et la Constitution civile du clergé. Le développement du richérisme. Sa propagation dans le bas-clergé: 1713–1791* (Paris, 1929); Charles-Louis Chassin, *Les cahiers des curés* (Paris, 1882); John McManners, *French Ecclesiastical Society under the Ancien Régime, a Study of Angers in the Eighteenth Century* (Manchester, 1960); and Maurice G. Hutt, "The Curés and the Third Estate: the Ideas of Reform in the Pamphlets of the French Lower Clergy in the Period 1787–1789," *Journal of Ecclesiastical History*, VIII (1957), pp. 74–92. I have relied particularly on the two latter works.

and precedence, theological quarrels rooted in the Jansenist controversy. Additional underlying factors no doubt included the growing social and pastoral separation of bishops and curés, and the vastly improved education of the curés, coupled with their greater self-awareness and their tendency to view the anachronisms and inefficiencies of the Church through increasingly "enlightened" eyes. But nowhere had the economic structures of the Church so essentially polarized the clergy, nowhere had the movements of parish priest protest attained such independence and scope, such a degree of organization, as in Dauphiné. The stream of pamphlets published in Grenoble and Vienne after 1760, not only by Henri Reymond but by other curés as well, would circulate widely throughout the country and be influential in the composition of curé grievance lists in 1789.[4] In fact, it is partly the extensive influence of the writings of the Dauphiné parish clergy that led many historians to mistakenly transpose to the kingdom as a whole ecclesiastical structures that were primarily characteristic of southeastern France.[5]

Until the late 1780's, this "insurrection" of the curés in Dauphiné and in France was fundamentally a struggle within the Church. The associations and assemblies of the Dauphiné parish priests, their appeals to the Parlement and to the royal government, had been activated primarily by injustices arising out of ecclesiastical institutions; and the ideological grounding had been largely theological. But the period 1787–1789 saw a transformation in the orientation and emphasis of this movement. The longstanding clash between upper and lower clergy developed into an overt so-

---

[4] See my paper, "The Ideas of Reform in the *Cahiers* of the Curés in 1789," written in partial fulfillment of the M.A. degree, Stanford University, 1969.

[5] Thus, many historians have assumed, wrongly, that the majority of all curés in France were on the *portion congrue*: see, for example, Marcel Marion, *Dictionnaire des institutions de la France aux XVIIe et XVIIIe siècles* (Paris, 1923), p. 446; and Préclin, p. 383.

cial conflict between the largely noble absentee tithe owners, including the bishops, and the commoner parish priests. The curés increasingly identified their struggle with the cause of the Third Estate.[6]

The "Pre-Revolution" in Dauphiné has often been described: the popular revolts against the edicts of May 1788, the Assembly of Vizille, the Provincial Estates of Romans.[7] Despite the relative difficulty of communications, the northern portion of the diocese of Gap was always closely associated with these events in Lower Dauphiné.[8] The three royal courts of the region, Gap, Embrun, and Saint-Bonnet, all followed Grenoble in refusing to register the May edicts.[9] In most of the important towns in the north and center of the diocese, the three orders met, against the wishes of the intendant, to express their sympathy for the *"parti grenoblois."* In Saint-Bonnet in the Champsaur, the symbolic colored ribbons, popularized in Grenoble, were flown throughout the town.[10] All the pamphlets published in the provincial capital were circulating in profusion in the subdelegation of Gap during the summer of 1788. The subdelegate, Delafont, counted more than sixty in August alone.[11] Within the Dauphiné portion of the diocese of Gap,

---

[6] This phenomenon has been studied, in particular, by McManners, pp. 208–239; and Hutt, pp. 89–92.

[7] Jean Egret, *Les derniers Etats de Dauphiné, op. cit.*; and *Le Parlement de Dauphiné et les affaires publiques dans la seconde moitié du XVIIIe siècle,* 2 vols. (Grenoble, 1942), II, 204–344.

[8] The best study of the period 1787–1789 in Gap is Joseph Roman, "La fin de l'administration de l'Ancien régime à Gap," *BHA,* XIX (1900), pp. 99–124.

[9] Letter from Caze de la Bove, intendant of Dauphiné, to Loménie de Brienne, June 4, 1788: A.N., B^a 43 (3). The other royal jurisdictions in Dauphiné refusing the registration were Romans, Valence, Montélimar, and Pierrelatte.

[10] Letter from Delafont to Caze de la Bove, Aug. 12, 1788: A.D.H.A., Collect. Roman, LI. Saint-Bonnet, Veynes, Serres, Tallard, Ribiers, Orpierre, Upaix, Ventavon, and Aspres were all said to have close relations with Grenoble.

[11] Letters, Delafont to Caze de la Bove, Aug. 8 and 19, 1788: A.D.H.A., Collect. Roman, LI.

only the Baronnies seem to have remained more submissive to the royal government.[12]

Many curés were closely following the events as they unrolled. Dominique Chaix read a large number of pamphlets loaned to him by Villars and the surgeon Serre; and he firmly took sides against the "yoke of oppression" imposed by the royal bureaucracy.[13] It is not known whether any of the curés of the diocese of Gap actually made political harangues from the pulpit—as did Galland and Goubet in the diocese of Grenoble.[14] But in four towns for which municipal records are preserved, we find curés and vicaires participating in the assemblies that voted approval for the resolutions of the city of Grenoble and that elected deputies to the assembly of Vizille.[15] During the following months, the two warring factions within the province—the royal bureaucracy and the conservatives, on the one hand, the liberals of the *parti grenoblois*, on the other—would avidly compete for the right to have their respective resolutions and decrees published by the curés from the pulpit.[16]

No parish priest from the diocese of Gap was present at

12 The three royal jurisdictions serving the Baronnies—Die, Le Buis-les-Baronnies, and Crest—all registered the May edicts: letter cited above: A.N., B^a 43 (3). Significantly, the Baronnies were later to be one of the focal points of counter-revolutionary activity in the Southeast.

13 Letter to Villars, Nov. 24, 1788: B.M.G., R 10073.

14 Egret, *Le Parlement de Dauphiné*, II, 267 and 313.

15 A. C. Veynes, BB 31, deliberations of June 23, 1788; A. C. Upaix, BB 2, delib. June 29, 1788; A. C. Ribiers, BB 37, delib. July 6, 1788; brochure *Délibérations du bourg de Corps, du 22 juin 1788* (n.p.).

16 On June 9, 1788, the Duke de Tonnerre, governor of Dauphiné, asked all the bishops and archbishops of the province to have their curés inform the people of the king's good intentions and of the obedience owed to royal authority: A.N., B^a 43, mentioned in Egret, *Le Parlement de Dauphiné*, II, 260. In April 1789, the Interim Commission of the Provincial Estates was attempting to use the curés to propagate its decrees: *Extrait du procès-verbal de la commission intermédiaire des États de Dauphiné, 17 avril 1789* (Grenoble, 1789). The vicars-general of Grenoble, solidly in the camp of the conservatives, attempted to prevent the parish clergy from complying: *Les vicaires généraux du diocèse de Grenoble . . . aux archiprêtres, curés et vicaires de ce diocèse* (Grenoble, 1789).

Vizille in July 1788. The twenty-six curés attending were mostly from villages near Grenoble.[17] The two curé members of the Gap tax board, Jean Abonnel of Saint-Bonnet and Henri Escallier of Sainte-Euphémie, recently elected by their colleagues via the cantonal assemblies, were both sent to Romans in September as representatives of the diocesan clergy.[18] Here they would sit with eleven other curé deputies, including Reymond and Hélie.[19]

For the parish priests, the assemblies in Romans were extremely frustrating. The upper and middle clergy, with a total of 37 deputies, were in a position to dominate the First Estate.[20] On the first day of the assembly, 31 curés from several dioceses arrived uninvited to protest the inadequate representation of the parish clergy.[21] Initially, their demands were favorably welcomed by the nobles and the Third Estate. But a political compromise developed in the course of the assembly that allowed each order to determine its own membership for the future Provincial Estates.[22] The upper clergy seized the opportunity and reduced the curés' representation even further. Only 2 of the 24 clerical deputies would, in the future, be parish priests, and both were to be tithe-owning rather than congruist curés.[23] The final disillusion came during the election in January 1789 of Dauphiné's deputies to the Estates General.

---

[17] The list of delegates is in J.-A. Félix-Faure, *Les assemblées de Vizille et de Romans en Dauphiné* (Paris, 1887), pp. 345–356.

[18] Deliberations of *bureau diocésain*. Aug. 27 and Sept. 1, 1788: A.D.H.A., G 2361.

[19] *Procès-verbaux des assemblées générales des trois ordres et des Etats du Dauphiné tenus à Romans en 1788* (reprint; Lyon, 1888), pp. 2–3.

[20] Egret, *Les derniers Etats de Dauphiné*, pp. 8–9.

[21] *Ibid.*, pp. 15–16. The curés appearing in Romans on Sept. 10 are listed in the *Procès-verbaux des assemblées des trois ordres*, p. 64. Some of these curés had procurations signed by the members of their own or other cantons: see, for example, those in favor of Goubet, curé of La Mure, given by the curés of the canton of Voreppe: B.M.G., O 425.

[22] Egret, *Les derniers Etats de Dauphiné*, pp. 15–16.

[23] *Ibid.*, pp. 28–29 and 35.

Not a single curé was among the 5 deputies of the first order. The clergy as a whole was represented only by an archbishop, two vicars-general, a cathedral canon, and a knight of the Order of Malta. At least 4 of the 5 deputies were nobles' sons.[24]

The situation was aggravated when a faction arose among the clergy and nobility that attacked the very principle of counting votes by head rather than by corporate Estate—one of the cornerstones of the Revolution in Dauphiné. Numerous canons, priors, and bishops signed the protest letter of "a portion of the clergy and the nobility" presented to the king, and the archbishop of Embrun emerged as one of the principal leaders.[25] This coalition of dissidents served to crystallize still further the opposition of the parish clergy toward their superiors. A state of affairs that the curés had probably long suspected now became manifestly clear: the tithe-owning upper clergy and the nobility were to be grouped together as the common enemies of the Third Estate and the parish clergy. In early 1789 an anonymous pamphlet entitled *Les curés du Dauphiné à leurs confrères les recteurs de Bretagne* was published and circulated in Dauphiné and throughout the kingdom.[26] One of the most radical statements published to date—going well beyond the theories of Reymond—it openly attacked the archbishop of Embrun and identified the cause of the

---

[24] The deputies were Le Franc de Pompignan, archbishop of Vienne; Monspey, *chevalier* of the Order of Malta; Gratet de Dolomieu, canon of Saint-Pierre-Saint-Chef, vicar-general of Vienne; Corbeau de Saint-Albin, dean of the metropolitan chapter of Vienne, vicar-general of Vienne; and Colaud de la Salcette, cathedral canon of Die: Armand Brette, *Recueil de documents relatifs à la convocation des Etats généraux de 1789*, 4 vols. (Paris, 1894–1915), II, 100, 120, 211, 300, 370–371, and 537.

[25] Egret, *Les derniers Etats de Dauphiné*, pp. 157–162. The clergymen who signed are listed in the letter sent to the king in Mar. 1789: A.N., B^a 75 (3); and the supplement of signatures dated Apr. 7, 1789: B^a 75 (4).

[26] (N.p., 1789.) I have had to rely on the extensive quotations of the pamphlet published by Charles-Louis Chassin, *Les cahiers des curés* (Paris, 1882), pp. 114–118.

curés with that of the Third Estate: "The interest of the people is inseparable from that of the curés. If the people rise up from their oppression, the curés will escape the degradation into which they have been thrust and so long held down by the upper clergy. . . . In fighting for themselves, the people are also fighting for the curés."[27]

The position of the bishop of Gap, La Broüe de Vareilles, was at first ambiguous. He arrived at Romans only in late December after a six-month visit with his family in Poitou.[28] At that time, he argued in committee in favor of the vote by head and even served as spokesman for the committee before the Estates.[29] But by early 1789 he and six of the Gap cathedral canons had definitively joined forces with the archbishop of Embrun.[30] On January 16 Vareilles wrote a long letter to Necker, explaining his position and arguing at length against the decisions of the Provincial Estates. He had been shocked by the lack of respect shown to the privileged classes and by the "excessive liberty" in the election of deputies. And the bishop went further: ". . . it was, for example, a travesty to see an unenlightened curé, with neither birth nor talent, competing on a ballot with the prelates."[31]

---

27 Cited in Chassin, p. 116.

28 After faithfully residing in Gap for the first four years of his tenure, he had chosen the inopportune period of May-December 1788 to take a vacation: see Antoine de Vareilles-Sommières, *Les souvenirs et les traditions de Sommières* (Poitiers, 1938), pp. 85 and 132–141. He had returned only on the summons of Le Franc de Pompignan. He had refused the "long, difficult, and expensive" journey to the first assembly of Romans, fearing that the meeting would never, in fact, take place: letter to Delafont, Sept. 8, 1788: A.D.H.A., Collect. Roman, LI.

29 *Extrait du procès-verbal de la commission intermédiaire des Etats de Dauphiné, 17 avril 1789* (Grenoble, 1789).

30 He signed the *mémoire* of the dissident clergy and nobility along with canons Blanc, Gautier, Reymond, Puy du Sandrais, Robin, and St. Genis. Also signing was the vicar-general, La Villette: see above, note 25. Four other Gap canons—La Bastie, Busco, Marchon, and Tournu—were described by Delafont as members of the *parti grenoblois*: letter to the intendant, Aug. 27, 1788: Collect. Roman, LI.

31 Letter, Jan. 16, 1789: A.N., H 670.

Somehow the bishop's letter escaped into the hands of the *parti grenoblois*, and a printed version, complete with a pamphleteer's commentaries, arrived in Gap about the middle of March.[32] Dominique Chaix received a copy from Villars. His response to his friend must have expressed the feelings of many of the curés of the diocese: "In a free and monarchical state, despotism invariably arises from time to time, and [of late] the aristocracies of the nobility and of the clergy have exercised their tyranny against their respective subordinates. May the Supreme Judge of empires break at last the yoke of oppression! *Suscitans a terra inopem, et de stercore erigens pauperem.*"[33]

The following Sunday, March 22, 1789, a riot against the bishop broke out in Gap. The causes of the riot were complex. The bishop, as the seigneurial lord of the city, had recently won a court order, requiring all Gap merchants to pay a grain tax that had formerly been imposed only on out-of-town buyers.[34] A hard winter and rising prices had caused growing unrest among the lower classes.[35] When the bishop's letter was published, filled with condescension and disdain for both the curés and the Third Estate, it was easy

32 Vareilles to Necker, Mar. 19, 1789: A.N., H 670. The bishop said that the pamphlet had just been published and begun circulating in the province. A manuscript copy had earlier been circulated in private.

33 Letter to Villars, Mar. 21, 1789: B.M.G., R 10073.

34 This tax, the *cosse*, had previously been levied at the market place. Since the government's free grain edicts, the Gap merchants had been able to create private granaries and thus avoid paying the tax. The bishop sought to impose the tax even on the private granaries: letter from Calonne to Delafont, Oct. 5, 1786: Collect. Roman, LII; and the report by Marchon, mayor of Gap in 1788: A.D.H.A., F 1437. On Mar. 8, 1789, the city issued a long statement of grievances against the bishop on a whole series of issues, of which the *cosse* was the most important: A.C. Gap, BB 82.

35 In a letter to the intendant on the eve of the riot, Mar. 20, 1789, Delafont had expressed anxiety over the situation. The daily export of grain south to Provence and the speculation of certain merchants had heightened the tensions: Collect. Roman, LI. Perhaps this riot is also to be related to the series of grain riots and attacks on the nobility which were spreading throughout Provence during the month of March: Michel Vovelle, "La Provence et la Révolution," in *Histoire de la Provence* (Toulouse, 1969), pp. 397–398.

for the rumor to spread that the bishop himself was hoarding grain or selling it secretly for export to Provence.[36] If we can believe the bishop's account of the riot, Gaspar Bonthoux, curé of Gap, was one of the immediate instigators.[37] He had perhaps intended only a symbolic insult to Vareilles. The trouble began when the pupils in Bonthoux's catechism class poured out of the church and began throwing rocks at the bishop's palace. Inciting children to riot against a priest was, as we have seen, a technique the parishioners themselves sometimes employed to show their disapproval of a curé.[38] Soon the children were joined by women and then by men, and the situation became much more violent. Only a few people were hurt, but the palace was left badly battered.[39]

As seigneurial lord and as bishop, Vareilles had lost the respect of both the priests and the parishioners of his diocese. A few weeks after the riot, as the Estates General was beginning its sessions in Versailles, the ten curés of the canton of Ancelle delivered a joint statement that was virtually an ultimatum to the bishop. They gave Vareilles fifteen days to liberate the parish clergy of all ecclesiastical taxes. The *décime* must fall only on the "useless" members of the diocese. If the bishop refused, the curés declared that their requests and their allegiance would henceforth be given principally to the king and to the Estates General. Vareilles

[36] Letter from the *lieutenant général de police* of Gap to the intendant of Dauphiné, Mar. 23, 1789: Collect. Roman, XXII.

[37] "Mémoire de Henri-François de la Broüe de Vareilles, évêque de Gap, sur sa conduite dans son diocèse depuis mars 1789 jusqu'en juillet 1792," *BHA*, XI (1892), 38. The curé is not mentioned by name; but the context leaves no doubt that the bishop is referring to Bonthoux. Bonthoux's temperament is known from a previous suit with the chapter of Gap. Vareilles himself had arbitrated the dispute in 1785 and had forced the curé to a virtual capitulation: A.D.H.A., G 1932 and 1938. Bonthoux was the brother of a tanner in Arzeliers: *titre clérical*: A.D.H.A., G 904.

[38] See above, Chapter VII.

[39] Vareilles, "Mémoire," pp. 35–39: and the letter from the *lieutenant général de police* cited above, note 36. The two versions of the riot seem generally in accord.

anticipated that many other cantonal conferences would soon follow the lead of the curés of the Champsaur.[40] The curés' ultimatum was, in effect, the final step in a century-long process during which the conferences had increasingly escaped the control of the episcopacy. In the context of the Gallican Church, it was a declaration of independence.

THE CAHIER OF THE CURÉS OF DAUPHINÉ

It was particularly ironic that the curés of Dauphiné, who had exercised so considerable an influence on the "revolt of the curés" throughout the kingdom, were not only excluded from representation in the Estates General, but were allowed no influence whatsoever on the mandate given to the province's deputies. This mandate, the only official *cahier de doléances* ever written in Dauphiné, made no mention of the problems of the Church and the clergy.[41] By contrast, in virtually every other region of France, the parish clergy participated in the composition of the cahiers for the First Estate and in the selection of clerical deputies. Thus, in the southern part of the diocese of Gap within Provence, numerous curés attended the local electoral assemblies and contributed to the writing of the grievance lists; and two of their members, Jean-Michel Rolland and Jean-Gaspar Gassendi, were elected representatives to Versailles.[42] Of the 303 deputies of the Clergy in May of 1789, 192 would be curés.[43]

As early as January a group of parish priests, including

[40] Vareilles to the agents-general, May 28, 1789: A.N., G⁸ 632 (Gap). Vareilles sent a copy of the curés' letter; it was dated May 9, 1789.

[41] *Archives Parlementaires de 1787 à 1860, recueil complet des débats législatifs et politiques des chambres françaises, 1ᵉ série (1787 à 1799)*, ed. Jérôme Mavidal, Emile Laurent *et al.*, 82 vols. (Paris, 1867–1913), III, 80–83; see also Gaston Letonnelier, "Les cahiers de doléances en Dauphiné," *Bulletin de l'Académie delphinale*, LXXI (1935), pp. 77–129.

[42] Joseph-Marie Maurel, *Histoire religieuse du département des Basses-Alpes pendant la Révolution* (Digne, 1902), pp. 44–52.

[43] Ruth F. Necheles, "The Curés in the Estates General of 1789," *Journal of Modern History*, XLVI (1974), p. 427.

Henri Reymond, had considered the composition of an independent *cahier de doléances* for the curés of Dauphiné.[44] But the plan was long delayed by legal difficulties. An *arrêt du conseil* of February 25, 1789, forbade all cahiers not specifically ordered by the king. The curés' efforts to obtain an exception were systematically thwarted by the upper clergy. Finally, on May 6, the committee of curés meeting in Vienne voted to begin writing their cahier even without official approval.[45]

The document that finally emerged was unmistakably the work of a single writer, Henri Reymond. It was a long text —over 200 pages in its printed version—and it was completed with elaborate justifications and footnotes. More than any other text written by Reymond, the *Cahier des curés de Dauphiné* was intended to reflect and to respond directly to the desires of his colleagues throughout the province.[46] Before the document was written, the committee on which Reymond sat actively solicited statements of grievances from individuals and groups of curés.[47] Reymond was sensitive to the opinions of his fellow curés even when he did not share these himself. In September 1789 he wrote a personal letter to Camus, the noted canonist and member of the National Assembly, arguing that the number of curés in certain of the smaller towns should be reduced.

[44] Chassin, pp. 400–401; [Henri Reymond], *Mémoire à consulter et consultation pour les curés du Dauphiné relativement aux Etats généraux* (Paris, March 31, 1789); and Reymond's letter to the president of the Interim Commission of the Estates of Dauphiné, Mar. 13, 1789: A.N., Bª 75 (6).

[45] Chassin, pp. 400–401.

[46] *Cahier des curés de Dauphiné adressé à l'Assemblée nationale et à Messieurs les députés de la province en particulier* (Lyon, Nov., 1789). On this document, see Chassin, pp. 399–415; and Michel Bernard, "Revendications et aspirations du bas-clergé dauphinois à la veille de la Révolution," *CH*, 1 (1956), pp. 327–346.

[47] Chassin, pp. 400–401; and *Cahier des curés*, p. iii. Alexandre Achard's "cahier," discovered in the archives of the cure of Serres, may well have been the rough-draft version of such a statement written on behalf of the canton of Serres and forwarded to Vienne. The other original cahiers used by Reymond have not been located.

He had not been able to insert this grievance into the *Cahier* because he knew it would displease some of his associates.[48]

Once the *Cahier* was completed in manuscript, Reymond personally carried it to be read and approved by parish priests in all parts of Dauphiné. In each town or village he visited, a meeting of the local ecclesiastical canton was held in the presence of municipal officers—and in the absence of ecclesiastical superiors. The text was read, discussed, and voted on. The curés were then invited to sign the document and to contribute money for its publication.[49] Probably not every parish priest read the entire text. But the chapters in the *Cahier* were conveniently divided into lengthy "observations" and much more concise "complaints" and "requests." By reading through the latter, listed at the end of each chapter, one could quickly comprehend the principal contents. Reymond had also listed the complaints and requests together on a single eighteen-page manuscript that closely resembled the form of a regular *cahier de doléances*. It was, in fact, this abridged version of the *Cahier* that was specifically considered and signed by the curés of the canton of Gap in the summer of 1789.[50] Other curés, however, seem to have read the *Cahier* in its entirety.[51]

Reymond spent July and August 1789 patiently discussing the document with as many curés as possible. Not all of the Dauphiné parish clergy signed the text. In the diocese of Gap, only priests in the eight northernmost cantons appear to have done so. In seven of the eight, nearly 80 per-

[48] Letter, Sept. 27, 1789: B.M.G., N 2375.

[49] *Cahier des curés*, pp. iii–viii; also Henri Reymond, *Analyse des principes constitutifs des deux puissances* (Vienne and Embrun, 1791), pp. 45–46.

[50] Undated manuscript: A.D.H.A., G 1537. The text would indicate that this abridged version was originally designed to be circulated among the deputies of the National Assembly.

[51] Ducros and Béranger, curés of Châteaudouble and Peyruis respectively, wrote to Camus discussing details of the *Cahier* which were not specifically mentioned in the abridged version: letter dated Aug. 12, 1789: B.M.G., N 2375.

cent of all of the curés signed.[52] It is not clear why the parish priests of the south of the diocese did not sign the document, nor even whether Reymond was able to reach these more remote parishes in the time at his disposal. In any case, many of the parishes were within the jurisdiction of Provence, and the curés would already have participated in the electoral process in the circumscription of Forcalquier. Other curés, approached by Reymond after the decrees of August 1789, did not participate because they thought that the *Cahier* was no longer relevant.[53]

A manuscript copy of the *Cahier des curés* was sent to the National Assembly on September 2, 1789.[54] It was not a regular *cahier de doléances*, but it was much like one, not only in form but in being a collective, considered statement. Many regular cahiers were, in fact, composed by individuals or by small groups of individuals and only afterward approved by the general membership of the body whose grievances the cahier was to represent. The *Cahier* of the curés can therefore be considered as a statement of the intentions and aspirations of a great many parish priests in Dauphiné in general and in the diocese of Gap in particular in mid-1789.[55]

The *Cahier des curés* laid down a sweeping and fully elaborated program of reform. It at once summarized the grievances of the curés of the province expressed during the three previous decades, and suggested proposals for a general reorganization of the Gallican Church. These pro-

---

[52] The seven well-represented cantons were Gap, Veynes, Saint-Bonnet, Ancelle, Saint-Firmin, Corps, and La Salle-en-Beaumont, where 52 of 67 (78 percent) signed. One curé in the canton of Aspres-lès-Veynes also signed.

[53] *Cahier des curés*, p. iv.

[54] Reymond to Camus, letter dated Sept. 1, 1789: B.M.G., N 2375. Camus was asked to circulate the manuscript to Agier, Dillon, and Grégoire, and to any others to whom he thought it would be useful.

[55] Préclin was mistaken in calling the *Cahier des curés de Dauphiné* a mere "brochure de propagande": p. 437n. He made his judgment only on the basis of the text itself, and had no other information on the process by which the document was composed and approved.

posals, if implemented, would also have had considerable ramifications for lay society.

All the well-known economic grievances of the parish priests were presented once again. The curés' salary must be raised, clerical taxes assessed more justly, the *casuel* abolished, old-age pensions provided, and money for church upkeep, sacred ornaments, and the "little cleric" supplied. There was a lengthy and well-documented study of grain prices designed to demonstrate that the curés in 1789 should have salaries of at least 1,200 *livres* per year if they were to have the same real income as their predecessors in 1686. Arguments were also advanced in favor of those tithe-owning curés who received incomes much below the established *portion congrue*. In another section of the *Cahier*, there was a specific proposal of 1,500 *livres* per year for all curés.[56]

A plan for the total redistribution of the Church's wealth was established. The *Cahier* appealed to the writings of the early Fathers to prove that all of the Church's capital should be divided into four equal portions. The first portion was for the bishops and the upkeep of the cathedral, the second for the parish clergy, the third for the poor, and the fourth for the parish treasury. The National Assembly was to be given full and sole authority to effect the redistribution. The curés seem not to have perceived the implications of granting such all-inclusive powers to the National Assembly. The existing system of tithes and benefices was not put into doubt in the original text, and it was assumed that the Church would continue to have independent sources of revenue. In two footnotes added after the resolutions of the night of August 4, the abolition of the tithes was welcomed and even justified by Scripture. A stance was taken, however, against plans to expropriate the Church's property.[57]

---

[56] *Cahier des curés*, pp. 72–75, 91–92, 102–116, 124–126, 140–143, 177.

[57] *Ibid.*, pp. 94–99, 162–190. The footnote, on p. 183, was added on Oct. 30, 1789, before Church property was put "at the disposal of the nation."

It was evident to the curés that no such redistribution of ecclesiastical property could come about without a vast reorganization of ecclesiastical institutions. The curés were urging a veritable revolution within the Church. The existing clergy was beset by: ". . . a disease at once religious, moral, and political, which cannot be cured by any ordinary remedies such as the modification of the laws. . . . The National Assembly must therefore apply itself to the rigorous regeneration of the entire clergy."[58] There was a need for a "cutting away" of all of those benefices not useful to Church and society—especially the simple benefices and the benefices *in commendam*—and a major reduction in the numbers of canonries and monasteries. Both in its administration and in its pastoral activities, the Church was to be decentralized and democratized. The General Assemblies of the Clergy would be abolished and replaced by national and provincial councils meeting every twenty-five and every five years, respectively. In each of these councils, the parish clergy would have full membership and voting rights. The dioceses would be governed in close collaboration between the bishop and the curés, the bishop's natural "co-operators." Vicars-general were to be replaced by the "episcopal advisors," elected from among the most experienced curés during biennial synods.[59]

Finally, an entirely new kind of clerical career was envisioned, a career that would be open to talent from all social classes: ". . . [high posts] must not be the exclusive appanage of the nobility, but through a just return to canonical rules . . . personal merit must be able to aspire to all positions."[60] The benefice system would be rationalized. All positions would henceforth be filled through the joint decision of the bishop and his advisors. Every clergyman would be required to serve successively in each position of the hierarchy. No one could ascend to the episcopate without

[58] *Ibid.*, pp. 191–192.
[59] *Ibid.*, pp. 42–43, 131, 175–180, and 195.
[60] *Ibid.*, p. 130.

having first served as vicaire, curé, and episcopal advisor. The canonries would be exclusively reserved to elderly priests retiring from active pastoral care.[61] The *Cahier* also contained grievances and observations concerning the parish priest's role in lay society. The theme of the curé as the perfect citizen and patriot was developed far more than in any previous document written in Dauphiné: "No one is more a citizen by profession than a curé. . . . He is the leader of a parish, a public servant, and his personal interests are identical with those of the *patrie*. . . . His day-to-day experiences, his ceaseless preoccupation with the public welfare will necessarily give rise to a patriotism which, all things being equal, is more to be expected in him than in a man of any other profession."[62] The curé's civic virtues were listed and extolled: his functions in linking the government to the people, in preaching civil obedience, in spreading technological innovations. Every curé should be given a plot of land in the village, specifically for demonstrating techniques of enlightened agriculture to the peasants. The curés' efforts to calm the panic of the Great Fear of 1789 were noted as an example of their utility to the state.[63]

Yet, despite what they felt was their natural position of leadership in the rural community, despite their continuing efforts to promote the happiness and well-being of the people, the curés believed that they were misunderstood and unappreciated. They were frustrated that they had been misrepresented to public opinion as being merely men of God, "simple ecclesiastical workers, whose learning and talents are limited to theological knowledge and the instruction of elementary religion." They were indignant against "this type of political nullity, altogether humiliating for such warm patriots," into which they were now reduced. The principal authors of the curés' debased condition were said to be the upper, tithe-owning clergymen who were

[61] *Ibid.*, pp. 91n, 130–131.   [62] *Ibid.*, pp. 118–119.
[63] *Ibid.*, pp. 89–90, 115–116.

264

seeking only to subject the parish clergy. Yet the grievances seemed to be directed against all of those lay groups and individuals who were undermining the curés' authority in the rural community. There was an obvious reference to the confraternities of the Penitents, those "pious mascarades," which "congregating outside of the parish church, form a kind of isolated flock, independent from the rest of the fold." Confraternities of this kind should be abolished and their possessions turned over to the parish. The priest should also be given greater power in relation to the local municipal leaders: "The line that separates our ministry from the functions of political officials should be redrawn a bit more in our favor." Thus, for example, it was the curé rather than the municipal officers who would best serve as local correspondent of the Interim Commission of the Provincial Estates. The parish priests should be given back the rights they had formerly held to notarize certain simple documents for their parishioners. There was a plea for extensive police powers for the parish priests, powers they had already possessed in theory under the Old Regime, but that were rarely observed by the civil authorities. The archenemies of both religion and the state were the tavern keepers and the prostitutes. The curé's testimony alone should suffice to have women of ill repute locked up; and all cabaret owners should be required to produce regular affidavits, signed by the curés, proving that legal hours were being kept and that the cabarets were closed to the public on Sundays. In general, any wrongdoer who threatened the public tranquillity should be arrested on the simple denunciation of the parish priest.[64]

Finally, the curés should be confirmed in their rightful position as guardians of the poor and as principal authorities in social welfare. They should be readmitted to the hospital administration boards where they were now sometimes excluded. They should be declared directors of all local poor relief: "The poor are not to be cared for by the

[64] *Ibid.*, pp. 77, 79, 119, 122, 126–127.

people, but by the clergy." "It is this fundamental truth, so little understood . . . in our century, that we must substantiate before all else."[65] There followed a lengthy proposal for the total reform of poor relief. It would be financed by the "*quarte canonique*"—one-fourth of all Church revenues—and administered by the curés serving as presidents of local charity boards to be established in each parish in the realm.

In brief, the curés were to be reinstated in all the powers they felt were rightfully theirs. They were to become nothing less than the tutors of local society. As directors of souls, their pastoral functions were truly all-inclusive: "What does this government by the Church include? Reason again gives the reply: it includes instructing the people in the truths of religion; teaching them their duties to God and to the *patrie*; showing them the road that leads to happiness; setting them on that road, directing their steps, putting them back again whenever they have the misfortune of leaving it; in short, of watching over them continually that they do not go astray."[66]

A curious mixture of diverse lines of thought buttressed the requests and proposals of the *Cahier*. Whenever possible, assertions were justified by an appeal to authority: Holy Scripture, the Church Fathers, decisions of the councils. Frequent references were made to the primitive Christian Church as the standard by which all later institutions should be judged. There was something of a poetic vision—for which little documentation was given—of the gradual perversion and degeneration of a primal perfection. Similar appeals to the ideals of early Christianity had found their way into most of the great reform movements within the Church. But a much more "modern" kind of logic was also employed. The Enlightenment concepts of *reason* and *nature* were invoked. It was through a critical examination of the present system in the light of reason—albeit, reason "enlightened by Scripture"[67]—that one came to compre-

65 *Ibid.*, pp. 127, 146–190.   66 *Ibid.*, p. 193.
67 *Ibid.*

hend the injustice, absurdity, and inefficacy of this system. Here, as in earlier documents of curé protest, it was the principle of utility that served as the fundamental standard of judgment. The curés were shown as the most *useful* members of the Church and, perhaps, of society in general. They were continually juxtaposed with the useless and parasitic non-resident tithe owners. If only the tissue of abuse were cut away, how much more valuable their office would be for the state and the society! At times, the curés' civic virtues seemed to be placed even above their sacerdotal functions in the parish priests' image of themselves. It was the parishioners' happiness, more than their salvation, which seemed to represent the principal goal of the curés' labors.

There was also an ambiguity in the *Cahier* between self-interest and genuine reforming zeal. This same ambiguity had existed in the whole movement of curé protest—at least since Henri Reymond had declared himself the leader of the parish clergy. The reforms advocated would have produced enormous economic and career benefits for the parish priest. Yet it is impossible to disentangle calculation of personal advantage from altruistic moral fervor. If the curés demanded an increased income and auxiliary benefits for themselves, it was so that they might more effectively carry out their pastoral functions, care for the poor, and keep up the decor of their churches. It was part and parcel of the total program for redirecting the Church's wealth to better serve the needs of the people and the advancement of religion. If they asked for careers open to talent without distinction of birth, it was to end the scandalous abuses within the Church, which, they felt, were promoting the irreverence and indifference of the layman; it was to help to create a corps of experienced Church leaders, directly responsive to the needs of the faithful. The curés' hopes for the coming regeneration of religion and society had no bounds. The abuses that had so long burdened and disfigured the Church would be shorn away and only the essential "solidity and beauty of the edifice of the Church" would remain. The irreligious would be silenced, perhaps even the Protestants would return to the fold.[68]

"To ensure due respect for our profession, respect from which religion itself will profit; to re-establish order in the Church and thereby recover all that we have lost in the eyes of public opinion through the introduction of abuses; to thrust aside all of the humiliating prejudices shown toward the pastoral ministry and restore it to its due competence; in brief, to regain our essential and imprescriptable rights which we wish to enjoy only for the happiness of the people confided to our care: such is the nature of our proposals."[69]

In many of the documents of curé protest written during the three previous decades, there had been a characteristic alternation in the inspiration for change between what had been, what was now, and what should be. But the tensions between the will to change and the will to preserve were particularly striking in the *Cahier des curés* of 1789. In their ecclesiology, in their proposals for change in Church structures, they were profoundly radical. Perhaps not since the period of the Reformation had such revolutionary transformations been advocated by so large a segment of the Catholic clergy. It was all the more noteworthy in that the impetus was coming from the lowest echelons of the ecclesiastical hierarchy. Yet in their vision of the position the Church was to occupy in society, the curés were essentially defensive. They themselves would be established as the cornerstones of the Church, but the Church would be preserved as the cornerstone of society.

[68] *Ibid.*, pp. 15–16, 80, 193.   [69] *Ibid.*, pp. 22–23.

CHAPTER XI

The Civil Constitution
and the Oath of 1791

By the time the *Cahier des curés* was received in Versailles, momentous events had already begun unfolding in the French capital. The parish clergy of the diocese of Gap watched the opening stages of the Revolution with much the same tense excitement—bordering on religious enthusiasm—exhibited by the lay population. Curés Bonthoux and Escallier of Gap both attended meetings supporting the National Assembly held in the local Penitents' chapel, and Bonthoux actively participated in the proceedings.[1] In Corps, priest and parishioners assembled before the altar of the parish church to swear a solemn oath of loyalty to the king and to the national deputies.[2] In Upaix, curé Brun and his vicaire Gérard headed the list of those vowing to defend the Assembly's decisions "as long as a drop of blood still flowed in their veins."[3] When news arrived in Ribiers of the Decrees of August 4—suppressing the tithes and the *casuel* and abolishing the "feudal regime"—the village assembly, led by curé Nicolas, reconvened in the parish church to hear a *Te Deum* and to "combine its prayers in favor of the representatives of the Nation with the thanksgiving which it owed to the Almighty."[4] During the following weeks, many clergymen further affirmed their support of the Revolution through "patriotic gifts" to the government of as much as 250 *livres*.[5] Others, like Guieu of La Baume-des-Arnauds,

[1] Deliberations of July 19, 1789: A. C. Gap, BB 82.
[2] Deliberations of July 17, 1789: H. Durand, *Notes sur l'histoire de Corps et son mandement depuis les origines jusqu'à nos jours* (Tunis, 1918), pp. 112–113.
[3] Deliberations of July 26, 1789: A. C. Upaix, BB 2.
[4] Deliberations of Aug. 23, 1789: A. C. Ribiers, BB 37.
[5] The following curés mentioned donations in their declarations of revenues of 1790: Rouy of Châtillon-le-Désert, Achard of La

publicly renounced the surplice fees in August 1789, even though they could legally have been collected through the end of 1790.[6]

The curés waited with anticipation as the National Assembly set about the reorganization of the Gallican Church. Following the suppression of the tithes and the *casuel* on August 4, later decrees would end the taking of religious vows and put all Church lands "at the disposal of the nation." Having thus abolished or confiscated the Church's traditional sources of revenue, the National Assembly promised to support the clergy through public funds. But it then proceeded to establish a "civil" constitution of the clergy (by the decree of July 12, 1790), unilaterally restructuring ecclesiastical discipline and administration and diocesan boundaries—henceforth made to coincide with the civil departments. In November of 1790 the deputies took the fatal step of requiring all clergymen performing public functions—bishops, vicars-general, teachers, and parish clergymen—to swear an oath of allegiance to the new French constitution, including, of course, the Civil Constitution of the Clergy.

There is good evidence that until 1790 the parish clergy all over France reacted to the Revolution with much the same exuberant approval shown by the curés of Dauphiné.[7]

Chapelle, Joannais of Saint-Michel-en-Champsaur, Cogourdan of La Fare, Avon of Buissard, Ruynat-Gournier of Saint-Maurice, Sambain of Saint-Pierre-de-Chaillol, Rambaud of Montmorin, and Brun of Le Bersac: A.D.H.A., L 1024, I Q I 108, and ms. 399.

[6] A.D.H.A., L 1024. The date for the suppression of the *casuel* was established by the decree of July 24, 1790: *Archives Parlementaires de 1787 à 1860, recueil complet des débats législatifs et politiques des chambres françaises, 1ᵉ série (1787–1799)*, ed. Jérôme Mavidal *et al.*, 82 vols. (Paris, 1867–1913), XVII, 317.

[7] See, for example, Maurice Giraud, *Essai sur l'histoire religieuse de la Sarthe de 1789 à l'an IV* (Paris, 1920), pp. 161–173; Jean Eich, *Histoire religieuse du département de la Moselle pendant la Révolution* (Metz, 1964), p. 77; Charles Tilly, *The Vendée* (2nd ed.; New York, 1967), p. 228. Each of these studies deals with an area in which the clergy would eventually be largely refractory, but in which the curés

Civil Constitution

Yet with the nationalization of ecclesiastical property, the reorganization of the French Church, and, above all, the necessity of taking an absolute and unambiguous stand for or against the totality of the Civil Constitution, the parish clergy in wide sections of the kingdom was thrown into an agonizing dilemma. A careful, nationwide study of the incidence of the oath remains to be made. Clearly, there was considerable variation from region to region. Yet it is probable that by the summer of 1791, after the Pope's condemnation of the Civil Constitution had become known, the French parish clergy had split approximately in half, between those accepting and those refusing the oath.[8]

Within the dioceses of the former province of Dauphiné, however, the new constitution was approved unhesitatingly by the vast majority of curés and vicaires. From 85 to 90 percent initially took the oath in the new departments of the Isère, the Drôme, and the Hautes-Alpes—into which Dauphiné had now been divided.[9] Even after the papal condemnation, the proportion of the constitutional clergy re-

---

clearly welcomed the Revolution in its early stages. See also Philippe Sagnac, "Les curés et le patriotisme pendant la Révolution, 1789–1792," *La Révolution française*, XVIII (1939), p. 168.

[8] John McManners, *The French Revolution and the Church* (New York, 1970), pp. 48–50.

[9] The basic although oversimplified study by Philippe Sagnac, "Etude statistique sur le clergé constitutionnel et le clergé réfractaire en 1791," *Revue d'histoire moderne et contemporaine*, VIII (1906), pp. 97–115, can be complemented for the Drôme by Jules Chevalier, *L'église constitutionnelle et la persécution religieuse dans le département de la Drôme pendant la Révolution* (Valence, 1919); for the Isère by A.-M. de Franclieu, *La persécution religieuse dans le département de l'Isère de 1790 à 1802*, 3 vols. (Tournais, 1904–1905) and J. Martenelli, "Les serments de 1790 à 1792 dans l'Isère" (D.E.S., Université de Grenoble II, 1971); and for the Hautes-Alpes, by Paul Guillaume, "Notes sur l'histoire du clergé du diocèse de Gap pendant la Révolution," A.D.H.A., ms. 399; Chanoine Roger de Labriolle, "Le clergé de Gap et Embrun pendant la Révolution," ms. loaned to me by the author; and my own research in series L of the departmental archives. The book by Joseph Roman, *Le clergé des Hautes-Alpes pendant la Révolution. La Petite Eglise* (Paris, 1899) is filled with errors and virtually unusable.

mained close to 80 percent.[10] Within the territory of the former diocese of Gap—portions of which were to be attached to five newly created dioceses[11]—88 percent of the parish clergy (260 of 296 members) swore their allegiance and had still not retracted in late 1793.[12] In examining the option taken by the curés of Gap, we must attempt to explain, above all, this exceptional consensus of opinion, this massive affirmation of the Revolutionary organization of the Church.

Invariably, economic gain was a factor in the curés' evaluation of the new ecclesiastical constitution—especially for those curés, the majority in the diocese, who had never held

[10] The clergymen retracting their oaths are more difficult to identify. For the Drôme, the list of juring and non-juring priests established by the departmental administration, was sent to Paris on Sept. 2, 1791, long after the Pope's condemnation had become known. A number of retracted oaths are specifically mentioned. Nevertheless, 87 percent of the parish clergy remained constitutional: A.N., D XIX 21. Within the Isère, the initial 15 percent of the parish clergy refusing the oath had grown to about 21 percent by 1792—including those curés who refused to recognize the constitutional bishops: Martenelli, annexe XIX. Within the former diocese of Embrun, in the departments of the Hautes-Alpes and the Basses-Alpes, about 20 percent of the parish clergy would be refractory by 1792.

[11] The boundaries of the new dioceses were made to correspond with the departments. The former diocese of Gap was partitioned among the departments of the Hautes-Alpes, the Basses-Alpes, the Isère, and the Drôme. The two parishes belonging to the Papal territory of the Comtat-Venaissin were to fall under the jurisdiction of the diocese of the Vaucluse after the annexation of this territory by the French in 1791.

[12] See note 9. For the portion of the former diocese within the Basses-Alpes, see Joseph-Marie Maurel, *Histoire religieuse du département des Basses-Alpes pendant la Révolution* (Marseilles, 1902). I have also made use of the personal card files of the abbé Adrien Loche, for the Drôme, and the abbé Jean Godel, for the Isère. Approximately 17 refused immediately and 19 more retracted before the end of 1793. They represented about 12 percent of the corps of curés and 11 percent of the corps of vicaires in 1790. Bishop Vareilles later claimed that, before he emigrated in 1792, he had convinced "une cinquantaine" of his curés to retract: "Mémoire de Henri-François de la Broüe de Vareilles, évêque de Gap sur sa conduite dans son diocèse depuis mai 1789 jusqu'en juillet 1792," *BHA*, XI (1892), p. 50. But clearly this was an exaggeration.

vested interests in the tithes and beneficed lands that the clergy as a whole was forced to relinquish. The National Assembly now fully granted the curés' longstanding demands for higher salaries, giving all parish priests a minimum income of 1,200 *livres*, and progressively higher salaries for priests in parishes of over one thousand inhabitants.[13] Not more than a dozen curés in the diocese of Gap, including those receiving the tithes, had earned this much under the Old Regime. Perhaps equally important was the creation of guaranteed pensions for all priests who were too old or infirm to fulfill their functions. Dominique Chaix found that his economic condition was considerably better than it had ever been. He was especially pleased that every curé would be allowed to keep a small garden in addition to his rectory.[14] "I give thanks to Heaven," wrote curé Sambain of Chaillol to the district officials, "for at last having listened to our cries for mercy."[15]

In this respect, the situation of the curés of Dauphiné makes a striking contrast with that of the overwhelmingly refractory clergy in certain regions of western France such as Maine and Southern Anjou.[16] Here, following the Revolutionary legislation, the majority of the parish priests saw their ecclesiastical revenues diminished, some by a third or more.[17] They not only lost their rights to the tithes—for

---

[13] The text of the Civil Constitution of the Clergy is in *Archives Parlementaires*, XVII, 55–60.

[14] Letter to Dominique Villars, June 3, 1791: B.M.G., R 10073.

[15] Letter to the district of Gap, Nov. 27, 1790: A.D.H.A., I Q I 108.

[16] On the question of the oath in Southern Anjou: Tilly, *The Vendée*, pp. 227–262 and "Civil Constitution and Counter-Revolution in Southern Anjou," *French Historical Studies*, I (1959), pp. 172–199. On the province of Maine: Giraud, pp. 210–264 and Paul Bois, *Les paysans de l'Ouest* (abridged ed.; Paris, 1971), pp. 282–294; also my own research in A. D. Sarthe. On the wealth of the clergy in these areas, see above, Chapter V.

[17] The salaries of those curés in parishes of under 1,000 inhabitants who had earned more than 1,200 *livres* under the Old Regime was fixed at 1,200 *livres* plus one half of the declared revenues above 1,200 *livres*. Thus, for example, a clergyman previously earning 3,600 *livres* might see his revenues cut by one third to 2,400 *livres*.

only a small percentage in these areas were salaried—but they were also deprived of substantial tracts of Church lands that many had "owned" and cultivated for years. As one embittered tithe-owning curé was quick to point out, the Civil Constitution would effectively reduce all curés to the *portion congrue*.[18] When additional studies have been completed, the variations in the economic structures of the Church may prove to be one important factor in the broad regional patterns of reactions to the oath.

Nevertheless, for the parish clergy of Dauphiné, as for other members of the juring clergy in France, it was not merely a question of economic advantage. Many of the basic non-temporal demands advocated by the curés of the province during the previous decades were also instituted by the national legislature. The canons and priors *in commendam*, the curés' "natural adversaries," who had received so large a share of Church revenues under the Old Regime, were now expropriated and disbanded. Careers in the clergy were made open to talent. The bishoprics would eventually be held only by priests who had served at least fifteen years in pastoral functions or in other functions involving spiritual care, and all bishops would be required by law to maintain residence in their dioceses. The episcopal council was to be chosen by the bishop—not by the curés, as requested in the *Cahier des curés*. But the members would consist primarily of former parish priests who would hold considerable power over episcopal decisions. The curés were also confirmed in the right of choosing their own vicaires.

In other provisions—the sale of all Church property, the destruction of the monastic vows, the lay election of curés and bishops—the ecclesiastical legislation of the National Assembly went even beyond the demands contained in the *Cahier des curés*. Yet the more radical transformations in this legislation were, in some ways, the logical conclusions

[18] Alphonse Aulard, ed., *Lettres de l'abbé Barbotin, député à l'Assemblée constituente* (Paris, 1910), p. 52, cited in McManners, p. 26.

274

of the curés' invitation to the Estates General to totally reorganize ecclesiastical structures and redistribute the
Church's wealth. Thus, for example, there had been no
mention in the original *Cahier* of the sale of all Church
property or the suppression of the tithes. But there *were*
requests for the redistribution of "superfluous" Church possessions, and for the reapportioning of the tithes towards
the support of the parish clergy and the relief of the poor;
and this reapportionment was to be accomplished locally
by mixed committees of clergymen and laymen.[19] Once
Church lands had been nationalized, curé Chaix was ready
with a number of theological arguments in favor of ecclesiastical poverty, which was seen as a positive step toward
the purification and regeneration of the Catholic clergy:
"As for the confiscation of the clergy's land, I say that in the
Mosaic law the Levites were not included in the distribution of the promised land; that Jesus Christ, author of the
evangelical law, . . . deprived of all property those who
chose to follow him and become his ministers. When benefice holders are shown the banner of poverty to which they
should have rallied when they entered the clergy, it is only
to recall to them their original institution."[20] And
Chaix recalled an essay he had written in 1788, advocating that a portion of Church revenues be redirected for the
use of the poor.[21] Of all the transformations brought by the
new legislation, only the total suppression of monastic vows
left some misgivings in his mind: "Though I have long
anticipated the fate of the regulars, I could not but tremble
on reading of the general suppression of all religious orders. I would have much preferred that, in accordance with
their original institution, they all be reduced to work, retreat, and poverty, in the manner of the orders of Sept-Fons
or La Trappe; but that the door should not be closed to
those who genuinely wished to espouse this life. . . . If all

[19] *Cahiers des curés du Dauphiné* (Lyon, 1789), pp. 114–115, 206–208.
Also, see above, Chapter X.
[20] Letter to Villars, Dec. 22, 1789: B.M.G., R 10073.
[21] *Ibid.*

simple benefices were alone abolished, benefices which offer the state nothing but the vain glory of titles, a great abuse would be reformed."²² Chaix was thinking, above all, of his pious and learned friends in the Bochaine, the Carthusians of Durbon. Most parish clergymen had probably had far less positive experiences with the essentially "useless" monks and friars, and few regrets were expressed when most of the regulars were disbanded.

One of the most difficult provisions for some curés to accept was the creation of lay elections for pastors with cure of souls. Yet the curés of Dauphiné could view such a measure as another step in the return to the conditions of early Christianity that they had long been reading and thinking about. "Reason and justice return to you [the right to elect your pastor] which had been stolen from you by force": such was the conclusion of curé Nicolas as he swore his oath of allegiance in Ribiers. "The priesthood is thus returned to its primitive dignity; the glorious functions which we fulfill among you regain their true prestige."²³ The Constitution, wrote the abbé Cazeneuve, "tends only to revive among us the glorious days of the early Church by destroying the abuses introduced by superstition."²⁴ Chaix explained his general position on the oath of 1791 in another letter to Villars:

"I will have no difficulty in pronouncing my civic oath. I have already done so in our [municipal] assemblies and I will do it again for the new constitution of the clergy. The changes in discipline and administration do not alarm me. Were it to be a question of dogma, I would, by the grace of God, walk to the scaffold to uphold its inviolability. But Christian beliefs have in no way suffered from all that has been decided in the National Assembly. In abolishing abuses [in the Church], the august diet has merely

²² Letter to Villars, Mar. 18, 1790: B.M.G., R 10073.
²³ Deliberations of Jan. 20, 1791: A. C. Ribiers, D 1.
²⁴ Speech pronounced Feb. 6, 1791: *Procès-verbal de la prestation de serment de Messieurs les curés et autres ecclésiastiques fonctionnaires publics de la commune de Gap* (Gap, 1791).

recalled the organization and practices of the primitive Church."[25]

To be sure, the National Assembly had ignored and perhaps never really understood many of the curés' grievances concerning the priest's authority within lay society. The quasi-theocracy proposed in the *Cahier* was not taken seriously by the legislators in Paris. Yet it seemed clear to many parish priests of Dauphiné that in ending the abuses that had so discredited the pastoral functions, in making the curés undisputed masters of the parishes and virtually the peers to their bishops, and in conspicuously increasing their yearly revenues (for wealth was, of course, related to status), the Civil Constitution had markedly raised their position in the community. It was invariably a boost to their self-esteem that they were no longer paid by pompous non-resident tithe owners but by the "French Nation." For a time, the curés would even be the chosen agents of the nation in the publication of new laws and decrees.[26] In early 1791, it was still possible to believe that the reforms in ecclesiastical government and discipline might lay the foundation for future, more extensive "moral" reforms.

What is more, if the Assembly did not establish the curés as the tutors of local society, it did open the possiblity of overt participation in village and regional government to any clergyman who so desired. The Civil Constitution of the Clergy was explicit in this regard: any bishop, curé, or vicaire could serve as a member of the electoral or administrative assemblies in the village, district, or department. A priest could also be elected mayor, municipal officer, or member of a district or departmental directory,

[25] Letter, Jan. 18, 1791: B.M.G., R 10073.
[26] By vote in the National Assembly, Feb. 23, 1790. Some curés in certain areas of France refused to comply, especially in regard to the reading of decrees to which they were opposed. There is, however, no evidence of such opposition in Upper Dauphiné. See Albert Mathiez, "La lecture des décrets au prône," in *La Révolution et l'Eglise, études critiques et documentaires* (Paris, 1910), pp. 26–65.

although if he accepted any of the latter positions after the publication of the Civil Constitution, he was supposed to resign his pastoral functions.[27] Under the Old Regime, the curés of Dauphiné had been effectively excluded from official positions in civil government by virtue of their membership in the first order; but after the suppression of all orders, they could be admitted to many of these positions. During the first years of the Revolution, many curés from the former diocese of Gap participated in local and regional government. Dozens of parish clergymen from all regions of the diocese took part in the primary elections of 1790;[28] in some cases, virtually the entire local cantonal assembly was present and voting.[29] At least eight curés or vicaires were chosen as presiding officers or secretaries, and at least ten were named as departmental electors.[30] Several parish clergymen were also elected to municipal offices, including the office of mayor.[31]

The community deliberations of Ribiers illustrate the

27 Title IV, articles 6 and 7: *Archives Parlementaires*, XVII, 60.

28 Minutes of the elections: A.D.H.A., L 127; A.D.B.A., L 288–337; Joseph Estienne and Jacques de Font-Réaulx, *Inventaire sommaire des archives départementales. Drôme. Tome 10. Archives de la Révolution. Série L* (Valence, 1933), appendix, pp. 686–692. The minutes have been lost for the Isère. Fifty-six parish clergymen are *known* to have been present; but this figure is certainly a minimum, since the names of participants were not recorded in some of the elections.

29 *E.g.*, in the cantons of Aspres-sur-Buëch and Saint-Julien-en-Champsaur.

30 Priests chosen as electors were Bertrand, curé of Saint-Laurent-du-Cros; Borelly, curé of La Motte-en-Champsaur (who declined); Chaix, curé of Les Baux; Nicolas, curé of Ribiers; Bilhion, curé of La Roche-sur-le-Buis; Gleize, curé of Verclause; Roux, curé of Villebois; Laugier, curé of Valernes; Truphème, vicaire of Mison; Dalmas, curé of Saint-Geniez; Bertrand, curé of Reynier. Marchon and Cazeneuve, former canons in Gap were also elected.

31 *E.g.*, Bougerel, curé and mayor of Barret-le-Bas; Pellegrin, vicaire and mayor of Ribiers; Rouy, curé and mayor of Châtillon-le-Désert, Dalmas, curé and mayor of Saint-Geniez; Jean-Pascal, curé and mayor of Lazer; Mauduëch, curé and mayor of Eourres; in addition, the abbé Cazeneuve was mayor of Gap for a time: A.D.H.A., ms. 399 and various other sources. I have been unable to obtain a systematic count of the priest-mayors throughout the former diocese of Gap.

political authority the parish clergy might assume in the village under the new constitution.[32] Since 1788, curé Honoré Nicolas had been involved in a feud with the town officials over the location of Ribiers' new cemetery.[33] Prior to the Revolution, neither he nor his predecessors seem to have been admitted to formal participation in community assemblies. But from August 1789, both Nicolas and his vicaire, Joseph Pellegrin, began appearing regularly. In a dramatic meeting, at which most of the village was present, Nicolas defeated the town officials and won approval of his plan for the new cemetery. Thereafter, the two priests took increasingly important roles in village affairs, heading special municipal delegations, presiding over city elections, and consistently signing the registers of community deliberations. In 1792 Pellegrin became "vicaire and mayor" of Ribiers—despite the interdiction in the Civil Constitution—while Nicolas was elected district judge of Serres.[34]

Whether the political participation of the parish clergy was more extensive in Dauphiné than elsewhere is difficult to determine in the present state of research. There was probably a smaller proportion of curé-mayors in the department of the Hautes-Alpes than in such western departments as the Sarthe and the Morbihan.[35] On the other hand, an equal or even greater proportion of clergymen were apparently chosen electors in the Hautes-Alpes than in the Sarthe, the Vendée, or the southern Maine-

[32] A. C. Ribiers, BB 37 and D 1.
[33] See above, Chapter VII.
[34] Deliberations of Dec. 2, 1792: A. C. Ribiers, D 1; also A.D.H.A., F 987.
[35] In the former diocese within the Hautes-Alpes—where data is probably most complete—we have found 6 mayor-priests in 121 communities (4 percent). In the Morbihan at least 18 percent of the mayors were priests in 1790: Claude Langlois, *Le diocèse de Vannes au XIXe siècle, 1800–1830* (Paris, 1974), p. 45. There were also 18 percent priest-mayors (23 of 131 communities) in 11 cantons of the western portion of the Sarthe: data compiled from A. D. Sarthe, L 198 bis, A–N. The general question of the curé-mayors in France during the early Revolution has never been studied.

et-Loire.[36] Participation in such governmental activities was indicative not only of the confidence of a priest's parishioners and of the interest and ambition of the priest himself, but also of the tacit acceptance by the district and department-level administrators. It seems probable that in Upper Dauphiné, where the curé's position was relatively untroubled by competing urban elites—as in the Vendée and the Sarthe[37]—and where anti-clericalism and the polarization of political opinion were probably slow in developing, any ambitious parish clergyman might find paths for advancement within the new bureaucracy.

Whatever the ecclesiastical, economic, and social advantages of the Civil Constitution, there was still the fundamental theological difficulty: the authority of the Church had been spurned; the new system had been dictated by the deputies in Paris, without consulting the Pope, without even seeking the opinion and approval of the French clergy. This was no doubt the ultimate reason for the rejection of the oath by many clergymen who, in most other respects, found the Civil Constitution a desirable improvement over the Old Regime. Yet in Dauphiné, the traditional independence and the long-developing politicization of the clergy had well prepared the parish priests to confront this dilemma. A significant number had been thinking critically about the problems and injustices of ecclesiastical structures for several decades. As a group, they had already drawn the political lines and resolved many of the issues that the curés of most other areas of the kingdom would be forced to confront in 1791. Disinherited from the wealth of the Church and ignored and unappreciated by the upper

---

36 In the former diocese of Gap within the Hautes-Alpes, Basses-Alpes, and Drôme, 13 of approximately 185 electors in 1790 were clergymen: about 7 percent. At the same period, 3 percent of the electors in 26 cantons of the Sarthe were clergymen: Paul Bois, *Les paysans de l'Ouest* (Le Mans, 1960), p. 259; about 4 percent were clergymen in 4 districts of southern Maine-et-Loire: Tilly, *The Vendée*, pp. 270–271; and about 6 percent were clergymen in the department of the Vendée: data compiled from A. D. Vendée, L 168.

37 Bois; and Tilly, *The Vendée, passim.*

clergy, they had increasingly come to seek recognition by lay society not only as men of God, but as public servants, as "the first and most perfect citizens." They had long grown accustomed to bypassing the bishops and the ecclesiastical hierarchy and to appealing directly to such civil authorities as the Parlement or the royal ministers for redress of grievances in both material questions and questions of clerical discipline. In the age-old struggle for authority between Church and State, the Dauphiné curés had, in a sense, already opted for the state. They had embraced the very position of Parlementary Gallicanism that the upper echelons of the clergy had relentlessly combatted under the Old Regime. By 1789, Henri Reymond and the various local leaders of the curés, organized by cantonal conferences, had become, more than any of the bishops, the true directors of the parish clergy of the province. The traditional system of ecclesiastical authority had broken down in Dauphiné before the Revolution. In their grievances and in their political activities, they had already anticipated the Civil Constitution of the Clergy.

But what of those parish priests who did not accept the oath or who later retracted it? Undoubtedly, the motives behind the decisions of this small minority were various and complex. It is of interest that the greatest number of the non-jurors were serving in the southwestern portion of the diocese of Gap (see Figure U). Within the natural region of the Northern Baronnies, the refractories represented thirty-two percent of the parish clergy. This was probably the area of the diocese in which the lay population itself was the least attached to the Revolution: an area that had shown little enthusiasm for the *parti grenoblois* in 1788 and that would reveal counter-revolutionary tendencies as early as 1790-1791.[38] Such a regional correlation would seem to support the contention of Paul

[38] See above, Chapter X. Also, Michel Vovelle, "La Provence et la Révolution," in *Histoire de la Provence* (Toulouse, 1969), pp. 407, 412–413.

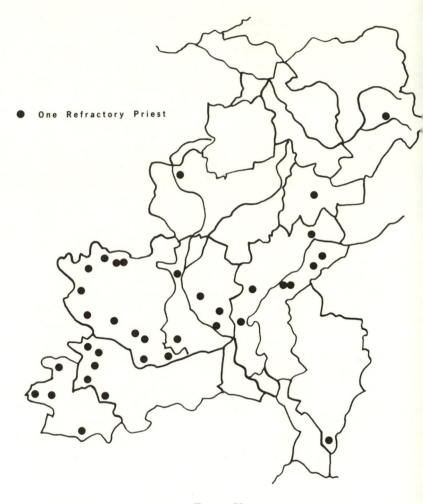

FIGURE U.
Regional distribution of the refractory parish clergy, 1791–1793

Bois and others that the clergymen's attitudes toward the oath were strongly influenced by pressures exerted from the lay milieux in which they lived.[39]

Yet a number of other factors were almost certainly involved in the decisions of the non-jurors. At the beginning of the Revolution, the curés of the Baronnies were, as a group, the least politicized of any in the diocese, having taken part in neither the discussions of the *Cahier des curés du Dauphiné*, nor the electoral process of the First Estate in Provence. In general, no refractory clergyman in the diocese of Gap had signed the *Cahier* in 1789. Moreover, in their collective biography, the small group of 36 non-jurors seemed distinctly atypical of the diocesan parish clergy as a whole. They tended to originate in relatively higher levels of the social hierarchy: over half (10 of 19 for which data is available) were from families of "notables" —nobles, "bourgeois," officeholders, or members of the liberal professions—compared to 33 percent for the parish clergy of the diocese as a whole. They were also generally older men: more than half (16 of 29) were above 50 years of age in 1790, as compared to 41 percent of the total diocesan clergy (see Figure V). They represented 15 percent of all living parish clergymen ordained before 1765 —before curé political activities became most intense—and only 8 percent of those ordained after 1765. There is also some indication that a large proportion had spent time in Avignon during their training period: about 40 percent (15 of 36)—compared to 15 percent overall—are known to have received university degrees or to have received one or more of their ordinations in this papal enclave. Possibly graduates from schools or seminaries in Avignon would have felt a greater deference toward Roman authority than those trained entirely in the seminary of Gap.[40] In terms of

---

[39] Bois, p. 292.

[40] In all, 4 of the 36 (11 percent) are known to have held university degrees: no significant difference from the percentage for the diocesan clergy as a whole: see above, Chapter III.

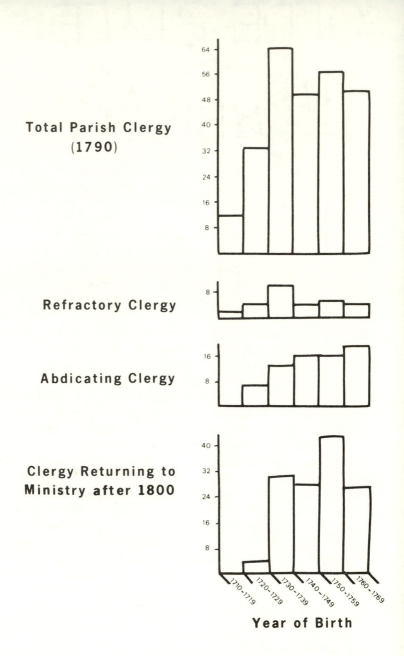

FIGURE V.
Age distribution of the parish clergy of the Old-Regime diocese
of Gap during the Revolution

their absolute revenues in 1790, the refractory curés were neither richer nor poorer than the rest of the curés of the diocese. Significantly, however, the non-jurors did hold more vested interests in the ecclesiastical structures of the Old Regime: 54 percent (15 of 28)—compared to 38 percent overall—had been in possession of tithes and Church lands prior to 1789.

Perhaps in other areas of France, with very different ecclesiastical structures and traditions, such correlations will not be found. But among the highly politicized and group-conscious clergymen of the diocese of Gap, the Civil Constitution was often rejected by those priests who, in their social origins, political and pastoral experience, and mode of ecclesiastical revenues, stood most aloof or apart from the general corps of the parish clergy.

The ultimate break with the Old Regime of the Church took place in the spring of 1791 when the departmental electors assembled in Dauphiné and throughout France to choose replacements for the refractory bishops (only 4 of the 139 diocesan bishops and archbishops of the Old Regime took the oath).[41] The elections in the Isère were particularly significant. The first bishop elected was Joseph Pouchot, one of the principal leaders of the curés in the diocese of Grenoble; when Pouchot died a year later, he was replaced by Henri Reymond.[42] There was thus a clear continuity between the real leadership of the parish clergy at the end of the Old Regime and the formal, institutional leadership of the Revolution. In the Hautes-Alpes, where the newly created diocese would have its seat in Embrun, no one individual had exercised the influence of Reymond or Pouchot. At first there was a movement for the election of Dominique Chaix, but the curé botanist indicated he would never accept, and the electors eventually

---

[41] André Latreille, *L'Eglise catholique et la Révolution française*, 2 vols. (2nd ed.; Paris, 1970), I, 106.

[42] Jean Godel, *La reconstruction concordataire dans le diocèse de Grenoble après la Révolution (1802-1809)* (Grenoble, 1968), p. 30.

opted for Ignace de Cazeneuve.[43] Son of a bourgeois of Gap, Cazeneuve had held the poorest canonry in the cathedral prior to the Revolution. In 1788 he had been one of the members of the cathedral chapter who had deserted Vareilles and backed the *parti grenoblois,* and in 1790 he had been chosen mayor of Gap.[44]

On the evening of March 8, 1791, the new bishop-elect arrived at the "ex-cathedral" of Gap to accept the nomination, ". . . accompanied by the town national guard and an immense crowd. Cries of joy reverberated from every direction and mixed together with the sound of drums; the church bells rang out and the organ played music appropriate to the circumstances."[45]

[43] Minutes of the election of the bishop of the Hautes-Alpes, Mar. 6–8, 1791: A.D.H.A., L 130. See also Dominique Villars, "Notice historique sur Dominique Chaix," *BHA,* III (1884), p. 21.

[44] See above, Chapter X. Also, Félix Allemand, *Dictionnaire biographique des Hautes-Alpes* (Gap, 1911), entry for "Cazeneuve." Cazeneuve's total ecclesiastical revenues in 1790 were a mere 904 *livres,* less than any other canon in the cathedral of Gap: A.D.H.A., I Q I 108 (1).

[45] A.D.H.A., L 130.

CHAPTER XII

De-Christianization and the End of an Era: An Epilogue

The religious and political events in the diocese of Gap after 1791 are, for the most part, beyond the scope of the present study. The history of the Revolution and the Empire in Upper Dauphiné remains to be written.[1] Yet our collective biography of the eighteenth-century curés would not be complete without a brief account of their careers through the later stages of the Revolution. In particular, we must focus on the experience of the Terror and the movement of "de-Christianization." For if the settlement of the Civil Constitution marked at least a partial victory for the citizen curés of Dauphiné, that victory was to be short-lived. Within three years after Ignace de Cazeneuve had made his triumphant entry in Gap, virtually all of the clergymen of the former diocese would have been forced from their posts, and a significant minority would have abdicated the priesthood altogether. The Constitutional Church, so painstakingly constructed by the ecclesiastical committee of the National Assembly in 1790, would be nearly reduced to ruin.

To be sure, an observer living in Upper Dauphiné during the early years of the Revolution might never have anticipated this impending crisis. Initially, most of the region was little perturbed by the partisan struggles, political passions, and anti-clericalism sweeping across other areas of the

---

[1] The most useful studies are Théodore Gautier, *La période révolutionnaire, le Consulat, l'Empire, la Restauration dans les Hautes-Alpes* (Gap, 1895); *Histoire de la ville de Gap* (Gap, 1966), pp. 227–265; Pierre Barral, "Le Dauphiné des notables (1790–1870)" in *Histoire du Dauphiné* (Toulouse, 1973), esp. pp. 339–351; consult also Vovelle, "La Provence et la Révolution," in *Histoire de la Provence* (Toulouse, 1969), pp. 397–438.

nation. The refractory clergy, a major catalyst in the formation of counter-revolutionary sentiments in many parts of France, was scarcely noticeable among the large numbers of clergymen in the Alps who accepted the Civil Constitution. Most inhabitants felt reassured in the fact that the local curé remained in the parish and apparently embraced the principles of the new regime.[2] The mixture of religion and revolution, in evidence at the election of the constitutional bishop, remained a characteristic theme in most public ceremonies in the Hautes-Alpes even into 1792 or 1793 —an obvious holdover from the intermingling of Christian and civic ritual under the Old Regime.[3] It was a measure of the tolerance and general lack of political polarization in the department that the refractory bishop, La Broüe de Vareilles, was able to reside in Gap until July 1792, long after most of the Old-Regime bishops had emigrated.[4]

[2] Georges Lefebvre argued that the peasants were little interested in the problems of the Civil Constitution as long as their curé remained with them. Their passions were aroused only if the curé was forced to leave or if they had to make a choice between a juring and a nonjuring curé: *Les paysans du Nord pendant la Révolution française* (2nd ed.; Paris, 1972), p. 780.

[3] Thus, for example, a solemn mass was the central event during the Federation Day festivities on July 14, 1791. The various parts of the mass were punctuated by drum rolls, cannon shots, and salutes by the armed national guard: *Consigne générale pour la journée du 14 juillet 1791* (Gap, 1791). In both 1791 and 1792 the elections of national deputies opened with speeches by Dominique Chaix, in which the curé inspired his listeners with a curious mélange of sermonical oratory and Rousseauist, humanist rhetoric: *A l'assemblée électorale, à Gap, le 29 août 1791* (Gap, 1791) and *A l'assemblée électorale convoquée à Embrun, le 2 septembre 1792* (Gap, 1792). As late as August 1793, the citizens of Corps continued to preface the ceremonies of allegiance to the Nation with high masses performed by the curé: H. Durand, *Notes sur l'histoire de Corps et son mandement depuis les origines jusqu'à nos jours* (Tunis, 1918), pp. 124–125.

[4] Vareilles at first obstinately refused to leave his residence in Gap and excommunicated Cazeneuve and his episcopal council. In June 1791 he was denounced by one of the curés of the diocese for attempting to distribute a pastoral letter that opposed the Civil Constitution: "Mémoire de Henri-François de la Broüe de Vareilles, évêque de Gap sur sa conduite dans son diocèse depuis mai 1789 jusqu'en juillet 1792," *BHA*, x (1892), p. 50; also *Extrait des registres du conseil*

Yet, by the summer of 1793, the local political climate was evolving rapidly. The first major Savoyard offensive through the Alpine passes had made the war a tangible reality in Upper Dauphiné,[5] while the collaboration of certain public officials with the Federalists of Marseilles was inciting vigorous countermeasures by the representatives on mission from the Convention.[6] In the meantime, the Vendée revolt in western France had given rise to an increasingly clear association between religion and counterrevolution. Everywhere, the earlier enthusiasm for national unity was replaced by fear, suspicion, and repressive violence.

As in most departments of France, it was apparently the representatives on mission who first introduced the de-Christianization movement into the Hautes-Alpes. Joseph Beauchamp, deputy from the Allier, arrived in early November 1793 with the ostensible purpose of requisitioning horses for the army. He had soon gone beyond his commission by ordering arrests of suspects, establishing popular societies, and overseeing the creation of a revolutionary army.[7] On the afternoon of November 8, 1793 he

épiscopal du département des Hautes-Alpes (Gap, 1791). Vareilles arrived in Fribourg, Switzerland, on Oct. 26, 1792. No other clergyman of the diocese of Gap accompanied or joined him there: Archives de l'Etat de Fribourg, Fonds Raemy, card file on emigrant priests in Fribourg.

5 France had been at war with the Kingdom of Sardinia since 1792, but the Sardinian forces posed a serious threat to Dauphiné only in the summer of 1793: Barral, p. 342.

6 See Joseph Roman, "La proscription des Girondins et ses effets dans les Hautes-Alpes," *BHA*, xxvii (1908), pp. 271–291. The role played by the clergy in the Federalist movement in the Hautes-Alpes is not known. Roman mentions only Jean-François Pellenc, vicaire of Gap, sent by Gap as deputy to the Federalists in Marseilles: *ibid.*, pp. 277, 282–283. On the other hand, several parish clergymen—the abbés Nicolas, Bastide, Joubert, Pellegrin, and Jacques—opted for the Jacobin side and were sent to Gap as delegates of the popular societies in Nov. 1793: A.D.H.A., L 279.

7 Beauchamp was commissioned on Oct. 8, 1793 to supervise the requisitioning of horses in the Drôme, the Hautes-Alpes, and the

entered the former cathedral of Gap, had it emptied of its "tainted remains of feudalism" (the religious ornaments and vestments), and converted into a "stable for the horses of the Nation." Almost simultaneously, curé Escallier of Gap became the target of a series of accusations for lack of patriotism—he had reportedly hidden some of the church's ornaments.[8]

In late December Beauchamp was replaced by Pierre-Jacques Dherbez-Latour, who was already operating in his native department of the Basses-Alpes. Even more energetic than his predecessor, Dherbez-Latour traveled through the countryside on horseback to insure that everywhere, "Reason is dissipating the prejudices of fanaticism."[9] He began a systematic effort to oust all priests from their posts and to convert the churches into temples of Reason: ". . . the priests were the greatest enemies of liberty; they held sway over man's conscience, entirely dominated the people and put a halt to their enthusiasm

---

Basses-Alpes. Barras and Fréron had, in fact, been charged with political questions in the Hautes-Alpes, but they were entirely preoccupied with the pacification of the Marseilles-Toulon area: see Auguste Kuscinski, *Dictionnaire des conventionnels* (Paris, 1910), pp. 42–43; and *Recueil des actes du Comité de salut public, avec la correspondance officielle des représentants en mission et le registre du conseil exécutif provisoire*, 28 vols., ed. F.-A. Aulard (Paris, 1889–1933), VII, 300; VIII, 570–571; and IX, 197–198. Also, Richard Cobb, *Les armées révolutionnaires, instrument de la terreur dans les départements, avril 1793–floréal an II*, 2 vols. (Paris, 1961–1963), I, 233, 245.

[8] Entry in the parish register of Gap by curé Escallier, Nov. 11, 1793: Archives of the cathedral of Gap; also *Histoire de la ville de Gap*, p. 255. A first warrant for Escallier's arrest was issued about Nov. 11; but there appears to have been no actual arrest until Mar. 5, 1794. He remained in detention until Nov. 3, 1794: A.D.H.A., L 1175 and ms. 399. Eventually it was decided to use the cathedral only for grain storage.

[9] Letter to the Committee of Public Safety, Nov. 24, 1793: Aulard, *Recueil*, VIII, 687–688. See also the letter of Apr. 22, 1794: *ibid.*, XII, 790–791. Representative to the Convention from the Basses-Alpes, Dherbez-Latour was sent on mission to his home department on June 28, 1793. On Dec. 29, 1793 he received an additional commission for the Hautes-Alpes: Kuscinski, pp. 207–208.

for the Revolution. Under the cloak of religion, they incited [the people] to revolt or to treason at the slightest whim."[10] There seems little doubt that the representative's ultimate desire was that the clergymen not only resign their pastoral functions but renounce and abdicate the priesthood as well. In the end, approximately 30 percent of the parish clergy within the former diocese of Gap would abjure the clerical profession and join the laity (see Figure W).[11]

In recent years a certain historical debate has arisen concerning the abdicating priests of the Year II and the motives governing their decisions.[12] It is impossible, in the case of the diocese of Gap, to enter into the inner thoughts and feelings of the individual clergymen involved. But when they are examined as a group, certain broad patterns of reactions do seem to emerge. Thus, it seems evident that the direct pressure exerted by Beauchamp and Dherbez-

[10] Letter to the Committee of Public Safety, May 10, 1794: Aulard, *Recueil*, XIII, 426.

[11] Seventy-five of an estimated 253 parish clergymen (30 percent) serving within the areas of the former diocese of Gap for which data is available are known to have abdicated. Principal sources: for the Hautes-Alpes, A.D.H.A., ms. 399, L 256, L 1510, F 987, and A.N. F[19] 880 and F[19] 891; for the Basses-Alpes, Joseph-Marie Maurel, *Histoire religieuse du département des Basses-Alpes pendant la Révolution* (Marseilles, 1902), and A.D.B.A., L 886; for the Isère, A.D.I., L 806, the personal card file of the abbé Godel, and Charles Pinel, La déchristianisation dans l'Isère de 1792 à 1795 (D.E.S., Université de Grenoble II, 1971). Lists of abdicating priests have been lost for the district of Le Buis, department of the Drôme, so that the patterns of de-Christianization in the southwest of the former diocese of Gap are not clear. But Jules Chevalier, *L'église constitutionnelle et la persécution religieuse dans le département de la Drôme pendant la Révolution* (Valence, 1919), p. 250, estimated that some 50 priests—a substantial percentage —abdicated in the district of Le Buis. Only 2 priests of the former diocese are known to have married: Jean-Baptiste Calvet, vicaire of Corps, and Jean-Joseph Jacques, curé of Serres.

[12] See the series of articles by Marcel Reinhard *et al.* in *Actes du 89e Congrès national des sociétés savantes, Lyon, 1964* (Paris, 1965), pp. 27–228. I have relied especially on Michel Vovelle, "Prêtres abdicataires et déchristianisation en Provence," pp. 63–98; and on Bernard Plongeron, "Les prêtres abdicataires parisiens," pp. 27–62. See, in addition, Vovelle, "Essai de cartographie de la déchristianisation sous la Révolution française," *Annales du Midi*, LXXVI (1964), pp. 529–542.

FIGURE W.
Regional distribution of parish clergy abdicating the priesthood,
1793–1794

292

Latour or by zealous local administrators at the district level was an important factor in prompting the decision to abdicate.[13] Two clergymen—Gueydan, secondary in Les Infournas, and Brun, vicaire of Saint-Bonnet—specifically mentioned the presence of one of the representatives on mission at the moment they relinquished their letters of ordination.[14] The importance of administrative boundaries in the geographic distribution of the abdicating clergy is apparent: the heavier concentration, for example, within the district of Grenoble, and the total absence in the district of Digne. It may also be noted that of 46 abdications for which the exact dates are known, over half (27) were grouped between March 13 and 18, 1794, precisely the period at which Dherbez-Latour was exerting his maximum efforts in the district of Sisteron.[15]

But to what extent might the parishioners themselves have cooperated in these de-Christianizing activities? Greater research will be necessary before a definitive answer can be given. One is impressed by the exceptionally large percentage of parishes in the region of the Durance that were affected by abdications (see Figure X), a pattern that seems to have been characteristic of the entire Durance basin into Lower Provence.[16] The major socio-economic and cultural dichotomy between north and south that manifested itself in so many ways within the Old-Regime diocese of Gap was apparently brought into focus once again by the issue of de-Christianization. Both Dherbez-Latour

13 On the activities of Dherbez-Latour in the Basses-Alpes, see Vovelle, "Prêtres abdicataires," pp. 71–74.

14 Correspondence of the district of Gap to the *Comité de salut public* of Gap, Feb. 27, 1794: A.D.H.A., L 1175.

15 The exact dates of the abdications in the district of Serres have not generally been determined. The earliest known abdication was that of Honoré Nicolas, former curé of Ribiers, on Nov. 6, 1793; the last was on April 15, 1794 (curé of Vaumeilh). Note, however, that the abdications in the Beaumont, department of Isère, came at the end of February, about two weeks earlier than the peak for the diocese as a whole.

16 Vovelle, "Prêtres abdicataires," p. 76.

Legend:

☐ Unaffected
☐ 1-35% of Parishes
▨ 36-70% of Parishes
■ Over 70% of Parishes

(Average for region studied: 35% of parishes affected)

Beaumont 54%

Valgaudemar Haut-Champsaur 0

Champsaur 17%

Dévoluy 0

Gapençais 13%

Bochaine 22%

Serrois 26%

Middle Durance 41%

Northern Baronnies 19%

Sasse-Vançon 74%

INSUFFICIENT DATA

Southern Baronnies 66%

Lower Durance 83%

FIGURE X.
Percentage of parishes (by natural region) affected by abdications of the priesthood, 1793-1794

294

and the earlier representatives on mission, Barras and Fréron, were convinced of a difference in political culture between the region north of Gap and the valley of the Durance. They waxed eloquent in their descriptions of the patriotism, the revolutionary fervor, the *esprit public* of the Basses-Alpes. In contrast, they found that the city of Gap and the northern portion of the Hautes-Alpes were characterized by political lethargy and apathy. "One might say that their patriotism is still covered with snow like the summits of their mountains."[17]

There may also have been a relation between the broad distribution of sacerdotal abdications and local popular attitudes toward religion. It is perhaps more than a coincidence that the region of the Durance, the site of such widespread de-Christianization in 1794, had already shown signs of a rapid decline in religious fervor in the two or three decades prior to the Revolution.[18] We have seen ample evidence of the kinds of pressures that, under the Old Regime, parishioners might bring to bear on the curé, urging him into conformity with their standards and opinions on a number of local issues.[19] Many of the parish clergymen of the Durance basin who abdicated in the Year II may have done so under pressure in order to maintain the acceptance of their flocks and to preserve their positions in the community. Only after having thus followed their parishioners—even to the ultimate extreme of renouncing the priesthood itself—could the curés hope to remain their leaders.

In the north, however, where religious vitality appears to have been strong and even increasing, the efforts toward de-Christianization were generally less effective. An exception must be recorded for the Beaumont, in the district of Grenoble, where abdications took place in over 50 percent

---

[17] Barras and Fréron to the Committee of Public Safety, May 10, 1793: Aulard, *Recueil*, IV, 92–95; *cf.* letter from Dherbez-Latour to the same, Apr. 22, 1794: *ibid.*, XII, 790–791.
[18] See above, Chapter II.
[19] See above, Chapters VII and VIII.

of the parishes.[20] Generally, however, in the Champsaur
and the Gapençais, the efforts of Beauchamp and Dherbez-
Latour and the surveillance committees in Gap and Saint-
Bonnet could obtain little more than the curés' agreement
to cease performing their pastoral functions; and even this
limited success was achieved only with great difficulty.
Communities like Saint-Julien-en-Champsaur, Saint-Laurent-du-Cros, or La Roche-des-Arnauds might be warned
that priests were public enemies; they might well be cited
the example of the counter-revolutionary curés of the
Vendée.[21] Yet many of these villagers continued to defend
their priests. They found it difficult to believe that their
curés, who had long backed and participated in the Revolution, could now pose this kind of a threat: "Friends and
brothers [wrote the Popular Society of La Roche-des-
Arnauds to the District of Gap], if the recently-read order
concerning priests were carried out in our department, a
large number of priests who have acted in a truly patriotic
and republican manner would be treated as suspects and
enemies of the Republic. We request, therefore, that the
departmental administration not put into effect the above
order, or that it do so only in regards to those who are
actually guilty."[22] In his efforts to provoke abdications in
the Champsaur, Dherbez-Latour would largely fail, in
much the same way as he would fail in the high-mountain
valley of Barcelonnette in the Basses-Alpes. Dherbez dis-
dainfully referred to the latter region as "a seminary, a
sewer of priests."[23] An analysis of clerical recruitment sug-

[20] A.D.I., L 806. It is significant, however, that none of these
priests in the Beaumont actually turned over their letters of priesthood, in contrast to a considerable number of their colleagues elsewhere in the district who did so.

[21] See the exchange of letters between the district of Gap and the
communities of Saint-Julien-en-Champsaur and Saint-Laurent-du-
Cros: A.D.H.A., L 256 and L 1175. The two communities had been
denounced by the Surveillance Committee of Saint-Bonnet for refusing
to oust their priests.

[22] Letter of Apr. 9, 1794: A.D.H.A., L 1513.

[23] Letter of 9 Prairial, Year II: A.D.B.A., L 131, cited in Vovelle,
"Prêtres abdicataires," p. 72.

gests that both the valley of the Drac and the region of Barcelonnette were indeed "seminaries" of clergymen before the Revolution.[24]

In the decision of some of the clergymen to renounce the priesthood, external pressure was not the only factor. The abdicating clergy was notably younger as a group than the clergy as a whole (see Figure V).[25] Only 30 percent had been over 50 in 1790, compared to 41 percent of the overall parish clergy and 55 percent of the non-jurors. Perhaps it was easier for a younger man to abandon his profession and take up a new status in life.[26] It is also clear that the younger priests were precisely of that generation, ordained after 1765, which stood to have been the most influenced by the political movement among the curés and by the image of the priests as a public servant of the community.[27] A few of the priests who went beyond stereotyped formulas in their abdication statements emphasized the continuity between their previous profession as pastors and their new role as citizens dedicated to the principles of the Revolution. They neither condemned their former vocation, nor renounced their belief in a deity; they declared rather that in the new France of the First Republic there

[24] See my article, "Le clergé de l'archidiocèse d'Embrun à la fin de l'Ancien régime," *Annales du Midi,* LXXXVIII (1976), pp. 177–197.

[25] Compared to the group of the non-jurors, the priests who abdicated in the Year II were much more typical of the parish clergy as a whole. Thirty-three percent of the abdicating clergymen originated in families of "notables" (nobles, "bourgeois," officeholders, or members of the liberal professions), the same percentage as for the overall group of parish clergymen in 1790. The percentages were also identical (37 percent) for the portion of the abdicating clergymen and the portion of the parish clergy as a whole who had possessed the tithes. There is no evident correlation between region of origin and the decision to abjure.

[26] There was perhaps a similar age pattern among the abdicating priests in the diocese of Fréjus: Vovelle, "Prêtres abdicataires," pp. 68 and 85–87; the nature of the data presented by Vovelle, however, makes comparisons difficult.

[27] The abdicating clergy represented 18 percent of the corps of clergymen serving in 1790, ordained before 1765; 32 percent of that corps ordained in 1765 or later.

was simply no longer a need for priests. Etienne Grimaud, who a few years earlier had declined the inheritance of his father's office of notary in order to become a priest,[28] abjured his sacerdotal status "without false pretension of shame . . . for a profession which I followed only to strive for the betterment of society"; and he vowed to continue his service toward his fellow-citizens by taking up arms for the defense of the nation.[29] Honoré Nicolas swore before "the Lord" that he had lived an exemplary life as a priest, but that now, with the progress of Reason, "to be a priest and a republican seems incompatible to me . . . ; I opt for the status of citizen."[30] The abbé Pellegrin was even more explicit:

"To console the people for their affliction in the days of their humiliation and slavery; to launch them toward the conquest of their sovereignty and independence when they wished to be free; to preach virtue, the love of mankind and the hatred of despotism: such is the use to which I have put my ministry.

"Today the people are magnanimous, generous, just, and worthy of themselves; in their fundamental laws they have consecrated eternal morality under the auspices of the Supreme Being; they are coming to know, by themselves, the principal truths and the principal virtues; they no longer need any priests."[31]

Grimaud, Pellegrin, and Nicolas were undoubtedly exceptions. The latter two were on ascending political careers that were certainly enhanced by their public abdications.[32] Priests who, like Dominique Chaix, refused to abdicate, could soon find themselves forced out of political participation. But whatever the motives of opportunism or even of

[28] Act of sale before notary Didier in Gap, Dec. 12, 1789: minutes deposited in A.D.H.A.
[29] Statement made Mar. 29, 1794: A.D.H.A., L 256.
[30] *BHA* (1969), pp. 74–75.
[31] Statement of Mar. 8, 1794: Gautier, pp. 36–37.
[32] See above, Chapter XI. We lose track of Grimaud after he left to join the army.

fear involved in the decision to abjure the priesthood, we should not overlook, in the case of some individuals, a measure of idealistic, religious dedication to the "Republic of Virtue" that was now to be born.

For the majority of the clergymen of the former diocese of Gap who had neither refused the oath nor abdicated the priesthood, the year 1794 marked the end of an era. To be sure, the original Revolutionary enthusiasm had begun to wane before that date. By 1793 the curés' 1,200 *livres* salary, which had once seemed such a large sum of money, had been reduced in real value by inflation to below the salary level of 1789.[33] Invariably, the curés were also disconcerted when they lost the right of registering births, marriages, and deaths; when they were forbidden to wear clerical dress in public; when the Christian calendar was suppressed by the state. Having long preached the necessity of civil obedience and the peaceful settlement of differences, many were bewildered by the waves of violence, riots, and civil war they read about or saw with their own eyes. Nevertheless, for most of the curés of Upper Dauphiné, it was the de-Christianization of the Year II, not the initial Revolution nor the oath of 1791, that brought the ultimate crisis of conscience. By the end of Germinal (April 1794), the "progress of Reason" had obliged virtually all parish clergymen to cease their functions and to abandon their rectories.[34] Some were even incarcerated in the former seminary of Gap, converted into a prison. The curés, who had so prided themselves in their role of public service to the nation, were now told by the nation that they were no longer needed, no longer wanted.

[33] Chaix calculated that his 1,200 *livres* paid in *assignats* (paper money) in 1793 would have been worth about 400 *livres* in money of 1789: letter to Villars, Mar. 13, 1793: B.M.G., R 10073. This was, in fact, an exaggeration, but the statement reflected the general state of mind in a period of apparently endless inflation.

[34] The register of the district of Gap claimed on April 13 that all curés had abdicated or resigned: A.D.H.A., L 149. This was not entirely correct: Dominique Chaix resigned only on Apr. 18, Urbain Laurent (curé of Saint-Didier) in Apr. 22.

The statements written by clergymen at the time of the de-Christianization—whether abdications or simple resignations—are usually quite formal; but occasionally we catch a glimpse of the deep sadness and dismay that must have accompanied many of the departures. The curé of Sigoyer, François Bonthoux, resigned his functions "since it was no longer possible for him to be useful to his parishioners."[35] Callandre of Montmaur proudly added that he had served the parish for a full twenty years; Pierre Sambain, who had been curé of Saint-Firmin for forty-four years, made a speech recounting his service in the community and then donated a parting gift of 300 *livres* for distribution to the poor—not unlike the legacies left by curés in their wills under the Old Regime.[36] Escallier of Gap was bitter against the "worthy sans-culottes of my parish" who had denounced him: "Let them tell you whether I have not helped them to sow their fields, to buy their tools!"[37] Dominique Chaix, who had participated in several electoral assemblies and who had been a charter member of his parish's popular society, was particularly dejected. Villars visited him not long after the curé had been forced from his rectory: "I never expected that the National Convention would go so far as to forbid me to say mass. Take my manuscripts, my specimens, and my books. Nothing is of use to me now."[38]

Many of the priests would now return to their villages of origin to begin an early retirement. Others, both those who had simply resigned their ecclesiastical functions and those who had abdicated the priesthood, were forced to look for new professions. The trend toward the participation of the clergy in secular professions—which had begun

[35] Resignation statement of Mar. 25, 1794: A.D.H.A., L 1172.

[36] Resignation statements of Mar. 19, 1794 and Dec. 8, 1793: A.D.H.A., L 1172.

[37] Letter to the *Comité de surveillance*, Feb. 23, 1794: *AA*, IX (1905), p. 50.

[38] Dominique Villars, "Notice historique sur Dominique Chaix," *BHA*, III (1884), p. 21.

in 1789—now became much more pronounced. It is impossible to follow the careers of all the clergymen through the later stages of the Revolution, but thirty-three have been found serving as city or departmental officials, judges or justices of the peace, even notaries, lawyers, and merchants.[39] Five are known to have served in the army.[40] At least three, including the ex-national deputy, Rolland, became teachers at the secondary school for the Hautes-Alpes, established in Gap in 1795.[41] Another, Jean-Joseph Jacques, the wealthy curé-entrepreneur of the Old Regime, served in the key post of *agent national* for the district of Serres.[42] Especially among the younger clergymen or ex-clergymen, the transition from religious notable to lay notable seems to have been made with relative ease. Of the 33 priests described above, only 6 (18 percent) had been over 50 years of age in 1790.

Following the Terror and the decree of 3 Ventôse, Year III (February 21, 1795), permitting open religious practice, many priests would quietly take up their functions once again. But as refractory priests returned from exile and as many disillusioned jurors retracted their oaths or refused the succeeding oaths, the once strongly constitutional clergy became sharply divided between two warring factions, the jurors and the nonjurors. In the Year IV, Dominique Chaix and a number of his colleagues attempted to rejuvenate the constitutional clergy of the diocese, but they were

[39] From numerous sources (especially those described in note 9 in the previous chapter) we have identified five mayors, three city officials, two cantonal officials, one district official, one member of the *comité de surveillance* of Gap, one "agent national," one member of the Patents Bureau (in Marseilles), one *agent de salpêtre*, six judges, four teachers, one merchant, one notary, one lawyer, and five soldiers. These professions were identified at various dates between 1794 and 1800.

[40] Peloux, Martin, Robin de la Flotte, Garagnon, and Grimaud: A.D.H.A., F 987 and L 256.

[41] The other two were Bonthoux, ex-curé of Sigoyer-sur-Tallard, and Martin, ex-curé of Le Saix.

[42] Roman, pp. 273–276, 280, 282.

constantly harassed by the group of refractories.[43] In the meantime, successive waves of official anti-clericalism sent many priests to prison in Gap, Digne, or Grenoble.[44] With the *Concordat* of 1801, negotiated between the Napoleonic government and the Pope, a new national Church was to be instituted in France. But only 45 percent of the corps of the parish clergy of 1790 would take up their posts once again. Included were 58 percent of the former refractory clergymen, many of whom were now in their late sixties or seventies, and 42 percent of those who had once renounced the priesthood, but who subsequently made amends with the Church.[45] Many members of the pre-Revolutionary corps had died during the intervening years. Many others, even some who had not abdicated the priesthood, remained in the secular positions they had now assumed, with no apparent desire to rejoin the ministry. In general, it was those who were in the prime of life in 1801 who returned in the greatest numbers: exactly two-

[43] Chaix described the situation of the diocese to Villars in letters dated Aug. 5 and Oct. 27, 1795, and Nov. 19, 1797: B.M.G., R 10073. He complained bitterly about the opposition of the refractories in the letter of 1797: "Un réfractaire est, à mon sens, un rebelle, un révolté, un ennemi de la patrie, un traître, un fourbe, un aristocrate, ou un royaliste." In 1797 a constitutional priest in Embrun wrote that there were very few priests in the districts of Gap and Serres who still maintained "les bons principes": letter from the abbé Tirant to Grégoire, Sept. 13, 1797: Bibliothèque de Port-Royal, Fonds Grégoire, dossier "Hautes-Alpes."

[44] *E.g.*, Antoine Augier, ex-vicaire of Claret, imprisoned in Digne before Aug. 2, 1798; Jean-Pierre Tourniaire, ex-curé of Le Noyer, arrested in Gap on numerous occasions; Joseph Davin, ex-curé of Moydans, imprisoned in Gap in 1798 and 1799; Jean Bonthoux, ex-curé of Le Glaizil, arrested in Corps in Nov. 1798 and deported to the Isle-de-Ré. Each of the priests in question had taken the required oaths before 1794: A.D.H.A., ms. 399, A.D.B.A., L 422.

[45] Altogether, 133 of the 296 parish clergymen serving in 1790 returned to service in 1801 or shortly thereafter; 21 of the 36 refractories returned, as did 27 of the 65 abdicating clergymen: A.D.H.A., ms. 399; Maurel, *passim*; and the card files established for the Drôme and the Isère by, respectively, the abbé Loche and the abbé Godel. Compare this percentage with the 39 percent of the parish clergy in the Isère in 1790 that returned after the Concordat: Jean Godel, *La reconstruction concordataire dans le diocèse de Grenoble après la Révolution (1802–1809)* (Grenoble, 1968), p. 244.

thirds of those between the ages of 42 and 61 returned to ecclesiastical functions. In contrast, only 31 percent of those over 61, and 53 percent of those under 42 served after the Concordat.[46]

None of the former canons or non-resident priors would reappear in the service of the Church. Bishop Cazeneuve, after having resigned the episcopacy in 1798, would die in obscurity and virtual poverty in 1806.[47] In the meantime, La Broüe de Vareilles, thundering against the "stinking beasts" infecting the country, would remain in exile in Switzerland and Bavaria and return to his native Poitou only with the Restoration. He refused to accept the Concordat and was still addressed as the "Bishop and Count of Gap" when he died in Poitiers in 1831.[48]

Most of the individual curés whose careers we have followed with particular attention would rapidly disappear after 1800. Several—both those who returned to the ministry and those who had taken up lay careers—went to their deaths with a sense of profound disillusionment over the outcome of the Revolution. Dominique Chaix never wavered in his allegiance to the Constitutional Church, but his last letters to Villars were somber and fatalistic. He inquired about the fate of bishop Henri Reymond,[49] and he wrote "black reflections" on the "instability of revolutions." He succumbed to a stroke while saying mass in July 1799.[50] The irascible curé Jean of Montjai, who had renounced the priesthood in 1794, mused in his note-

---

[46] Of those aged 42 to 61 in 1801, 71 of 108 returned; of those over 61, 34 of 110 returned; of those under 42, 27 of 51 returned.

[47] After his death, his total wealth was evaluated at 320 *Francs*: declaration of succession, Dec. 18, 1806: A.D.H.A., II Q CVIII 64.

[48] See Vareilles' "Mémoire"; also the letter from Vareilles in Fribourg to Achard de Germane, ex-*parlementaire* in exile in Lausanne, Apr. 19, 1793: A.D.I., J 572 (Chaper); and Antoine de Vareilles-Sommières, *Les souvenirs et les traditions de Sommières* (Poitiers, 1938).

[49] Imprisoned in Grenoble in 1793 and expecting to be executed, Reymond was saved by the fall of the Robespierrists and survived the Revolution to become bishop of Dijon. He died in Dijon in 1820.

[50] Letters of Aug. 29, 1797 and Jan. 31, 1798: B.M.G., R 10073. On Chaix's death, see the letter from Serre to Villars, July 24, 1799: B.M.G., N 2785.

J.M. ROLLAND
Député des Sénéchaussées
Digne, Sisteron, -

CURÉ DU CAIRE.
de S.t Forcalquier,
et Barcelonette.

Jean-Michel Rolland, curé of Le Caire at the beginning of the Revolution and deputy from Provence to the Estates General. (*Bibliothèque municipale de Grenoble*)

304

book over the ravages wrought by Voltaire, "who spent his entire life jeering at solemn ideals and the virtues of modesty"; and he penned cynical aphorisms: "the *esprit public* was never anything other than the *esprit des factions* which have tyrannized us." He later became a lawyer —probably his true calling—and died in Nyons in 1800, murdered in his bed, as legend would have it.[51] Curé Jean-Michel Rolland, who had also abjured the priesthood and who had served briefly as commissioner in the canton of La Motte in the Basses-Alpes, soon abandoned his political career. After serving as a teacher of rhetoric in Gap, he devoted his later years to poetry and entertained the Gap Literary Society with Platonic love sonnets (his earlier Rococo style was now transformed into a wistful romanticism). At his death in 1810, he had once again assumed the title of "abbé."[52] Of all the Old-Regime clergymen, perhaps none would have a more varied and successful career than Joseph Pellegrin, who served successively as vicaire, mayor, member of the departmental Surveillance Committee during the Terror, and justice of the peace and principal notable of Ribiers under the Empire and the Restoration. Yet he too would look back with some trepidation on the "violence of those unparalleled events" at the time of the Terror; on the "shipwreck" of the Revolution during which everyone had been forced to scramble for the first plank that floated near his reach.[53] Before he died in 1843, he was again preaching and saying mass in the parish church of Ribiers.[54]

By the time of Pellegrin's death, an entirely new parish clergy and a new period in the history of the Church had already emerged in Dauphiné and in France. The utopian

---

[51] Manuscript journal: A.D.H.A., F 2923; also A.D.H.A., ms. 399.

[52] See *Mélanges littéraires . . . de la société d'émulation des Hautes-Alpes* (Gap, 1807).

[53] Letter to Count Alexis de Noailles, minister in Paris, Dec. 22, 1823: A.D.H.A., F 1004.

[54] Joseph Chauvet, *La véritable vie et carrière d'un vicaire savoyard: l'abbé Joseph Pellegrin (1763–1843) et son temps* (Grenoble, 1920).

ideals of a generation of clergymen for the regeneration of society based on the regeneration of the Church had been largely shattered in the winter of the Year II. The alliance between parish priest and lay authority, between religion and revolution, had come to an end; the citizen curé, the curé patriot, had been pushed aside and denounced by the Revolution that he himself had helped to set in motion. In the nineteenth century, he would be replaced by a very different type of parish priest, increasingly originating in lower-class peasant milieux, held in closer subservience to episcopal authority, more strongly attached to Rome, and generally opposed to political radicalism. The *bon curé* of the Old Regime had ceased to exist.

Sources and Bibliography

I have not included all the documents and studies examined, nor all those mentioned in the footnotes. Only the more important materials on which the study is based are listed below.

MANUSCRIPT SOURCES

1. *Archives Nationales*

Series G

G³ 30, responses to an inquiry by the agents-general into the diocesan tax boards, 1770.

G⁸ 68, 74, 80, 81, reports by diocese concerning the increase in the *portion congrue*, for the ecclesiastical provinces of Aix, Embrun, and Vienne, *ca.* 1767–1786.

G³ 632, 634, 661, letters to the agents-general from clergymen—bishops, curés, canons, syndics of the clergy—in the cities of Gap, Grenoble, and Vienne, second half of eighteenth century.

G⁸* 2451–2466, written briefs by the Council of the Clergy of France, 1766–1788.

G⁸* 2467, alphabetical table for the preceding materials.

G⁸* 2468–2554, memoranda and requests sent to the agents-general, 1727–1788.

G⁸* 2555, table for the preceding materials.

G⁸* 2557–2621, letters written by the agents-general, 1727–1787.

G⁸* 2622–2626, tables for the preceding materials.

G⁸* 2627–2632, letters received by the agents-general from members of the royal bureaucracy.

G⁸* 2632 (end), table for the preceding materials.

G⁸* 2781–2833, consultations and deliberations of the Council of the Clergy of France, 1727–1788.

G⁸* 2832 and 2834, tables for the preceding materials.

Series D

D XIX 21–22, lists of priests taking and refusing the oath of 1791, by department.

Bibliography

D XIX 24, letters from Gap concerning the Civil Constitution of the Clergy, 1790–1791.

Series B

Bᵃ 41, *cahiers de doléances* and *procès-verbaux* concerning the elections to the Estates General in the *sénéchaussées* of Sisteron and Digne.

Bᵃ 43–44, reactions to the laws of May 1788 in Dauphiné.

Bᵃ 74–75, various letters and reports concerning events in Dauphiné in 1788–1789, including many by clergymen.

Series F

F¹⁰ 872–893, lists of abdicating clergymen by town, district, and department.

Series H

H 670, correspondence received by Necker concerning elections to the Estates General in Dauphiné.

2. Archives des Affaires étrangères

Mémoires et documents, France.

1386 and 1388, letters concerning the *portion congrue* and other ecclesiastical matters received from Dauphiné and Provence, 1778–1781.

1563, miscellaneous ecclesiastical affairs, Dauphiné, 1750–1788.

3. Bibliothèque de la Société de Port-Royal

Fonds Grégoire.

Carton "Hautes-Alpes," letters received by abbé Grégoire, late eighteenth and early nineteenth centuries.

4. Archives départementales des Hautes-Alpes

Series B

B 48–105, registers of insinuations of donations *inter vivos*.

B 543–579, civil and criminal cases before bailliage of Gap, 1750–1790.

Series II C and II Q

Alphabetical tables of acts subject to *enregistrement* and *contrôle des actes*.

Bibliography

Series I E
Notary minutes.

Series II E
Parish registers.

Series VII E
Jarjayes, 142–145 and 155, correspondence received by the Tournu family (of which several members were clergymen).

Series F
F 676, division of the estate of Dominique Chaix, Year VIII.

F 779, documents concerning the *collège* of Embrun, eighteenth century.

F 987, priests in the district of Serres who abdicated the priesthood in the Year II.

F 1004–1015, papers of Joseph Pellegrin, vicaire and mayor of Ribiers, eighteenth and early nineteenth centuries.

F 1344–1347 and 1350, letters of Augustin Millon, curé of Laye, to baron Des Preaux, 1772–1780.

F 1443, papers of curé Martin, of Saint-Michel-de-Chaillol.

F 1494, papers concerning a suit between the curé and the notary of Saint-Julien-en-Bochaine, 1759–1760.

F 2908, *inventaire d'après décès* of Marchon, curé of Le Noyer, 1748.

F 2923, notes and letters of Jean-Joseph Jean, curé of Montjai, end of eighteenth century.

Series G
G 785–792, registers of pastoral visits, 1685–1788.

G 800–828 and 1550, registers of the bishop's secretariat, 1691–1789 (with lacunae).

G 829–830, registers of approbations, 1745–1777.

G 870–880, registers of *insinuations ecclésiastiques*, 1687–1771.

G 896 and 1810, notifications of university degrees.

G 898–908, registers of ordinations, 1616–1790 (with numerous lacunae before 1707).

G 925, formation of the cantonal conferences, *ca.* 1686.

G 939, register of confraternities, 1695.

G 952, papers on the *petit séminaire* of Tallard.

G 960, statutes of the Dames de la Charité et Miséricorde of Malijai, 1738.

G 966, ordinance on *casuel*, 1762; statutes of Pénitents of Reilhanette, 1764.

G 969, register of signatures of clergymen accepting the bull *Unigenitus*.

G 973–987 and 995–996, correspondence, inquests, and reports to and from bishop Vareilles, 1784–1790.

G 988–993, registers of ordinances by bishop Vareilles, 1784–1789.

G 1037, papers concerning Protestants in the diocese of Gap, early eighteenth century.

G 1098–1104, "Etat des paroisses," 1706–1707.

G 1107, *pouillé* of 1729.

G 1108, *pouillé* of 1755.

G 1109, list of vicaires in the diocese in 1764.

G 1537, résumé of the principal contents of the *Cahier des curés* of 1789.

G 1932 and 1938, papers concerning a dispute between the curés and the chapter of Gap, 1776–1785.

G 2086, 2089, 2092, 2166, correspondence received by the chapter of Gap, second half of the eighteenth century.

G 2328, benefices in the nomination of the bishop of Gap, 1741.

G 2337–2339, declarations of revenue of the parish clergy, 1772.

G 2358–2361, deliberations of the diocesan tax board of Gap, eighteenth century.

G 2362–2363 and 2365–2366, procurations for elections of curé deputies to the diocesan tax board, 1780–1788.

G 2420, copies of leases of ecclesiastical possessions, eighteenth century.

G 2485–2492, *décime* rolls, 1766–1789.

G 2668, various cases before episcopal court of Gap, eighteenth century.

G 2669, register of the episcopal court of the diocese of Gap, 1774–1778.

G 2692, documents and reports concerning the seminary of Gap, seventeenth and eighteenth centuries.

Series H

3 H² 1, "Livre des archives du couvent des Pères Capucins de la ville et cité de Gap."

Bibliography

Series L

L 127, minutes of the primary assemblies of elections of 1790, districts of Gap and Serres.

L 130, minutes of the election of the bishop of the Hautes-Alpes, 1791.

L 256, abdications and resignations of the curés of the district of Gap, Year II.

L 356–357, census of the Year IV.

L 499, 1234, 1388, *capitation* rolls, districts of Gap and Serres, 1790.

L 563, *matrices de rôles* of land tax, district of Gap, 1792.

L 1007, list of botany books owned by Dominique Chaix, Year III.

L 1024, declarations of revenue of the clergy of the Hautes-Alpes, 1789.

L 1043–1047, individual dossiers on priests during the Revolution.

L 1053, report on the seminary of Gap, *ca.* 1791.

L 1172 and 1362, deliberations of the districts of Gap and Serres.

L 1175, register of correspondence of the revolutionary surveillance committee in Gap.

L 1232 and 1380, deliberations on the division of communal property, districts of Gap and Serres, Year II.

L 1391, land tax rolls for the district of Serres, 1791.

L 1512–1513, deliberations of the popular societies of Gap and La Roche-des-Arnauds.

Series Q

I Q I 78, report on the seminary of Gap, *ca.* 1790.

I Q I 107, declarations by the communities concerning Church lands, 1790.

I Q I 108–109 and 137, declarations of revenue by the clergy of the Hautes-Alpes, districts of Gap and Serres, 1790–1791.

I Q I 110, *fabriques* of the district of Gap, Year III.

I Q I 111, confraternities in the district of Gap, 1792.

I Q I 290–291, inventories of possessions confiscated from emigrants during the Revolution.

Series V

V 21, censuses of Protestants, nineteenth century.

Collection Roman

Tomes XLVI–LIII, archives of the sub-delegation of Gap, eighteenth century.

Bibliography

Other Manuscripts

Ms. 85, notes by Jules Chérias on La Bâtie-Neuve.

Ms. 120, "Extrait des mémoires et abrégé historique de l'église et des évêques de Gap," annotated by Jean-Michel Rolland.

Ms. 342, "La Landriade," probably written by Jean-Michel Rolland.

Ms. 377, notes by Paul Guillaume on benefice holders of the diocese of Gap, sixteenth to eighteenth centuries.

Ms. 385, "L'histoire des biens nationaux dans les Hautes-Alpes," by Paul Guillaume.

Ms. 399, notes by Paul Guillaume on the clergy of the diocese of Gap during the Revolution.

5. Archives départementales de l'Isère

Series B

"Procès criminels, Parlement de Dauphiné," partially classed court records.

Series C

II C 34–43, tables of marriages, births and deaths in Dauphiné, 1690–1701 and 1752–1763.

II C 52–62, monthly prices of grain in several cities in Dauphiné, 1755–1790.

III C 34, cahier de doléances of Upaix and response to the Interim Commission by Beaufin, 1789.

Series J

14 J 212, letters by Joseph-François Mévouillon, curé of Manteyer, to Pinet de Manteyer, 1777–1787.

14 J 226, letters by Jean-Baptiste Allard, curé of Rambaud, to Pinet de Manteyer, 1770–1776.

Series L

L 604–624, declarations of revenue of the clergy, 1790–1791.

Series V

IX V^1 1, censuses of Protestants, early nineteenth century.

6. Archives départementales de la Drôme

Series B

B 2185–2196 and 2201–2214, civil and criminal cases before the bailliage of Le Buis-les-Baronnies, 1775–1790.

Bibliography

Series C
C 3–5, responses to the Interim Commission by the communities of the Drôme, 1789.

Series D
D 41–44, *nominations de grades* sent by the University of Valence, 1768–1789.

Series G
XXVII G 1, "Mémorial" of parish of Sahune by curé Bernardin Tronquet, first half of eighteenth century.

Series L
L 87–89, declarations of revenue of the clergy, 1790–1791.

Series V
53 V 1, censuses of Protestants, early nineteenth century.

7. Archives départementales des Alpes de Haute-Provence

Series C
C 57 and 59, *affouagement* of 1728 for the *vigueries* of Digne and Sisteron.
C 78, *capitation* rolls, 1789.

Series L
L 421, priests abdicating the priesthood, district of Sisteron, Year II.
L 30, pensions paid to priests, district of Sisteron, Year III.

8. Archives communales

Deliberations of municipalities:
Bruis, BB 1.
Gap, BB 76–78 and 82.
Montmaur, BB 19 and D 1–2.
Ribiers, BB 37 and D 1.
Saint-Laurent-du-Cros, BB (unclassified).
Upaix, BB 2.
Veynes, BB 31–32.

Confraternity records:
Barcillonnette, GG 1.
Bruis, GG 1 and 4.
Châteauvieux, GG 1.

Neffes, GG 3.
Ribiers, GG 9–10.

9. *Archives de l'évêché de Gap*

Registers of ordinations, nineteenth century.
Liasse on Penitents of Gap, eighteenth century.
Ms. by abbé Louis Jacques on the confraternities in Serres.
Ms. by abbé Louis Jacques on the religious history of Serres.

10. *Archives de l'évêché de Valence*

O 18, "livre ou catalogue des Pénitents blancs de Chauvac."

11. *Bibliothèque municipale de Grenoble*

R 10073, 3 vols., copies of letters from Dominique Chaix to Dominique Villars, 1772–Year VIII, transcribed from the originals by Georges de Manteyer, archivist of the Hautes-Alpes.
N 2046 and 2783, letters from Chaix to Villars and Liottard.
N 2375, letters from Henri Reymond to various individuals.
N 2785, letter from Serre to Villars on the death of Dominique Chaix, 1799.
Vh 1095, pastoral letter from bishop Condorcet to the parish clergy of the diocese of Gap, July 28, 1745.

12. *Archives de la cure de Rémuzat*

Fonds Marcellin, assorted family papers, eighteenth century.

13. *Private Research Files*

Ms. card file on the clergy of the Isère during the Revolution by abbé Jean Godel, loaned to me by the author.
Ms. card file on the clergy of the Drôme during the Revolution by abbé Adrien Loche, loaned to me by the author.
Ms. alphabetical list of the clergy of the former dioceses of Gap and Embrun during the Revolution by abbé Roger de Labriolle, loaned to me by the author.

PRINTED SOURCES

1. *Document Collections. Almanac*

Archives Parlementaires de 1787 à 1860, recueil complet des débats législatifs et politiques des chambres françaises, 1ᵉsérie (1787 à

1799), ed. Jérôme Mavidal, Emile Laurent *et al.*, 82 vols. Paris, Librairie Dupont, 1867–1913.

Procès-verbaux des assemblées générales des trois ordres et des Etats du Dauphiné tenus à Romans en 1788, ed. André Lebon. Lyon, 1888.

Recueil de documents relatifs à la convocation des Etats généraux de 1789, ed. Armand Brette, 4 vols. Paris, Imprimerie nationale, 1894–1915.

Recueil des édits, déclarations, lettres patentes, et ordonnances du roi, arrêts des Conseils de S.M. et du Parlement de Grenoble concernant en général et en particulier la province de Dauphiné, 27 vols. Grenoble, Giroud, 1690–1790. [Cited as "*Recueil Giroud.*"]

Recueil général des anciennes lois françaises depuis l'an 420 jusqu'à la Révolution de 1789, eds. François-André Isambert, N. Decrusy, Alphonse-Henri Taillandier, and Athanase-Jean-Léger Jourdan, 29 vols. Paris, 1821–1833.

Almanach général de la province de Dauphiné pour l'année 1789, Grenoble, 1789.

2. Legal Treatises

Durand de Maillane, Pierre. *Dictionnaire de droit canonique et de pratique bénéficiale*, 5 vols. Lyon, 1776.

Ferrière, Claude-Joseph de. *Dictionnaire de droit et de pratique, contenant l'explication des termes de droit, d'ordonnances, de coutumes & de pratique. Avec les jurisdictions de France, nouvelle édition.* Paris, 1755.

Fleury, Claude. *Institution du droit ecclésiastique de France.* Paris, 1677.

Héricourt, Louis de. *Les lois ecclésiastiques de France dans leur ordre naturel.* Nouvelle édition. Paris, 1756.

Jousse, Daniel. *Traité du gouvernement spirituel et temporel des paroisses.* Paris, 1769.

3. Documents on Economy and Society

Recueil des réponses faites par les communautés de l'élection de Gap au questionnaire envoyé par la Commission intermédiaire des Etats du Dauphiné, ed. Paul Guillaume. Paris, Imprimerie nationale, 1908.

"Documents relatifs à la vie économique et sociale de la Révolution. Election de Grenoble, partie comprise dans le département des Hautes-Alpes. Le Champsaur et le Valgaudemar en 1789," ed. Paul Guillaume, *BHA*, xxxi (1912), 1–46, 103–150, 294–335.

"Les communautés du Poët et de Rousset, 1789," ed. Paul Guillaume, *AA*, xiv (1910), 1–11.

"Situation économique du département des Hautes-Alpes en 1801," ed. Paul Guillaume, *BHA*, xxxii (1913), 166–197, 226–252; xxxiii (1914), 23–48.

Delafont, Pierre-Joseph-Marie. "Mémoire sur l'état de la subdélégation de Gap en 1784," ed. Joseph Roman, *BHA*, xviii (1899), 73–93, 167–186, 247–264; xix (1900), 19–53. [Cited as "Subdel. Gap-1784."]

Expilly, Jean-Joseph d'. *Dictionnaire géographique, historique et politique des Gaules et de la France*, 6 vols. Paris, 1762–1770.

Farnaud, Pierre-Antoine. *Exposé sur les améliorations introduites depuis environ cinquante ans dans les diverses branches de l'économie rurale du département des Hautes-Alpes*. Gap, 1811.

4. Synodal Statutes. Pouillé

Ordonnances synodales du diocèse de Gap publiées en l'année 1712 par Mgr. de Malissoles, 2 vols. Grenoble, 1712. [Cited as "Ord. syn."]

"Pouillé ou état général des bénéfices séculiers et réguliers du diocèse de Gap avant 1789," ed. Paul Guillaume, *BHA*, x (1891), 113–165.

5. Protests by Curés. French Revolution

Cahier des curés de Dauphiné adressé à l'Assemblée nationale et à Messieurs les députés de la province en particulier. Lyon, 1789.

"Cahier de doléances des curés du diocèse de Gap, 1789–1790," ed. Paul Guillaume, *AA*, xiii (1909), 201–212. [Probably written by Alexandre Achard.]

Chaix, Dominique. *A l'assemblée électorale à Gap, le 29 août 1791*. Gap, 1791.

———. *A l'assemblée électorale convoquée à Embrun, le 2 septembre 1792*. Gap, 1792.

———. *A MM. élus pour le Convention nationale à Embrun, le 6 septembre, 1792*. Gap, 1792.

Les curés de Dauphiné à leurs confrères les recteurs de Bretagne. N.p., n.d.

Bibliography

Procès-verbal de la prestation de serment de messieurs les curés et autres ecclésiastiques fonctionnaires de la commune de Gap. Gap, 1791.

Reymond, Henri. *Analyse des principes constitutifs des deux puissances, précédée d'une adresse aux curés des départements de l'Isère, de la Drôme, et des Hautes-Alpes.* Embrun, 1791.

——. *Les droits des curés et des paroisses considérés dans leur double rapport spirituel et temporel.* Paris, 1776.

——. *Mémoire à consulter et consultation pour les curés du Dauphiné relativement aux Etats généraux.* Paris, 1789.

——. *Mémoire à consulter et consultation pour les curés de la province du Dauphiné.* Paris, 1780.

——. *Mémoire pour les curés de France relativement à la convocation des Etats généraux.* Avignon, 1788.

6. Legal Briefs

Requête du syndic des curés de la province de Dauphiné, contre les abbés, chapitres, monastères, prieurs, au sujet de l'exiguïté des portions congrues et arrêt du 22 décembre 1664. N.p., 1664.

Consultations, vu les pièces du procès des consuls et communautés d'Arzeliers et Laragne contre les sieurs prieurs-curés des paroisses d'Arzeliers et Laragne. Grenoble, 1782.

Mémoire pour sieur Alexandre Achard, archiprêtre et curé de Serres contre M. de Bardonnenche, évêque de Vence, prieur de Serres. Grenoble, 1780.

Mémoire pour la communauté de Montjai contre M. Tournu, prieur-majeur. Grenoble, 1782.

7. Other Writings by Clergymen

Albert, Antoine. *Histoire géographique, naturelle, ecclésiastique, et civile du diocèse d'Embrun,* 2 vols. Embrun, 1783–1786.

Chaix, Dominique. *Récit historique et moral sur la botanique.* Gap, 1793.

La Broüe de Vareilles, Henri-François. "Mémoire de Henri-François de la Broüe de Vareilles, évêque de Gap, sur sa conduite dans son diocèse depuis mars 1789 jusqu'en juillet 1792," ed. Paul Guillaume, *BHA,* XI (1892), 34–54.

Reymond, Henri. "Notice biographique de Monseigneur Reymond, évêque de Dijon," *Chronique religieuse,* IV (1820), 364–380, 385–395.

Bibliography

Réguis, Léon. *La voix du pasteur, discours familiers d'un curé pour tous les dimanches de l'année*, 2 vols. Lyon, Girard et Josserand, 1855. (The first edition was in Paris, 1766.)

SECONDARY WORKS

1. *Bibliography*

Aimès, Paul. *Guide bibliographique des Hautes-Alpes.* Gap, Clavel, 1959.

——. *Initiation aux recherches d'histoire locale pour le département des Hautes-Alpes.* Gap, Clavel, 1961.

Chomel, Vital. "Le Dauphiné sous l'Ancien régime. Publications relatives à l'histoire moderne de la province de 1935 à 1962," *CH*, VIII (1963), 303–339.

Guillaume, Paul. *Notice sur les sources historiques des Hautes-Alpes.* Gap, Jouglard, 1882.

Latouche, R. "Histoire du Dauphiné (bibliographie)," *RH*, CLXXV (1935), 546–570.

Maignien, Edmond. *Bibliographie historique du Dauphiné pendant la Révolution française*, 3 vols. Grenoble, Imprimerie dauphinoise, 1891.

——. *Dictionnaire des ouvrages anonymes et pseudonymes du Dauphiné.* Grenoble, Drevet, 1892.

2. *Dictionaries*

Allemand, Félix. *Dictionnaire biographique des Hautes-Alpes.* Gap, Alpine, 1911.

Brun-Durand, Justin. *Dictionnaire biographique et biblioiconographique de la Drôme*, 2 vols. Grenoble, Falque et Penin, 1901.

Marion, Marcel. *Dictionnaire des institutions de la France aux XVIIe et XVIIIe siècles.* Paris, Picard, 1923.

Rochas, Adolphe. *Biographie du Dauphiné*, 2 vols. Paris, Charavay, 1856–1860.

3. *Religious History: Diocese of Gap and Dauphiné*

"Quotité des dîmes en Gapençais en 1791," *AA*, XIII (1909), 212–215.

Bibliography

Albanès, J. H. *Gallia christiana novissima. Histoire des archevêchés, évêchés, et abbayes de France*, t. I (province of Aix). Mont-béliard, Hoffman, 1895.

Allemand, Félix. "Notice sur les sources minérales, les fonts saints, et les fonts bénits dans les Hautes-Alpes," *BHA*, xxiii (1904), 65–83, 205–225.

Arnaud, Eugène. *Histoire des Protestants du Dauphiné aux XVIe, XVIIe, et XVIIIe siècles*, 3 vols. Paris, Grassart, 1875–1876.

Avezou, Robert. "La vie religieuse en Dauphiné du XVIe au XVIIIe siècle," *Procès-verbaux mensuels de la Société dauphinoise d'ethnologie et d'archéologie*, xxxi (1955), 22–60.

Bermond, J. "Etude sur la dîme et les biens ecclésiastiques dans l'ancien diocèse de Gap," *BHA*, xlvi (1928), 242–276.

Bernard, Michel. "Revendications et aspirations du bas-clergé dauphinois à la veille de la Révolution," *CH*, i (1956), 327–347.

Charronnet, Charles. *Les guerres de religion et la société protestante dans les Hautes-Alpes, 1560–1789*. Gap, Jouglard, 1861.

Chauvet, Joseph. *La véritable vie et carrière d'un vicaire savoyard: l'abbé Joseph Pellegrin (1763–1843) et son temps*. Grenoble, Allier, 1920.

Chevalier, Jules. *L'église constitutionnelle du département de la Drôme (1790–1801)*. Valence, Céas, 1919.

Chomel, Vital. "Les paysans de Terrebasse et la dîme à la fin de l'Ancien régime," *Evocations*, xviii (1962), 98–103.

Delattre, Pierre. "Embrun" in *Les établissements des Jésuites en France depuis quatre siècles, fasc. 6*. Wetteren, Belgium, Imprimerie de Meester Frères, 1950.

Font-Réaulx, Jacques de. "Les pouillés de la province de Vienne," *BD*, lxix (1943), 17–33.

Franclieu, A.-M. de. *La persécution religieuse dans le département de l'Isère de 1790 à 1802*, 3 vols. Tournais, Imprimerie Notre-Dame des Prés, 1904–1905.

Gangneux, Gérard. "Le bas-clergé sous l'Ancien régime. L'exemple d'une cure aux XVIIe et XVIIIe siècles," *Annales E.S.C.*, xiv (1959), 745–749.

Gautier, Théodore. *Histoire de la ville de Gap et du Gapençais*, ed. Paul Guillaume, 2 vols. Gap, Imprimerie alpine, 1910. (The first edition of volume I was published in 1844.)

Bibliography

Geisendorf, Paul F. "Recherches sur les conséquences démographiques de la révocation de l'Édit de Nantes en Dauphiné," *CH*, VI (1961), 245–264.

Grimaud, Pierre. L'état des esprits en Dauphiné et la question religieuse à la fin de l'Ancien régime. L'édit de novembre 1787, typewritten *mémoire* submitted for the D.E.S., Faculté de droit, Aix-Marseilles, 1959.

Godel, Jean *et al. Le cardinal des montagnes, Etienne Le Camus, évêque de Grenoble (1671–1707). Actes du Colloque Le Camus, Grenoble, 1971*. Grenoble, Presses universitaires de Grenoble, 1974.

Godel, Jean. *La reconstruction concordataire dans le diocèse de Grenoble après la Révolution (1802–1809)*. Grenoble, chez l'auteur, 1968.

Guillaume, Paul. "Introductions" to *Inventaire sommaire des Archives départementales antérieures à 1790. Hautes-Alpes. Séries G*, Imprimerie alpine and Jean et Peyrot, 1891–1913.

———. *Clergé ancien et moderne du diocèse de Gap. Abbés, prieurs, curés, vicaires, chapelains, etc., de toutes les paroisses du diocèse actuel*. Gap, Jean et Peyrot, 1909.

———. *Bénéfices et bénéficiers du Beaumont aux XVIe, XVIIe, et XVIIIe siècles*. Grenoble, Biratier et Dardelet, 1896.

———. *Bénéfices et bénéficiers de l'ancien diocèse de Gap, archiprêtré de Provence. XVIe, XVIIe, et XVIIIe siècles*. Digne, Chaspoul, 1896.

———. *Bénéfices et bénéficiers du Rosanais aux XVIe, XVIIe, et XVIIIe siècles*. Valence, Céas, 1895.

Jacques, E. *Le séminaire de Gap, 1577–1789*. Gap, Jean et Peyrot, 1924.

Ladoucette, Jean-Charles-François. *Histoire, antiquités, usages, dialectes des Hautes-Alpes*. Paris, Hérissant Le Doux, 1820.

Lemas, T. *Ignace de Cazeneuve*. Paris, Gaston Née, 1890.

Lovie, Jacques. "La vie paroissiale dans le diocèse de Die à la fin de l'Ancien régime," *BD*, no. 245 (Oct. 1932), pp. 358–382; no. 257 (Jan. 1933), pp. 31–51; no. 260 (Oct. 1933), pp. 169–183; no. 265 (Jan. 1935), pp. 17–28; no. 269 (Jan. 1936), pp. 274–289; no. 272 (Oct. 1936), pp. 446–470.

Martenelli, J. Les serments de 1790 à 1792 dans l'Isère, typewritten *Mémoire* for the *Maîtrise*, Université de Grenoble II, 1971.

Bibliography

Maurel, Joseph-Marie. *Histoire religieuse du département des Basses-Alpes pendant la Révolution.* Marseilles, P. Ruat, 1902.

Nicollet, F. N. "Le collège communal de Gap avant la Révolution," *Bulletin des sciences économiques et sociales du comité de travaux historiques et scientifiques* (1895), pp. 10–24.

——. "Les biens et revenus du collège d'Embrun avant la Révolution," *BHA*, XI (1892), 310–324.

Pinel, Charles. La déchristianisation dans l'Isère de 1792 à 1795, typewritten *mémoire* for the D.E.S., Université de Grenoble II, 1971.

Pisani, Paul. "Vingt-six ans d'épiscopat: Monseigneur Jean-Baptiste de Maillé de La Tour-Landry," *Revue des questions historiques*, XCII (1912), pp. 404–435.

Rance, A. J. *Jacques-Marie de Condorcet, évêque de Gap, 1741–1754.* Paris, Librairie Catholique, 1885.

Roure, H. "Le clergé du sud-est de la France au XVIIe siècle," *RHEF*, XXXVII (1951), 153–187.

Tackett, Timothy. "Le clergé de l'archidiocèse d'Embrun à la fin de l'Ancien régime," *Annales du Midi, LXXXVIII* (1976), 177–197.

——. "Le recrutement du clergé dans le diocèse de Gap au XVIIIe siècle," *RHMC*, XX (1973), 497–522.

Taillas, A. de. "Etude historique sur le pouvoir temporel des évêques de Gap," *Bulletin de l'Académie delphinale*, 3ᵉ série, XIV (1878–1879), 201–252.

Vareilles-Sommières, Antoine de. *Les souvenirs et les traditions de Sommières.* Poitiers, Basile, 1938.

Villars, Dominique. "Notice historique sur Dominique Chaix," *BHA*, III (1884), 291–319.

4. Political History: Region of Gap and Dauphiné

Anonymous. *Histoire de la ville de Gap.* Gap, Librairie alpine, 1966.

Baratier, Edouard *et al. Histoire de la Provence.* Toulouse, Privat, 1969.

Bligny, Bernard *et al. Histoire du Dauphiné.* Toulouse, Privat, 1973.

Conrad, Pierre. *La Peur en Dauphiné.* Paris, Billais, 1904.

Egret, Jean. *Les derniers Etats de Dauphiné. Romans (1788–1789).* Grenoble, Arthaud, 1942.

Bibliography

Egret, Jean. *Le Parlement de Dauphiné et les affaires publiques dans la seconde moitié du XVIIIe siècle*, 2 vols. Grenoble, Arthaud, 1942.

Esmonin, Edmond. "Les intendants du Dauphiné des origines à la Révolution," *Annales de l'Université de Grenoble*, xxxiv (1923), 37–90.

Faure, Léon. *Une page des origines de la Révolution en Dauphiné. Gap en 1788*. Gap, Fillon, 1888.

Félix-Faure, J.-A. *Les assemblées de Vizille et de Romans en Dauphiné durant l'année 1788*. Paris, 1887.

Gautier, Théodore. *La période révolutionnaire, le Consulat, l'Empire, la Restauration dans les Hautes-Alpes*, ed. Paul Guillaume. Gap, Guillaume, 1895.

Letonnelier, Gaston. "Les cahiers de doléances en Dauphiné," *Bulletin de l'Académie delphinale*, LXXI (1935), 77–129.

Meizel, Joseph. *Essai historique sur les Hautes-Alpes des origines à 1820*, 2 vols. Gap, Jean, 1927.

Queyrel, Camille. Un modèle de l'administration éclairée, Pierre Delafont et Pierre-Joseph-Marie Delafont, derniers subdélégués de Gap, typewritten *mémoire* for the D.E.S., Faculté des lettres de Grenoble, 1933.

Roman, Joseph. "La fin de l'administration de l'Ancien régime à Gap," *BHA*, xix (1900), 99–124.

——. *Histoire de la ville de Gap*. Gap, Richaud, 1892.

——. "La proscription des Girondins et ses effets dans les Hautes-Alpes," *BHA*, xxvii (1908), 271–291.

5. Economy, Society, and Demography: Diocese of Gap

Agulhon, Maurice. *La vie sociale en Provence intérieure au lendemain de la Révolution*. Paris, Clavreuil, 1970.

Arbos, Philippe. *La vie pastorale dans les Alpes françaises. Etude de géographie humaine*. Paris, Colin, 1922.

——. "L'évolution économique des Baronnies," *La géographie*, xxxi (1916–1917), 89–112.

Baratier, Edouard. *La démographie provençale du XIIIe au XVIe siècle (avec chiffres de comparaison pour le XVIIIe siècle)*. Paris, SEVPEN, 1961.

Blache, J. "L'essartage, ancienne pratique culturelle dans les Alpes dauphinoises," *RGA*, xi (1923), 553–575.

Bibliography

Blache, J., C. Carcel, and M. Rey. "Le troupeau bovin dans les Alpes de Dauphiné et de Savoie au milieu du XVIIIe siècle," *RGA*, XXI (1933), 419–431.

Blanchard, Raoul. *Les Alpes occidentales*, 13 vols. Paris, Arthaud, 1938–1956.

Chianéa, Gérard. *La condition juridique des terres en Dauphiné au XVIIIe siècle (1700–1789)*. Paris, Mouton, 1969.

Gibert, A. "Le Valgaudemar," *RGA*, XI (1923), 663–782.

Guillaume, Paul. "Mouvement de la population du département des Hautes-Alpes au XIXe siècle," *BHA*, XXVII (1908), 203–217.

Léon, Pierre. *La naissance de la grande industrie en Dauphiné (fin du XVIIe siècle–1869)*, 2 vols. Paris, PUF, 1953.

Livet, M. R. "Le bocage du Champsaur," *Bulletin du comité de travaux historiques et scientifiques, section de géographie*, LXXI (1958), 169–182.

Mercier, J. "La basse Durance alpestre de Sisteron à Mirabeau," *RGA*, XXIX (1941), 579–705.

Moralis, D. "Les phénomènes d'habitat dans le massif des Baronnies," *RGA*, XII (1924), 547–644.

Sauvan, E. "Gap et ses foires," *RGA*, XX (1932), 1–57.

Sclafert, Thérèse. *Le Haut-Dauphiné au Moyen-Age*. Paris, Sirey, 1926.

Vallentin du Cheylard, Roger. *Essai sur la population des taillabilités de Dauphiné d'après les mémoires des intendants*. Valence, Céas, 1912.

Van Gennep, Arnold. *Le folklore des Hautes-Alpes, étude descriptive et comparée de psychologie populaire*, 2 vols. Paris, Maisonneuve, 1946–1948.

Veyret, Paul. *Les pays de la moyenne Durance alpestre*. Grenoble, Allier, 1944.

———. "Le commerce des produits agricoles dans les pays de la moyenne Durance vers la fin du XVIIIe siècle," *RGA*, XXIX (1941), 283–305.

6. Studies of Individual Parishes: Diocese of Gap

Orpierre et son canton: histoire de la Baronnie d'Orpierre-Trescléoux. Gap, Ribaud, 1953.

Achard, l'abbé. "Histoire religieuse de Trescléoux," *BHA*, XXXV (1917), 140–168, 203–227, 310–328; XXXVI (1918), 28–29.

Bibliography

Bermond, J. *Monographie de Lagrand*. Gap, Jean et Peyrot, 1925.
——. "Saint-André-de-Rosans," *Quinzaine religieuse du diocèse de Gap*. (1926.)
Durand, H. *Notes sur l'histoire de Corps et son mandement depuis les origines jusqu'à nos jours*. Tunis, Niérat et Fortin, 1918.
Feraud, Jean-Joseph-Maxime. *Souvenirs religieux des églises de la Haute-Provence*. Digne, Vial, 1879.
Imbert, Jean. *Histoire de Serres et des Serrois*. La Tronche-Montfleury, Editions des cahiers de l'Alpe, 1966.
Maurel, Joseph-Marie. *Histoire de l'Escale*. Forcalquier, Crest, 1893.
Roman, Joseph. *Histoire de Ribiers*. Gap, Richaud, 1892.
Taillas, A. de. *Notice historique sur l'ancienne communauté de Tallard*. Grenoble, Allier, 1868.

7. The Parish Clergy in France: Origins, Careers, Revenues, and Social Position

Ageorges, J. *Le clergé rural sous l'Ancien régime, sa vie et son organisation*. Paris, Bloud, 1906.
Berthelot du Chesnay, Charles. "Le clergé diocésain français au XVIIIe siècle et les registres des insinuations ecclésiastiques," *RHMC*, x (1963), 241–270.
Châtellier, Louis. "Société et bénéfices ecclésiastiques. Le cas alsacien (1670–1730)," *RH*, ccxliv (1970), 75–98.
Desaive, Jean-Paul. "Clergé rural et documents fiscaux, les revenus et charges des prêtres de campagne au nord-est de Paris, d'après les enquêtes fiscales des XVIIe et XVIIIe siècles," *RHMC*, xvii (1970), 921–952.
Ferté, Jeanne. *La vie religieuse dans les campagnes parisiennes (1622–1695)*. Paris, J. Vrin, 1962.
Fracard, M. L. *La fin de l'Ancien régime à Niort, essai de sociologie religieuse*. Paris, Desclée de Brouwer, 1956.
——. "Le recrutement du clergé séculier dans la région niortaise au XVIIIe siècle," *RHEF*, lvii (1971), 241–265.
Gagnol, P. *La dîme ecclésiastique en France au XVIIIe siècle*. Paris, Librairie générale catholique, 1910.
Girault, Charles. *Les biens d'Eglise dans la Sarthe à la fin du XVIIIe siècle*. Laval, Goupil, 1953.
Gutton, Jean-Pierre. "Notes sur le recrutement du clergé séculier

Bibliography

dans l'archidiocèse de Lyon (1589–1789)," *Bulletin du Centre d'histoire économique et sociale de la région lyonnaise*, no. 2 (1974), 1–19.

Join-Lambert, M. "Pratique religieuse dans le diocèse de Rouen de 1707–1789," *Annales de Normandie*, v (1955), 35–49.

Julia, Dominique. "Le clergé paroissial dans le diocèse de Reims à la fin du XVIIIe siècle," *RHMC*, xiii (1966), 195–216.

——. "Le clergé paroissial du diocèse de Reims à la fin du XVIIIe siècle; de la sociologie aux mentalités; le vocabulaire des curés: essai d'analyse," *Etudes ardennaises*, no. 49 (Apr.–June 1967), pp. 19–35; no. 53 (Oct.–Dec. 1968), pp. 41–66.

Julia, Dominique, and Denis McKee. Le clergé paroissial dans le diocèse de Reims sous l'épiscopat de Charles-Maurice Le Tellier, origine, carrière, mentalités, paper presented at the Colloque sur le curé Meslier et la vie intellectuelle, politique, et sociale à la fin du XVIIe et au début du XVIIIe siècle, Reims, octobre 1974.

Léouzon le Duc, Claude. "La fortune du clergé sous l'Ancien régime," *Journal des Economistes*, 4e série, xv (July–Sept. 1881), 217–240.

Le Pennec, Y.-M. "Le recrutement du clergé séculier dans le diocèse de Coutances au XVIIIe siècle," *Revue du département de la Manche*, xii (1970), 191–234.

Loupès, Philippe. "Le casuel dans le diocèse de Bordeaux aux XVIIe et XVIIIe siècles," *RHEF*, lvii (1972), 19–52.

——. "Le clergé paroissial du diocèse de Bordeaux d'après la grande enquête de 1772," *Annales du Midi*, lxxxiii (1971), 5–24.

McManners, John. *French Ecclesiastical Society under the Ancien Régime. A Study of Angers in the Eighteenth Century*. Manchester, Manchester University Press, 1960.

Marion, Henri. *La dîme ecclésiastique en France au XVIIIe siècle et sa suppression*. Bordeaux, Imprimerie de l'Université, 1912.

Pérouas, Louis. *Le Diocèse de la Rochelle de 1648 à 1724: sociologie et pastorale*. Paris, SEVPEN, 1964.

Plongeron, Bernard. *La vie quotidienne du clergé français au XVIIIe siècle*. Paris, Hachette, 1974.

Poyer, Alex. Les curés de la Quinte du Mans au XVIIIe siècle (1723–débuts de la Révolution), typewritten *Mémoire* for the *Maîtrise*, Université du Mans, 1974.

Bibliography

Rébillon, Armand. *La situation économique du clergé à la veille de la Révolution dans les districts de Rennes, de Fougères, et de Vitré.* Rennes, Oberthur, 1913.

Roy, Jean. Le prêtre paroissial dans deux diocèses provençaux: Aix et Arles au XVIIIe siècle. Société et religion, typewritten *Thèse de troisième cycle*, Université d'Aix-Marseilles I, 1975.

Schaer, André. *Le clergé paroissial catholique en Haute-Alsace sous l'Ancien régime, 1648–1789.* Paris, Sirey, 1966.

Schmitt, Thésèse-Jeanne. *L'organisation ecclésiastique et la pratique religieuse dans l'archidiaconé d'Autun, 1650 à 1750.* Autun, L. Marcelin, 1957.

Sévestre, Emile. *L'organisation du clergé paroissial à la veille de la Révolution.* Paris, Picard, 1911.

Sicard, Augustin. *La nomination aux bénéfices ecclésiastiques avant 1789.* Paris, V. Lecoffre, 1896.

Vaissière, Pierre de. *Curés de campagne de l'ancienne France.* Paris, Spes, 1933.

——. "L'état social des curés de campagne au XVIIIe siècle," *RHEF*, xix (1933), 23–53.

Venard, Marc. "Pour une sociologie du clergé au XVIe siècle. Recherche sur le recrutement sacerdotal dans la province d'Avignon," *Annales E.S.C.*, xxiii (1968), 987–1016.

Viala, André. "Suggestions nouvelles pour une histoire sociale du clergé aux temps modernes" in *Etudes d'histoire du droit canonique dédiées à Gabriel Le Bras*, 2 vols. Paris, Sirey, 1965, vol. ii, 1471–1481.

Vovelle, Michel. "Analyse spectrale d'un diocèse méridional au XVIIIe siècle: Aix-en-Provence," *Provence historique*, xxii (1972), 352–451.

8. *The Revolt of the Curés in France and the Civil Constitution of the Clergy*

Chassin, Charles-Louis. *Les cahiers des curés.* Paris, Charvay, 1882.

Eich, Jean. *Histoire religieuse du département de la Moselle pendant la Révolution. Première partie. Des début à l'établissement de l'église constitutionnelle.* Metz, Le Lorrain, 1964.

——. *Les prêtres mosellans pendant la Révolution*, 2 vols. Metz, Le Lorrain, 1959–1964.

Bibliography

Giraud, M. *Essai sur l'histoire religieuse de la Sarthe de 1789 à l'an IV.* Paris, Jouve, 1920.

Hutt, Maurice G. "The Role of the Curés in the Estates General of 1789," *Journal of Ecclesiastical History,* VI (1955), 190–220.

——. "The Curés and the Third Estate: The Ideas of Reform in the Pamphlets of the French Lower Clergy in the Period 1787–1789," *Journal of Ecclesiastical History,* VIII (1957), 74–92.

La Gorce, Pierre de. *Histoire religieuse de la Révolution française,* 5 vols. Paris, Plon, 1909–1923.

Latreille, André. *L'Eglise catholique et la Révolution française,* 2nd ed., 2 vols. Paris, Editions du Cerf, 1970.

McManners, John. *The French Revolution and the Church.* New York, Harper and Row, 1970.

Mathiez, Albert. *La Révolution et l'Église, études critiques et documentaires.* Paris, Colin, 1910.

——. *Contributions à l'histoire religieuse de la Révolution française.* Paris, Félix Alcan, 1907.

Necheles, Ruth F. "The Curés in the Estates General of 1789," *Journal of Modern History,* XLVI (1974), 425–444.

Préclin, Edmond. *Les Jansénistes du XVIIIe siècle et la Constitution civile du clergé. Le développement du richérisme. Sa propagation dans le bas-clergé: 1713–1791.* Paris, Gambier, 1929.

Plongeron, Bernard. *Conscience religieuse en révolution. Regards sur l'historiographie religieuse de la Révolution française.* Paris, Picard, 1969.

Porée, Charles. *Cahiers des curés et des communautés ecclésiastiques du bailliage d'Auxerre pour les Etats généraux de 1789.* Auxerre, Imprimerie l'Universelle, 1927.

Reinhard, Marcel. *Religion, révolution et contre-révolution.* Paris, Centre de Documentation Universitaire, 1960.

Sagnac, Philippe. "Les curés et le patriotisme pendant la Révolution, 1789–1792," *La Révolution française,* XVIII (1939), 166–177.

——. "Etude statistique sur le clergé constitutionnel et le clergé réfractaire en 1791," *Revue d'histoire moderne,* VIII (1906), 97–115.

Tilly, Charles. "Civil Constitution and Counter-Revolution in Southern Anjou," *French Historical Studies,* I (1959), 172–199.

Williams, William H. "Perspectives on the French Parish Clergy on the Eve of the French Revolution" in *Proceedings of the*

Bibliography

Fourth Annual Colloquium on Revolutionary Europe, 1750–1850. Gainesville, University of Florida Press, 1976.

——. *The Priest in History: A Study of Divided Loyalties in the French Lower Clergy from 1776 to 1789.* Ph.D. dissertation, Duke University, 1965.

9. Other Studies in Religious History and Rural Culture

Agulhon, Maurice. *Pénitents et Francs-Maçons de l'ancienne Provence (Essai sur la sociabilité méridionale).* Paris, Fayard, 1968.

Babeau, Albert. *Le village sous l'Ancien régime,* 3rd ed. Paris, Didier, 1882.

Bien, David D. "Catholic Magistrates and Protestant Marriage in the French Enlightenment," *French Historical Studies,* II (1961–1962), 409–429.

Billacois, François *et al. Crimes et criminalité en France sous l'Ancien régime.* Paris, Colin, 1971.

Bois, Paul. *Paysans de l'Ouest,* abridged ed. Paris, Flammarion, 1971.

Bouchard, Gérard. *Le village immobile. Sennely-en-Sologne au XVIIIe siècle.* Paris, Plon, 1972.

Carrière, Victor. *Introduction aux études d'histoire ecclésiastique locale,* 3 vols. Paris, Letouzey et Ané, 1934–1940.

Castan, Yves. *Honnêteté et relations sociales en Languedoc, 1715–1780.* Paris, Plon, 1974.

Chaunu, Pierre. "Une histoire religieuse sérielle: à propos du diocèse de La Rochelle (1648–1724) et sur quelques exemples normands," *RHMC,* XII (1965), 5–34.

——. "Jansénisme et frontière de catholicité (XVIIe et XVIIIe siècles)," *RH,* CCXXVII (1962), 115–138.

Christian, William A., Jr. *Person and God in a Spanish Valley.* New York, Seminar Press, 1972.

Cobb, Richard. *Les armées révolutionnaires, instrument de la Terreur dans les départments, avril 1793–Floréal An II,* 2 vols. Paris, Mouton, 1962–1963.

Dégert, A. *Histoire des séminaires français jusqu'à la Révolution,* 2 vols. Paris, Beauchesne, 1912.

Delumeau, Jean. *Le Catholicisme entre Luther et Voltaire.* Paris, PUF, 1971.

Bibliography

Font-Réaulx, Jacques de. "La structure comparée d'un diocèse," *RHEF*, xxxvi (1950), 182–187.

Gargan, Edward T. "The Priestly Culture in Modern France," *Catholic Historical Review*, lvii (1971), 1–20.

Goubert, Pierre, *L'Ancien régime*, 2 vols. Paris, Armand Colin, 1969–1973.

Greenbaum, Louis S. *Talleyrand, Statesman-Priest, The Agent-General of the Clergy and the Church of France at the End of the Old Regime*. Washington, D.C., Catholic University of America Press, 1970.

Groethuysen, Bernard. *The Bourgeoisie; Catholicism vs. Capitalism in Eighteenth-Century France*, trans. Mary Ilford. New York, Holt Rinehart and Winston, 1968.

Gutton, Jean-Pierre. *La société et les pauvres. L'exemple de la généralité de Lyon, 1534–1789*. Paris, Les Belles Lettres, 1971.

Julia, Dominique. "La crise des vocations, essai d'analyse historique," *Les Etudes*, no. 326 (1967), pp. 238–251.

———. "Le prêtre au XVIIIe siècle, la théologie et les institutions," *Recherches de science religieuse*, lviii (1970), 521–534.

———. "La réforme posttridentine en France d'après les procès-verbaux de visites pastorales: ordre et résistances" in *La società religiosa nell'età moderna. Atti del convegno studi di storia sociale e religiosa. Cupaccio-Paestum, 18–21 maggio 1972*. Naples, Guida Editori, 1973, pp. 311–397.

Langlois, Claude. *Le diocèse de Vannes au XIXe siècle, 1800–1830*. Paris, Klincksieck, 1974.

Le Bras, Gabriel. "Les confréries chrétiennes—problèmes et propositions," *Revue historique de droit français et étranger*, 4e série, xix–xx (1940–1941), 310–363.

———. *Introduction à l'histoire de la pratique religieuse en France*, 2 vols. Paris, PUF, 1942–1945.

———. *Etudes de sociologie religieuse*, 2 vols. Paris, PUF, 1955–1956.

Léonard, Emile G. *La question du mariage civil et les Protestants français au XVIIIe siècle*. Aix, Numéro spécial de la *Revue de Théologie*, 1942.

Lewy, Guenter. *Religion and Revolution*. New York, Oxford University Press, 1974.

Mandrou, Robert. *Introduction à la France moderne. Essai de psychologie historique, 1500–1640*. Paris, Albin Michel, 1961.

Bibliography

Mitchell, Harvey. "Resistance to the Revolution in Western France," *Past and Present*, no. 63 (May 1964), 94–131.

Palmer, Robert R. *Catholics and Unbelievers in Eighteenth-Century France*. Princeton, N.J., Princeton University Press, 1939.

Peltier, H. *Séminaires et formation du clergé au diocèse d'Amiens du Concile de Trente au Concordat de 1801*. Paris, Picard, 1946.

Peronnet, Michel. "Les assemblées du clergé de France sous le règne de Louis XVI, 1775–1788," *Annales historiques de la Révolution française*, xxxiv (1962), 8–35.

——. "Les problèmes du clergé dans la société de l'Ancien régime de 1700 à 1789" in Roland Mousnier, *Société française de 1700 à 1789*, 2 vols. Paris, Centre de documentation universitaire, 1970, vol. I, 17–58.

Pérouas, Louis. "Le nombre des vocations sacerdotales, est-il un critère valable en sociologie religieuse historique aux XVIIe et XVIIIe siècles," pp. 35–40 in *Actes du 87e congrès national des sociétés savantes, Poitiers, 1962*. Paris, Imprimerie nationale, 1963.

Plongeron, Bernard. *Théologie et politique au siècle des lumières, 1770–1820*. Geneva, Droz, 1973.

Poland, Burdette C. *French Protestantism and the French Revolution. A Study in Church and State, Thought and Religion, 1685–1815*. Princeton, N.J., Princeton University Press, 1957.

Ravitch, Norman. *Sword and Mitre. Government and Episcopate in France and England in the Age of Aristocracy*. The Hague, Mouton, 1966.

Reinhard, Marcel *et al.* "Les prêtres abdicataires pendant la Révolution," in *Actes du 89e congrès national des sociétés savantes, Lyon, 1964*. Paris, Imprimerie nationale, 1964, pp. 27–228.

Sage, Pierre. *Le "bon prêtre" dans la littérature française d'Amadis de Gaule au Génie du Christianisme*. Geneva, Droz, 1951.

Sicard, Augustin. *L'ancien clergé de France*, 3 vols. Paris, V. Lecoffre, 1893–1903.

Tilly, Charles. *The Vendée*, 2nd ed. New York, Wiley, 1967.

Viguerie, Jean de. *Une oeuvre d'éducation sous l'Ancien régime. Les Pères de la Doctrine chrétienne en France et en Italie (1592–1792)*. Paris, La Nouvelle Aurore, 1975.

Bibliography

Vovelle, Michel. "Le chapitre cathédral de Chartres," in *Actes du 85e congrès national des sociétés savantes, Chambéry-Annecy, 1960.* Paris, Imprimerie nationale, 1961, pp. 235–277.

——. "Essai de cartographie de la déchristianisation sous la Révolution française," *Annales du Midi,* LXXVI (1964), 529–542.

——. *Piété baroque et déchristianisation en Provence au XVIIIe siècle, les attitudes devant la mort d'après les clauses des testaments.* Paris, Plon, 1973.

——. "Prêtres abdicataires et déchristianisation en Provence," in *Actes du 89e congrès national des sociétés savantes, Lyon, 1964.* Paris, Imprimerie nationale, 1965, pp. 63–98.

——. "Problèmes méthodologiques posés par l'utilisation des sources de l'enregistrement dans une étude de structure sociale," *Bulletin de la section d'histoire moderne et contemporaine du Comité des travaux historiques et scientifiques,* fasc. 3 (1961), pp. 49–106.

——. "Y a-t-il eu une révolution culturelle au XVIIIe siècle? A propos de l'éducation populaire en Provence," *RHMC,* XXII (1975), 89–141.

Williams, William H. "Voltaire and the Utility of the Lower Clergy," *Studies on Voltaire and the Eighteenth Century,* LVIII (1967), 1869–1874.

Index

The following abbreviations are used in the index: c. = curé; v. = vicaire; pr. = prior; cn. = canon; bs. = bishop; p. = priest; H.A. = Hautes-Alpes; B.A. = Basses-Alpes; D. = Drôme; I. = Isère; V. = Vaucluse. Note that the positions indicated are those held by priests in 1789 or at the time of death.

Index